**Literary Structure
and Rhetorical Strategies
in the Hebrew
Bible**

Literary Structure and Rhetorical Strategies in the Hebrew Bible

Edited by

L.J. de Regt
J. de Waard
and
J.P. Fokkelman

Van Gorcum

Eisenbrauns

ISBN 90 232 2995 9

Library of Congress Cataloging-in-Publication Data

Literary structure and rhetorical strategies in the Hebrew Bible /
    edited by L.J. de Regt, J. de Waard, and J.P. Fokkelman
            p.   cm.
    Includes bibliographical references and index.
    ISBN 1-57506-011-6 (alk.paper)
    1. Bible: O.T.-Language, style. 2. Rhetoric in the Bible.
3. Intertextuality. I. Regt, L.J. de, 1960- . II. Waard, Jan de.
III Fokkelman, J.P.
BS 1171.2.L567   1996
221.6'6-dc20   96-9273
                                           CIP

Printed by: Van Gorcum, Assen, The Netherlands

CONTENTS

III. Epilogue

PREFACE

Analysis of text structures has been a dominant feature in Biblical studies for quite some time. More recently, scholars have focused on rhetorical strategies that have been employed in Biblical texts. In the present volume, rhetorical as well as structural approaches to the Hebrew Bible have been brought together. It contains studies on a range of topics and on a good many texts and textual corpuses.

Interpretation culminates in translation. The contributors to this volume were asked to discuss the implications of their findings for Bible translators. Many of these translational implications have been put together in the epilogue. The volume thus not only intends to show the present state of our knowledge of literary and rhetorical techniques employed in the Bible; on these points it aims to be a selective guide to translators as well.

We are very grateful to the contributors for their co-operation in bringing together such a wealth of information and very much hope that students, exegetes, and translators will benefit from it.

Lénart de Regt
Jan de Waard
Jan Fokkelman

FOREWORD

The *Shorter Oxford English Dixtionary* defines 'rhetoric' as "the art of using language so as to persuade or influence others; the body of rules so as to be observed by a speaker or writer in order that he may express himself with eloquence." Margot, who contributes a study on Joshua 6, clearly represents such a concern, being interested not only in an informative function of a written text, but also in its expressive function.

When such an approach is applied to our corpus, namely the biblical literature with special reference to the Old Testament, one needs to bear in mind a number of special circumstances.

a) Whereas it is hardly to be doubted that ancient Israelites also cultivated this art in order to put their case in most persuasive manners and to couch their inner experiences, thoughts and emotions in outwardly attractive and appealing forms, they have not left behind any treatise laying down rules of rhetoric and containing discussions or expositions of them, as theoreticians and practicioners of the art of the classical world did. This means that rules of ancient Hebrew rhetoric need to be identified and ferreted out through a close study of the texts which we assume to embody them. The present volume speaks volumes of the serious difficulty and intellectual challenge presented by this exercise.

b) Those who cannot resist this challenge are confronted at almost every turn with considerable difficulties of interpretation of our ancient Hebrew literary sources. Despite the fact that this body of literature has attracted over the centuries some of the brightest philologists and exegetes attracted to any body of literature, the number of interpretive cruces remains uncomfortably high despite, and largely because of, its modest size in comparison with, say, the classical Greek and Latin literature. This aspect is also eloquently testified by every contribution to the present volume. See Eslinger's study on Exodus 6.3 in particular.

c) Again compared with the classical literature, our ancient Hebrew literature, because of its primarily religious message and Sitz im Leben, it has remained until relatively recently the preserve of theologians to a large extent. It has been looked upon as sacred literature par excellence. Though its literary forms as well as its contents have never ceased to influence and inspire minds with literary and artistic predilections and sensibilities, it is only in recent times that this body of literature has begun to become an object of serious scholarly investigation as a piece of literature in a broad sense. Among leading figures who have been spearheading this new direction one thinks of names such as Robert Alter and L. Alonso Schökel. In this volume one finds Fokkelman contributing a fine study on

Genesis 37 and 38, which also has important implications for the traditional literary criticism of this book. This latter aspect also holds true of Boadt's study on mythological themes and the unity of the book of Ezekiel.

d) A serious study of the biblical text in its original languages very often has important implications for its translators. This is not only true of a study of the grammar and lexicon of those languages, but also of questions pertaining to features of its style and rhetoric. Most contributions to the present volume show awareness of this issue in varying degrees. The contribution of De Waard, one of the editors, takes the issue head-on, accompanied by some observations of his on select contributions to the volume from this vantage-point.

The emergence of the new trend just mentioned has coincided with the emergence of discourse analysis or text linguistics as a recent, promising development in the science of linguistics. Scholars such as R.E. Longacre who advocate this approach to a written text stress the importance of studying a biblical text, not with individual words or even grammatical sentences as the minimum unit for study and analysis, but with much larger literary units, entire discourse. De Regt's study on rhetorical question attempts to demonstrate that one needs to study such a type of utterance not only per se, but also pay attention to an important function it fulfils in structuring the whole document it forms a mere fragment of.

The interest in intertextuality, namely mutual interaction and influence within a given text or a corpus of affiliated texts, is obviously a facet of this larger concern. Beentjes's study deals with cases where the original sequence of two given components, AB, is later quoted in the inverted sequence, BA. This illustrates in a way how scholars interested in rhetoric and style take up where grammarians leave off, namely possibilities of arranging multiple constituents of more or less identical grammatical standing, questions of coordination and the question of their literary effect. These concerns are central to De Regt's second study on the order of participants. Tsumura's study is concerned with a variation on the same theme, interrupted coordination.

Parunak studies the question of the presence or absence of a deictic element in a Hebrew relative clause, an element referring back to the antecedent of the relative clause. It is an attempt to go beyond the not infrequent ad hoc suggestion that a certain grammatical phenomenon is a variation for the sake of style, a claim not buttressed by any serious enquiry.

An interaction takes place not only between authors, but also between writer or narrator and reader or hearer. It is here that the art of rhetoric and narration comes to play a significant role. Van Wolde's study of Genesis 1 is a stimulating text-linguistic analysis of the creation story, showing how the narrator relates to the outside world, makes use of dramatis personae, and allows the reader to penetrate the narrator's world by going beyond the conventional meanings of linguistic codes and decoding the iconic message of linguistic symbols, and literary or stylistic features. Fokkelman's above-mentioned study and Bailey's study on inverted parallelisms and encased parables illustrate this interest in specific literary and narratological devices and their implications for interpretation of biblical texts.

Magonet explores another possibility, namely that of reading a biblical narrative from the standpoint of its characters, and not that of its narrator himself.

As Margot, in his piece on Joshua 6, justly emphasises, and also skilfully demonstrated by Gitay's study of Psalm 1 where a well-known message is cast in an engaging style coupled with a powerful argumentative style, one ought not to dissociate form from meaning, for literary and rhetorical devices constitute part of the meaning and message. Without purporting to be a handbook of Classical Hebrew rhetoric, this collection of essays representing a broad range of literary, stylistic, and rhetorical concerns, should appeal to anyone interested in seeking and discovering the *whole* message of a biblical text.

T. Muraoka
Leiden University

I. STUDIES ON TOPICS

CHARACTER/AUTHOR/READER
THE PROBLEM OF PERSPECTIVE IN BIBLICAL NARRATIVE

RABBI JONATHAN MAGONET

There is a paradox at the heart of this enterprise that must be acknowledged at the outset. The editors have invited contributors to look at rhetorical features and structures in 'Old Testament' texts. But accompanying this task is the additional request to 'pay attention to some of the implications of their findings for Bible translation in particular'. The problem is that the more attention is drawn to the rhetoric of the Hebrew Bible, the less possible does translation of a particular passage become. This is because an analysis of the rhetoric reveals the multilayered nature of the composition, the variety of possible meanings and nuances of particular words and the myriad interactions with other texts within the Hebrew Biblical corpus. Add to this the additional layers of understanding and commentary that are imposed by readers throughout the centuries and the translator is likely to become paralysed!

I do not point this out with any subversive intent but out of the painful experience, as a Bible exegete, of having had the task of translating a number of the Psalms for a Jewish prayerbook. The more I tried to indicate the inner connections within the particular Psalm, as shown, for example, by the repetition of particular key words, the more impossible ('overstuffed', 'pregnant') the translations became. Let me give an illustration.

Psalm 90:3 contains a word play on the root *shuv*, with its multiplicity of meanings - 'turn', 'turn back', 'return'. *tashev enosh ad-dakka vattomer shuvu v'nei adam.* Literally (if one dare use such a term), 'You "turn" mortal beings to dust, and/but You say "turn", sons of Adam.' Is the verb intended to have the same meaning in both parts of the verse? Thus we have the somewhat banal, but nevertheless powerful, sentence: 'You, God, return human beings back to the dust from which they came (though the word '*dakka*', inert dust, is not actually the *aphar* of Genesis 2:7) and You say (to them) "Go back, sons of Adam, (to the dust from which you came)"'. The use of 'sons of Adam' evokes the '*adamah*' from which the first 'man' was taken. Given the centrality to the Psalm of the theme of the transience of human life, it is perfectly reasonable to assume that this is indeed the intention of the verse and, for example, translate the verb *shuv* with the word 'return' for both uses.

But it is equally clear that the theme of the transience of life is intimately bound up with that of seeking to make that transient life valuable so that we acquire a 'heart of wisdom' (v 12). Since there is a further emphasis on the risk of being consumed in God's anger, it is also very possible that the second use of the verb '*shuv*' in verse 3 is to have God intend instead, 'return (to Me)', 'repent', 'do *teshuvah*'('repentance'). There is no way at this early stage of the Psalm to decide which of these two meanings is the intended one - and it might be closer to the intent of the author to suggest that the word play between these two meanings was deliberate. Thus the tension within the two meanings of the words, with their diametrically opposite implications - a return to lifelessness or a return to life close to God - will indeed continue to echo through the Psalm.

To complicate matters further, it is not even certain that the word *dakka*, which literally means 'crushed material', does mean 'dust'. Thus the word appears in Psalm 34:19 in a metaphorical sense in parallel with the phrase 'a broken heart'. ('The Lord is nigh unto them that are of a broken heart, and saveth such as are of a *contrite* spirit' - *dakk'ei ruah*). Hence the Jewish Publication Society of America translation of 1917 reads our verse as:

> Thou turnest man to contrition:
> And sayest: 'Return, ye children of men.'

(The New JPS Translation gives 'dust' in the text, but offers 'contrition' in a footnote.)

But having recognised the complexity of this early verse in the Psalm, what do we make of the third appearance of the verb *shuv*, in verse 13, when the Psalmist appeals to God to 'return' and '*take pity* on Your servants'. Again the terminology surrounding the verb is open to different understandings. The verb '*niham*', 'take pity', has the sense of exchanging one emotional mind set for its opposite. God can 'regret' having created human beings (Gen 6:6), or 'change His mind' about the punishment He intends to bring upon them (Exod 32:14), or call out words of 'comfort', a change of emotional state from despair to hope, to Israel because of the end of exile (Isa 40:1). What is the 'comforting' that God is to do in our Psalm? Is this 'comforting' related to the general theme of human frailty and death, or much more specifically here to ending some aspect of Israel's suffering which is itself a punishment for wrongdoing that has 'distanced' God from them - hence the need to appeal to God Himself to 'return' (to them). It is also possible that the request is that God 'turn away' from His current anger (Jonah 3:9) and 'repent'.

Moreover, what effect, if any, does this last appearance of the verb have on our understanding of the two previous uses in retrospect - and will it affect our understanding of verse three the next time we read it - perhaps enhancing the view that God is calling for a return to Him rather than simply to the dust?

There is, of course, no answer to this conundrum. Any translation of any of the phrases will be based on a personal decision about how far to seek to translate these complex interactions; whether to find a term that is sufficiently ambiguous in the English as to permit the same range of associations and options (possibly playing at the very least on 'turn/return') (so Buber/Rosenzweig 'Bis zum Mulm lässest den Menschen du *kehren*, und du sprichst: *Kehrt* zurück, Adamskinder!'/'Kehre um, DU! bis wann!'); or instead to give up that particular struggle and decide for one particular view of the Psalm as a whole and follow that line through with heroic single-mindedness, oblivious to the word-plays! Of course many, provided they see the problems in a given instance, will seek out some kind of middle way, perhaps relying on the particular purpose of the translation to enable them to make their choices at each point of divergent or convergent meanings.

The following sampling of translations shows the various approaches:

> You can turn man back into dust
> by saying, 'Back to what you were, you sons of men!'...
> Relent! Yahweh! How much longer do we have?
> Take pity on Your servants! (Jerusalem Bible)

> Thou crumblest man away,
> summoning men back to the dust,...
> Relent, O thou Eternal, and delay not,
> be sorry for thy servants. (Moffatt)

> Thou turnest man back into dust;
> 'Turn back,' thou sayest, 'you sons of men'...
> How long, O Lord?
> Relent, and take pity on thy servants. (New English Bible)

> You return man to dust/contrition;
> You decreed, 'Return you mortals!'
> Turn, O LORD!
> How long?
> Show mercy to Your servants. (New JPS)

In my particular case the liturgical context became the final arbiter for pushing the translation towards simplicity (because of the need for public recitation) and the more 'spiritual' understanding. Thus verse 3 became:

> You turn mankind back to dust
> yet You say: 'Sons of man, turn back to Me!'

(I should note that in this same context, and some twenty years later, I would be struggling also to find more 'gender-inclusive' language for terms like '*enosh*' and '*b'nei adam*'. The translator has his or her social or political context no less than the author.)

The problem of reading 'character' - the case of Naomi

It might be argued that precisely the 'density' of 'poetic' writings leads to such inner complexity and hence the problems for the translator. Surely with simple narrative prose we are on safer ground. In some sense we are, in that there may be a greater degree of certainty about what the author is seeking to convey and less possibility of cross-referencing to other passages or words. But precisely when we enter the area of narrative, and particularly given the apparent simplicity and directness of Hebrew narrative prose with its emphasis on action rather than the explicit description of character, the reader is confronted with major problems of interpretation. What motivates the characters? How does the author indicate this? Does the author actually do so? Are we perhaps imposing modern categories of thought on the ancient writer when we seek nuances in the mode of expression, the use of repetitions, in our filling of the gaps?

I would like to illustrate some of these problems with an example from the Book of Ruth. In chapter one we are told about the journey of Elimelech to Moab during a time of famine. We are introduced to his wife and sons and then told, in verse three, of his death. The verse ends with the phrase 'there *remained* she and her two sons (*baneha*)'. The following verse describes how the two sons marry Moabite women and subsequently die. Verse five ends with a similar phrase involving once again the verb meaning 'to remain': 'there *remained* the woman from her two children (*yeladeha*) and her husband.' The two sentences (describing these events from her perspective - surviving first the death of her husband, and then of her two sons and husband) by their usage of the identical form of the verb and general construction are so similar that one's attention is drawn to them. But a closer examination reveals one distinction between the two - in verse three it is her 'sons' who die, in verse five they are described as her 'children', from the verb *yalad* which means to give birth.

We may approach this difference in a number of ways. The first is at least to acknowledge it as a fact, irrespective of the meaning we may come to place upon it. (Not all translations take the difference into account - thus the New JPS simply reads 'sons' in both cases, whereas the older 1917 edition uses 'sons' in the first case and 'children' in the second.)

The next step may indeed be to assume that this 'fact' has no particular significance - the author simply chose two words at random. Our present approach to the text would lead to a second assumption, that the author did not like to repeat the same word within such a short space and so produced a stylistic variation - an aesthetic choice with no other significance. But the next stage, presumably determined by our interest in the story as a whole and the quest to understand it, leads us to wish to interpret this fact. Here two options present themselves. The first is that this information, which is presented as part of the narrator's description of events is meant to remain part of the narrator's perception alone - a perception that the narrator has chosen to share with the reader for our information and evaluation. However the alternative is to see in this an intention to indicate something of the effect of these deaths on Naomi herself. If this be the case, then the wording reflects a change in her inner state, so that she is the one who perceives her living 'sons' as 'children', now that they are dead. They are no longer for her the independent married adults they were in life but have regressed in her mind to the children they once were who have now been taken from her. Such a psychological reading is very suggestive. Thus I remember the devastating effect on my own grandmother when my mother died. Though my mother was in her fifties, for my grandmother it was 'her little girl' who had died, and she never recovered from the blow.

If we read the story in that light, then we have a major key to understand Naomi's mentality in this difficult time of bereavement and it will affect our reading of all that follows in her treatment of her daughters-in-law. Clearly we already know that she must be in mourning after these tragic deaths, and, depending on our ability to empathise with her situation, will take this into account as we read on. But if we read with this particular nuance in mind it will deepen our understanding of, and increase our sensitivity to, her situation.

A rabbinic perspective

We have traced here already a number of levels of interpretation brought to our attention through the replacement of a single word, each level being determined by the assumptions we bring to the text. We will see subsequently how these different perspectives can lead to quite dramatic differences of opinion about a particular Bible character. But before examining this it is instructive to examine a totally different set of presuppositions that colour the reading of a text in the same section. This time we will look at a Rabbinic reading, by the great mediaeval Bible exegete Rashi (Rabbi Shlomo Yitzhaki, 1040-1105). The value of this, apart from the intrinsic interest of his comments, is to give a necessary perspective on the presuppositions that we too bring to the text out of our own cultural conditioning.

Verse three begins with the statement: 'Elimelech died, the husband of Naomi'. Those who are aware of the Rabbinic approach to exegesis will immediately recognise a problem in this simple statement. Since we already know that Elimelech is the husband of Naomi - it was made explicit in the preceding sentence - what is the point in giving this information again? Such a question is itself dependent on a Rabbinic view that since each word of Scripture came ultimately from God, nothing is redundant, so each apparent duplication or seemingly unnecessary addition must be scrutinised in the greatest detail for the particular message it was conveying to us. ('Turn it (the Torah, the Pentateuch) and turn it again for everything is in it' Mishnah Avot 5:25) This kind of approach is not that different from the 'close reading' that a modern scholar might apply, even though the underlying presuppositions and the goal of such interpretation may be radically different. If we were to ask why this apparent redundancy is necessary, a literary appproach might lead us to suggest that until now the perspective of the story has been the fate of Elimelech, the patriarch who has set events in motion by leaving his land and taking his family with him. Now the focus of attention is changing to Naomi, so that her name is introduced ('Elimelech died, the husband of Naomi') in order to put her into centre stage. If until now events have been described from his perspective, they will now be described from hers. (This would already serve to reinforce the view expressed above that the author, though not ascribing either the change in words (son/child) or any particular emotional set, to Naomi, has led us to see certain key events through her eyes.)

On this verse Rashi chooses to turn to the tradition of Rabbinic exegesis, *midrash*, in explaining this apparent redundancy of information. He does it most elegantly by quoting a passage from the Babylonian Talmud, Sanhedrin 22b.

> *The husband of Naomi*: Why is this expressly stated? From here they derived the
> teaching: 'No man dies except to his wife'.

That is to say, the person who is most affected by the death of a man is his wife and companion of so many years. This poignant remark, logical within the approach of the Rabbis to apparently redundant words, serves also to set precisely the necessary emotional tone we have considered above in taking seriously the suffering of Naomi that must colour her subsequent actions.

But there is a second quotation in Rashi, one not present in all editions so its source must be questioned, which reads the same 'redundancy' in a totally different way. To understand it we need a little more background on the Rabbinic reading of this chapter. The Rabbis criticised Elimelech for leaving the land of Israel during a famine (Baba Batra 91a, Genesis Rabba 28:3). They explained that he was a wealthy man who could have sustained many but left so as to avoid all the demands being made upon him. This in turn explains his early death - a punishment for failing to live up to his responsibilities. But this raises a major problem which Rashi's comment addresses.

> And it says, 'the husband of Naomi' as if to say that because he was Naomi's husband
> and ruled over her and she was attached to him, therefore the divine judgment came
> on him but not on her.

By this reading the redundant phrase is there to resolve a problem and at the same time reflect a legal issue. In a 'patriarchal' society, the adult male was the one responsible under the law - for his own actions and those of his household. By such a reasoning, Naomi had no choice but to follow her husband in his departure from the land and so she was exempt from the punishment that befell him.

Here again the remark, however weak the peg on which it is hung appears to be, addresses an issue in the text - at least from the Rabbinic point of view and in the light of their own overview of the Book. It is consistent, coherent and convincing - within that particular kind of discourse.

A current controversy

These kinds of issue were somewhat dramatised in an exchange of views that occurred in a couple of issues of the *Journal for the Study of the Old Testament* and it is instructive to see on what the debate was based.

In issue 40 of the Journal Danna Nolan Fewell and David M. Gunn published an article '"A Son is Born to Naomi!": Literary Allusions and Interpretation in the Book of Ruth.' Their starting point is the literary critical and feminist reading of the Book of Ruth by Phyllis Trible in her book *God and the Rhetoric of Sexuality*.

> Like many other commentators, Trible finds Naomi to be a model of selflessness, her
> dominant concern being for the welfare of her daughters-in-law. Her support of Ruth,
> like Ruth's devotion to her, is exemplary. We would suggest a less sanguine reading.
> (99)

Their analysis focuses on five 'silences' 1. Naomi's silence at Ruth's final determination to go on with her to Bethlehem; 2. Naomi's silence about Ruth on her arrival in Bethlehem; 3. Naomi's silence about her kinsman Boaz, until prompted by Ruth's story of success at gleaning; 4. Ruth's silence about her own part in the threshing floor scene when she returns to Naomi the next morning; 5. Naomi's silence about Ruth at the birth of Obed.

We will restrict ourselves to the first example. The authors ask:

> But *why* does Naomi so withdraw, if she is so selfless, so wholly motivated by her regard for others?...Why should the altruism of Ruth reduce an altruistic Naomi to silent withdrawal? For she speaks not a word either to, or about, Ruth, from this point to the end of the scene in the arrival at Bethlehem. If Ruth's famous 'Where you go, I go; your god, my god' speech can melt the hearts of a myriad preachers and congregations down the centuries, why not Naomi's heart? (100)

They also note the literary allusions that lie behind the story - particularly the Moabite background of Ruth which implies a negative attitude to her by the Israelites. But also the story of Judah and Tamar (Gen 38) which has many parallels including, they argue, Judah's suspicion of Tamar the Canaanite considering the harm she has done to his first two sons. They conclude:

> On this reading, Naomi's silence at Ruth's unshakeable commitment to accompany her emerges as resentment, irritation, frustration, unease. Ruth the Moabite is to her an inconvenience, a menace even. (104)

This explains Naomi's embarrassed silence before the women of Bethlehem. Moreover they see 'A Naomi with a prejudice against foreigners, a Naomi who thinks like Judah, is also consistent with a Naomi who sends Ruth to the harvest field without advice or warning.' (105) Such concern as Naomi does show for Ruth, they argue, only emerges when she experiences her as a useful breadwinner, and she is even prepared to send her off to the threshing floor at night in a highly risky attempt to entrap Boaz, forcing him to marry this Moabite woman who would not otherwise be a suitable spouse. Even when her plot succeeds and eventually a child is born, Naomi's silence points to her unhappiness.

> She owes her restoration to a woman, to Ruth the Moabite woman, to Ruth the woman whose radical action challenges the male-centered values that permeate both the story and Naomi's worldview. (107)

Not surprisingly such a radical reading of the character of Naomi evoked a response. Issue 45 of the Journal contained the article 'Was Naomi a Scold?: A Response to Fewell and Gunn' by Peter W. Coxon.

> This interpretation fails to recognize the shifting levels of reality employed by the narrator, fails to respond to the restrained narrative voice and consequently fails to do justice to Naomi's true response. Naomi's thoughts are unexpressed in the words of a set speech, but this is not altogether surprising. The narrative has already contained expressions of emotional indulgence: in v. 9 Naomi kissed Orpah and Ruth, 'and they

lifted up their voices and wept' and in v. 14 'they lifted up their voices and wept again'. The three widows are bound together in a common expression of sorrow and the pressure exerted by Naomi on the two younger women in vv. 8-9,11-13 is motivated by an altruistic regard for their welfare which she saw as being best served by remaining within the social structure of their own Moabite family life. Ruth's confession goes beyond the domestic responsibility she may feel for her mother-in-law and thoroughly Judaizes her with a notable future genealogy very much in mind. A further comment by Naomi at this point might or might not have been appropriate. The text itself conveys its own deep impression and the narrative description serves to indicate thoughts which remain unexpressed in *actual speech*. First when Naomi saw Ruth's determination 'she said no more' (v. 188) which means probably she ceased to argue the point. The narrative voice takes over and mention is made of the *activity* of the two women:

> So *the two of them* went on until they came to Bethlehem (1:19).
> So Naomi returned, and Ruth the Moabitess her daughter-in-law *with her* (1:22).
> (26)

Coxon also acknowledges the structural similarities to the Judah-Tamar story in Genesis 38 but concludes:

> However, to go beyond this and see in Judah's cynical reticence in doing anything to help Tamar the mainspring of Naomi's silence towards Ruth is quite unacceptable. The reason for Judah's behaviour is clearly stated in the narrative (38:11) whereas in the book of Ruth we are presented with a series of intentional silences. (31-32)

Again it is no surprise that Fewell and Gunn reply to Coxon's paper though the emotional temperature goes up somewhat. They question his use of the term 'Scold' being applied to their view of Naomi and suggest that 'it does, however, say something about Coxon's propensity to reduce, overstate or caricature the nuanced complexity of character that we sketch.' (40)

> Moreover, that desire for simple androcentric models meshes with his desire for a 'proper understanding', of 'deeper levels of reality and truth' through unerring interpretation of a character's 'true response'. This is not the time for a discussion of hermeneutics and critical theory; let us just say that such phrases indicate a naive understanding of the business of intepretation. There is, we would say, no 'true' understanding of the character of Naomi, though some reconstructions will resonate more with some readers, seem 'truer' to the text, than others. The rules by which the critical game is played will make a difference, as will the point of view of the reader. Our reading obviously reflects these differences - as does Coxon's. It is hardly insignificant, for example, that, as he seeks to reassert a vision of stereotypical patriarchal relationships, he also assumes that the narrator is a 'he' and believes that all the readers are 'he'. (At least one of us has some difficulty thinking of herself as 'the reader himself'.) (40)
>
> Coxon's reading strategies (the rules of the game) are naturally convenient for the case he is asserting. (40)
>
> In reference to Naomi's silence in the face of Ruth's determination to go with her (her 'confession' as he quaintly terms it) Coxon is eager to discover here silent but willing consent. We do not know, however, what Naomi is thinking. Here is a gap in the text which, from his reading of the context (amongst other resources), Coxon fills with willing consent just as, from ours, we fill it with apprehension, resignation, even resentment. Our problem with Coxon's reading method is not the gap-filling but his

claim that 'the narrative description serves to indicate actual thoughts which remain unexpressed in actual speech'. He refers to the narrator's report that the women proceed on together to Bethlehem (v. 19) and to the narrator's summary (though Coxon does not recognize this as summary), 'so Naomi returned, and Ruth the Moabitess, her daughter-in-law, with her' (v. 22). These statements, he asserts , are 'vehicles of Naomi's feelings'. Nothing in the text, however, indicates that these statements by the narrator represent Naomi's point of view. If Coxon is to collapse together the narrator's and Naomi's points of view at least he needs to recognize that this is in fact what he is doing and to justify his move. (40-41)

The paper goes on to evaluate some inner contradictions in Coxon's article. These three papers together make a valuable contribution to recognizing the problem before us, and their detailed arguments about how such a literary approach might be conducted are very helpful. For someone outside the particular debate they are also fascinating documents reflecting two quite radically different starting points and assumptions. (I have addressed the issue of perspective in more detail in *A Rabbi's Bible* 'How a Donkey Reads the Bible - On Interpretation', 60-72.) Moreover, since the rhetoric goes beyond the customary scholarly detachment, they are highly entertaining as well.

At the risk of becoming embroiled myself, it is worth drawing attention to a couple of textual details that contribute to this particular discussion, in particular the delicate one of the relationship between the perspective of the narrator and of the characters.

For example, the narration is quite consistent in making Naomi the single initiator in the early stages of her journey home.

> *She* arose and her daughters-in-law and *she* returned from the fields of Moab (v. 6).
> *She* went out from the place where *she* was and her two daughters-in-law with her and *they* went along the way..... (v. 7)

Following Ruth's declaration, Naomi saw that she was intent on staying with her and the following verse begins literally, '*They* went, the two of them, till they came to Bethlehem....' (v. 19).

Rashi on this verse, again quoting *midrash*, recognizes this switch to the plural form as reflecting a new relationship between the two. Within the Rabbinic tradition he interprets it on the basis that Ruth's declaration was an expression of her formal conversion to 'Judaism'.

> Come and see how beloved are converts before God. The moment she decided to convert, Scripture ranks her equally with Naomi.

But on the level of the narrative, how are we to interpret this change? Does it imply mutual agreement and some kind of bonding as they continue the journey together, as Coxon would suggest. Or is it simply a neutral statement that they went together? How is it to be linked to the use of the same verb, 'to go' in the plural form in verse 7? Do they reflect Naomi's ambivalence about the presence of her daughters-in-law, one that changes with Ruth's insistence? The reader will fill in the gaps dependent on his or her understanding of the story as a whole, and may choose to ascribe meaning to such nuances or not.

Since the issue of Naomi's feelings about her daughters-in-law seems crucial to the understanding of the chapter, perhaps another literary detail can be introduced that relates to this. Here the language is that of Naomi and not the narrator but as in all the examples we have seen, it is evocative but raises as many questions as it answers.

When Naomi tries to send them away the narrator has her addressing her 'two daughters-in-law':

> Go (*lekhna*), return (*shovna*) each woman to the house of her mother..... (v. 8)

The two women protest and Naomi speaks to them again. However this time she addresses them as 'my daughters'. Do we see this as unrelated to the narrator's description of them as 'daughters-in-law' prior to the previous speech? Or do we take the narrator's view as also reflecting that of Naomi, a view that has changed because their affirmation of loyalty has moved her to see them as truly her daughters? The latter possibility is reinforced by a further word play in her actual speech.

> Return (*shovna*), my daughters, why will you go (*telakhna*) with me....... Return (*shovna*), my daughters, go (*lekhna*) for I am too old..... (vv. 11,12)

The three-fold repetition of the verb *shovna*, (the same root *shuv*, turn, return, that we have examined before), together with a three-fold use of the root *halakh*, to go, twice in the same feminine imperative plural form, is striking. In *Ruth Rabbah 2:16* the repetition of *shovna* is interpreted by the Rabbis to indicate that one should turn away a potential convert to Judaism three times, but if they persist, then they should be accepted. Again the Rabbinic view has a particular legal colouring, but it rightly draws attention to this three-fold repetition.

However within the context of the story itself, there is another possible dimension. The sequence of verbs puts *lekhna*, 'go', before *shovna*, 'return', when Naomi first speaks, but reverses the order after the response of her daughters-in-law. It is therefore possible to see in her opening remarks a desire to send them away - 'go!' It is only subsequently that she expresses sufficient concern for their welfare that she tells them to 'return' to their mother's house. Only after their response does she put their welfare before her own immediate concerns, twice emphasising that they should 'return' to their home and 'go'.

Such a combination of details would suggest a deeply hurt and self-absorbed Naomi, suffering from a bereavement that leaves her wishing to be left utterly alone, who nevertheless can be taken out of herself sufficiently to be concerned with the welfare of her daughters-in-law. On such a reading Ruth's persistence could be resented, tolerated and welcomed at one and the same time - a position somewhere between that of Fewell-Gunn and Coxon.

Is such a conclusion any more legitimate than either of the extremes presented by these papers? More to the point, in the context of this paper, the effect of these widely divergent readings has helped focus on certain, though not all, elements that need to be addressed in evaluating the character of Naomi as depicted in the chapter. It has also drawn our attention to the question of the 'rules of the game'. What details of the narrative should legitimately be considered, and how do we determine what to select? How does the voice of the narrator relate to that of the characters? Granted there is no 'true reading', what is the best strategy to pursue? Presumably one that allows for the maximum flexibility and openness to the richness of the narrative. (I have attempted my own view of the characters in the Book of Ruth in *Bible Lives*, 33-47.)

This paper has offered more questions than answers. This modern awareness of the 'multidimensionality' of the text is a rediscovery of the old Rabbinic dictum, '*shiv'im panim la-torah*', that there are 'seventy faces to Torah', to Scripture. This is an uncomfortable view but a liberating one. The responsibility is firmly placed back on the reader to make of the text what he or she can. There is no one view but rather a variety of perspectives that have to be taken into account. The best one can hope for is some degree of probability - and the possibility of being surprised again and again into rediscovering the text afresh. As Marcel Proust expressed it:

> While he is reading, every reader is the reader of his own self. The writer's work is merely a kind of optical instrument, which he offers to the reader, to enable him to discern what, without this book, he would perhaps never have perceived for himself.

Bibliography

Coxon, Peter W. 'Was Naomi a Scold? A Response to Fewell and Gunn' *JSOT* Issue 45, 1989, 25-37.
Fewell, Danna Nolan and Gunn, David M. '"A Son is Born to Naomi!": Literary Allusions and Interpretation in the Book of Ruth' *JSOT* Issue 40, 1988, 99-108.
Fewell, Danna Nolan and Gunn, David M. 'Is Coxon A Scold? On Responding to the Book of Ruth' *JSOT* Issue 45, 1989, 39-43.
The Holy Scriptures: According to the Masoretic Text: A New Translation with the Aid of Previous Versions and with Constant Consultation of Jewish Authorities (Philadelphia 1917).
The Jerusalem Bible General Editor Alexander Jones (London, 1966).
James Moffatt *A New Translation of the Bible Containing the Old and New Testaments* (London 1934).
Magonet, Jonathan *A Rabbi's Bible* (SCM Press; London, 1991).
Magonet, Jonathan *Bible Lives* (SCM Press; London, 1992).
The New English Bible (Oxford and Cambridge 1970).
The Writings Kethubim: A New Translation of The Holy Scriptures According to the Traditional Hebrew Text (Philadelphia 1982) (*The New JPS Translation*, (Philadelphia 1985)).

"INVERTED PARALLELISMS" AND "ENCASED PARABLES" IN ISAIAH AND THEIR SIGNIFICANCE FOR OT AND NT TRANSLATION AND INTERPRETATION

KENNETH E. BAILEY

The extensive use in Biblical literature of a wide variety of rhetorical devices is well-known.[1] Within this broad field of scholarly endeavor is the narrower focus on the inter-locking of the Hebrew parallelisms in a variety of texts to form larger cohesive units. It is this latter concern that was James Muilenburg's focus as he coined the phrase "Rhetorical Criticism."[2]

It appears to me that Muilenburg's interests are significant for the translator's task. If in a Biblical narrative one is able to identify plot, character development, comedy, tragedy, irony and the like, such identifications are significant for the *interpreter*. They may be less important for the *translator*. However, the translator is obliged to *format* the text on the printed page. This inevitably involves paragraphing and presenting the text as a series of parallel lines or as non-structured prose. For more than a century there has been general agreement that the Hebrew parallelisms of the Psalms and the Prophets should be presented appropriately to the eye of the reader to assist that reader in identifying those pairs of ideas and thus be able to react to them. Consequently for decades Isaiah 55:6-7 has been formatted as follows:

> *Seek* the Lord while he may be *found*,
>   *call* upon him while he is *near*;
> let the wicked forsake his *way*,
>   and the unrighteous man his *thoughts*;
> let him return to the *Lord*, that he may have *mercy* on him,
>   and to our *God*, for he will abundantly *pardon*.
>   PLATE ONE: ISAIAH 55:6-7

---

[1] J.L. Bailey and L.D. Vander Broek, *Literary Forms in the New Testament* (Louisville: Westminster/John Knox, 1992); K.E. Bailey, *Poet and Peasant and Through Peasant Eyes* (Grand Rapids: Eerdmans, 1980) 44-75; J. Dewey, *Markan Public Debate: Literary Technique, Concentric Structure, and Theology in Mark 2:1-3:6* (Chico: Scholars Press, 1980) 5-39; J.L. Kugel, *The Idea of Biblical Poetry: Parallelism and Its History* (New Haven: Yale University Press, 1981).

[2] James Muilenburg, "Form Criticism and Beyond," *JBL* 88 (1969) 8.

The simplest reader can easily perceive the three "synonymous parallelisms" in the text and this long accepted formatting assists that discovery. The six lines form a whole. We will call them a "stanza." In the first two the sinner is called on to seek the Lord. The following two lines tell the readers to abandon their own way/thoughts. The last two complete the sequence by urging a return to the merciful Lord. The climax appears at the end in the call to *return*.

However the two following verses also form a clearly delineated stanza. These five lines can be formatted as follows:

ISAIAH 55:8-9

A.	For my *thoughts* are not your *thoughts*,	THOUGHTS
B.	neither are your *ways* my *ways*, says the Lord.	WAYS
C.	For as the *heavens* are higher than the *earth*,	PARABLE
B.	so are my *ways* higher than your *ways*,	WAYS
A.	and my *thoughts* than your *thoughts*.	THOUGHTS

(The capitalized words on the right summarize the ideas that repeat)

PLATE TWO

Isaiah has taken "ways" and "thoughts" out of the *middle* of the previous six lines, doubled them, split them and placed a concrete simile in the center. The material presents the pattern of: thoughts - ways - simile/parable/*mashal* - ways - thoughts. The two words "ways" and "thoughts" interlock this second stanza with the previous six-line construction. The parable in the center of the second stanza adds a new and important element to the whole. Thus the five lines exhibit both *inverted parallelism* and an *encased parable*. These two rhetorical devices are the subject of this essay.

The "inverted parallelism" of these five lines, to my knowledge, has not been set out in the formatting of any major English translation. It is understandable that translators are appropriately cautious and thereby prudently wait for some consensus before proceeding. Speculative subtleties can, and have, caused many rash interpretive acts in the name of "poetic structures." Yet the A-B-C-B-A form of the above five-line stanza is surely as clear and unmistakable as the AA-BB-CC structure of the previous six lines. Those initial six lines have been formatted in a manner appropriate to their parallelistic nature for nearly all of the 20th century. Why does the formatting of the latter five lines not offer the reader the same assistance that is now always offered for the preceding six lines?

It is the intent of this essay to examine a few examples of two clear and repetitive types of parallelistic structures in Isaiah that mark off identifiable stanzas and to see what difference these structures make for a clearer understanding of those texts. The significance of these OT structures for related NT passages will also be noted when appropriate. It is our intent to offer these examples to translators with the recommendation that they be translated with the parallelisms in mind, and also that they be seriously considered for formatting in a manner that allows the reader to identify parallels when they are clearly the conscious intent of the original writer.

The first type to be examined we prefer to call "inverted parallelism." The more common term, chiasm, can perhaps be used with greater precision if preserved for describing Greek rhetoric. The phrase "inverted parallelism" clearly identifies the rhetoric under consideration as being a development of Hebrew parallelism. Both cultures constructed larger literary units by presenting a series of ideas, coming to a climax and then repeating the series backwards. The distinctive feature of Hebrew style (as compared with Greek) is this use of Hebrew parallelisms as the building-blocks for such structures.

Turning then to a striking example of *inverted parallelism* we observe Isaiah 28:14-20 which is as follows:

ISAIAH'S PARABLE OF THE TWO BUILDERS - ISAIAH 28:14-20
Therefore hear the word of the Lord you scoffers,
who rule this people in Jerusalem.
Because you have said,

1 a. "We have made a *covenant* with *death*,		
b. and with *Sheol* we have an *agreement*;	COVENANT WITH	
c. when the *overwhelming scourge passes through*,	DEATH, SHEOL	
d. it will *not come* to *us*:		

2 a. for we have made *lies* our *refuge*	REFUGE
b. and in *falsehood* we have taken *shelter*."	SHELTER

Therefore thus says the Lord God,
3   "Behold, I am *laying* in *Zion* for a *foundation*, FOUNDATION
         a *stone*, a *tested stone*,   STONE
         a precious *cornerstone*, a sure *foundation*.

4   'He who *believes* (in it - LXX)   INSCRIPTION
         will *not* be *shaken*.'

5   And I will make *justice* the *line*,   BUILDING TOOLS
         and *righteousness* the *plummet*,

6 a. and *hail* will *sweep away* the *refuge* of *lies*,	REFUGE
b. and *waters* will *overwhelm* the *shelter*."	SHELTER

7 a. Then your *covenant* with *death* will be *annulled*,	
b. and your *agreement* with *Sheol* will *not stand*.	COVENANT WITH
c. When the *overwhelming scourge passes through*,	DEATH, SHEOL
d. *you* will be *beaten down* by *it*.	

PLATE THREE

The rhetorical features of this prophetic gem are clear. There are seven stanzas. These seven are inverted with an A-B-C-D-C-B-A interlocking pattern. But in addition to the overall connectedness of the seven stanzas, the parallel sections themselves interlock. This is particularly striking when #1 and #7 are compared. If the intervening material was missing the reader would find nothing amiss because each of the four lines in #1 is countered by a parallel line in #7. Seen together they would appear as follows:

1 a. "We have made a *covenant* with *death*,   DEATH
   b. and with *Sheol* we have an *agreement*;   SHEOL
   c. when the *overwhelming scourge passes through*,   SCOURGE
   d. it will *not come* to *us*:   NOT COME

7 a. (But) your *covenant* with *death* will be *annulled*, DEATH
   b. and your *agreement* with *Sheol* will *not stand*.   SHEOL
   c. When the *overwhelming scourge passes through*,   SCOURGE
   d. *you* will be *beaten down* by *it*.   BEATEN DOWN

                                    PLATE FOUR

It is virtually impossible to argue that the above parallels are an unconscious accident. Surely Isaiah of Jerusalem assumed that his reader/hearer could make the above connections. But the modern reader may need some help to do so. The finely crafted parallels between these two groupings of four lines each are not easy for a 20th century reader to identify because #1 and #7 are so far apart in the text. The ancient reader, presumably, was accustomed to spotting such things. These parallels carry a part of the theology as well as the artistry of the text. The text *does* make sense when read as a straight line progression of ideas. An additional layer of meaning is available when the above structure is discerned.

The above is like the counterpoint in the music of Bach, where two melodies are woven into the same musical line. A vocal duet provides a similar parallel. The melody is clear, but the harmony enriches the artistry of the song and, in addition, aids in the interpretation of the song's meaning.

In like manner, the straight line sequence of the above text can be likened to the melody of a song. When read from beginning to end as a progression of ideas the text makes good sense. This is not by accident. This flow of ideas is available to all and likely dominates any reader's consciousness when first exposed to the material. But the "harmony line" adds both art and meaning to what is being said.

This can be seen in the fact that with inverted parallelism the climax is usually in the center. Even so, in this text the center (#4) tells of an inscription to be written on the new cornerstone of the future promised building. This climax is encased with the other elements that lead into (#1,#2,#3) and out of (#5,#6,#7) that center. The center (in this case including #3, #4 and #5) is then given special prominence in both Rabbinic and NT literature.

As recorded in the *Mishnah*, while building the second temple the masons cleared the floor of the original Holy of Holies. In the center of that floor they found a single stone three fingerbreadths higher than the rest of the flagstones. They left it and the community named it *eben shetiyah*, "the foundation stone" (Mishnah. Moed, Yoma, 5:2. Danby Translation, p. 167). The text reads,

After the ark was taken away a stone remained there from the time of the early Prophets, and it was called 'Shetiyah'. (Lit. "Foundation".) It was higher than the ground by three fingerbreadths. On this he used to put [the fire-pan].

The previous passage in the *Mishnah* provides additional details (Yoma 5:1). On the great day of Atonement the high priest entered the Holy of Holies with a fire-pan and some incense. These were placed on this protruding stone in the middle of the floor. So why was this ancient stone in the center of the Holy of Holies called "the foundation"?

We cannot give a conclusive answer because no early Rabbinic commentary on Isaiah is extant. But it is highly probable that this especially honored stone was called *eben shetiyah* because the building of the second temple was seen as a fulfillment of the prophecy of Isaiah 28. They were building *in Zion*. Here was a *precious stone*, a *sure foundation* on which the entire temple complex, with its rich and meaningful liturgies, was based. Surely this stone was the gift of God promised in Isaiah! Such an identification would have been only natural. The importance of this "foundation stone" was not lost by Jesus and the NT writers.

Jesus' well-known parable in Luke 6:46-49 presents two builders. The one digs deep and lays a *foundation* upon the rock. The second builds without a *foundation*.

The text exhibits a "step parallelism" similar to what was observed above in the comparisons between the first and the seventh stanzas of the Isaiah passage. The Lucan text is as follows:

THE PARABLE OF THE TWO BUILDERS
LUKE 6:46-49

1	Every one coming to me and hearing my words	HEAR MY WORDS
	and doing them [I will show you what he is like].	DO THEM

2	He is like a man building a house	BUILT HOUSE
	[who dug down and went deep	FOUNDATION
	and laid a *foundation*] upon rock.	

3	And when a flash flood arose	FLOOD -
	the stream broke against that house,	HOUSE NOT SHAKEN
	and the stream was not strong enough to shake it	
	because it was *well built*.	

4	And the one hearing	HEAR
	and not doing,	NOT DO

5	he is like a man who built a house	BUILT HOUSE
	upon the [ground	NO FOUNDATION
	without any *foundation*];	

6	against which the stream broke	FLOOD -
	and immediately it fell,	HOUSE FALLS
	and the ruin of that house was great.	

PLATE FIVE

The [ ] indicate words that appear only in Luke. The parallel and more familiar story of Matt 7:24-27 tells of *sand* and rock. The account in Luke has no sand. As in Isaiah, the *foundation* is the key element. The storm symbol appears in Isaiah 28 and Luke 6 and in each case does its destructive work. However, in Isaiah's parable, one building is complete. It then collapses under the fury of the storm. The second building is only a promised future foundation. In Luke, both buildings are completed. The storm destroys the one without foundation. The one with foundation survives. The climactic center of the Isaiah passage (#3, #4) becomes the focus of the new parable in Luke 6. Jesus is thus remembered in Luke's sources as having claimed to be, in his teachings and thereby in his person, the *eben shetiyah* promised by Isaiah, rather than the sacred stone in the center of the Holy of Holies. Was Jesus, like Isaiah, "discerning the times" politically and looking forward to the coming inevitable clash with Rome and expressing his convictions, like Isaiah, as to who would prove the stronger? At his trial he was accused of having threatened "to destroy the temple" (Matt 26:61 // Mark 15:29). Was that accusation perhaps a doctored form of what he implied in this parable? It is easy to see how "There is a storm coming and the temple will fall when it strikes" could be garbled into "He has threatened to destroy the temple." In any case, Jesus' parable was not forgotten by his followers.

In 1 Cor 3:10-17, now for the third time in the tradition, Paul follows the same story line. The text is as follows:

PAUL'S PARABLE OF THE TWO BUILDINGS
1 COR 3:10-17

1 According to the commission of God given to me,
       like a skilled master builder
    I laid a *foundation* and another is building upon it.   JESUS CHRIST IS
       Let each take care how he builds upon it.   THE FOUNDATION
    For *no other foundation* can anyone lay
       than that which is laid, which is *Jesus Christ.*

2   Now if anyone *builds* on *the foundation*   BUILT ON
            with *gold, silver, precious stones,*   FOUNDATION OF:
            wood, hay, straw -   Gold?
            each person's work will become manifest,   Wood?

3   for the day will disclose it
            because it will be *revealed* with *fire.*   TESTED
            And the *fire* will *test*   BY FIRE
            what sort of work each one has done.

4   If anyone's work *built* on *the foundation* survives,
            he will receive a reward.   BUILD ON
            If any person's work is burned up,   FOUNDATION:
            he will suffer loss,   Survive?
            though he will be *saved,*   Burn?
            but only as through *fire!*

5 Do you not know that *you are God's temple*
       and that *God's spirit* dwells in you?
    If *anyone destroys God's temple*   YOU ARE
    God will *destroy him.*   THE TEMPLE
    For *God's temple* is *holy*
    and *that temple are you.*

PLATE SIX

A striking number of artistic and theological themes are shared in some combination among the three texts. These can be seen as follows:

1. Two builders and two buildings (Jesus and Paul)
    Isaiah has one "shelter" complete. The second is only a promised foundation. Jesus has two buildings. Paul has one house built of non-flamable materials (gold, silver, precious stones). The second is constructed of flamable substances (wood, hay, stubble).

2. Precious stones (Isaiah and Paul)

3. The foundation is critical (Isaiah and Jesus)

4. An exterior force attacks the building(s)
Isaiah and Jesus - the storm; Paul - the fire

5. One building is destroyed/burned (Isaiah, Jesus, Paul)

6. A second building stands (Jesus, Paul)

7. To hear/believe/obey is central to the parable
(Isaiah/Jesus/Paul)

8. The temple is implied or mentioned
As interpreted by the *Mishnah*, the temple is central to Isa 28. In the parable of Jesus, the temple is most likely in mind. In the parable of Paul, the temple is mentioned in the text.

9. God's act in the future is critical for all three.

This same subject appears again in Ephesians 2:20 where Jesus is referred to as the cornerstone of the "household of God." Finally, 1 Pet 2:6 quotes the whole of Isa 28:16 and applies it to Jesus Christ.

The intertextuality of these five Biblical passages is extensive and important both for the interpreter and the translator. The question is not merely that of *formatting* the material to clarify its nature and meaning. But the *translation* of these texts should surely be influenced by the interrelatedness evidenced among them. The present writer must confess that he always saw the "precious stones" of 1 Cor 3:12 as gemstones. This can hardly be missed when those stones appear in a list which includes "gold, silver, precious stones, ..." However, it was not until I saw the inner connection between 1 Cor 3 and Isa 28 that I discovered the "precious stone, cornerstone" of Isaiah 28:16 in like manner to be a gemstone.

In summary, what we have thus far observed may have significance for translators in three directions. These are:

1. When *stanzas* are interrelated in a single text in a clear discernible pattern to form a whole, the question of formatting must surely be seriously considered.

2. In the case of "inverted parallelism" and "step parallelism" such as we have observed above, the words and phrases chosen for translation of one side of a parallel must be kept in mind when the other side of the parallel is translated. If the original provides verbal clues to connect the two sides those clues should not be lost.

3. Intertextuality brings to light cases of where it is reasonable to assume that a later author has an earlier text in mind as he/she composes. This inner Biblical

connectedness perhaps should influence the translator's choice of words and phrases in all of the texts involved.

Isaiah 45:22-25 is a second case of an influential and structured text. It is as follows:

ISAIAH 45:22-25

1	"Turn to me and *be saved*,	BE SAVED
	all the ends of *the earth*!	ALL THE EARTH
2	For *I* am *God*, and there is *no other*.	
	By myself I have sworn,	ONLY GOD
	from my mouth has gone forth in *righteousness*	RIGHTEOUSNESS
	a *word* that shall not return;	
3	'To me *every knee* shall *bow*,	EVERY KNEE
	every tongue shall *swear*.'	EVERY TONGUE
4	*Only* in the *Lord*, it shall be said of me,	
	are *righteousness* and strength;	ONLY THE LORD
	to him shall come and be ashamed,	RIGHTEOUSNESS
	all who were incensed against him.	
5	In the Lord they shall be *justified*	BE JUSTIFIED
	and shall glory - *all* the *offspring* of *Israel*."	ALL ISRAEL

PLATE SEVEN

This brief five-stanza unit has a striking interior structure. Like the five-line stanza of Isaiah 55:8-9 examined above, this larger unit has a simple A-B-C-B-A pattern. One hesitates to take on the giants, but the above structure indicates that the material is intended by the author to be a single unit, whether it be called a paragraph, stanza, prophetic homily or hymn. Yet JB, RSV, NRSV and NIV all break the material into separate paragraphs. Here the rhetorical structure is far more than simply an esthetically pleasing balancing of ideas into a semantic whole. Rather, significant aspects of the theological content are built into this self-authenticating structure. This is true on two counts.

First, the opening and the closing of such a semantic unit are points of special emphasis and are often two sides of a single coin. This is profoundly true in this case. The opening two lines tell the reader of God's concern to be the saviour of "*all* the ends of *the earth*." The concluding two lines affirm *justification* (i.e. salvation) for "*all* the seed of *Israel*." Thus Isaiah presents two sides of the coin of God's saving purposes; one side is *all nations* and the other side is *all* the *seed* of *Israel*. When this rhetorical balancing act is not perceived, the translation of the last two lines is critically affected. The above is my own literal rendering of the Hebrew. RSV reads,

> In the Lord all the offspring of Israel
>   shall triumph and glory.

From this translation no English reader can possibly catch Isaiah's presentation of God's balanced concern for the salvation of the *nations* and the justification of the seed of *Israel*.

This same pair of ideas reappears in Paul, where he describes the Gospel as "for the Jew first and also for the Greek," only Isaiah's order is reversed.

Second, the climax is again in the center where the word from the mouth of God is,

> "To me every knee shall bow,
>   and every tongue shall swear."

This climax reappears in the great Christological hymn in Phil 2:5-11, to which we now turn.

Indeed, both of the above mentioned rhetorical features, with their attached theological significance, can be seen to influence the hymn, which exhibits the following form:

THE HYMN OF EXALTATION
PHIL 2:5-11

Have this mind in you which is in Christ Jesus,

1	who, being in *the form of God,*	ORIGINAL STATUS
	did not consider it worth plundering	EQUAL WITH GOD
	to be equal with God.	
2	But he *emptied himself,*	A SERVANT
	taking the *form of* a *servant*	TO OTHERS
	and in the *likeness of men* he became;	
3	and being found in *human form* as man	HUMILIATION
	he humbled himself, becoming *obedient unto death,*	TO DEATH
	even death upon a *cross.*	
4	Therefore *God* has *highly exalted him*	HIGHLY
	and *graced* upon *him*	EXALTED
	the *name above every name,*	
5	that at the name of Jesus	ALL BOW
	every knee might *bow,*	TO HIM
	in the heaven and on the earth and under the earth,	
6	and every tongue confess,	
	"Jesus Christ is *Lord,"*	FINAL STATUS
	to the glory of God the Father.	AS LORD

PLATE EIGHT

It has long been recognized that this passage is a hymn. A variety of structures have been suggested for it by different scholars. These are carefully summarized and reviewed by Martin.[3] My own analysis of this question leads me back to Isaiah.

The Philippian text moves from exaltation to humiliation, suffering and death, and returns to glory. This pattern is most likely borrowed from Isa 52:13-53:12. Yet the conclusion in #5 and #6 of the Philippian hymn is taken from the climax of Isa 45:22-25 (cf. Plate 7, #3 above). The author of the Philippian hymn was apparently aware of the five stanza semantic unit in Isa 45:22-25 that we have identified. He borrowed its center and then incorporated the universal message of its opening and closing by adding to the quote.

---

[3]   Ralph P. Martin, *Carmen Christi: Philippians ii. 5-11 in Recent Interpretation and in the Setting of Early Christian Worship* (Cambridge: The University Press, 1967) 24-41.

Our point is that Paul, or the author of the hymn, is not merely lifting an isolated double line from Isa 45:23. Rather, in the Isaiah text, that divine oath is the climax of a stanza that opens by affirming God's saving intentions for "all the ends of the earth" (cf. Plate 7, #1), and concludes with reference to justification for "all the seed of Israel" (cf. Plate 7, #5). This universal vision is reflected and indeed expanded in the Philippian hymn. The author begins with:

> To me every knee shall bow
> and every tongue confess.

Into the middle of these two lines he adds "in heaven and on earth and under the earth." With the inclusion of this addition, the all-inclusiveness of Isaiah is broadened and given a cosmic dimension. Thus it is possible to affirm that the author of the Philippian hymn was aware of and influenced by the content *and structure* of the entire Isaiah "hymn" noted above.

This same careful balancing of God's concern for the *nations* and his commitment to *Israel* occurs again in the opening verses of the first of the servant songs, which is rhetorically structured in the same A-B-C-B-A fashion. The servant song opens as follows:

ISAIAH 42:1-9

1	Behold *my servant*, whom I uphold,	
	my chosen, in whom my soul *delights*;	MY SERVANT
	I have put *my spirit* upon him,	JUSTICE
	he will bring forth *justice* to the *nations*.	TO THE *NATIONS*
2	He *will not cry* out or lift up his voice,	HE WILL NOT
	or make it heard in the street;	CRY OUT
3	a bruised reed he *will not* break,	PARABLES OF
	and a dimly burning wick he will not quench;	REED & WICK
	he will *faithfully* bring forth *justice*.	BRING JUSTICE
4	He *will not fail*	HE WILL NOT
	or be discouraged	FAIL
5	till *he* has established *justice* in the *land*;	JUSTICE
	and the *coastlands* wait for *his law*.	IN THE *LAND*

PLATE NINE

Again five semantic units come together to form a single stanza. As in Plate 8, this stanza opens with a universal - an affirmation of justice for the *nations/gentiles*. Here also the closing can be seen to focus on the inner circle of God's concern - justice in *the land*.

In this text *ha-aretz* is often translated as "the earth." But when a Hebrew prophet talks about "the land," the first assumption is that he is discussing "the land of Israel." That probable meaning is further reinforced in v. 6 which reads,

> I have given you as a covenant to the *people*,
>   a light to the *nations*.

This particular pair of ideas, "the people [*'ammim*]" and "the nations/gentiles [*goyim*]," is known to reflect the Jews and the Gentiles. Thus this text repeats the literary device observed in Isa 55:6-9, where two stanzas are interlocked with ideas appearing in the center of one stanza and then reflected at the beginning and at the end of a second adjoining stanza.

A second feature of Isaiah 55:6-9 also appears in the above text. This I have chosen to call an "encased parable." In Isa 55:8-9 the concrete simile (*mashal*) about the *heavens* and the *earth* was *encased* in four matching lines referring to thoughts and ways. Here the "encased parable" is identical in structure, only the semantic units are longer. That is, we are again dealing with an A-B-C-B-A form, only here each of the letters represents multiple lines rather than a single line. In this text the concrete images are that of a bruised reed and a burning wick. Justice is mentioned in #1, #3, and #5, and in the center (#3) that justice is defined *by parables*.

Often justice is perceived to be "equal application of law." But here justice becomes "compassion for the weak and the bruised." The two images are carefully balanced. In the first, the reed is subjected to *external* bruising. The second, the wick, is smoldering due to an *internal* lack of oil. The two together present a sensitive pair of pictures that complement each other in their description of the human predicament. We will return to an examination of other instances of the "encased parable" but first, one final example of the balancing of Jew and gentile in the text needs brief examination.

Isaiah's vision of God's broadly focused compassion appears again towards the end of the second Servant song. The rhetorical style shifts to step parallelism and appears as follows:

ISAIAH 49:5-6

| 1 | And now the *Lord says*, | GOD SAYS: |
| | *who formed me* from the womb to be *his servant*, | HIS SERVANT |

| 2 | to *bring Jacob back* to him, | JACOB-RETURN |
| | and that *Israel* might be *gathered* to him, | ISRAEL-GATHERED |

| 3 | for *I am honored* in the eyes of the Lord, | SERVANT HONORED |
| | and my *God* has become *my strength*. | MADE STRONG |

| 4 | *He says*: "It is *too light* a thing | HE SAYS: ONLY |
| | that you should be *my servant* | MY SERVANT? |

| 5 | *to raise up* the tribes of *Jacob* | FOR JACOB |
| | and *to restore* the preserved of *Israel*; | AND ISRAEL |

6	I will give *you* as *a light to the nations*,	TO NATIONS
	that my salvation may reach to the end	END OF EARTH
	of the earth."	

PLATE TEN

The repetitive ideas are again summarized to the right of the text. In the first three pairs of lines the Servant affirms that his task is to bring *Jacob* and *Israel* back to *him*, that is, back to *God*.

In itself this affirmation is remarkable. On the eve of the people's political liberation from exile the "return" that was surely on the lips of all was the political return to the land. But the servant of Yahweh understands that his calling is to challenge the people to return to *God*.

The second series of six lines is carefully balanced with the first six. As double lines they have an A-B-C, A-B-C structure. In this second set of six lines, God responds. The servant's task is *more* than a rescue and recovery responsibility for Jacob and Israel. Such is "too light a thing" for the servant. Indeed he is to become "a light to the nations, that my salvation may reach to the end of the earth." Thus once again a vision for Israel is balanced with a concern for the nations/gentiles. Hebrew parallelisms appear, but they are presented to the reader in a simple discernible pattern that reinforces the meaning of the overall stanza. Thus the rhetorical and theological balancing of God's concern for *Israel* and for the *nations/gentiles* has been discovered in three different texts in Isaiah.

We return now to the "encased parable" such as was observed in a simple form in Isa 55:8-9 (Plate 2) and in a more extended form in Isa 42:1-5 (Plate 9).

Throughout Isa 40-66 I have identified more than 25 occurrences of this particular rhetorical device.[4] It is also extensively used in 1 Corinthians.[5]

Three further examples appear in rapid succession in the well-known servant song of Isa 52:13-53:11. All of these encased parables reflect a distinctive Middle Eastern cultural love for concrete language. In other cultures thinking is done in abstractions that may or may not then be "illustrated." The Middle Eastern mind turns this equation on its head. Here in the Middle East, as I have known it for over 40 years, creative thinking is done in concrete picture language. Meaning is created via visible images rather than through abstract ideas. But the Middle Eastern world is not adverse to extracting concepts out of the story, metaphor, simile or dramatic action. Rather, such picture language lends itself to interpretation and, in scripture, the interpretation is often attached to the picture.

This appears to be the case in what we are here observing. The *primary* language of the picture is placed in the climactic center. Around that center is a series of interpretive semantic "envelopes," which provide direction to the reader's imagination as he/she reflects on the metaphor. That is, the parable/metaphor is not like a balloon that is launched and left to drift in whatever direction the ideological wind happens to blow. Rather the author, by providing the "semantic envelopes," provides specific direction for any interpretive reflection. The first of this trilogy is Isa 53:3-4. The text is as follows:

1	He was *despised*	DESPISED/REJECTED
	and *rejected by men*;	BY *MEN*
2	a man of *sorrows*	SORROWS
	and *acquainted with grief*;	GRIEF
3	and *as one from whom men hide* their faces	PARABLE OF THE
	he was *despised*, and we *esteemed* him not.	SUFFERING MAN
4	Surely *he* has *borne our griefs*	GRIEFS
	and *carried* our *sorrows*;	SORROWS
5	yet we esteemed him *stricken*,	STRICKEN/SMITTEN
	smitten by God and *afflicted*.	BY *GOD* (?)

PLATE ELEVEN - ISAIAH 53:3-4

The appearance of the words "as" or "like" indicate some form of a comparison. What usually follows is a simile. The simile, along with metaphors,

---

[4]   See Isa 40:12-17; 41:1-5; 42:13-17; 43:16-19; 44:1-5; 45:1-3; 47:13-15; 48:9-11, 48:17-20; 49:8-13; 50:5b-8, 8-11; 53:5-6, 7-8; 54:1-3; 54:9-11; 55:8-9; 58:1-9; 58:9c-14; 59:1-13; 61:9-11; 63:12c-14; 64:1-3; 65:8-12; 66:10-14.

[5]   See 1 Cor 2:10-11; 3:5-9a, 10-17; 4:8-10; 4:18-5:2; 5:6-8; 12:1-31; 13:8-13; 14:6-12; 15:42-50.

parables, proverbs and many other Biblical forms of concrete speech, falls under the umbrella of the Hebrew word *mashal* (parable). It is in this larger sense that the word "parable" is used to describe these occurrences of "encased parables."

As regards the parable in this text, there are forms of violence in any culture whether they be witnessed, heard of in description or viewed in films, that are so horrifying that one instinctively turns away or covers the face with the hands. Pictures of a deeply grieving person at the scene of some tragedy with hands covering the face are all firmly implanted in the memories of all of us. Such is the parable that the prophet here presents to the reader. The matching lines are clear and the associations between pairs are strong. The witnesses to the suffering of the servant are *sure* that he is rejected by *men* (#1). Yet his suffering is more than that. Indeed, it almost appears that he is also stricken by *God* (#5)! We *know* the first is true. The second is frightening in its contemplation, but yet unavoidable and thus expressed but with some hesitancy. In like manner there is a progression between #2 and #4. In #2 we are told "he suffers." Number 4 informs the reader, "he suffers *for us*." The RSV and the NRSV have the above material broken into two separate paragraphs. Thus the English reader of those translations is virtually prevented from observing the above. Yet the encased parable form is clear and strong.

Verses 5-6 of chapter 53 offer yet another example of an encased parable. The text is as follows:

ISAIAH 53:5-6

1	But he was *wounded* for *our transgressions,*	HE SUFFERED
	he was *bruised* for our *iniquities*;	FOR US
	upon him was the *chastisement* that made *us whole,*	HIS SUFFERING =
	and with *his stripes we* are *healed.*	OUR HEALING
2	*All* we *like sheep* have *gone astray*;	PARABLE OF
	we have turned every one to his own way;	LOST SHEEP
3	and the *Lord* has *laid on him*	HE SUFFERED
	the *iniquity of* us *all.*	FOR US

PLATE TWELVE

The stanzas of this great song exhibit a progression. The reader is first told: he *suffers* (52:14-53:2). The next stanza affirms: he suffers *for us* (53:3-4, cf. Plate 11). This stanza moves the discussion one step further and says: His suffering for us *heals us* (cf. Plate 12 above). This is followed by a parable (#2). The stanza concludes (#3) with a reaffirmation of the first half of #1.

The chapter continues (v. 7-8a) with yet a third encased parable. Six lines form into three inverted parallelisms. The text is as follows:

ISAIAH 53:7-8a

1	He was *oppressed*, and he was *afflicted*,	OPPRESSED
2	yet he *opened not* his *mouth*.	SILENT
3	Like a *lamb* that is led to the slaughter,	PARABLE OF
4	and like a *sheep* that before its shearers is dumb,	LAMB/SHEEP
5	so he *opened not* his *mouth*.	SILENT
6	By *oppression* and judgment he was *taken away*.	OPPRESSED

PLATE THIRTEEN

The simile of sheep again appears in the center. This parable/*mashal* is encased with double references to the servant's silence. The outer envelope tells the reader that he is oppressed. The nature of the above stanza was missed by Robert Stephens when he added verse numbers to the text in 1551. His influence appears to still be with us in that often line #6 above is translated in a fashion that breaks its links with what precedes and attaches the sentence to what follows. The connections noted above are surely the intent of the prophet and through translation and formatting should be presented in some clear fashion to the modern reader.

The double use of sheep as a parable is not by accident. In the first case (Plate 12) the stanza climaxes with the affirmation that *we* are like sheep. In the second instance (Plate 13) the *suffering servant* of Yahweh is likened to a sheep. The inference is clear. *He* is *like us*. The prominence of these parables in such constructions adds to their theological significance. Furthermore, the double use of the image of sheep as climaxes to these stanzas can be seen as having a profound influence on the Christology of the NT.

In conclusion, here we have observed that the book of Isaiah exhibits clusters of parallelistic couplets that are brought together in carefully structured stanzas. Some such stanzas are held together by inverted parallelism. Others present a series of parallelisms and then repeat the same series in the same order. This style we have called "step parallelism." In yet other cases a parable is placed in the center of a number of semantic envelopes. In three cases examined, the theme of God's concern for the nations was balanced with expressions of divine favor for Israel. Influence on style and content in related NT passages is significant. Issues relating to both translation and the formatting of the printed page were seen to be affected by the semantic patterns discovered.

DISCOVERING A NEW PATH OF INTERTEXTUALITY:
INVERTED QUOTATIONS AND THEIR DYNAMICS

PANCRATIUS C. BEENTJES

Introduction

In the Postscript to his very exciting novel *Il Noma della Rosa* the famous Italian semiotic scholar and novelist Umberto Eco states that books are always referring to other books. Within the corpus of the New Testament this phenomenon is frequently met. In the opening chapters of Saint Matthew's Gospel, e.g., four explicit quotations from the Old Testament have been incorporated into a solid literary and theological structure. All four quotations are introduced with the help of an introductory formula which identifies the subsequent texts as being adopted from the Old Testament:
- 'All this happened in order to fulfil what the Lord declared through the prophet' (Matt 1:23; cfr Isa 7:14).
- 'For this is what the prophet wrote ...' (Matt 2:6; cfr Mic 5:1).
- 'This was to fulfil what the Lord had declared through the prophet ...' (Matt 2:15; cfr Hos 11:1).
- 'So the words spoken through Jeremiah the prophet were fulfilled' (Matt 2:18; cfr Jer 31:15).

Within the Old Testament similar explicit introductory formulae are met relatively scantily. One of the most clear cases is to be found in 2 Chr 36:21: 'All the time that it lay desolate it kept the sabbath rest, to complete seventy years in fulfilment of the word of the LORD by the prophet Jeremiah' (cfr Jer 25:11; 29:10).

Apart from such explicit references both the Old Testament and the New Testament rather often display a more restrained stylistic feature which is not always sufficiently paid attention to: a literary phenomenon that by the present author is called 'inverted quotation'.

The first encounter with this stylistic feature was caused by examining a small text in Ben Sira's famous 'Hymn in Praise of the Fathers' (Ben Sira 44-50) relating to Samuel. The description of Samuel (Sir 46:13-20) has completely been set in the *third person* singular. The only exception, however, is the third bicolon of verse 19, in which suddenly the *first person* singular is used: כופר ונעלם ממנ [תי ('Ransom and sandals, from whom did I take [them]?).[1] Ben Sira here refers to 1 Sam 12:3, where it says: ומיד מי לקחתי כפר ואעלים

Now the issue is not the famous text-critical question relating to the Hebrew verbal form ואעלים.[2] It is sufficiently known that in 1 Sam 12:3 the Septuagint did not translate a verbal form, but a substantive ($\dot{υ}ποδήμα$). This justifies the supposition that, in the Hebrew text, it found the word נעלים ('sandals'). And it is precisely *this* textual form which one meets with in the Hebrew as well as in the Greek text ($\dot{υ}ποδημάτων$) of Sir 46:19c. So apparently in very early days, already *two* Hebrew text forms of 1 Sam 12:3 were in circulation.

The Masoretes preferred the reading ואעלים עיני בו ('and I did blind my eyes with it') to the textual form with נעלים 'sandals'),[3] that has been handed down in the Septuagint version of 1 Sam 12:3 and also in the Hebrew and Greek text of Sir 46:19c. In the three latter cases the combination עיני בו is understood as ענה בו ('to answer').[4]

Much more interesting than this text-critical matter, however, is the question how Ben Sira in his text has remodelled the phrase from 1 Sam 12:3. For he did not just simply copy these words from Samuel's valedictory address, but he introduces an interesting change in the sequence of the parts of the sentence. As a matter of fact he takes them over in precisely the *reversed* sequence:[5]

ומיד מי לקחתי כפר ואעלים
כופר ונעלם ממן] תי[

A current term for this remarkable literary phenomenon does not exist. In view of the most striking characteristic of this stylistic figure, the notion *inverted quotation* would be the most suitable name for it.

After having discovered such a striking intertextual relationship, the first question to be answered would be whether this phenomenon is showing up more often within the Book of Ben Sira. A closer examination brings to light that indeed a number of such 'reversed texts' can be established. Most of them are found within the chapters 44-

---

[1] With respect of the Hebrew text of Sir 46:19-20 (Ms.B.) Hebrew text editions of the Book of Ben Sira are rather inaccurate in their rendering of the exact position of the stichs. Sir 46:19a-d which in Ms.B. is *one* extremely lengthy verse is always divided by the editors into two lines. Sir 46:20, however, which is extremely lengthy too, is printed most of the time on one single line! In fact one should constantly consult *Facsimiles of the Fragments hitherto recovered of the Book of Ecclesiasticus in Hebrew* (Oxford: Oxford University Press, 1901) and the photographs of the newly discovered Hebrew Ben Sira texts.

[2] See *BHS*, and H.J. Stoebe, *Das erste Buch Samuelis* (KAT VIII,1; Gütersloh: Gerd Mohn, 1973) 232.

[3] For sandals as a symbol of bribery: E.A. Speiser, 'Of Shoes and Shekels', *BASOR* 77 (1940) 15-18.

[4] In 1 Sam 12:3 the Vulgate left the term ואעלים untranslated, which is also an indication for the textual problem. In the *Nova Vulgata* from 1979, however, this was remedied: *ut oculos meos clauderem*.

[5] There is no single commentary on the Book of Ben Sira which has ever paid attention to this remarkable change.

50, being the 'Hymn in Praise of the Fathers'. This should not be surprising, because Ben Sira in this particular section of his book is offering a portrayal of biblical heroes, who of course to a high degree are described with the help of biblical vocabulary.

The passage devoted to the prophet Elijah (Sir 48:1-12) not only at the end contains an explicit parallel quotation from Mal 3:24 (להשיב לב אבות על בנים), it also at the opening lodges an intriguing formula: ודבריו כתנור בוער ('his words blazed like a torch'; 48:1b).[6] There can be no doubt that Ben Sira has adopted this rare expression from Mal 3:19, where the same words have been used in a *reversed order* (בער כתנור) to indicate the Day of the Lord to come. Although all commentators of course mention Ben Sira's use of Scripture here, no one however has drawn attention to the fact that this use of Scripture, being a reversed quotation, should be marked off from the parallel quotation in Sir 48:10.

In the same way Sir 48,19b (ויחילו כיולדה) must be considered an inverted quotation from Isa 13:8 (כיולדה יחילון). In Sir 45,15ab the ordination of Aaron is described with the help of an inversion of the vocabulary of Exod 28:41.[7] As the word-pair משח - מלא יד everywhere in the Old Testament is presented in that fixed order, the reversed order in Sir 45:15 points to a deliberate use of inverted quotation by Ben Sira.[8]

It is rather strange to ascertain that a remarkable literary phenomenon such as the inverted quotation in the Book of Ben Sira has never been noticed, let alone be described. A possible reason for it might be that one could think such a literary feature does not occur within the so-called 'protocanonical' literature. The present author, however, will provide solid proof that this is an untenable theory.

Before offering a series of proof texts, however, we should shortly discuss two publications which can be considered as a starting point to the issue of the 'inverted quotation' as such.

As far as can be ascertained, the 'inverted quotation' as described so far has never systematically been set out in detail. Two Jewish scholars, however, have raised the matter of more or less comparable literary phenomena. Moshe Seidl in a series of four articles has collected a large number of text-pairs from Isaiah and Psalms which should be solid proof that the prophet Isaiah has constantly adopted texts from the Book of Psalms and reworked them into his own concept in a *chiastic* way.[9] Not once does Seidl take into account that such a chiastic parallel could have been created the other way around, and he therefore does not reckon at all with the

---

[6] Many translations (e.g. BJ, TOB, REB) have a singular ('his word') which reflects the Greek and Syriac.

[7] This observation is on firm ground, as Sir 45:6-14 has also been modelled upon Exodus 28 as a kind of structural use of scripture. See my doctoral thesis *Jesus Sirach en Tenach* (Nieuwegein, 1981) 180-182.

[8] Beentjes, *Jesus Sirach en Tenach*, 83-87 provides some further occurrences of inverted quotations within the Book of Ben Sira.

[9] M. Seidl, מקבילות בין ספר ישעיה לספר תהילים ('Resemblances between the Book of Isaiah and the Book of Psalms'), *Sinai Yarhon* 19 (1955-1956) 149-172; 229-240; 273-280; 333-353.

possibility that texts of the Book of Isaiah could have been adopted from other biblical compositions than the Psalms. More important, however, is the question of the quality of the evidence. Seidl has brought together no less than 321 text pairs which should support his theory. Upon further consideration, however, it appears that a large majority of text pairs either do not expose a chiastic pattern, or even do not have any relation with each other. In fact there remain only *five* pairs in which a real 'chiasm' shows itself.[10] Undoubtedly Seidl's most vivid example is to be found in Isa 17:13-14 and Ps 83:14-16.

Both passages deal with the same theme: God's intervention against the enemies. Furthermore, לגלג has the unusual meaning 'whirling dust' only in these two texts of the Old Testament.[11] If one sets the words which occur in Ps 83:14-16 as well as in Isa 17:13-14 in columns next to each other, then it is striking that no less than four words in a row (A-B-C-D) from Psalm 83 can be found in precisely the *reverse sequence* (D-C-B-A) in Isa 17:13-14.

Ps 83:14-16		*Isa 17:13-14*	
A.	כגלגל	D.	ורדף
B.	לפני רוח	C.	הרים
C.	הרים	B.	לפני רוח
D.	תרדפם	A.	וכגלגל
E.	ובסופתך	E.	סופה
F.	תבהלם	F.	בלהה

The terms under F. also require attention. They belong to two different roots (בהל and בלה), but strangely enough they have a nearly identical meaning ('to frighten', resp. 'fright'). It cannot be excluded that the changing of the radicals was done on purpose in order to give extra (visual) force to the *reversion of terms*. Seidl, paying attention to this text pair, does not enter at all into the transposition of the radicals under F. He does not even indicate that there are two different radices involved.[12] It is very conspicuous that Seidl only in passing has drawn some attention to the literary device of the 'chiasm' in the Old Testament in a rather general way.[13] The

---

[10] Isa 30:26/Ps 147:3 (p. 150; p. 230); Isa 17:13-14/Ps 83:14-16 (p. 163); Isa 26:1-2/Ps 118:19-21 (p. 168); Isa 51:17/Ps 75:9 (p. 336); Isa 61:10/Ps 35:9 (p. 347).

[11] In Isa 5:28 (Isa 28:28), Jer 47:3; Ezek 10:2.6; 23:24; 26:10; Ps 77:19, and Qoh 12:6 the word regularly has the meaning 'wheel'.

[12] Studies which pay attention to Isa 17:12-14 do not mention Ps 83:14-16 at all, let alone speak of a relationship between both texts: J. Vermeylen, *Du prophète Isaïe à l'Apocalyptique* (EBib; Paris: Gabalda, 1977) I, 313-316; H. Barth, *Die Jesaja-Worte in der Josiazeit* (WMANT 48; Neukirchen-Vluyn: Neukirchener Verlag, 1977) 180-183; 205-207; 227-232; W. Dietrich, *Jesaja und die Politik* (BEvT 74; München: Chr. Kaiser Verlag, 1976) 135-137.

[13] Seidl, 'Resemblances' 150-151.

four examples which he adduces as evidence[14] unfortunately are not specific enough to convince his audience.[15]

Shemaryahu Talmon in an extensive article dealing with the textual study of the Bible,[16] in the sixth paragraph is describing 'Stylistic Metathesis and Textual Inversion'.[17] In the first part of this paragraph Talmon comes across the 'inversion' - or 'chiastic arrangement of reiterative components' - as a genuine literary activity employed by a creative writer within a parallelistic sentence structure, either of adjacent cola (e.g. Prov 1:26 and 1:27) or of distant cola, arching over at least one intervening verse (e.g. Jer 16:4 and 16:6). In the second part he emphasizes that 'inversion' is also used as a 'recensionist' technique, i.e. during the process of text transmission. He wants us to be very careful not immediately to postulate the existence of a second Hebrew *Vorlage* when in the Old Versions we meet upon a sequence of words which apparently is an inversion of the Hebrew Masoretic standard text.

Although Talmon, in his dealing with the textual study of the Bible, has quite rightly paid attention to these two different functions of the 'inversion', the existence of 'inverted quotations' as a *deliberate* result of a creative literary process has hardly been discussed by him.[18]

In this contribution it will be demonstrated that one meets here with a widespread literary phenomenon, which is not only to be found in many biblical texts, but in extra-biblical literature as well. One can only guess at the reason(s) why this literary device for such a long time has escaped the attention of both exegetes and other scholars examining literary documents.

I. Old Testament Evidence

The Hebrew Old Testament in fact keeps a large number of inverted quotations. Probably the most convincing documentary evidence is handed down in the Book of Ezekiel.

---

[14] Isa 43:23/Ps 51:18; Hos 5:3/Ps 106:39; Exod 33:13/Ps 25:4; Isa 1:2/Deut 32:1.

[15] Specific observations and critical comments upon Seidl's choice of these four Old Testament examples are discussed by Beentjes, *Jesus Sirach en Tenach*, 69-71.

[16] Sh. Talmon, 'The Textual Study of the Bible - A New Outlook', *Qumran and the History of the Biblical Text* (ed. F.M. Cross & S. Talmon; Cambridge Mass. 1975) 321-400.

[17] Talmon, 'Textual Study', 358-378.

[18] Without reaching any conclusion at all he in fact only points at Deut 7:5/Deut 12:3, and Deut 13:10-11/Deut 17:5-7; Talmon, 'Textual Study', 361.

Ezek 8:12	*Ezek 9:9*
כי אמרים	כי אמרו
אין יהוה ראה אתנו	עזב יהוה את הארץ
עזב יהוה את הארץ	ואין יהוה ראה

"For they say:	For they have said:
The LORD does not see (us),	The LORD has forsaken the land,
the Lord has forsaken the land'.	the Lord does not see'.

Commentaries on the Book of Ezekiel usually remark that Ezek 9:9 resembles Ezek 8:12, but it is hardly ever remarked that here we have excellent proof of the existence of an inverted quotation as a deliberate literary feature. Both texts belong to the same composition, viz. Ezekiel 8-11, and both times they refer to the situation in which the prophet finds himself.[19] The *qatal*-form of the introductory *verbum dicendi* in Ezek 9:9 (אמרו) hardly leaves any doubt that here words are repeated which have been spoken before, viz. in Ezek 8:12. There is certainly a very definite tie between both texts: Ezekiel 8 voices the accusation and hereupon, in Ezekiel 9, the punishment is carried out. The two cornerstones of prophetic speech (accusation and announcement of judgement) are bound together indissolubly in Ezek 9:9 precisely by the *inverted quotation*.[20]

When one compares Gen 27:29b to Num 24:9b, one notices that, besides the similarity in words, the elements in this saying have changed places with regard to one another.

Gen 27:29	*Num 24:9*
אררי ך ארור	מברכי ך ברוך
ומברכי ך ברוך	ואררי ך ארור

It is hardly coincidence that these two texts are so similar. They both belong to a passage wherein Jacob/Israel's position with regard to the nations is described very explicitly. But not only the contents are the same both times, the form also shows a remarkable similarity. Within the larger frame of the prose narrative wherein they are set, Gen 27:29 and Num 24:9 are distinguished by their short, terse poetic style. This could indicate that the relevant curse and blessing are very ancient. There is no answer to the question which passage was the model for the other one. Probably the saying in Num 24:9 is older than the one in Gen 27:29. But one of the most difficult

---

[19] W. Zimmerli, *Ezekiel* (BKAT XIII/I; Neukirchen-Vluyn: Neukirchener Verlag, 1969) 188-253, esp. 208-209.

[20] As far as I am aware, only Moshe Greenberg has drawn attention to the inversion: 'The reverse of the elements of the saying of 8:12 indicates a purposeful reference to it'; M. Greenberg, *Ezekiel, 1-20* (AB 22, New York: Doubleday, 1983) 178.

questions regarding the Balaam cycle (Numbers 22-24) is precisely that of a more or less trustworthy dating of the various parts.[21]

No one doubts that there is a clear connection between the Book of Ezekiel and the Holiness Code in Leviticus 17-26. Thus there is an unmistakable relationship between Lev 26:3-13 and Ezek 34:25-30. This is especially apparent in a strong resemblance regarding vocabulary.[22] If we take a closer look, we at once notice an *inverted quotation* in these passages:

Lev 26:4b	*Ezek 34:27a*
ונתנה הארץ יבולה	ונתן עץ השדה את פריו
ועץ השדה יתן פריו	והארץ תתן יבולה

There is no unanimous opinion regarding the question which of these two passages must be considered the original source.[23] Nonetheless the following remarks could be important.

(1) Zimmerli, who is convinced that the prophet Ezekiel was clearly influenced by Leviticus 17-20, has another opinion regarding Leviticus 26: 'dass die Prophetie Ezechiels auf die Ausgestaltung von H zurückgewirkt hat ...'.[24]

(2) In his analysis of Leviticus 26, Elliger has clearly demonstrated that, as far as composition is concerned, the chapter is no unity but that, in a gradual process of tradition, it has absorbed all kinds of new themes.[25] One could compare the chapter with which the Holiness Code in Leviticus 26 ends to a magnet drawing all sorts of different material. Therefore for the present author it is indubitable that the passage in Ezek 34:27b served as a model for the *inverted quotation* in Lev 26:4b.[26]

If one compares Hag 1:10 and Zech 8:12 one finds a quite different *inverted quotation*. Haggai's preaching is meant to convince his audience that the bad

---

[21] See W. Gross, *Bileam* (SANT 38; München: Kösel, 1974).

[22] Ezek 34:25b/Lev 26:6b; Ezek 34:27a/Lev 26:4b; Ezek 34:27b/Lev 26:13b; Ezek 34:28b/Lev 26:5b-6b.

[23] A survey of opinions is to be found in Zimmerli, *Ezekiel*, 77*-79*. See also: K. Elliger, *Leviticus* (HAT 4; Tübingen, 1966); R. Kilian, *Literarkritische und formgeschichtliche Untersuchungen des Heiligkeitsgesetzes* (BBB 19; Bonn: Peter Hanstein Verlag, 1963); E.S. Gerstenberger, *Das 3.Buch Mose: Leviticus* (ATD 6; Göttingen: Vandenhoeck & Ruprecht, 1993).

[24] Zimmerli, *Ezekiel*, 78*.

[25] Elliger, *Leviticus*, 364-367.

[26] In Lev 26:42 there is another remarkable formulation, in which the sequence of traditional elements is reversed: 'Then I will remember my covenant with Jacob, and my covenant with Isaac too, and my covenant with Abraham I will also remember, and I will remember the land'. This is the only time in the entire Old Testament that the traditional sequence (Abraham - Isaac - Jacob) is given in a *reversed order*. Unanimously Lev 26,42 is viewed secondary. It is considered to be an addition, probably caused by verse 45, where the impression is created that 'covenant' could only be connected with the departure from Egypt; the Priestly Code does not agree with this at all. The wording of Lev 26:42 with the names of the Patriarchs in a reversed sequence can be meant to draw the reader's attention and to stress what is going to be said. One should also take note of the unique word-combination 'the covenant with the former men' (Lev 26:45).

economic situation (crop failure) must be seen as a punishment of God, because the people have stopped rebuilding the temple.

Hag 1:10	*Zech 8:12*
כלאו שמים מטל	והארץ תתן את יבולה
והארץ כלאה יבולה	והשמים יתנו טלם

The commentaries unanimously hold the view that the images in Zech 8:12 have been adopted from Hag 1:10.[27] Zechariah is reversing the negative formulation of Haggai, and the inverted quotation reinforces stylistically the expression of the change from negative to positive.[28]

Many scholars have noticed that there is a remarkable resemblance between Zeph 3:4b and Ezek 22:26. No one however claims it is an inverted quotation:

Zeph 3:4b	*Ezek 22:26*
כהניה חללו קדש	כהניה חמסו תורתי
חמסו תורה	ויחללו קדשי

Although Zimmerli in his commentary in fact is even describing the characteristics of an inverted quotation,[29] he does not define it as such. That an interdependence is absolutely certain here is proved, first, by the word pair חמס תורה which within the Old Testament is handed down in these two texts only; and, second, by the way the author of Ezek 22:23-31 has elaborated and amplified the accusation of Zeph 3:3-4 in a rather general way. But even if this Zephaniah text should depend on Ezekiel, in any case it would be an example of an inverted quotation!

The inverted quotations mentioned so far are all inner-Hebrew examples: one Hebrew text is remodelled into another Hebrew composition. Inverted quotation as a literary phenomenon is showing up, however, in other combinations too. Documentary evidence can be adduced, for instance, that the *Greek translator(s)* of the Hebrew Bible rather often purposely reversed the sequence of words:

Ps 121:8a (TM)
יהוה ישמר צאתך ובואך

Ps 120:8a (LXX)
κύριος φυλάξει τὴν εἴσοδόν σου καὶ τὴν ἔξοδόν σου

---

[27] W.A.M. Beuken, *Haggai-Sacharja 1-8* (SSN 10; Assen: Van Gorcum) 156-183 and 184-207, esp 166 and 213, note 1.

[28] In this connection one could also point to the word combination הבהמה/האדם ('man/cattle') that in Zech 8:10 precedes the text dealt with, and comes *after* in Hag 1:11.

[29] 'Die Priester ... werden zunächst wie in Zeph 3,4b, *nur in umgekehrter Aufzählung ...*'(Italics by me, PCB); Zimmerli, *Ezekiel*, 524.

That the Greek word order must be considered a deliberate inversion can be inferred from other Septuagint texts in which the order is always the other way around (ἔξοδος- εἴσοδος).[30]

Another example is given by Mal 2:10:

> *Mal 2:10 (TM)*
> הלא אב אחד לכלנו
> הלא אל אחד בראנו

> *Mal 2:10 (LXX)*
> οὐχὶ θεὸς εἷς ἔκτισεν ὑμᾶς;
> οὐχὶ πατὴρ εἷς πάντων ὑμῶν;

The usual explanation that the Greek translator of Mal 2:10 should have inverted the sequence of the Hebrew cola in order to apply the notion 'Father' to Abraham in place of God[31] must be reconsidered now. The structure of Mal 2:10, both in TM and in LXX being a mere *parallelismus membrorum*, makes it very unlikely that 'Father' in the LXX should not be identified with God. A more plausible inference therefore should be that in Mal 2:10 (LXX) we are dealing with an inverted quotation.

Biblical scholars, and Bible translators as well, should also take into account the possibility of 'inner-Septuagint' inverted quotations. Sir 1:27a can be cited as an example:

> σοφία γὰρ
> καὶ παιδεία
> φόβος κυρίου

Here we have a splendid inverted quotation from Prov 15:33a (LXX, Codex A):

> φόβος κυρίου
> παιδεία
> καὶ σοφία

A very striking inverted quotation is found in Sir 24:15:

---

[30] 1 Kgdms 29:6; 2 Kgdms 3:25; 3 Kgdms 3:7; 4 Kgdms 19:27 = Isa 37:28; 1 Chr 16:1. The only exception is to be found in Wis 7:6, which has εἴσοδον - ἔξοδον. This latter text, however, should be considered an inverted allusion to 3 Kgdms 3:7!

[31] E.g. A.S. van der Woude, 'Malachi's Struggle for a Pure Community: Reflections on Malachi 2:10-16', *Tradition and Re-interpretation in Jewish and Early Christian Literature. Essays in Honor of Jürgen C.H.Lebram* (SPB 36; eds J.W. van Henten et al.; Leiden: Brill, 1986) 65-71.

Sir 24:15a
ὡς κιννάμωμον καὶ ἀσπάλαθος ἀρωμάτων
καὶ ὡς σμύρνα ἐκλεκτὴ διέδωκα εὐωδίαν

Exod 30:23 (LXX)
καὶ σὺ λαβὲ ἡδύσματα, τὸ ἄνθος σμύρνης ἐκλεκτης
πεντακοσίους σίκλους καὶ κινναμώμου εὐώδους

Sir 24:15b
ὡς χαλβάνη καὶ ὄνυξ καὶ στακτὴ
καὶ ὡς λιβάνου ἀτμὶς ἐν σκηνῇ

Exod 30:34 (LXX)
λαβὲ σεαυτῷ ἡδύσματα, στακτήν, ὄνυχα, χαλβάνην ἡδυσμοῦ καὶ
λίβανον διαφανῆ ...

Sir 24:13-17 can be considered the 'Praise of Lady Wisdom' proper. Within the structure of these verses Sir 24:15 strikes the eye, not only because of its length, but also by its position: it forms the *heart* of the passage. G.T.Sheppard[32] wonders why Ben Sira's grandson - being the Greek translator - did not copy the sequence of the word order of Sir 24:15 from the Septuagint; however, he does not answer this question at all. The most obvious reason would be that already in his grandfather's Hebrew text there was an inverted quotation from Exodus 30, which has subsequently been translated carefully by the grandson.[33] There is also a possibility that Ben Sira with the reversal of the word order wanted to draw his reader's attention to the point that he in his own composition was using the texts of Exodus on a different, viz. allegorical level. For in Sir 24:15 with the help of these Exodus verses he is not describing the cult, but the activities of Lady Wisdom.

II. Qumran

It is rather a discovery to observe that the inverted quotation as a stylistic feature is not confined to the Old Testament alone. Several times the Dead Sea Scrolls, for instance, contain Old Testament material which must be considered inverted quotations. Michael Fishbane, who wrote a fine and extensive article about the use,

---

[32] G.T. Sheppard, *Wisdom as a Hermeneutical Construct* (BZAW 151; Berlin: W. de Gruyter, 1980) 58, note 94.

[33] In his doctoral thesis B. Wright unfortunately gives no attention at all to the phenomenon of the inverted quotation as a translation technique in the Greek text of the Book of Ben Sira; B.G. Wright, *No Small Difference* (SBLSCS 26; Atlanta: Scholars Press, 1989).

authority and interpretation of the Old Testament at Qumran,[34] does not mention the inverted quotation as one of the options of Qumran use of Scripture. There is no doubt, however, that inverted quotations from the Old Testament have been used by the scribes of the Qumran community as a stylistic feature.

In the War Scroll (1 QM 11:6-7) a large quotation from Num 24:17b-19 has been inserted. As it is introduced by an explicit introductory formula (לאמור), there can be no doubt about the intention(s) of the author. It is a very interesting quotation, because the first part of it (1 QM 11:6) is completely identical to Num 24:17b,[35] whereas the second part (1 QM 11:7) has inverted the sequence of the cola of Num 24:18-19:

Num 24:17b-19		*1 QM 11:6-7*
דרך כוכב מיעקב 17b		6 דרך כוכב מייקוב
וקם שבט מישראל		קם שבט מישראל
ומחץ פאתי מואב		ומחץ פאתי מואב
וקרקר כל בני שת		וקרקר כול בני שית
והיה אדום ירשה 18		7 וירד מיעקוב
והיה ירשה שעיר איביו		והאביד שריד [מ]עיד
וישראל עשה חיל		והיה אויב ירשה
וירד מיעקב 19		וישראל עשה חיל
והאביד שריד מעיד		

As the Qumran scribe has altered the name of אדום into the more general notion אויב, he had to leave out the second colon of Num 24:18 in his text.

Irrefutable evidence relating to the practice of inverted quotation is adduced by the Damascus Document where a very interesting use of an Ezekiel text is found:

CD 6:17-18		*Ezek 22:26*
ולהבדיל בין הטמא לטהור		בין קדש לחל לא הבדילו
ולהודיע בין הקודש לחול		ובין הטמא לטהור לא הודיעו

There can be no doubt that the Damascus Document goes back to this text from the Book of Ezekiel. Both texts are dealing with the same subject, viz. the Sabbath. They also have the same unique combination of elements, which do not occur elsewhere. The reason why the Qumran text has inverted the elements of the biblical passage could be the same as was the case in the example of Hag 1:10/Zech 8:12 mentioned above. Whereas Ezek 22:26 describes the situation in the land in a *negative* way, the Qumran text has altered these prophetic words into a relatively positive statement or

---

[34] M. Fishbane, 'Use, Authority and Interpretation of Mikra at Qumran', *Mikra* (CRINT II/1 ed. M.J. Mulder; Assen: Van Gorcum, 1988) 339-377.

[35] Num 24:17b is also quoted in CD 7:19, and in 4QTestim 12-13.

command.[36] That is the reason why I do disagree with S.Talmon who states 'that CD VI,17 presents a *paraphrased* inverted quotation of Ez 22:26' (Italics by me, PCB).[37]

III. New Testament

In the New Testament one also repeatedly finds the inverted quotation. In Rom 10:20-21 Paul quotes a rather lengthy passage from Isa 65:1-2 (LXX), and there, in an intriguing manner, he allots a different place to certain specific parts:

Rom 10:20-21	*Isa 65:1-2 (LXX)*
(a) εὑρέθην τοῖς ἐμὲ μὴ ζητοῦσιν	(b) ἐμφανὴς ἐγενόμην τοῖς ἐμὲ μὴ ζητοῦσιν
(b) ἐμφανὴς ἐγενόμην τοῖς ἐμὲ μὴ ἐπερωτῶσιν	(a) εὑρέθην τοῖς ἐμὲ μὴ ἐπερωτῶσιν
[ ]	[ ]
(c) ὅλην τὴν ἡμέραν	(d) ἐξεπέτασα τὰς χεῖάς μου
(d) ἐξεπέτασα τὰς χεῖάς μου	(c) ὅλην τὴν ἡμέραν
(e) πρὸς λαὸν ἀπειθοῦντα καὶ ἀντιλέγοντα	(e) πρὸς λαὸν ἀπειθοῦντα καὶ ἀντιλέγοντα

We meet the same phenomenon of the inverted quotation in Rom 11:3, where the apostle starts quoting the words of the prophet Elijah from 3 Kgdms 19:10 (LXX) in an inverted way:

3 Kgdms 19:10 (LXX)	*Rom 11:3*
(a) τὰ θυσιαστήριά σου κατέσκαψαν	(b) τοὺς προφήτας σου ἀπέκτειναν
(b) καὶ τοὺς προφήτας σου ἀπέκτειναν ἐν ρομφαίᾳ καὶ ὑπολέλειμμαι ἐγὼ μονώτατος καὶ ζητοῖσι τὴν ψυχήν μου λαβεῖν αὐτήν	(a) τὰ θυσιαστήριά σου κατέσκαψαν κἀγὼ ὑπελείφθην μόνος καὶ ζητοῖσιν τὴν ψυχήν μου

Within Romans 9-11 there is at least once more an inverted quotation:

Rom 9:25
(a) καλέσω τὸν οὐ λαόν μου λαόν μου
(b) καὶ τὴν οὐκ ἠγαπημένην ἠγαπημένην

---

[36] Relating to Qumran literature D.F. Miner has pointed at 'inversion of words within quotations and allusions'. The examples given by him, however, are very meagre (4QTestim 19/Deut 33:11; 4QSa 2:2/Num 16:2; 1QH 5:23-24/Ps 41:10b; 1QH 15:10/Deut 6:5). D.F. Miner, 'A Suggested Reading for 11Q Melchizedek 17', *JSJ* I-III (1970-1972) 144-148 (147).

[37] Talmon, 'Textual Study', 377.

The text from Hos 2:25, quoted here by Paul, does *not* follow the words that can be read in most of the Greek manuscripts. But it is very similar to a textual form that can be found in Codex Vaticanus and Codex Venetus:[38]

Hos 2:25
(b) καὶ ἀγαπήσω τὴν οὐκ ἠγαπημένην
(a) καὶ ἐρῶ τῷ οὐ λαῷ μου λαός μου εἶ σύ

Commentaries mostly do note that in the three passages from the letter to the Romans mentioned above (Rom 9:25; 10:20-21; 11:3), Paul's sequence deviates from the Septuagint. But they rarely give an explanation why this is so. The few times that someone really looks for a solution, *theological* explanations nearly immediately start to mystify the issue. Paul reversed the sequence of sentences and words - so one contends - because in the order of salvation drastic changes took place regarding the place of the heathen. Explanations like these, which are to be found e.g. in the commentaries of O. Kuss and E. Käsemann,[39] seem untenable to me. The authors mentioned above would only be right, if the stylistic figure of the inverted quotation could *only* be found in Romans 9-11.

One also meets the inverted quotation, however, in other letters of Paul, for instance in 2 Cor 6:17, where Isa 52:11 is quoted 'upside down':

Isa 52:11 (LXX)	*2 Cor 6:17*
(a) καὶ ἀκαθάρτου μὴ ἅπτεσθε	(b) διὸ ἐξέλθατε ἐκ μέσου αὐτῶν
(b) ἐξέλθατε ἐκ μέσου αὐτῆς	καὶ ἀφορίσθητε [ ]
ἀφορίσθητε	(a) καὶ ἀκαθάρτου μὴ ἅπτεσθε

Those scholars who try to explain the inverted quotations in Romans 9-11 according to *theological* grounds, in my opinion seem to miss an elementary step, namely that Paul is using an evidently accepted *literary* process: the inverted quotation. And by using this literary technique exactly within the very heavily laden and important digression of Romans 9-11, he had at his disposal the extra *rhetorical* means to enforce his radical message. In other words: it is not the inverted quotations which bring about a theological turn-about in Romans 9-11. Even *without* them Paul would have been able to formulate his message. But the apostle uses this *literary* device in order to accentuate his theology in an expressive way.[40]

---

[38] For more detailed information about the Greek texts: J. Ziegler, *Duodecim Prophetae.* (Septuaginta auctoritate Societatis Litterarum Gottingensis editum Vol. XIII (Göttingen: Vandenhoek & Ruprecht, 1943) 152.

[39] O. Kuss, *Der Römerbrief III* (Regensburg 1978) 780; E. Käsemann, *An die Römer* (HNT 8a; Tübingen 1973) 284-285.

[40] Other (less extensive) examples of inverted quotations can be found in Rom 3:14; 9:13; 11:9; 14:11; 15:11.21; 2 Cor 8:15; 1 Tim 5:18. In a reaction to my article 'Inverted Quotations in the Bible', *Bib* 63 (1982) 506-523, my colleague P. van Boxel has reexamined Paul's use of inverted quotations in Romans 9-11. In his contribution he mentions a further example of inverted quotation in Phil 2:10-11/Isa 45:23; P.W. van Boxel, 'Israël en de volken in Rom. 9.25-29', *Reflecties op Schrift. Opstellen*

Exegetes' opinions are divided whether the description of the vineyard in Mark 12:1 goes back to Isa 5:2 (LXX).[41] But when one compares both texts in Greek, a *model* becomes visible. Curiously enough nobody has ever described this model.

Isa 5:2 (LXX)	*Mark 12:1*
(a) καὶ φραγμὸν περιέθηκα καὶ ἐχαράκωσα	(b) ἀμπελωνα ἄνθρωπος ἐφύτευσεν
(b) καὶ ἐφύτευσα ἄμπελον σωρηχ	(a) καὶ περιέθηκεν φραγμὸν
(c) καὶ ᾠκοδόμησα πύργον ἐν μέσῳ αὐτοῦ	(d) καὶ ὤρυξεν ὑπολήνιον
(d) καὶ προλήνιον ὤρυξα ἐν αὐτῷ	(c) καὶ ᾠκοδόμησεν πύργον

In the Parable of the vineyard-workers in Mark 12:1 we find a more or less consequent reversal of the text from Isa 5:2 (LXX). In Mark's passage parts of the sentences from Isa 5:2 (LXX) have changed places mutually (the sequence a-b-c-d in Isa 5:2 has become b-a-d-c in Mark 12:1). But that is not all, the sequence of *words* has been changed:

Isa 5:2 (LXX)	*Mark 12:1*
a - 1 - 2	b - 2 - 1
b - 1 - 2	a - 2 - 1
c - 1 - 2	d - 2 - 1
d - 1 - 2	c - 1 - 2

It is most improbable that such a composition by Mark would be a coincidence. Moreover various scholars[42] see in the question τί ποιήσει that concludes the parable (Mark 12:9) a parallel with τί ποιήσω in Isa 5:5 (LXX), so that the *entire* passage in Mark 12:1-9 refers to the Song of the Vineyard in Isa 5:1-7.

The fact that Mark, in the beginning of his Parable of the bad vineyard-workers (12:1), was able to transform the text from Isa 5:2 (LXX) into a very special inverted

---

voor Prof. Dr. Gijs Bouwman (eds. B. Hes a.o., Cahiers voor Levensverdieping 44; Averbode: Altiora 1983) 113-126.

[41] 'The vineyard's structure is evidently based on that of the vineyard from Isa. 5:2 (LXX)'; J.D. Crossan, 'The Parable of the wicked husbandmen', *JBL* 90 (1971) 452. 'The Parable of the Vineyard-Workers (Mk. 12:1-12), ... is introduced by an unmistakable reference to the allegory of the vineyard (=Israel) from Isa 5:1-2 ...'; H.C. Kee, 'The Function of Scriptural Quotations and Allusions in Mark 11-16', *Jesus und Paulus. Festschrift für W.G. Kümmel* (Göttingen 1975) 176.
Quite differently: 'Der durchweg verbreitete Ansicht, dass in V 1 Jes 5,2 LXX zitiert sei, ist als irrig abzuweisen'; R. Pesch, *Das Markusevangelium* (HTKNT II,2; Freiburg, 1977) 215. Among others who definitely deny a connection between Mark 12:1 and Isa 5:2 LXX: e.g. J. Blank, 'Die Sendung des Sohnes', *Neues Testament und Kirche. Festschrift für R. Schnackenburg* (Freiburg, 1974) 11-41, esp. 14; R.H. Gundry, *The Use of the Old Testament in St. Matthew's Gospel* (Leiden, 1967) 13.

[42] J. Jeremias, *Die Gleichnisse Jesu* (Siebenstern-Taschenbuch 43; München 1965) 72; M. Hengel, 'Das Gleichnis von den Weingärtern in Mc 12:1-12 im Lichte der Zenonpapyri und der rabbinischen Gleichnisse', *ZNW* 59 (1968) 7 and 18; J. Gnilka, *Das Evangelium nach Markus* (EKKNT II/2; Zürich: Benzinger 1979) 143. 147; P.J. Farla, *Jezus' oordeel over Israël* (Kampen: Kok, 1978) 195 and 450.

quotation is all the more remarkable, because in all the other instances of his gospel where he quotes the Old Testament, he follows more or less closely the Septuagint (cfr Mark 1:2-3; 7:6-7; 12:10-11; 12:36 etc.).

When one takes the parallel account in Matt 21:33, one notes that Matthew goes back to Mark 12:1, as far as the sequence of the sentence parts is concerned (b-a-d-c). But Matthew brings the sequence of the *words* as much as possible in harmony with the text of Isa 5:2 (LXX). Martin Hengel's hypothesis - Matthew and Mark have used two different Greek translations of the Old Testament - seems rather untenable.[43] First of all there are no manuscripts[44] which support his point of view and second, in the rest of his gospel Mark quotes rather accurately from the Septuagint. At present it is not yet clear why he did not do that in Mark 12:1, but the present author is quite sure that there must be a very special reason for it. A further investigation into the use and function of the inverted quotation is much needed; this goes for the Old Testament, the New Testament,[45] and the early Christian literature.

In Luke 11:27 it is reported that, while Jesus was speaking, a woman in the crowd called out:

μακαρία ἡ κοιλία ἡ βαστάσασα σε
καὶ μαστοὶ οὓς ἐθήλασας

'Happy the womb that carried you
and the breasts that suckled you'.

This saying is not invented by Luke himself. The tradition from which Luke has most probably adopted this saying is reflected in *Tg. Neofiti, Tg. Pseudo-Jonathan/ Tg. Yerushalmi I* on Gen 49:25, be it that the lines in Luke 11:27 have been remodelled into an inverted quotation![46]

An inverted quotation can also been recognised in the passage where Luke describes Jesus on his way to his execution:[47]

---

[43] Hengel, 'Das Gleichnis', 19.

[44] Cf. J. Ziegler, *Isaias* (Septuaginta ...Vol. XIV; Göttingen: Vandenhoeck & Ruprecht, 1939) 137.

[45] For the question whether and in what way the synoptic gospels quote each other: G. Howard, 'Stylistic inversion and the synoptic tradition', *JBL* 97 (1978) 375-389.

[46] See M. McNamara, *The New Testament and the Palestinian Targum to the Pentateuch* (AnBib 27; Rome: Biblical Institute Press, 1966) 133-138; R. le Déaut, *The Message of the New Testament and the Aramaic Bible (Targum)* (SubBib 5; Rome: Biblical Institute Press, 1982).

[47] In Codex Alexandrinus, and Minuscel 106 as well, the Greek text of Hos 10:8 however is identical with Luke 23:30. See J. Ziegler, *Duodecim prophetae*, 170. See also Rev 6:16.

Luke 23:30   Hos 10:8 (LXX)
λέγειν τοῖς ὄρεσιν   καὶ ἐροῦσι τοῖς ὄρεσι
πέσατε ἐφ' ἡμᾶς   καλύψατε ἡμᾶς
καὶ τοῖς βουνοῖς   καὶ τοῖς βουνοῖς
καλύψατε ἡμᾶς   πέσατε ἐφ' ἡμᾶς.

Within the New Testament Hab 2:4 is quoted several times (Rom 1:17; Gal 3:11; Heb 10:38). Only in the latter text it has been adopted in its complete form; moreover, it has been remodelled into an inverted quotation:

Heb 10:38   *Hab 2:4 (LXX)*
ὁ δὲ δίκαιός μου ἐκ πίστεως ζήσεται ἐὰν ὑποστείληται
καὶ ἐὰν ὑποστείληται   οὐκ εὐδοκεῖ ἡ ψυχή μου ἐν αὐτῷ
οὐκ εὐδοκεῖ ἡ ψυχή μου ἐν αὐτῷ   ὁ δὲ δίκαιος ἐκ πίστεώς ζήσεται

IV. Further documentary evidence

It would be a misconception to consider the inverted quotation as just an *inner-biblical* literary phenomenon. As a literary feature it can be documented in series of texts originating from different periods in Antiquity.

In ancient Egypt, for instance, in *Merikare 44* (9/10th dyn.) one comes across the sentence:

sjqr jst=k nt jmtt / smnḫ ḥwt=k nt ḫrt-nṯr[48] ('Make splendid your mansion of the West (the cemetery)/ Embellish your place of the necropolis')[49] which is an inverted quotation from the famous Djedefhor-saying (4th dyn.):

smnḫ pr=k nt ḫrt-nṯr / sjqr jst=k nt jmtt.[50]

Two examples from ancient Greek texts can adduce documentary evidence to the existence of such a literary feature as inverted quotation. Herodot in his *Hist.* 1,47 describes an oracle by the Pythia of Delphi, which text has been inverted by Maxim

---

[48] W. Guglielmi, "Zur Adaption und Funktion von Zitaten", *Studien zur altägyptischen Kultur* 11 (1984) 347-364; the transcription is to be found on p. 352.

[49] Translation by Prof. D. van der Plas (Utrecht University). I would like to thank him for his assistance and advice.

[50] Here *pr* has been used as a synonym to *ḥwt*. In *Ostracon Wien Aeg. 14*, however, which is considered the eldest text, the feminine form of the genitival adjective after the lacuna makes it very plausible that this lacuna should be reconstructed as *ḥwt*. More information: H. Brunner, 'Eine neue Entlehnung aus der Lehre des Djedefhor', MDAIK 14 (1956) 17-19; H. Brunner, 'Ein weiteres Djedefhor-Zitat', MDAIK 19 (1963) 53; H. Brunner, 'Djedefhor in der römischen Kaiserzeit' (Festschrift für Vilmos Wessetzky), Budapest 1974, 55-64; H. Brunner, 'Zitate aus Lebenslehren', *Studien zu altägyptischen Lebenslehren* (OBO 28; eds. E. Hornung & O. Keel; Freiburg: Universitätsverlag. 1979) 112-115. More examples of Egyptian 'inverted quotations' are given by H. Brunner, 'Zitate', *Lexikon der Aegyptologie* Vol. 6 (eds H.W. Helck, E. Otto & W. Westendorf; Wiesbaden: O. Harrassowitz, 1986) 1415-1420.

of Tyre in a twofold way. Not only the cola of the parallelismus membrorum itself, but also the internal sequence of the word pairs have been inverted:

Herodot 1,47
οἶδα δ᾽ ἐγὼ ψάμμου τ᾽ ἀριθμὸν καὶ μέτρα θαλάσσης

Maxim of Tyre 11,6
ἀλλ᾽ οὐδὲ θαλαττης μέτρα οὐδὲ ἀριθμὸν ψαμμου

There is a saying from Aristotle that 'it is not possible for fire to be cold or snow to be black'. This saying has been adopted by the Greek doxographer Aetius (ca. 50-118) in just the reversed order:

Aristotle, Cat. 12b 40-41
οὐ γὰρ ἐνδέχεται τὸ πῦρ ψυχρὸν εἶναι οὐδὲ τὴν χιόνα μέλαιναν

Aetius, De placitis 1.7.3
εἰ θεὸς ἐστι ποιείτω τὴν χιόνα μέλαιναν τὸ δὲ πῦρ ψυχρὸν ...

Irenaeus, bishop of Lyons, concludes a paragraph of the Third Book of his *Adversus Haereses* (2,3) with the words:

'sed omnimodo impossibile est
errorem effugere
apposita veritate'.[51]

Although it has many times been observed that Irenaeus is quoting here from the *First Apology* of Justin the Martyr (*Apol.* 1,12,11), nobody has ever paid attention to the inversion of the elements:

οὐκ ἀδύνατον
ἀληθείας παρατεθείσης
ἄγνοιαν φυγεῖν

In a Treatise on Jerusalem[52] which bishop Eucherius of Lyons (died 449) sent to the priest Faustus the exordium closes with the typically Christian salutation 'Vale in Christo', and then continues: 'Decus et praesidium meum'.[53] This phrase undeniably goes back to the opening of Horace's *Odes* (1,1-2):

---

[51] 'Still it is not absolutely impossible to put error to flight by putting the truth beside it.'
[52] For the text: CSEL 39 (1898) 125-134; CCL 175 (1965) 237-243.
[53] The question whether or not one should speak of *Pseudo*-Eucherius, and whether or not the addressee is the famous Faustus of Reji, does not affect the analysis of the inverted quotation as such which is discussed here.

'Maecenas atavis edite regibus,
o et praesidium et dulce decus meum'.

Ilona Opelt, who was the first scholar to connect these texts with each other,[54] does not pay any attention to the fact that the bishop in his treatise has inverted the words from Horace. Opelt only speaks of 'The somewhat remodelled quotation from Horace'.[55] And even a quotation from Prudentius' *Apotheosis* (393f.): 'O nomen preadulce mihi et lux et decus et spes praesidiumque meum', did not lead her to the observation that in Eucherius' case an *inverted quotation* plays a part.[56]

V. Final remarks

If we survey the examples of the inverted quotation, given up till now, it becomes evident that not all of them have the same *structure*. In view of certain characteristics, one could arrange them in five types.

1) Of course the most spectacular is the inverted quotation that is the *exact reflection* of another text (e.g. Gen 27:29/Num 24:9; Ezek 8:12/Ezek 9:9).

2) Then there are texts which, besides the characteristics of the first group, have an *extra* characteristic: through the inverted quotation the negative content of a text is transformed into a text with a positive message (e.g. Hag 1:10/Zech 8:12) or the other way around (Herodot 1,47/Maxim of Tyre 11,6).

3) Quite often one sees an inverted quotation, in which a number of words (including the verb) from sentence *a* changes places with a number of words (including te verb) from sentence *b* (e.g. Rom 10:20-21/Isa 65:1-2 LXX).

4) A considerable number of words (but not all) from a specific text returns in a passage with a similar theme, but in a *different sequence*. This type could be well described by the name *selective* inverted quotation (e.g. Ps 83:14-16/Isa 17:13-14).

5) The last group is probably the hardest to recognize, because in this type of inverted quotation the *parallelismus membrorum* is not used as it is in group 1,2, and 3. Neither are there rather long passages (as in group 4) but it is simply a question of small changes in sequence of merely a few (mostly two, three, or four) words (e.g. Sir 48:1b/Mal 3:19).

Seeing some examples of inverted quotations (Gen 27:29/Num 24:9; Lev 26:4/Ez 34:27), the question could arise whether such a stylistic figure is not the mere result

---

[54] Il. Opelt, 'Ein Horazzitat bei Pseudo-Eucherius', *JAC* 5 (1962) 175-176.

[55] 'Das etwas umgeformte Horazzitat ...'; Opelt, 'Ein Horazzitat ...', 176.

[56] A large number of inverted quotations could be passed. From antiquity two further examples should be sufficient.
'Caelum, non animum mutant qui trans mare currunt' (Horace, *Epist.* 1,11,27) / 'animum debes mutare, non caelum' (Seneca, *Ep.* 28,1). 'Et oleum et operam perdidi' (Plautus, *Peon.* 332) / 'Confitetur se et operam et oleum perdidisse' (Cicero, *Ad Fam.* 7,1,3).
Even in various periods of the *Dutch literature* one comes across the literary device of the inverted quotation. For some striking examples see Beentjes, *Jesus Sirach en Tenach*, 99-101.

of a free rendering within an oral tradition and must be traced to a common tradition of formulaic pattern[57] or set phrases which can be used variously. In the present author's opinion the problem cannot be solved in that way. If the inversion of phrases had been a common pattern in oral biblical literature indeed, it may be wondered why this literary phenomenon then does occur only a few times in the Old Testament as well as in the New Testament. Neither can the inverted quotation as a stylistic pattern in the Bible be put aside with the disparaging remark that, in those places, the authors were quoting untidily. They are extremely accurate otherwise in their quotations in most other places of their books! Reading some examples of inverted quotations, it is hard to avoid the impression that the biblical author did rework the original text *on purpose*. The fact that now and then we meet an inverted quotation must therefore mean something special. It will take much time and much study of detail before all the mysteries of this stylistic figure will have been laid open. At this moment we can say that in an existing formulation (a sentence, a colon, an established expression, a rare combination of words) the author reverses the sequence. And by this *deviating* model he attains a moment of extra attention in the listener (or the reader), because the latter hears something else than the traditional words.

VI. Implications for Bible translation

• In biblical literature repetitions are never without reason.
• When a biblical author is using formulae, sayings, sentences which also show up elsewhere in the Bible, translators are advised to signalize such repetitions for themselves immediately.
• They should also be very careful, then, in their effort to translate as much as possible all pecularities which are presented by such texts.
• Especially quotations, marked or unmarked, must be translated very carefully, because smaller or larger variations might have been introduced into the 'target text' in order to create special effects. Should a translator smooth out such variations, the author's intentions could be mutilated or even completely destroyed.
• Bible translators should therefore have at their disposal a simple and user-friendly computer search programma, e.g. such as QUEST, to be absolutely sure that during their work of translation they will not overlook potential intertextual relationship(s).[58]

---

[57] Cfr W.R. Watters, *Formula Criticism and the Poetry of the Old Testament* (BZAW 138; Berlin: W. de Gruyter, 1976).

[58] I wish to thank Prof. Bob Becking, Prof. Piet van der Horst, Prof. Arie van der Kooy, Dr. Gerard Mussies, Prof Cornelis Verhoeven, and many others, who - shortly after the publication of my doctoral thesis in 1981 - have supplied me with so many texts in which inverted quotations show up.

VII. Some further literature

J.B. Bauer, "Vexierzitate," *Grazer Beiträge* 11 (1984) 269-281.
C. Kuhl, "Die 'Wiederaufnahme' - ein literarkritisches Prinzip?," *ZAW* 64 (1952) 1-11.
E. Staiger, "Entstellte Zitate," *Trivium* 3 (1945) 1-17.
W.G.E. Watson, "Reversed Word-Pairs in Ugaritic Poetry," *UF* 13 (1981) 189-192.

DISCOURSE IMPLICATIONS OF RHETORICAL QUESTIONS IN JOB, DEUTERONOMY AND THE MINOR PROPHETS

LÉNART J. DE REGT

Abstract

In this article some characteristics of rhetorical questions (henceforth RQs) in Biblical Hebrew are presented, paying attention to their definition, recognition, forms and structuring functions, bias, and implied meanings. Many of the examples are from the book of Job. For comparison, a discussion of the RQs in Deuteronomy and many of the Minor Prophets is included at the end of the article. In the book of Job, relatively many RQs are found of different kinds. RQs play a part in the structuring of the poems into sections. Careful interpretation of these aspects of RQs is important for their translation.

1. Introduction: RQs in parallelism

As is often the case in Job, the disjunctive RQs in 38:28-29 are parallel in meaning.

> Has (ה) the rain a father,
> or who (או מי) has begotten (הוליד) the drops of dew?
> From whose (מי) womb did the ice come forth,
> and (ו) who (מי) has given birth (ילדו) to the hoarfrost of heaven?
> (Job 38:28-29 NRSV)

There is "morphological parallelism of word pairs of different conjugation" (Berlin 1979:23-27) as well because of הוליד (*hiphil*) in v. 28b and ילדו (*qal*) in v. 29b. The verse relations in this RQ series could be described as follows: *{RQ // RQ} // {RQ // RQ}*.

Although the question in 38:28a primarily presupposes a negative answer more than one level of implied meaning is involved. Alter observes "a sort of riddling paradox (no one is the father of the rain, but the rain is the father of life)" (Alter 1985:101). Unlike Alter however, Mitchell (1992:xxv) sees a different meaning here: "*Does* the rain have a father? The whole meaning is in the lack of an answer ... God's humor is ... subtle beyond words".

These are two variant interpretations of the same RQ. Such observations may be valid but they do call for a more linguistic treatment of RQs. The fact that RQs in

Job often occur not only in parallelism but in series[1] raises the issue of their relations and implications. What function does the RQ have in its context, particularly in a context of RQs?

1.1 Definition

Generally, RQ definitions have the following elements in common. "In an ordinary conversation ... a question is assumed to be a request for information. When it becomes evident to the hearer that the "information" in question is already well known to both of them, he understands that the speaker must be deliberately flouting the expected pattern, and thereby doing something else, namely emphasizing a point" (Koops 1988:418) which might have been neglected. The (implicit) answer/statement is made all the stronger by the RQ form. The emotional reaction of the hearers and readers is stimulated, as it is evident that the interrogative form is unnecessary (Lausberg 1967:145). If the answer to a question is common knowledge, it is probably a RQ (Beekman & Callow 1976:236), rather than a real question.

The real question is used to elicit information, whether known or unknown; the rhetorical question is used to convey or call attention to information, expressing the speaker's attitudes, opinions, etc. (Beekman & Callow 1976:229, 244). (This is not to say that real questions cannot express emotion. The real questions in Habakkuk 1:2,3 and 1:13,17 are a complaint as well as a request for some answer, which is given in 1:5-11 and 2:2-4, respectively.) A RQ functions as a reminder of information that the speaker considers relevant to the hearer (Sperber & Wilson 1986:251-252).

A RQ implies that the audience itself knows the answer. In fact, a RQ is a way of implying that the audience will be fully cognizant of its implications. A speaker or writer may thus identify with the audience by implying that the audience will obviously agree (Nida et al. 1983:167).[2] In short, RQs "have the form of a question but are not designed to elicit information. The intent, therefore, is not to ask for a response but to make an emphatic declaration." (Nida et al. 1983:39).

A RQ can be a persuasive device. Because the speaker implies more than the words as such and expects no response, the hearer is impressed by the thought processes that would logically lead to the kind of answer the speaker intends the hearer to reach (Frank 1990:726). The hearer "is forced to frame the expected answer in his mind" (Labuschagne 1966:23) and thus to agree with the speaker. The speaker may gain a position of power from this. RQs are thus likely to be found in contexts where rhetoric is desired for accomplishing *persuasion*, for instance in monologues (Frank 1990:726). This is illustrated by the speeches in Job.

---

[1] Examples are mentioned in Watson (1984:339-340).

[2] E.g., "... the double question in wisdom serves to establish a consensus of obvious fact to which various parties may give assent. In more disputational contexts and uses, the subsequent argument builds upon the consensus." (Brueggemann 1973:371).

With regard to the implied answer, Watson's definition contains a sligthly different aspect: "either the speaker or listener (or even both of them) already knows the answer." (Watson 1984:338).

1.2 Formally unmarked RQs

In cases where an interrogative particle does not occur, the context may still call for interpreting the clause as a question, for instance a RQ. Job 2:10, 10:9, 10:11, 11:11, 17:4b, 17:16a, 23:17, 30:24, 38:8, 40:24,25 and probably 12:12 and 21:16 are generally taken to be genuine unmarked RQs, functioning as the "equivalent to asseveration" (Pope 1973:86). Job 10:11 simply depends on what precedes, as it is a continuation of the הלא-question in 10:10 (van Rensburg 1991:242). Job 2:10 and 10:9 illustrate that the interrogative particle is often lacking when the clause is connected with a preceding sentence by ו (Gesenius §150a). This applies to Joel 4:21 as well (see section 1.3). In 11:11, as Mitchell (1992:109) points out, Theodotion, the Targum and the Vulgate ("*nonne*") translate as an interrogative.

In 2:10 Job thus speaks interrogatively rather than positively as in 1:21. This in itself does not mean, however, that his certainty is replaced by insecurity, as van Wolde (1994:34) suggests. On the contrary, in 2:10 he speaks for the first time explicitly about accepting evil from God. The above definition of a RQ as a persuasive device applies here.

An interesting example of how to recognize an unmarked RQ is provided by Job 38:8. Here the RQ is formally unmarked: no interrogative particle occurs in it. But if it were a statement, v. 10 would be unnecessary. Moreover, it would not go with the first person reference in vv. 9-11. The particle מי in v. 5a is implied or continued here in v. 8. The RQ functions as a challenge and is followed by the speaker's answer in the form of subordinate clauses in vv. 8b-11 (cf. Job 21:30 in section 3.1.1): *RQ + subordCl/answer*.

> Who shut up the sea behind doors
> when it burst forth from the womb,
> when I ... fixed limits for it
> and set its doors and bars in place ... (Job 38:8-11 NIV)

Hos 13:14 starts with two unmarked RQs, expecting a negative answer. Neither the preceding nor the following context makes it probable that they are declarations of God's intention to rescue Israel (Davies 1992:295). In their context they are rather to be interpeted as a threat. The last two RQs, then, summon death to send its plagues on the people.

Shall I ransom them from the power of Sheol?
Shall I redeem them from death? (Hos 13:14a NRSV)
Where (אהי) are your plagues, O Death?
Where (אהי) is your destruction, O Sheol? (13:14b)[3]

1.3 RQs with an explicit answer

Job 38:8-11 thus illustrate that a speaker may answer his own RQ in a monologue
(Longacre 1976:171). Syntactically, the answer in these verses is a subordinate
clause to the RQ in the main clause. Although "rhetorical use of question-answer
sequences" (Schmidt-Radefeldt 1977:379) is not obligatory as it is sometimes in
certain languages, RQs in Job and elsewhere in the Old Testament are frequently
followed by their answer (Labuschagne 1966:27), given by the speaker.

   Habakkuk 3:8 contains another example. In this verse, it is important to take the
word order into account in translation.

Was (ה) your wrath against the rivers, O LORD?
Or (אם) your anger against the rivers,
or (אם) your rage against the sea ...? (Hab 3:8 NRSV)

It seems in this translation as if the prophet asks whether God is angry. But in
Hebrew, the rivers and the sea occur at the beginning of their clauses. Some
translations, e.g. the Good News Bible and the Bible de Jérusalem rightly take this
word order into account.

Est-ce (ה) contre les fleuves (בנהרים), Yahvé, que flambe ta
colère,
ou (אם) contre la mer (בים) ta fureur ...? (Hab 3:8 BdJ)

The answer to these RQs is negative: God's anger is not directed against the
rivers and the sea which are, in fact, instruments of his anger in vv. 9 and 10. On
the contrary, God came out with his anger to save his people (v. 13). Thus, the
prophet seems to give the answer to his own RQs in v. 13. This treatment of the
questions in v. 8 as rhetorical is different from Clark's and Hatton's approach.
They state that "the fact that the answer comes at all shows that the questions in
verse 8 are not rhetorical. In translation, therefore, they should be kept as
questions and not changed into statements." Clark & Hatton (1989:123). RQs
might be treated as statements, as is explained in the next section.

   In Allen's (1976:117) syntactic analysis of Joel 4:21, this verse contains a RQ
with an answer as well, in a way very similar to Jeremiah 25:29.

---

[3] Compare Isa 63:15 and 2 Kgs 2:14 (van Leeuwen 1968: 264). For a discussion of אהי and other
issues in Hos 13:14 see, e.g., Davies (1992:292,295-296).

ונקיתי דמם And shall I leave their bloodshed impunished?
לא־נקיתי I will not, as surely as the Lord has his home in Zion!
(Joel 4:21 Allen)

2. Form and function

RQs take the form of questions. At the same time they are assertions (or the like) by conversational implication. Thus both the interrogative form of RQs and their function must be accounted for (O'Connor 1980:12). "It is commonly believed that a declarative sentence is automatically a statement, that an interrogative sentence is invariably a question, and that an imperative sentence must essentially be a directive. In fact, the relation between grammatical form and communicative function is far more complex, and for the translator this is a vital insight. A so-called rhetorical question, for example, is in fact an *interrogative sentence* with the force of an emphatic *statement* ... Thus form and function exist in *dynamic tension* with each other, and what is important for translation is the fact that this tension varies from one culture, and hence language, to another." (Snell-Hornby 1988:87). Along with the terms form and function the terms content and intent may also be used (Nida et al. 1983:39).

An example of the use of an imperative sentence functioning as a condition is to be found in Ephesians 4:26 (quoting Psalm 4:5 in the Septuagint) where the first imperative "is not a command but a type of concessive condition meaning 'even if you do get angry' followed by the result 'still you must not sin' " (de Waard & Nida 1986: 108). Questions which function as a condition occur in James 5:13,14: 'if anyone among you is suffering, ...'.

Parallel texts in the Old Testament itself sometimes indicate the function a RQ has. A RQ with a certain function is sometimes met with some other construction expressing the same function in the parallel text. Examples of such parallels are to be found in Samuel/Kings and Chronicles. Some of these are mentioned below. In each instance, the RQ is mentioned first. It has the same content as its counterpart in the parallel text.

2 Sam 7:5 ה	and 1 Chr 17:4 לא (negative command)
2 Sam 23:19 הכי	and 1 Chr 11:21 (declarative statement)
1 Kgs 22:45 הלא־הם	and 2 Chr 20:34 הנם (declarative statement)
2 Kgs 15:36 הלא־הם	and 2 Chr 27:7 הנם (declarative statement)
1 Kgs 12:16 מה	and 2 Sam 20:1 אין (negative statement)
and 2 Chr 10:16 מה	

Such functions of RQs on their own are not to be confused with the relations of RQs to their contexts. For example, König (1900:229) says that Ruth 2:9 contains a question instead of a causal clause. Rather, the RQ in Ruth 2:9, being a question in form (הלוא ...), functions in itself like a declarative statement and is the reason for what is said in the preceding context. Similarly, the RQs in Mark 4:30

(Hollenbach 1984:32) and Luke 13:18,20 are formally a question but their function is to introduce a topic.

> And again he said, "To what should I compare the kingdom of God?" (Luke 13:20 NRSV)

Especially when RQs function as the introduction of a topic, or a new aspect of a topic (Barnwell 1992:172), they play a part in the structuring of a passage. This will be discussed in section 3.

2.1 Levels of implication
The terms content, function and intent may be rather confusing. Koops' distinction between different levels, or stages, of implied meaning of RQs is more precise.

> (1) the *rhetorical*, in which the negative-positive polarity is reversed
> (2) the *conventional*, in which a connection is made between a physical state (old or young), or an attitude (you limit wisdom to yourself) and a mental state (wise, foolish or proud)
> (3) the *pragmatic*, in which the conclusion is drawn that certain behavior should follow from certain conditions. (Koops 1988:420).

At the conventional level, the RQ refers to general conventions that are often moral. The physical or mental state of the addressee (or the speaker) is compared with these conventions.

It has already been mentioned that the RQ in Job 38:8 functions as a challenge and is answered in the following verses. The levels of implied meaning apply here. First, it is made clear that it is God who shut in the sea with doors. Second, this implies that Job or any other human could not possibly have done it. Third, the RQ functions as a challenge.

These levels of implied meaning are relevant to Alter's remarks on the RQs in Job 15:7-8.

> Are (ה) you the first man ever born?
> (ו) Were you brought forth before the hills? (Job 15:7 NIV)
> Have (ה) you listened in the council of God?
> And (ו) do you limit wisdom to yourself? (15:8 RSV)

"Eliphaz, in one of the Friends' frequent appeals to the antiquity of received wisdom, upbraids Job" in a "sarcastic hyperbole" (Alter 1985:88). At the rhetorical level, it is implied that Job is not the first man that was born, and that he has not listened in the council of God. At the conventional level, it is implied that wisdom is in the council of God only. At the pragmatic level, Eliphaz makes clear that Job should not be so presumptuous.

In Job 11:7 it is implied at the conventional level that the deep things of God are beyond man. At the rhetorical level, then, a negative answer is implied.

Pragmatically, it is implied that Job should stop pretending that he can understand God.

> Can (ה) you find out the deep things of God?
> Can (אם) you find out the limit of the Almighty?
> (Job 11:7 NRSV)

Other relevant examples are the RQs in 1 Samuel 28:9,12. The woman "is not asking, she is chastising" king Saul, as he turns out to be, accusing him of endangering her life (Craig 1994:230). At the rhetorical level, it is implied that the king is laying a snare for her life (v. 9) and that he has deceived her (v. 12). At the conventional level, it is implied that someone who consults a medium must be laying a snare for her life because these practices are forbidden. At the pragmatic level, she implies that the king should not endanger her life and should not deceive her.

The remarks in Clark & Mundhenk (1982) on Micah 2:7, a series of four RQs (Watson 1984:339), can be related to these levels of contextual implication.

> ... Do not (הלוא) my words (דברי, MT) do good to one who walks uprightly? (Micah 2:7 NRSV)

At the rhetorical level, it is implied that Micah's words do good to those who do right. The conventional implication is that the rich oppressors do not walk uprightly, as "people who are upright will find the prophet's message acceptable, and ... those who do not find the message acceptable cannot be walking uprightly" (Clark & Mundhenk 1982:89). At the pragmatic level, the question "becomes a further probe into the consciences of the rich".

2.1.1 Implied meaning of a RQ and its function in (embedded) discourse
The RQ in Job 31:3, introduced by הלא, constitutes the supposed answer to the preceding RQ in v. 2.

> Is it not ruin for the wicked, disaster for those who do wrong?
> (Job 31:3 NIV)

In v. 3, then, a "virtual quotation" is used by which Job presents the general belief "he formerly held in the justice of God, that served as the basis of his code of moral behavior" (Gordis 1978:545). In v. 2 the NIV translated 'For what is *man's* lot ... *his* heritage' [italics mine] probably to introduce this general belief. Job, however, no longer shares that belief.

At the rhetorical level of implied meaning, according to the general belief the bias of the RQ in v. 3 is indeed that it is "expected to be answered in the affirmative", as Brongers (1981:179) maintains. Hence the particle הלא. On the other hand, the rhetorically implied meaning according to the speaker of this passage is that the RQ has a negative bias. He doubts this belief of the people whom he virtually quotes in his direct discourse.

In the Revidierte Lutherübersetzung this dual nature of the RQ has brought out
by the subjunctive form *Wäre*.

> Wäre es nicht Verderben für den Ungerechten und Unglück für den
> Übeltäter? (31:3 RLU)

2.2 Bias

Job 12:12 illustrates that it is sometimes difficult to establish whether a RQ is
involved; the interpretation of this verse is complex. One could, for instance,
maintain that v. 12 is a RQ implying an affirmative answer, still depending on
הלא in v. 11. This is what the NIV has translated and what is suggested in
Bobzin (1974:188).

> Does not (הלא) the ear test words
> as the tongue tastes food?
> Is not wisdom found among the aged?
> Does not long life bring understanding?
>   To God belong wisdom and power;
>   counsel and understanding are his. (Job 12:11-13 NIV)

This rendering of v. 12, however, would cause it to contradict v. 13. One cannot
solve this contradiction and change it into an analogy by using Webster's analysis.
In his view, vv. 10-12 are a strophe with a concentric pattern: "The truth in vv.
10 and 13 is as certain as that of the more mundane statements within the ring."
(Webster 1983:42). V. 10, however, is a relative clause: "In whose hand (אשר
בידו) *is* the soul of every living thing, and the breath of all mankind." (KJV).
This suggests that v. 10 is connected with what precedes rather than with what
follows and thus does not form a ring with v. 13.

If 12:12 is not treated as an unmarked RQ, but as a declarative sentence, it does
not contradict v. 13 at all. Rather, it is a contrast: the aged may have wisdom, but
only God has the power that goes with it. The Bible de Jérusalem has translated
vv. 12-13 in that way.

> L'oreille n'apprécie-t-elle pas les discours,
> comme le palais goûte les mets?
> La sagesse est l'affaire des veillards,
> le discernement le fait du grand âge.
> Mais en Lui résident sagesse et puissance,
> à lui le conseil et le discernement. (12:11-13 BdJ)

The passage seems most coherent, maintaining the contrast with v. 13, if v. 12 is
taken to be a RQ that implies a negative answer. The RQ could have been marked
with the particle ה. It gives the reason for the preceding RQ in v. 11 and is
followed by an answer starting in v. 13. The New JPS Translation and

Averincev's translation of Job into Russian have treated v. 12 as such.

> Does not (*Ne...li*) the ear try words, like the mouth
> that tastes food?
> Is wisdom really (*Razve*) among the old
> or is understanding apparent among the aged?
> Wisdom as well as power are all His:
> His is counsel, His is understanding. (12:11-13 Averincev)

Mitchell has translated these verses in the same way and like BdJ and the Groot Nieuws Bijbel (The Bible in Today's Dutch) has assumed that a new paragraph starts with the RQ in v. 11.

> Doesn't the mind understand
> as simply as the tongue tastes?
> Do all men grow in knowledge?
> Are they wise because they are old?
> Only God is wise;
> knowledge is his alone. (12:11-13 Mitchell)

The Bible in Today's Dutch translates these verses in the same way, except for v. 11: 'Should one not test statements, as one carefully tastes food?' (backtranslation). The relations of vv. 11-13 can be described as follows: *RQ + RQ/reason + answer*.

In v. 12, the conventional belief that wisdom comes with age is implicitly referred to. On the rhetorical level of implied meaning this belief is repudiated. Koops' rhetorical and conventional levels of implied meaning seem to apply here in reverse order.

At this point something must be said about the bias of RQs. Generally, by asking a yes-no question the questioner often expresses his bias. He does not consider both possible responses to be equally valid but implies or expects that only one of them is right. This can apply to RQs as well as to real questions.[4]

In Biblical Hebrew in general, הלא occurs in questions when an affirmative answer is implied (cf. Latin *nonne*) whereas ה is used when a question implies a negative answer (cf. Latin *num*). ה is also found in real questions where the

---

[4] In English, "the questioner's bias is signalled by various linguistic means such as tags, particles, negative questions, etc. For example, *Bill is coming tonight, isn't he? Isn't Bill coming tonight? Has she gone to bed already? Did someone call last night?* Normally, in cases when the questioner's expectations are not fulfilled, a more elaborate answer is required." (Kiefer 1988:259). Hence real questions (those asked to elicit information) can be biased, too: a speaker expresses his "belief that a particular answer is likely to be correct" and requests "assurance that this belief is true." (Sadock & Zwicky 1985:180). Similarly, in questions in Serbo-Croatian certain conjunctions or adverbials like *dakle* 'so' and *verovatno* 'probably' may be used to indicate the speaker's presumption that something is true (Rakić 1984:696,697,704).

answer is uncertain (cf. Latin *-ne*) (Lettinga 1976:143 §61b). In addition however, ה-questions are found that imply an affirmative answer. This is acknowledged by van Rensburg: RQs with ה as well as with הלא can "elicit a preconceived positive response" (van Rensburg 1991:245). Such instances of ה in Job are found in 4:2, 6:26, 11:2 (ה ... לא), 13:25, 15:11, 20:4, 35:2 (disapproval), 41:1 and possibly 22:2-3 and 36:19. Drijvers & Hawinkels (1971) have interpreted 22:2-3 and 36:19 in this way.

> Isn't an able man of use to God? Is it no help to Him at all when
> someone is sensible? Does it not benefit the Almighty when you
> are righteous? ... (Job 22:2-3 Drijvers & Hawinkels)

The question of bias is important in translation. It would, of course, be wrong to translate a question with a certain bias literally into a language in which its bias would then be different. "... negative yes-no questions are often positively biased questions ... But in some languages ... they are neutral questions about the negative proposition." (Sadock & Zwicky 1985:182). If in a language there are different forms for questions according to whether the bias is positive or negative, the appropriate form must be used in the translation (Clark & Mundhenk 1982:88).

2.2.1 *The bias of* ה
Some RQs with ה that imply an affirmative answer will now be discussed. They are to be found in Job 13:25, 15:11 and 6:26. The section ends on a more controversial note with Amos 5:25.

In the RQ in Job 13:25, which starts with ה, an affirmative answer is implied: 'Will you still frighten a windblown leaf and hunt down a piece of straw?' (Drijvers & Hawinkels). This statement is then motivated in the כ-sentence of v. 26: 'that/For you write bitter things against me and make me inherit the iniquities of my youth'. The motivation contains, in fact, what the speaker objects to. The relation of vv. 25-26 can thus be described as follows: *RQ* ← *objection*. The actual question concerns the contents of the כ-sentence (Aejmelaeus 1986:202). V. 26, though not a RQ, could be translated as one if that should be the best way to express that its contents are being objected to. This is done in the Groot Nieuws Bijbel (The Bible in Today's Dutch): 'Why do you call me to account for so much and do I have to pay for the sins of my youth?' (backtranslation). Van Selms (1971/72:147 & 1978:31) refers to v. 25 as a motivated interrogative clause. If the particle ה is not taken as implying an affirmative answer, the RQ's relation with the כ-sentence would be awkward.

As for translating the כי-sentence of v. 26 as a RQ, the same is recommended by Held (1969:79) for Job 7:12b, 10:6, and other instances. In Hebrew a כ-sentence can actually be parallel to a RQ introduced by למה. This is illustrated by the chiastic synonymous parallelism of the first and fourth clauses in Micah 4:9, a RQ introduced by עתה למה and a כי-sentence, respectively. At the pragmatic level of implication, these questions "force the reader to think about what is happening to them'' (Clark & Mundhenk 1982:126). Both the first and fourth clause contain an admonition to personified Zion not to suffer anxiety (Gruber 1987:583-584).

> Now why (למה) do you cry aloud?
>   Is there no king in you?
>   Has your counselor perished,
> that (כי) pangs have seized you like a woman in labor?
> (Micah 4:9 NRSV)

In the second and third clause, it is implied that even though the king and counselor are there, ''they are as useless and helpless as if they were gone'' (Clark & Mundhenk 1982:127).

Job 15:11 shows another example of the particle ה in a RQ implying an affirmative answer.

> Are (ה) the consolations of God too small for you ...?
> (Job 15:11a NRSV)

Apparently the consolations of God are considered to be too small by Job. This is what is affirmed at the rhetorical level of implied meaning. At the conventional level it is implied that Job is too proud (Koops 1988:420) to accept that God's consolations are not too small for man and should be enough for him. Koops (1988:421) shows how this implication could be made explicit in translation.

> ... are you too proud to receive the consolation God offers you?
> (15:11a Koops)

This level of implied meaning has been made explicit in the Nije Fryske Bibeloersetting (New Frisian Bible Translation) as well.

> Do you consider yourself too great for God's comfort, and for the
> word that is gentle with you? (15:11 NFB)

At the pragmatic level, Eliphaz urges Job to accept the consolations of God rather than reject them. This level of implication is brought out in Today's English Version and, perhaps less clearly, in the Dutch Willibrord Translation and New JPS Translation.

> God offers you comfort; why still reject it? (15:11a TEV)

> Is God's comfort not sufficient for you,
> is his word too low for you? (15:11 Willibrord Translation)

> Are God's consolations not enough for you,
> And His gentle words to you? (15:11 JPS)

Translations sometimes bring out different contextual implications of the same RQ.

Job 6:25 shows that "the interrogatory and exclamatory characteristics are often very difficult to keep apart" (van Rensburg 1991:238). The interrogative pronoun מה occurs in v. 25a as well as in v. 25b. V. 25a, an exclamation, is antithetically paralleled by the RQ in v. 25b. This RQ expects a strongly negative answer which follows in v. 26.

> How forceful are honest words!
> But your reproof, what does it reprove?
> Do (ה) you think that you can reprove words,
> and treat the words of a despairing man as wind?
> You would even cast lots over the orphan ...
> (Job 6:25-27 NRSV, v. 26b NIV)

At the first level of implication, v. 26 is another example of a RQ with the particle ה implying an affirmative answer: Job's friends do think that they can reprove his words and treat them just like wind. This is what is implied at the rhetorical level. Koops' terminology is of use here as well. At the conventional level it is implied that the friends are hard on a desperate man as if his words are just wind, violating the convention that one should not be hard on a despairing man. This implication is continued in v. 27: they would even be hard on an orphan. At the same time, however, v. 26 implies that the friends cannot reprove Job because of his words. At this level, the RQ in v. 25b is answered in the negative by a RQ in v. 26: 'But your reproof, what does it reprove? You think you can reprove my words but you can't; and you are so hard as to treat the words of a desperate man as wind.' V. 26 has different implications at different levels and thus functions in more than one way in the context.

In Job 6:28-29 Job confronts his friends with a challenge.

> But now (ועתה), "look me in the face" (TEV) ...
> "my righteousness still stands" (NIV footnote)
> Is (ה) there any wrong on my tongue?
> Cannot (אם ... לא) my taste discern calamity? (Job 6:28-30)

Job can come up with this challenge for the reason stated in the parallel RQs of v. 30. In v. 30a the particle ה implies a negative answer; in v. 30b אם ... לא implies a positive answer. Watson (1984:339) quotes v. 30 as an illustration that in Hebrew poetry, which is largely composed of parallel couplets, RQs tend to come in pairs. Yet it is interesting to note that these RQs, though they are parallel, do not have the same bias at the rhetorical level. The verse relations of

6:25-30 could be described as follows: *RQ* (25b) + *RQ/answer* (26) + *impl. continued* (27) ¦ *challenge* (28-29) + *RQ/reason // RQ/reason* (30). This corresponds with the strophic division of the poem (Webster 1983:40): vv. 28-30 are a strophe and vv. 25-27 are part of the strophe of vv. 24-27.

After challenging his friends, Job continues his speech in chapter 7 with a complaint about his condition. The RQs in 6:30 thus constitute the closure of this part of Job's first answering speech.

A controversial RQ with ה is to be found in Amos 5:25. The present discussion will be limited to its bias which is sometimes seen as affirmative and often as negative. ה here is not an article, because otherwise it would have been repeated before the word מנחה (Soggin 1987:98). On the face of it, the following translation would seem quite in order.

> Did (ה) you bring to me sacrifices and offerings the forty years in
> the wilderness, O house of Israel? (Amos 5:25 RSV)

But this translation could sound like a condemnation for not bringing sacrifices and offerings, which is not the intention of the passage (de Waard & Smalley 1979:123). Many different interpretations and translations of this RQ and its context have been put forward which will not be repeated here.[5] According to most of them, the RQ implies a negative answer. This is illustrated by the Willibrord Translation.

> Did you (surely you did not) offer me sacrifices and meal-offerings
> in the desert, forty years long, house of Israel?
> (Amos 5:25 backtranslation of Willibrord Translation)

Few interpretations, however, take the word order of the RQ into account. The emphasis rests on the words זבחים and מנחה at the beginning of the sentence (Hammershaimb 1970:91). A very long single clause with no indication of poetic structure, it is intended to apply the question to the object and not to the total clause (Andersen and Freedman 1989:530-531). Although the Israelites did offer something in the desert, the RQ still implies a negative answer.

> Was it (only) sacrifices and offerings that ye brought me in the
> wilderness during forty years? (Amos 5:25 Harper)

Joüon - Muraoka (1991: §161b) are of the opinion that this RQ implies an affirmative answer, ה having an exclamatory nuance here.

---

[5] Summaries can be found in Harper (1979:136) and van Leeuwen (1985:227-235).

> Indeed, you offered me sacrifices and oblations in the wilderness!
> (Amos 5:25 Joüon - Muraoka 1991: §161b)

An affirmative bias of this RQ might as such be valid in its context. It would mean that during the ideal time in the desert Israel offered sacrifices to God and that, in contrast to that, it will go into exile with its idols (vv. 26-27). The contrast between Israel's relationship with God and its relationship to the idols would then be in focus. But this interpretation does not do justice to the word order of the RQ. And if one combines Joüon & Muraoka's interpretation with a focus on the word order, the result would not fit in the context, either:

> Indeed, sacrifices and oblations were what you offered in the wilderness ...!

The RQ's bias, then, is hardly affirmative, but negative. It is not denied that Israel offered sacrifices in the desert. It is denied, however, that such sacrifices were offered all the time as the central cultic expression. A translation like "you did not have to show your faithfulness to me by sacrifices and offerings during those forty years ..." can thus be used (de Waard & Smalley 1979:123). In contrast to this ideal situation in the desert (Jer 2:2, Hos 2:16-17), when true worship of the heart was most important, Israel now hypocritically offers burnt offerings and grain offerings (Amos 5:22).

3. RQs as a structuring device

Passages from Job 21, 15 and 31 will now be discussed in respect of form and function, levels of implied meaning, bias, and the structuring role of RQs. Observations on the structuring role of these RQs will be related to Webster's strophic divisions of the passages in which they occur.[6] This may be useful, as a strophe is "unified by a common theme as well as by various structural and rhetorical devices" (Andersen 1976:40).

In subsequent sections, RQs in Deuteronomy and the Minor Prophets will be discussed and compared.

---

[6] Other examples of RQs in Job with a structuring function, either starting a section or closing one, are 3:11-12, 4:2, 4:6-7, 4:17, 4:21, 6:11-13, 7:1, 8:2, 8:10, 8:11, 9:12, 10:18, 11:7 (de Regt 1994:327-328), 12:11-12 (see above), 13:7-8, 18:2-3, 19:2, 19:22, 22:2-3, 22:12, 24:25, 28:12, 28:20, 35:2, 38:2, 39:5, 39:9, 39:19, and 39:26. Reyburn (1992:16) mentions the use of RQs in Job as a discourse marker, while referring to the beginning of chapter 4, 5, 7, 8, 11, 15, 18, and 22. In fact, chapter 5 starts with an imperative before the RQs. Imperatives are another transition marker in Hebrew poetry (Bandstra 1995:46). Interrogative particles are one of the "categories of markers which primarily denote the beginning of a strophe." (van der Lugt 1995:41).

3.1.1. Job 21

Chapter 21 illustrates nicely what part RQs can play in the structuring of a text. In 21:2-3, Job announces that he will speak. He starts with disjunctive RQs in v. 4 (Gesenius 1910:§150g). A question, probably a RQ, in v. 7 is the beginning of a lengthy description of the wicked. A new strophe starts at each of these three points (Webster 1983:49). The virtual quotation put into the mouth of the wicked in vv. 14-15 largely consists of RQs. The description of the wicked ends with the RQ in v. 16 and the one in vv. 17-18.

V. 16 consists of an unmarked RQ: it is introduced with הן לא and not with הן הלא. If this verse is not taken as a RQ, the resulting negative statement - 'Their prosperity is not in their hand' - would not fit in the context of the chapter. Because of that, a RQ has to be recognized here.

> Behold, (הן לא) is not their prosperity in their hand?
> The counsel of the wicked is far from me. (Job 21:16 RSV)

As proposed in the Biblia Hebraica Stuttgartensia, one could read ממנו instead of ממני at the end of this verse. The whole of v. 16 could then be a RQ. That is how the Bible de Jérusalem has translated it.

> Ne tiennent-ils pas leur bonheur en main,
> et Dieu n'est-il pas écarté du conseil des méchants? (21:16 BdJ)

With the RQ in vv. 17-18 - 'How often (כמה) does calamity come upon the wicked ...?' - v. 16 is perhaps a transitional element; vv. 16-18 also seem to be an introduction to a discussion about punishment. This, in turn, ends with the RQ in v. 21 which gives a reason for what precedes it: 'For (כי) what (מה) does he care about the family he leaves behind ...?' (NIV). The RQ in v. 22 seems to be the beginning of a description of a certain state of affairs in vv. 23-26. Webster's division of these verses into strophes - vv. 16-18, vv. 19-21, vv. 22-26 (Webster 1983:49) - corresponds with this.

In 21:27 Job speaks to his friends again. This verse is closely connected with the RQs that follow. The RQs in Job 21:28 with the particle איה are virtually a quotation: it is explicitly put into the mouth of the friends: כי תאמרו 'For you say ...'. At the rhetorical level, it implies the negative statement that the house of such a prince and the tent of such prosperous wicked people are nowhere to be found. At the conventional level of implication, it is maintained that the wicked are never prosperous. At the pragmatic level, the view expressed by the quotation is condemned.

> Oh (הן), I know your thoughts,
> and your schemes to wrong me.
> For you say, 'Where (איה) is the house of the prince?
> Where (ואיה) is the tent in which the wicked lived?'
> Have you not (הלא) asked those who travel the roads,

and do you not (לא) accept their testimony,
that (כי) the wicked are spared in the day of calamity ...
(Job 21:27-30 NRSV)

The opposition to v. 28 is introduced in v. 29 by means of RQs, implying that the
view of those who travel is opposite to the view put into the mouth of Job's
friends. It is the testimony of those who travel that the wicked escape from
calamity. V. 29 is thus followed by the speaker's answer in the form of
subordinate clauses in v. 30 (cf. Job 38:8-11 in section 1.2). V. 30 is thus part of
the strophe that precedes (vv. 27-30). Webster (1983:49) admits that v. 30 "may
conclude this strophe".

The parallel RQs in v. 31 imply a negative answer: 'Who (מי) declares his way
to his face and for what he has done, who (מי) requites him?'. Nobody repays the
wicked for what they have done. This answer follows in vv. 32-33 which describe
what happens instead: 'He is carried to the grave, and watch is kept over his tomb
...' (NIV). Finally, the RQ in v. 34a with the particle איך constitutes the
conclusion of vv. 29-33 and forms the closure of the speech and indeed of the
second cycle (Webster 1983:39,49): 'How then can you console me with your
nonsense when nothing is left of your answers but falsehood?' The verse relations
of 21:28-34 are the following: *RQ/virtual quotation* (28) + *RQ/opposition* (29) +
subordCl/answer (30) + *RQ // RQ* (31) + *answer* (32-33) + *RQ/conclusion* (34).

3.1.2 Job 15:1-16

Chapter 15 is another passage in Job where RQs play their part in the structuring
of the text. It illustrates that RQs "appear in strategic collocations" and "often
provide the climactic line of the strophe" (Muilenburg 1969:16). The speech
starts with parallel disjunctive RQs in vv. 2-3 and another section seems to start
with parallel disjunctive RQs in vv. 7-8. The section of vv. 7-16 will now be
discussed. Vv. 7 and 8 consist of parallel disjunctive RQs with the particle ה. As
has been shown earlier, it is implied at the rhetorical level that Job is not the first
man that was born, and that he has not listened in the council of God. At the
pragmatic level, Eliphaz makes clear that Job should not be so presumptuous. Vv.
7-8 give the reason for the RQ with the particle מה in v. 9. V. 9 itself is
followed by a reason for it in v. 10.

What (מה) ... do you understand that is not clear to us?
Both the grey-haired and the aged are among us,
older than your father. (Job 15:9-10 RSV)

Vv. 7-10 together give the reason why in v. 11 Job should accept the comforts of
God as sufficient. As has been pointed out in section 2.2.1, it is at the pragmatic
level of implied meaning in v. 11 that Eliphaz urges Job to accept the
consolations of God rather than reject them. Vv. 7-10 thus constitute the reason
for this implication in particular. It would be more difficult to see how these
verses could be the reason for the rhetorical and conventional implications of v.

11. Where different levels of implied meaning are involved, one should try to understand which implication plays a part in the structuring of the context of the verse. Because of the context, then, translations of 15:11 which make the pragmatic implication explicit (see TEV and Willibrord Translation above) are to be preferred to those in which it is the conventional implication, Job's mental state of pride, that has been made explicit (see Koops and NFB above).

The Willibrord Translation not only makes the pragmatic implication slightly explicit but it closes this strophe with v. 11 as the conclusion, thus connecting v. 11 with vv. 7-10. The verse relations in 15:7-11 could be described as follows: *reason{ reason[RQ* (7a) // *RQ* (7b)] // [*RQ* (8a) // *RQ* (8b)]*reason* + *RQ* (9) + *reason* (10) }*reason* + *RQ/conclusion* (11).

Clines states that vv. 7-10 deal with ''Job's reaction to the friends (he claims superior wisdom to theirs)'' whereas vv. 11-13 deal with ''Job's reaction to God (he rejects what is positive from the divine side and insists on angry argument)'' (Clines 1989:351). Van Selms makes a similar division of the passage. In vv. 2-10 Job shows himself to be arrogant towards his friends, whereas his arrogance towards God in vv. 11-16 is worse (van Selms (1982:129, 131). Vv. 4 and 8 however, already seem to hint at Job's arrogance towards God. This division would therefore seem to be too clear-cut. This leaves room, then, to treat v. 11 as a conclusion of vv. 7-10, making a division after v. 11, as has been done in the Willibrord Translation, rather than before it. In fact, even on the grounds given by Clines and van Selms, the division could still be made after v. 11. This is done in Terrien (1963:127): ''Ce n'est pas seulement contre les hommes que Job a manqué de patience. Il a lancé son animosité contre Dieu lui-même.'' In any case, the RQ in v. 11 proves to be a transition from what precedes to what follows.

In translation, the RQs in v. 12 (Koops (1988:420) could be converted to statements, as in Today's English Version

> But you are excited and glare at us in anger.
> You are angry with God and denounce him. (Job 15:12-13 TEV)

or to exclamatory sentences, as in the Bible de Jérusalem.

> (מה) Comme la passion t'emporte!
> (ומה) Et quels yeux tu roules,
> (כי) quand tu tournes contre Dieu ta colère
> (ו) en proférant tes discours! (15:12-13 BdJ)

The connection between v. 12 and v. 13, a כי-sentence, is more transparent and makes more sense in the interpretations of van Selms (1978:32) and Mitchell. Although the questions in v. 12 may at first sight seem to be real rather than rhetorical, they are hardly a request for information.

To what (מה) does your heart carry you and to what (ומה) do
your eyes hint, that (כי) you turn your spirit against God, and (ו)
let such words proceed from your mouth? (15:12-13 van Selms)

What has taken hold of you?
What has made you so wild
that you spew your anger at God
and spit out such insolent words? (15:12-13 Mitchell)

The questions in v. 12, a motivated interrogative sentence, are motivated in the
כי-sentence of v. 13. As in 13:26 (section 2.2.1) and, e.g., Jeremiah 37:18 (van
Selms 1978:33), the motivation contains what the speaker objects to. V. 13,
though not a RQ, could be translated as one if that should be the way to express
that its contents are being objected to. Again, this is done in The Bible in Today's
Dutch: 'Why are you so excited, why do you turn against God?' The relations of
vv. 12-13 can thus be described as follows: *RQ // RQ ← objection.* The reason for
the objection in v. 13 is given in v. 14. In the *a-b-b-a* structure of v. 14, the
relation *RQ ← objection* applies twice. The RQ in element *a* "does not ask for
information about the object. Rather it serves as a basis for the conclusion in
element *b*. And the relationship between the two elements implies a negation for
the verb in element *b*." (Coats 1970:18).

What (מה) is man, that (כי) he could be pure,
or one born of woman, that he could be righteous?
(Job 15:14 NIV)

V. 14 is followed by an answer in vv. 15-16, in which v. 15 gives the reason for
v. 16. The relations of vv. 14-16 are the following: *RQ + {reason → answer}.*
Because of this relation with the RQ in v. 14, vv. 15-16 are connected with what
precedes rather than with what follows.

The relations in vv. 7-16 can be summarized as follows: *reason{ reason[RQ
(7a) // RQ (7b)] // [RQ (8a) // RQ (8b)]reason + RQ (9) + reason (10) }reason
+ RQ/conclusion (11) ¦ RQ (12)a // RQ (12b) ← objection (13) + RQ/reason (14)
+ {reason (15) → answer (16)}.* The section starts with the RQs in v. 7 and is
structured around the RQs in vv. 11 and 14.

3.1.3 Job 31:1-6

Finally, it will be shown how the issue of form and function bears on verse
relations and the structure of Job 31:1-6. In 31:1b, ומה - unless one reads
מהתבונן here as is proposed in the BHS - introduces a RQ. The RQ functions as
an "exclamation of indignation", as "the indignant refusal of a demand"
(Gesenius 1910: §148a).

I have made a covenant with my eyes;
how then (ומה) could I look upon a virgin? (31:1 NRSV)

The RQ in 31:2, introduced by ומה, is commonly interpreted as the reason for Job's behaviour in v. 1. The NIV translates it 'For what is man's lot from God above, his heritage from the Almighty on high?' A different interpretation of v. 2 is chosen by the Willibrord Translation (see below) and by Mitchell: 'But what good has virtue done me ...?' In this view, the conjunction ו introduces what after v. 1 would imply the unexpected.

The RQ in v. 3, introduced by הלא, constitutes the supposed answer to v. 2: 'Is it not ruin for the wicked, disaster for those who do wrong?' (NIV). In v. 3, then, a "virtual quotation" is used by which Job "presents the belief he formerly held in the justice of God, that served as the basis of his code of moral behavior" (Gordis 1978:545). It is a general belief, which is probably why the NIV translated '*man's* lot ... *his* heritage' [italics mine] in v. 2. The relations in 31:1-3 are thus as follows: *RQ + RQ/reason/unexpected + virtual quotation: {RQ/answer}*.

At the rhetorical level of implied meaning, according to the general belief the bias of the RQ in v. 3 is indeed that it is "expected to be answered in the affirmative", as Brongers (1981:179) maintains. On the other hand, the rhetorically implied meaning according to the speaker of this passage is that the RQ has a negative bias. As has been mentioned in section 2.1.1, the speaker disagrees with this belief of the people whom he virtually quotes in his direct discourse. Unlike the virtual quotation in Job 21:14-15 and 28 above, the virtual quotation is implicit: it is not formally introduced as such. In translating, it may be necessary to make this information explicit. This is what the Willibrord Translation does.

> And what is my lot from God,
> what does the Almighty decree from on high?
> Disaster for the bad people - they say -
> misfortune for everybody who does evil.
> (Job 31:2-3, backtranslation of Willibrord Translation)

The opposition to this is introduced by the RQ in 31:4: 'Does he not see my ways, and number all my steps?' (NRSV). Introduced by הלא, this RQ is expected to be answered in the affirmative at the rhetorical level: He, God, does see Job's ways and number his steps. At what might be called the conventional level, Job implies that he is blameless and this implication is continued in the rest of the chapter. At the pragmatic level it is perhaps implied that God should have rewarded him accordingly.

V. 5 starts with אם. If one takes v. 5 to be a conditional protasis, v. 6 can hardly be the apodosis of v. 5. One could then assume that v. 5 is part of a larger conditional structure, formed by a protasis in vv. 5 and 7 and an apodosis in v. 8. The protasis would then be interrupted by v. 6 (NRSV, Bobzin 1974:389-390) in which case the structure of the passage would be awkward. And to transpose v. 5 with v. 6, as Skehan (1971:117) does, would be too drastic.

It would seem more natural to treat 31:5 as Gordis (1978:544) does, as a RQ, implying a negative answer: 'Ai-je fait route avec le mensonge, pressé le pas vers la fausseté?' (BdJ). The answer, then, follows in v. 6: 'Let Him weigh me on the scale of righteousness; Let God ascertain my integrity.' (JPS).

V. 5 may illustrate the tension between form and function. The RQ in v. 5 probably functions as an oath. It is thus possible to translate vv. 5-6 as an oath: 'I swear I have never acted wickedly and never tried to deceive others ... he will see how innocent I am.' (TEV; The Bible in Today's Dutch).

The verse relations in 31:1-6 can be described as follows: *RQ* (1) + *RQ/unexpected* (2) + *RQ/'answer'/virtual quotation* (3) + *RQ/opposition* (4) // *RQ/oath* (5) + *answer/wish* (6).

3.2 Deuteronomy

It has been mentioned above that RQs are likely to be found in contexts where rhetoric is desired for accomplishing persuasion, for instance in monologues (Frank 1990:726). The book of Job is a case in point. It does not imply however, that in persuasive monologic texts many RQs are bound to occur. Deuteronomy, for instance, largely consists of what may be called persuasive monologues. One might then have expected a large number of RQs in Deuteronomy, but of the no more than 48 interrogative clauses in the whole book, only 29 are RQs. This difference between Deuteronomy and Job may be due to the fact that speeches in Deuteronomy, unlike those in Job, do not constitute a dialogue.

The figures in this section are partly based on de Regt (1988:32-34, 73-44, Supplement 28-29). Of the 14 yes/no-questions in Deuteronomy, 12 are RQs, and of the 34 wh-questions, 17 are RQs. These RQs are scattered through the book[7] and, with the exception of chapters 4 and 20, hardly occur in parallelism or in series like in Job.

The RQs in 20:5,6,7,8 are parallel in the sense that they each introduce a new subject in the officials' speech, another category of men to be exempted from battle.

> What man is there that (מי־האיש אשר) has built a new house and has not dedicated it? (Deut 20:5 RSV)

The same construction (מי־האיש אשר) is found in vv. 6 and 7. These are often believed to be examples of the indefinite use of מי, introducing a generalising relative clause: 'Whoever has built a house ... let him go home.' (Gesenius 1910:

---

[7] A list of the 29 RQs in Deuteronomy is given here, with their respective interrogative particles. ה: 4:32de, 4:33a, 4:34a, 20:19h (with the Septuagint and BHS), 32:6a; א(ו)הלא: 3:11b (qere), 11:30a, 31:17h, 32:6c, 32:34a; למה: 5:25a; אנה: 1:28a; מה: 10:12a; איכה: 1:12a, 7:17c, 32:30a; מי: 3:24c, 4:7a, 4:8a, 5:26a, 9:2c, 20:5b, 20:6a, 20:7a, 20:8d, 33:29b; אי: 32:37b; unmarked: 4:33d (after 4:33a). Except for 3:11b, 7:17c, and 11:30a, these RQs occur in a context of persuasion. The 19 non-rhetorical questions are to be found in 5:29a (מי), 6:20b (מה), 8:2g (ה), 12:30e (איכה), 13:4d (ה), 18:21b (איכה), 21:1f (מי), 28:67bd (מי), 29:23bc (מה), 30:12b (מי), 30:12cde (unmarked after 30:12b), 30:13b (מי), 30:13cde (unmarked after 30:13b). 5:29a and 28:67bd function as exclamations.

§137c; Waltke & O'Connor 1990: §18.2e). The Revidierte Lutherübersetzung has translated these verses in this way ('Wer ein neues Haus gebaut hat ...'). However, this interpretation is rather unlikely in v.8 (Joüon - Muraoka 1991: §145fa) where the article ה replaces the relative pronoun.

> What man is there that is fearful (מי האיש הירא) ...?
> (Deut 20:8 RSV)

In a majority of translations RQs are used here, as in the RSV, maintaining the parallel between vv. 5,6,7, and 8.

Again, it is important to distinguish between form and function. In terms of their syntactic form, 20:5b,6a,7a,8d are RQs, whereas they function as a generalising introduction to a new subject or even as a conditional protasis. It is because of this function and not for syntactic reasons that it may be useful to translate these verses the way the Revidierte Lutherübersetzung or TEV has done.

> Is there any man here who has lost his nerve and is afraid? If so,
> he is to go home. (20:8 TEV)

In Deuteronomy 4:7-8, the two parallel RQs constitute the closure of vv. 1-8, giving a reason for the preceding verses. In 4:32-34, parallel RQs are part of the closing section (vv. 32-40) of Moses' first speech in Deuteronomy.

> For (כי) ask ... from one end of heaven to the other:
> has (ה) anything so great as this ever happened
> or has (ה) its like ever been heard of?
> Has (ה) any people ever heard the voice of a god ...
> and lived?
> Or has (ה) any god ever attempted ...? (Deut 4:32-34 NRSV)

At the rhetorical level of implied meaning, it is clear that the answers are negative: "none, except X" (Labuschagne 1966:19). Elements of these RQs are still repeated as an answer in vv. 35-38, before the conclusion is given in vv. 39-40.

In different ways, then, RQs play a part in the structuring of sections in chapters 4 and 20. In these passages in Deuteronomy where RQs are frequent, their functions are similar to those of RQs in Job.

3.3 The Minor Prophets
As has been mentioned, the RQs in persuasive monologic texts may be less numerous than in Job. Although this applies to the books of the Minor Prophets the RQs in them have various important functions. RQs sometimes begin a new section, for example in Habakkuk 1:12 and in 2:6, introducing a series of taunts

against the wicked, and in Obadaiah v. 8.[8] But they fulfil other functions as well.

3.3.1 Amos

In two passages in Amos, RQs function as part of a comparison. Amos 3:3-8, which consists of a series of nine RQs, is built up from a series of general illustrations from natural life (3:3-6a) to a more specific illustration from God's actions (3:6b). V. 7, being a statement, seems to be a secondary element. It clarifies the relationship between v. 6b and the conclusion in v. 8 about the prophet's role (de Waard & Smalley 1979:66,202-204). Just as those disasters and relations of natural creatures cannot be denied, one has to reckon with the relation of God to man. One has to fear when God (the lion) gives warnings and to prophesy concerning God's actions (3:8).

According to de Waard & Smalley (1979:193,201), 3:1-2 would seem to be the final section of 1:3-3:2. The series of RQs in 3:3-8 would then constitute the beginning of a new section on the prophet's role and commission (3:3-4:3). On the other hand, 3:1-8 are the end of the first part of Amos as 3:8 forms an inclusio with 1:2 because of the roaring of the lion (Van Leeuwen 1985:41; Peter Booij, personal communication). This means that the first part of Amos closes with the RQs in 3:3-8. Once again, RQs are found to play a part in the structuring of the text.

In Amos 6:12, in which a comparison is made as well, the RQs imply a strongly negative answer. It is impossible for horses to run on rocks or for someone to plough the rocks with oxen. The second half of v. 12 then says that what the hearers do is just as impossible.

> Do (ה) horses run on rocks?
> Does (אם) one plough [them] with oxen?
> Yet (כי) you have turned justice into poison... (Amos 6:12)

With the KJV, Segond, and the Dutch Groot Nieuws Bijbel the Masoretic Text of the second RQ is adhered to here. To bring out clearly that impossibilities are being compared, the second half of v. 12 may have to be translated into a RQ as well.

> How then can you turn justice into venom
> and righteousness into bitter gall?
> (Amos 6:12b, backtranslation of NFB)

V. 12b is followed by two relative clauses in v. 13, the last of which introduces a RQ put into the mouth of those who are being spoken to. 6:2 is also most likely to be such a "quotation put by Amos in the mouth of the rulers to show their unlimited boasting." (de Waard & Smalley 1979:127).

---

[8] "... before a standard prophetic announcement as an exact synonym of *hinnē* and the like" (Brown 1987:216).

3.3.2 Micah, Zechariah and Haggai

Some of the RQs in Micah have been discussed earlier. It is in chapter 6, however, that RQs (and their answers) have a structuring function. In Micah 6:1-2, the Lord's controversy with his people in vv. 3-5 is introduced. In vv. 3-5 the Lord speaks in first person, and he begins by asking RQs.

> O my people, what (מה) have I done unto thee?
> and wherein (ומה) have I wearied thee?
> testify against me. (Micah 6:3 KJV)

The rhetorical implication is that the Lord has done nothing to give the people trouble. The people thus cannot give an answer to these questions. No answer of theirs is given in this paragraph. On the basis of this, Clark & Mundhenk (1982:156) maintain that these questions are real rather than rhetorical. In our opinion however, these questions are not a request for information but they function as a challenge to the people. Secondly, in contrast with the lack of an answer by the people, the Lord gives his own answer in vv. 4-5.

In reaction to this, real questions are put into the mouth of the people in vv. 6-7. Part of the answer to these questions is a RQ.

> ... and what (ומה) does the LORD require of you but (כי אם) to
> do justice ...? (Micah 6:8 NRSV)

It is to the answer in v. 8 that vv. 6-7 lead. This reply "completely ignores the sacrificial system" of vv. 6-7 (Clark & Mundhenk 1982: 162).

6:9-16 is another section where the Lord speaks in first person, and he starts with an imperative and with RQs.

RQs do not occur frequently in Zechariah but there is a series of RQs in 7:5-7 with a structuring function. The RQs, one in each verse, with a conditional protasis in vv. 5 and 6, give unity to this paragraph.

> When (כי) you fasted ..., was it (ה) for me that you fasted?
> And when (כי) you eat ..., do you not (הלוא אתם) eat ... only for
> yourselves?
> Were not (הלוא) these the words that the LORD proclaimed ...?
> (Zec 7:5-7 NRSV)

In Haggai, a RQ occurs at the beginning of every prophecy in which the people are challenged, after the introductory formulas: in 1:4 (ה), 2:3 (מי) and 2:12 (ה).

3.3.3 Nahum and Malachi

RQs are not so frequent in Nahum and Malachi. Nevertheless, RQs play a part in the structuring of the text. Nahum actually ends with a RQ. In Nahum 2:12-14, lions are a metaphor for Nineveh and its inhabitants. This section starts with a mocking RQ (Clark & Hatton 1989:36).

Where (איה) is the lions' den, ...? (Nahum 2:12 RSV)

According to most modern translations, a new paragraph starts with the RQ in Nahum 3:8. This means that the preceding section ends with the RQs in 3:7. In Malachi 1:6, a passage about the priests starts with metaphors and RQs.

> A son honours his father, and a servant his master.
> If I am a father, where (איה) is the honour due me?
> If I am a master, where (איה) is the respect due me?
> (Mal 1:6 NIV)

The description of the priests' offering practices is concluded with a RQ in 1:13 and a curse in 1:14. A passage about Judah's unfaithfulness (2:10-16) starts with RQs in v. 10. Finally, the RQs of 3:2 not only express the Lord's incomparability (Labuschagne 1966:26; compare also Nahum 1:6 and Micah 7:18) but introduce a description of the Lord's day (vv. 2-5) as well. ''The rhetorical question, whether used to initiate a new topic or to highlight some crucial attitude or emotion, was a mainstay in the Hebrew prophet's stock of poetic devices.'' (Wendland 1985:109).

There is another characteristic of RQs in Malachi. Remarks are frequently put into the mouth of those who are being spoken to. They are objections to what the Lord has said before (Wendland 1985:112). Most of them are RQs (1:2,6,7, 2:14,17, 3:7,8,13,14). Except for the RQ in 3:14 they are followed by an answer from the speaker. They introduce the answer, making it more persuasive. The parallel questions 'How (במה) have we despised your name?' and 'How (במה) have we polluted you?' (1:6,7) illustrate this. The RQ in 3:7 ('How (במה) shall we return?') is indeed followed by an answer but this starts with a counter-question ('Will (ה) man rob God?'). This applies to 1:2 as well.

Parts of Malachi are thus similar to dialogue although only one party speaks. Such stylized dialogues in which the other party is imagined to make hyperbolic claims, as well as the RQs strongly remind us of the diatribe, a style of literature from the Hellenistic world (Peterson 1995).

4.1 Translating a statement into a rhetorical question

As has been shown, RQs in Hebrew may become clearer in translation when rewritten as statements, or the like (compare section 2). But to remove them too frequently would lead to a loss of impact. On the other hand, some of that impact may be gained back elsewhere when a statement is translated with a RQ (Clark & Mundhenk 1982:16). They demonstrate this with Obadaiah v. 7, a negative statement in Hebrew, translated as a RQ in the TEV: 'Where is all that cleverness he had?'. The TEV has done the same in Haggai 1:5. In English, 'Don't you see what is happening to you?' (TEV) has much more impact than a translation which uses an imperative as in the Hebrew text, e.g., 'Give careful thought to your ways.' (NIV).

In the receptor language, RQs may have functions which are not attested in the source language. A RQ may thus have to be used in the translation even though the source text does not have a question at that point (Barnwell 1992:175-176).

4.2 Translating the answers to rhetorical questions

Job 6:25b-26 (see section 2.2.1) and other passages in the Old Testament (Labuschagne 1966:27 note 5) illustrate that it is possible to answer a RQ with a RQ that itself constitutes the full answer. This is different from passages like 2 Samuel 12:23, Job 1:9-10 and Matthew 11:7-9 in which after some supplementary RQs the full answer is given but not in the form of a RQ. In 2 Samuel 12:23 the conventional implication of 'Can I bring him [the child] back again?' follows as the answer: '... he will not return to me'. ''In some languages rhetorical questions always require answers. Such a series of questions as that in Matthew 11:7-9 is especially difficult to translate, for three of the questions are expanded by immediately appending supplementary questions, but the full answer is not given until the middle of verse 9'' (Nida 1964: 229). No answer to the RQ in Job 6:25b is given however, except the RQ in 6:26.

Loewen's translation advice needs to be amplified so as to include these instances. Not only is it necessary to decide how to translate a single RQ, ''whether you can use it unanswered as in the Bible, or whether you can retain it with its answer, or whether you should rewrite it as a statement'' (Loewen 1981: 149). This should be amplified to include deciding about sequences of RQs, whether all of them, only one or none of them should be followed by an answer or rewritten as a statement. For example, some of the RQs in Amos 3:3-8 might be grouped to avoid repeating an answer too much (de Waard & Smalley 1979:62). In Micah 1:5, two of the RQs - 'Is it not (הלוא) Samariah? ... Is it not (הלוא) Jerusalem?' - are used as an answer. It is better to make the answer a statement if the question would otherwise come over as a real question (Clark & Mundhenk 1982:59).

When receptor-language readers do not recognize that a given question is rhetorical, it may not be necessary to rewrite it as a statement. It may be possible to make the rhetorical character of the question explicit by using a special construction or particle in translation. The TEV has done this in 2 Samuel 11:20 ('Why, then, ...?'). The wording of a statement or answer should be in keeping with the emotional force of the RQ: 'Does a young lion growl...? Never!' (Amos 3:4, de Waard & Smalley 1979:62).

5. Conclusion

RQs in Job are frequently followed by their answer, which may itself take the form of a RQ. On the other hand, the answer is often left implicit in the RQ itself. A difference in function may or may not be involved.

Some of the functions of RQs in the book of Job are as follows: RQs can open or close a section and thus play a part in the (poetic) structuring of the text. They can provide a reason or answer, constitute an opposition or conclusion. RQs may have different implications at different levels and thus function in more than one way in their context. The bias of RQs affects the interpretation of passages in which they occur.

In Deuteronomy, RQs are more scattered. In the few passages where RQs occur frequently, they are similar in function to RQs in Job.

Finally, RQs have a structuring function in Micah 6, Zechariah 7, Nahum, Habakkuk, Haggai and Malachi. In Malachi they frequently constitute quotations put into the mouth of the hearers. In Amos, RQs mainly function as part of a comparison.

References

Translations
Authorized King James Version, 1611.
S.S. Averincev, "Kniga Iova: perevod i primečania," *Mir Biblii* 1 (1993) 37-64 (Moscow: Russian Bible Society). (= in: *Poetry and Prose of the Ancient East* (Moscow 1973).
Bible de Jérusalem: La Sainte Bible traduite en français sous la direction de l'École biblique de Jérusalem (Nouvelle édition), 1986.
P. Drijvers & P. Hawinkels, *Job* (Bilthoven, Netherlands: Ambo, 1971).
Groot Nieuws Bijbel (The Bible in Today's Dutch), 1983.
S. Mitchell, *The book of Job: Translated and with an introduction* (New York: HarperPerennial, 1992).
New International Version, 1978.
New Jewish Publication Society Translation, 1985.
New Revised Standard Version, 1989.
Nije Fryske Bibeloersetting (New Frisian Bible Translation), 1978.
Revidierte Lutherübersetzung, 1973.
Revised Standard Version, 1952.
La Sainte Bible traduite par Louis Segond, édition revue 1910.
Good News Bible: Today's English Version, 1976.
Willibrord Translation, revised edition, 1995.

Other References
A. Aejmelaeus, "Function and Interpretation of *ky* in Biblical Hebrew," *JBL* 105 (1986) 193-209.
L.C. Allen, *The Books of Joel, Obadaiah, Jonah and Micah* (NICOT; London: Hodder and Stoughton, 1976).
R. Alter, *The art of biblical poetry* (New York: Basic Books, 1985).
F.I. Andersen, *Job, An Introduction and Commentary* (Tyndale Old Testament Commentaries; London: Inter-Varsity, 1976).
F.I. Andersen & D.N. Freedman, *Amos* (AB 24A; New York [etc.]: Doubleday, 1989).
B.L. Bandstra, "Marking Turns in Poetic Text: Waw in the Psalms," *Narrative and Comment: Contributions to Discource Grammar and Biblical Hebrew presented to Wolfgang Schneider* (ed. E. Talstra; Amsterdam: Societas Hebraica Amstelodamensis, 1995) 45-52.
K. Barnwell, *Bible Translation: An introductory course in translation principles* (3rd ed.; Dallas: Summer Institute of Linguistics, 1992).
J. Beekman & J. Callow, *Translating the Word of God* (Grand Rapids: Zondervan, 1976).
Berlin, A., "Grammatical Aspects of Biblical Parallelism," *HUCA* 50 (1979) 17-43.
Biblia Hebraica Stuttgartensia. 1967/77. Stuttgart: Deutsche Bibelstiftung.
H. Bobzin, *Die 'Tempora' im Hiobdialog* (Dissertation Marburg an der Lahn, 1974).

H.A. Brongers, "Some remarks on the biblical particle הלא," *OTS* 21 (1981) 177-189.

M.A. Brown, " "Is It Not?" or "Indeed!"": *HL* in Northwest Semitic," *Maarav* 4 (1987) 201-219.

W.A. Brueggemann, "Jeremiah's Use of Rhetorical Questions," *JBL* 92 (1973) 358-374.

D.J. Clark & H.A. Hatton, *A Translator's Handbook on the Books of Nahum, Habakkuk, and Zephaniah* (New York: United Bible Societies, 1989).

D.J. Clark & N. Mundhenk, *A Translator's Handbook on the Books of Obadaiah and Micah* (London [etc.]: United Bible Societies, 1982).

D.J.A. Clines, *Word Biblical Commentary, Volume 17: Job 1-20* (Dallas: Word Books, 1989).

G.W. Coats, "Self-Abasement and Insult Formulas," *JBL* 89 (1970) 14-26.

K.M. Craig Jr., "Rhetorical Aspects of Questions Answered with Silence in 1 Samuel 14:37 and 28:6," *CBQ* 56 (1994) 221-239.

G.I. Davies, *Hosea* (New Century Bible Commentary; London: Marshall Pickering / Grand Rapids: Eerdmans, 1992).

J. Frank, "You Call That a Rhetorical Question? Forms and functions of rhetorical questions in conversation," *Journal of Pragmatics* 14 (1990) 723-738.

Gesenius' Hebrew grammar (ed. by E. Kautzsch, 2d English ed. revised and translated by A.E. Cowley; Oxford: University Press, 1910).

R. Gordis, *The Book of Job: commentary, new translation, and special studies* (Moreshet Series 2; New York: The Jewish Theological Seminary of America, 1978).

M.I. Gruber, "The Double Three-Part Question in the Book of Micah [Hebrew]," *Tarbiz* 56 (1987) 583-584.

E. Hammershaimb, *The Book of Amos: A Commentary Translated by John Sturdy* (Oxford: Basil Blackwell, 1970).

W.R. Harper, *A Critical and Exegetical Commentary on Amos and Hosea* (ICC; Edinburgh: Clark, 1979).

M. Held, "Rhetorical Questions in Ugaritic and Biblical Hebrew," *Eretz-Israel: Archaeological, Historical and Geographical Studies* 9 (1969) 71-79.

B. Hollenbach, Translation Study Guide on Discourse. *Notes on Translation* 99 (1984) 28-34.

P. Joüon, *A Grammar of Biblical Hebrew* (Subsidia Biblica 14, translated and revised by T. Muraoka; Roma: Pontificium Institutum Biblicum, 1991).

F. Kiefer, "On the pragmatics of answers," *Questions and Questioning* (ed. M. Meyer; Berlin/New York: de Gruyter, 1988) 255-279.

R. Koops, "Rhetorical Questions and Implied Meaning in the Book of Job," *The Bible Translator* 39 (1988) 415-423.

E. König, *Stilistik, Rhetorik, Poetik in bezug auf die biblische Literatur komparativisch dargestellt* (Leipzig: Dieterich'sche Verlagsbuchhandlung Theodor Weicher, 1900).

C.J. Labuschagne, *The Incomparability of Yahweh in the Old Testament* (Pretoria Oriental Series 5; Leiden: Brill, 1966).

H. Lausberg, *Elemente der literarischen Rhetorik* (München: Hueber, 1967).

C. van Leeuwen, *Hosea* (De prediking van het Oude Testament; Nijkerk, The Netherlands: Callenbach, 1968.

------, *Amos* (De prediking van het Oude Testament; Nijkerk, The Netherlands: Callenbach, 1985).

J.P. Lettinga, *Grammatica van het Bijbels Hebreeuws* (Leiden: Brill, 1976).

J.A. Loewen, *The Practice of Translating: Drills for training translators* (Helps for Translators; London [etc.]: United Bible Societies, 1981).

R.E. Longacre, *An Anatomy of Speech Notions* (Lisse, The Netherlands: de Ridder, 1976).

J. Muilenburg, "Form Criticism and Beyond," *JBL* 88 (1969) 1-18.

P. van der Lugt, *Rhetorical Criticism and the Poetry of the Book of Job* (OTS 32; Leiden [etc.]: Brill, 1995).

E.A. Nida, *Toward a Science of Translating* (Leiden: Brill, 1964).

E.A. Nida, J.P. Louw, A.H. Snyman & J. v. W. Cronje, *Style and Discourse: With special reference to the Greek New Testament* (Cape Town: Bible Society, 1983).

M. O'Connor, *Hebrew Verse Structure* (Winona Lake, IN: Eisenbrauns, 1980).

D.L. Peterson, *Malachi: The form-critical task* (Paper read at the 15th Congress of the International Organization for the Study of the Old Testament, Cambridge, 1995).

M.H. Pope, *Job* (AB 15; Garden City, New York: Doubleday, 1965, reprinted 1973).

S. Rakić, "Serbo-Croatian Yes/No-Questions and Speech Acts," *Journal of Pragmatics* 8 (1984) 693-713.

J.F.J. van Rensburg, "Wise Men Saying Things by Asking Questions: The interrogative in Job 3 to 14," *Old Testament Essays* 4 (1991) 227-247.

L.J. de Regt, *A Parametric Model for Syntactic Studies of a Textual Corpus, Demonstrated on the Hebrew of Deuteronomy 1-30* (Studia Semitica Neerlandica 24; Assen, The Netherlands: Van Gorcum, 1988).

------, "Implications of Rhetorical Questions in Strophes in Job 11 and 15," *The Book of Job* (ed. W.A.M. Beuken, BETL 114; Leuven: Peeters, 1994) 321-328.

W.D. Reyburn, *A Handbook on the Book of Job* (UBS Handbook Series; New York: United Bible Societies, 1992).

J.M. Sadock & A.M. Zwicky, "Speech Act Distinctions in Syntax," *Language Typology and Syntactic Description, Vol. I: Clause structure* (ed. T. Shopen; Cambridge: University Press, 1985) 155-196.

J. Schmidt-Radefeldt, "On So-Called 'Rhetorical' Questions," *Journal of Pragmatics* 1 (1977) 375-392.

A. van Selms, "Motivated Interrogative Sentences in Biblical Hebrew," *Semitics* 2 (1971/72) 143-149.

------, "Motivated Interrogative Sentences in the Book of Job," *Semitics* 6 (1978) 28-35.

------, *Job I* (De prediking van het Oude Testament; Nijkerk, The Netherlands: Callenbach, 1982).

P.W. Skehan, *Studies in Israelite Poetry and Wisdom* (CBQMS I), XVII 114-123: Job's Final Plea (Job 29-31) and the Lord's Reply (Job 38-41) (Washington D.C.: The Catholic Biblical Association of America, 1971). (= *Biblica* 45 (1964) 51-62.)

M. Snell-Hornby, *Translation Studies: An integrated approach* (Amsterdam [etc.]: Benjamins, 1988).

J.A. Soggin, *The Prophet Amos: A translation and commentary* (London: SCM Press, 1987).

D. Sperber & D. Wilson, *Relevance: Communication and cognition* (Oxford and Harvard: Basil Blackwell, 1986).

S. Terrien, *Job* (CAT 13; Neuchâtel, Switzerland: Delachaux & Niestlé, 1963).

J. de Waard & W.A. Smalley, *A Translator's Handbook on the Book of Amos* (New York/Stuttgart: United Bible Societies, 1979).

J. de Waard & E.A. Nida, *From One Language to Another: Functional equivalence in Bible translation* (New York: Thomas Nelson, 1986).

B.K. Waltke & M. O'Connor, *An Introduction to Biblical Hebrew Syntax* (Winona Lake, IN: Eisenbrauns, 1990).

W.G.E. Watson, *Classical Hebrew Poetry: A guide to its techniques* (JSOTSup 26; Sheffield: JSOT Press, 1984).

E.C. Webster, "Strophic Patterns in Job 3-28," *JSOT* 26 (1983) 33-60.

E. Wendland, "Linear and Concentric Patterns in Malachi," *The Bible Translator* 36 (1985) 108-121.

E.J. van Wolde, "A Text-Semantic Study of the Hebrew Bible, Illustrated with Noah and Job," *JBL* 113 (1994) 19-35.

THE ORDER OF PARTICIPANTS IN COMPOUND CLAUSAL ELEMENTS IN THE PENTATEUCH AND EARLIER PROPHETS: SYNTAX, CONVENTION OR RHETORIC?

LÉNART J. DE REGT

Introduction

Participants are mostly part of different syntactic constituents in a clause. But occasionally two (or more) participants are part of one and the same nominal constituent, e.g., of the subject in the clause. One may then ask what may be indicated by the order and form in which they are mentioned. Is the order determined by the grammar of the sentence and of the text, or does the order express an implicit comment? In this last case, the order would be significant in rhetorical analysis.

In the majority of compound constituents (see sections 1-1.4), the order is not rhetorically significant in the text but is syntactically determined by the text. It seems that the inflectional affix, pronoun or first proper name refers to the central, major participant in the context whereas other nominal descriptions refer to minor participants.[1] This may or may not be the only action these participants perform together, but this joint activity does not usually extend beyond a few clauses. A conjoined NP does not become more central than the first one in what follows in the context.

In other instances, the order in compound clausal elements is determined by factors such as chronological order and social conventions (see section 2-2.3). Finally, the reader is referred to section 3 for the instances where the order has to be explained otherwise and is indeed determined by rhetorical strategy.

It seems appropriate to analyze the Pentateuch and Earlier Prophets with a view to this problem. The Pentateuch does not only contain instructions, e.g., concerning the tabernacle, but many other passages of direct discourse and narrative sections as well. Narrative text and direct discourse are of course widely attested in the Earlier Prophets. The findings of this article are thus not characteristic of one textual corpus or one author only.

---

[1] See de Regt (1991-1992) for syntactic differences between major and minor participants.

1. Centrality

In the same constituent, Laban is mentioned before his father or mother in Gen 24:50,53,55 and unlike his parents he is indeed a major participant in what follows later. For the same reason Samson is mentioned before his father and mother in Judg 14:5. Rachel is mentioned before Leah in Gen 31:4,14 and the narrative continues not with Leah but rather with Rachel who steals her father's household gods. Esau is mentioned before Jacob in Gen 35:29 and is the major participant in what follows. One might say that Rachel and Esau are mentioned first so as to implicitly comment that they are Jacob's favourite wife and Isaac's favourite son, respectively. Rashi, for instance, comments on Gen 31:4 that Rachel is mentioned before Leah, as she was the major character of the house, because for her sake Jacob had become allied to Laban by marriage. On Gen 24:50 he comments that Laban was a wicked person and, in his great impudence, hastened to answer before his father. However, it is of interest to see how the order in which participants are mentioned seems to be determined by their relative centrality to the context, thus overruling other factors like social conventions. It is the centrality of a participant in the context that determines that in compound constituents he is mentioned first. Hence, the syntax of such constituents is influenced by the context at large.

Similarly, in 1 Kgs 1:32,34,38,44,45 Zadok the priest is mentioned before Nathan the prophet as Zadok actually performs the anointing of Solomon in v. 39 (Morešet 1967:259). In Gen 19:12, the men mention sons-in-law before sons and daughters.

> Have you anyone else here? Son(s)-in-law (חתן) and your sons and
> your daughters ... bring them out of the place. (Gen 19:12)

The daughters have already been mentioned to the men in v. 8; the future sons-in-law are referred to again in v. 14. Given the daughters, there are probably (future) sons-in-law as well. So they are more central whereas there may or may not be other children. The angels seem to know that the only male relatives of Lot's, who are mentioned first, are sons-in-law (van Selms 1967a:252). 1 Sam 27:3 mentions David's men and their families before his wives. V. 2 already mentions David and the men when they go to Gath. It is the general pattern that these men take their families with them; David's wives are only a specific example.

In Joüon - Muraoka (1991: §150q(1)) it is stated that Morešet (1967) "shows that it is not always correct to say that the person mentioned first is the principal person". But to be more specific, Morešet only shows that when a verb preceding two or more subjects is in the singular, this verb does not indicate that the first-mentioned subject - e.g., in Exod 29:32; 34:30 - is the initiator of the action (Morešet 1967:253). The lack of agreement of the verb is only a formal matter and has no bearing on the content (Levi 1987:45).

And saw (וירא) Aaron and all the children of Israel Moses
(Exod 34:30)

Irrespective of the verb, Morešet also briefly discusses the order of subjects in the compound subject as such. The first-mentioned subject is central in the actual context, or more important than his companion, and the principal factor in the action (Morešet 1967:254). Among other instances, he mentions here 'Miriam and Aaron' (Num 12:1), 'both (גם) you and (גם) this people with you' (Exod 18:18), 'Deborah and Barak' (Judg 5:1) and 'Samson and his father' (Judg 14:5) as such compound subjects. The compound subject in Num 12:1 is indeed striking because its order is different in vv. 4,5 where in the compound constituents Miriam is mentioned last. The earlier example Gen 31:4 ('Rachel and Leah') is valid as well, though this is not indicated by the singular verb ותען as Miller (1994:220) claims. A similar example occurs in Num 16:5 ('to Korah and to all his company') and 16:24,27 ('Korah, Dathan, and Abiram'). Korah is indeed the initiator in the action (16:1). Also, 1 Sam 18:3 and 20:39 ('Jonathan and David') occur in a context where Jonathan is the initiator of a development or course of action. In 1 Sam 20:39 he gives a sign to David by shooting arrows.

Compare also the subjects in Num 32:2,25,29,31 ('the children of Gad and the children of Reuben')[2] as opposed to the chronological order (of the tribes' ancestors) in v. 1 and many other places (including Deuteronomy) where Reuben is mentioned before Gad. In other passages Gad is only mentioned before Reuben in Josh 18:7 and 2 Kgs 10:33 ('Gadites'). Morešet (1967:258) states that in Num 32:2,25,31 the Gadites are the initiators. Similarly, in Deut 31:14 and 32:44-45, Moses is the initiator rather than Joshua/Hoshea. 2 Kgs 15:37 contains another, interesting example.

The Lord began to send *Rezin, king of Aram, and Pekah, son of Remaliah* against Judah (2 Kgs 15:37)

Although Rezin is a foreign king, he is mentioned first. He becomes more central in the context that follows (2 Kgs 16:5-9 // Isa 7:1-4).[3] All these examples show that the order of participants in a compound clausal element is not just determined by the syntax of only the clause or sentence but by the passage at large.

1.1 Moses and Aaron
In Exodus, Moses is introduced in Exod 2:2 and he remains the central participant in the book. He is a partner in most of the dialogues. Apart from 12:43 he is the

---

[2] At these points, the Rubenites are mentioned before the Gadites in the Septuagint, the Syriac Version, and (apart from v. 2) the Samaritan Pentateuch. One should thus not jump to conclusions on the basis of the order in which they are mentioned (Gispen 1964:242). On the other hand, the translators of these versions may have reversed the order in accordance with the places where the Masoretic Text mentions the Rubenites before the Gadites.

[3] Pekah is mentioned closer to 15:37, in 15:32 and 16:1, but only as part of a temporal phrase.

only one to whom the Lord speaks, even when it concerns Aaron as well. In the end this applies to 7:8-9 as well.

> And the Lord spoke to Moses and to Aaron, saying: When Pharaoh speaks to you (אלכם) ... you [Moses] will say (ואמרת) to Aaron ... (Exod 7:8-9)

Unlike Moses, Aaron is only introduced in 4:14. In 4:29 Aaron starts his supportive role. The only instance of the Lord speaking to Aaron as well as Moses occurs in 12:43: 'And said the Lord to Moses and Aaron: ...'. After 12:50, at the end of the first Passover, Aaron is not mentioned until 16:2 where the manna story begins. He is mentioned as a participant between 16:2 and 17:12, in 18:12, 19:24, in chapter 24, in 32:1-25, 34:30-33, and 40:31-32. He is mentioned not as a participant but only in connection with rules for the priests in chapters 28-29, 35:19, 39:1,27,41, and 40:12-13. So Aaron is mentioned in fewer passages than Moses and his function is primarily to help Moses. In 10:3 they both go to Pharaoh but v. 6 only says that 'he turned and left[4] Pharaoh' even though Aaron left with him (cf. v. 8).

Although Aaron is the less central participant of the two, one may say that Moses and Aaron are the two major participants in Exodus. Their joint activities extend over passages that are longer than a few clauses. It is thus important to discover how and when Moses and Aaron are referred to in one constituent. They meet in 4:27 and are mentioned in one constituent for the first time in 4:29. Not only the narrator refers to Moses first and then to Aaron; Pharao addresses them in the same order (5:4).

> Why, Moses and Aaron, do you take the people away from their work? (Exod 5:4)

To the king, they are the adopted son of his daughter with his brother (Cassuto 1967:67). Where they are referred to in one constituent, Moses is always mentioned before Aaron, except in 6:14-27, Num 3:1-4, and 26:59. In those contexts, which are genealogical, Aaron and Moses are mentioned chronologically (see section 2.1).

When, genealogies apart, Moses is mentioned before Aaron in compound constituents, this reflects that in the text as a whole Moses is more central than Aaron. This order continues to be used in the rest of the Pentateuch. (Aaron's son and successor, Eleazar, is mentioned after Moses as well, e.g., in Num 26:1.) Moses is, in fact, mentioned before Aaron even outside the Pentateuch (1 Sam 12:6,8, Psa 99:6, 105:26).

---

[4]   Plural in the Syriac Version.

1.2 Identification of a participant in terms of another
Frequently a group of participants is referred to and identified in terms of the
relationship to another, more central participant. In direct discourse this is often
the addressee.

as an ordinance for you and for your sons (Exod 12:24)

that he performed (אתכם ואת־אבותיכם) for you and for your
ancestors (1 Sam 12:7)

then the hand of the Lord will be (בכם ובאבתיכם) against you
and against your fathers (1 Sam 12:15)

in the hearing of your son and of your son's son (Exod 10:2)

as neither your fathers nor your father's fathers have seen
(Exod 10:6)

visiting the iniquity of the fathers upon the children and the
children's children (Exod 34:7)

They will be *to you* a sign... *and to your seed* for ever
(Deut 28:46)

The participant or group of participants closest to the addressee is mentioned after
him. Finally, at the end of the constituent, the group of participants is mentioned
that is only indirectly related to the addressee through the group that was
mentioned first. In Exod 34:7, the children are referred to in terms of the fathers.
The children's children, in turn, are referred to at the end in terms of their
relationship to the children. These examples are actually in accordance with the
Cooper-Ross semantic principle as summarized by O'Connor (1980:97), that in a
dyad the present generation is mentioned before another one. This also applies to
1 Sam 12:7,15.[5]
    In narrative texts a participant can be (re)introduced like this in relation to the
major, more dominant participant in the text. In Exodus 18, Jethro is reintroduced
and in the rest of the chapter is further referred to as the father-in-law of Moses,
the major participant. 1 Sam 4:19,21, about Eli's daughter-in-law, Phinehas' wife,
is another example. Not only is the loss of the ark mentioned first and foremost,
but in v. 19, the major participant in this context, Eli, is referred to before
Phinehas. Although they are both referred to in terms of their relationship to
Phinehas' wife, the order in which they are mentioned is not determined in

---

[5]   The order of participants apart, it seems strange in v. 15 that the hand of the Lord should be
      against generations of the past as well. (Hence the reading of the Septuagint: 'and against your
      king'.) The fathers have apparently been mentioned here under the influence of v. 7.

relation to her. From her point of view her husband would have come before her father-in-law. Instead, the narrator refers to Eli before Phinehas and identifies the woman first in relation to her father-in-law, who is the major participant, and after that in relation to her husband.

> And his daughter-in-law, the wife of Phinehas ... and that were dead her father-in-law and her husband (1 Sam 4:19)

1.3 Resumptive pronouns

The resumptive pronoun in, e.g., Exod 3:18 is not emphatic but obligatory, enabling the addition of further subjects (Joüon - Muraoka 1991:541, §146c2,3; Muraoka 1985:63). It serves to explicitly represent the referent of the resumptive pronoun as "the chief actor among other actors" (Waltke & O'Connor 1990:294, §16.3.2c). In Exod 12:4 and Ruth 1:6-7, for instance, the 'chief actor' is the participant in relation to which the other participant is referred to.

> She started out, she (היא) and her daughters-in-law (Ruth 1:6)

The same applies to Exod 20:10 and Num 20:8 where the other participants are referred to in terms of the addressee, the 'chief actor' as well.

> You shall not do any work, you (אתה) or your son or your daughter, your manservant or your maidservant, or your cattle or the alien... (Exod 20:10)

> And gather the assembly, you and Aaron your brother
> (Num 20:8, carried out in v. 10)

In Exod 35:34 the resumptive pronoun refers to Bezalel who has already been reintroduced in 35:30; Oholiab is only reintroduced as a conjoined proper name.

> He has also given him the ability to teach, him (הוא) and Oholiab
> (Exod 35:34)

Bezalel and Oholiab are mentioned in the same order in a compound subject in 36:1 and 2. Oholiab, if mentioned at all, only comes after Bezalel. This corresponds with the fact that in Exod 31:2-11, 35:30-36:2, and 38:22-23 Oholiab's competence is subordinate to Bezalel's. The order thus reflects that Bezalel is the more important one of these two in the text.

1.3.1 Resumptive suffix pronouns after prepositions

The conjoined proper names or nominal descriptions are sometimes followed by the preposition עם or את 'with' plus a pronominal suffix. Like a resumptive pronoun, such a pronominal suffix refers back to the first and major participant. Exod 19:24 contains an example.

> and you shall go up, you (אתה) and Aaron with (עמך) you
> (Exod 19:24)

Gen 19:30-38 illustrate that the conjoined participants can be as central as the first participant in the following context but do not become more central than him (Creason 1993).

> And he [Lot] lived ... and his two daughters with him (עמו) ... and
> he lived ... he (הוא) and his two daughters (Gen 19:30)

2 Sam 17:24 and Ruth 1:7,22 contain other examples.

> And she set out from the place ... and her two daughters-in-law
> with her (עמה) (Ruth 1:7)

After the clauses in Ruth 1:6-7 which still designate Naomi as "the chief actor among other actors", it is striking that the end of v. 7 ('and they went') does not distinguish the three participants at all.

Usually, resumptive suffix pronouns after prepositions refer to the 'chief actor'. Nevertheless, in Exod 18:6 the pronominal suffix after עם does not refer to the 'chief actor', Jethro, who is the speaker, but to Moses' wife (the first conjoined nominal description).

> I, your father-in-law Jethro come to you, and your wife and her
> two sons with her (ושני בניה עמה) (Exod 18:6)[6]

Instead of עמה 'with her', one might have expected עמי 'with me'. However, Jethro refers to these relatives only in terms of their relation to Moses and to one another.[7] This is, in fact, in line with what the narrator does (in vv. 2-3,5). Participants in this passage are thus referred to in terms of their relation to Moses, the major participant in Exodus.

1.4 Groups of participants

Often the cast consists of a group of participants in the plural and one individual participant who is more central in the context. As 2 Sam 2:17 ('Abner and the men of Israel') and a few of the earlier examples show, this individual is mentioned separately before the group in the same constituent. In Gen 44:14 Judah is reintroduced as an individual participant because of the dialogue between him and Joseph in the rest of this chapter (cf. vv. 16,18). Consequently, the others in this constituent are mentioned in terms of their relationship with him.

---

[6] It is implied that Jethro's words are passed on to Moses by a messenger (so Rashi). The Septuagint and Syriac Version facilitate the reading of the text by stating what the messenger(s) would have said: 'Word was sent to Moses: Lo, your father-in-law ...'.

[7] This also applies if ושני בניה עמה is to be treated as a separate circumstantial clause.

And came Judah and his brothers to Joseph's house (Gen 44:14)

In Exod 18:12 and 34:31, Aaron is mentioned before the elders and before the leaders, respectively. He is probably not seen as one of the elders or leaders, so that it is not surprising that he is mentioned separately. He is primarily Moses' supportive companion.

And came Aaron and all the elders of Israel (Exod 18:12)

In 1 Sam 13:16, two individuals are mentioned before the people.

And Saul and Jonathan his son and the people present with them
(הנמצא עמם) (1 Sam 13:16)

The second one is referred to in terms of the first. In Exod 18:8 Pharao is mentioned separately from the Egyptians. In the episodes to which this clause refers, Pharao was a central participant.

all that had done the Lord to Pharao and to the Egyptians for
Israel's sake (Exod 18:8)

In Gen 47:12, 50:14 (resumptive pronoun), Exod 1:6 (see section 3), 17:3 and other instances, the reference to the individual is followed by references to two groups of participants. In such instances, the first group is smaller and more specific than the last, of which it is part.

And got up Pharao ... he and all his servants and all the Egyptians
(Exod 12:30)

to kill me (אתי) and my children and my cattle with thirst?
(Exod 17:3)

However, all this does not apply when emphasis is put on the individual. In 2 Sam 17:26 Absalom is only mentioned after Israel. This unexpected order may emphasize that it is Absalom who goes on campaign with his troops,[8] thus taking Hushai's advice of 17:11 (Mauchline 1971:283).

And encamped Israel and Absalom in the land of Gilead
(2 Sam 17:26)

The same may be true of 2 Sam 3:22: 'David's servants and Joab' come back from a raid. It is underlined that Joab came back as well as the soldiers, thus

---

[8]   Absalom, not Amasa (v. 25), is the real commander (Goslinga 1962:313).

implying that he has not been with David and Abner in the preceding episode.

In some instances, two (or more) groups are mentioned in the constituent without a reference to an individual. Again, when no numbers occur, the first group of participants is more specific than the last.

...brothers and ...father's house (Gen 46:31; Judg 16:31)

on the magicians and on all the Egyptians (Exod 9:11)

the priests and the people (Exod 19:24)

of Benjamin and of the men of Abner (2 Sam 2:31)[9]

When Israel and Judah are mentioned together, Israel usually comes first: 'over Israel and over Judah' (2 Sam 3:10). This may seem a counterexample because Judah was smaller than Israel. On the other hand, Israel includes Judah so that the two are one entity: 'he reigned over all (על כל) Israel and Judah' (2 Sam 5:5).[10] 'Judah' precedes 'Israel' in 1 Kgs 4:20 and 5:5.[11] A real, more serious counterexample is to be found in 2 Kgs 10:19 where one would have expected the worshippers to be mentioned last.

all the prophets of Baal, all his worshippers (כל־עבדיו) and all his priests (2 Kgs 10:19)

However, it is of interest to see that this has indeed become a text-critical problem.[12] In the Lucianic recension of the Septuagint, the worshippers are mentioned at the end.

To summarize, the order of participants will be as follows: individual, specific group, largest group.

Exod 6:13 contains an interesting exception to this pattern. In Exod 6:13, the Israelites are more central in the context than Pharaoh.

---

[9] Whether the Benjaminites and Abner's men are mentioned in apposition or not - the prepositions are different (מבנימין ובאנשי אבנר) - the latter group is wider than the first (Goslinga 1962:56).

[10] The whole of Israel, including Judah. Considering the one preposition על, they are not two separate kingdoms (Goslinga 1962:215). Other instances of 'Israel and Judah' are 1 Sam 18:16, 2 Sam 11:11, 12:8, 21:2.

[11] This may be a "clue to extreme lateness ... (in the post-exilic period, 'Judah' began more and more to assume precedence because the returnees from exile were almost all Judahites)." (De Vries 1985:72).

[12] The generalizing term עבדי הבעל appears again in vv. 19-23 and may be a reading introduced from those verses (Cogan - Tadmor 1988:115; Brongers 1970:103).

> And he gave them orders concerning the Israelites and concerning
> Pharao king of Egypt (Exod 6:13)

Other exceptions are Gen 42:35 ('And they saw ... they and their father'), Num
31:6, and 16:16, which are resumptive pronoun examples.

> And Moses sent them (אתם) to the war, a thousand from each
> tribe, them (אתם) and Phinehas ... (Num 31:6)

The thousands from each tribe have already been mentioned in Num 31:4-5. In v.
6, they are thus more central than Phinehas. The resumptive pronoun refers to
them.

> *You and all yours*, be before the Lord, *you and them and Aaron*,[13]
> tomorrow (Num 16:16)

Moses is speaking to Korah. Korah and those who are on his side are more
central in the context of this conversation than Aaron.

2. Conventions

The order of participants in one constituent is often determined by conventions of
family and social hierarchies, unless these are overruled by centrality of a
participant in the context. Sections 2.1-3 deal with the hierarchies that can be
found.

2.1 Chronological order
The order of participants can be simply chronological. In one constituent,
Abraham, Isaac, and Jacob are always mentioned in that order in our corpus (for
Lev 26:42 see section 3). This order may be merely formulaic in character in,
e.g., Exod 6:3,8, Deut 9:5,27. But it is certainly determined by chronology in
Exod 32:13 and 1 Kgs 18:36 where Jacob is referred to not as Jacob but as Israel
in a series of conjoined proper names and a nominal description.

> Remember Abraham, Isaac, and Israel, your servants (Exod 32:13)

Other examples are Gen 11:26,27 ('Abram, Nahor, and Haran'), Gen 46:20 and
48:1 ('Manasseh and Ephraim'), Num 3:4 ('And-died Nadab and Abihu'), Num
26:9, 16:1,24,27, Deut 11:6 ('Dathan and Abiram'), 32:1 ('... Reuben and ...

---

[13] This is actually one of the discontinuous subjects mentioned by Driver. "... it must be recognized
as a feature of Hebrew style, when two subjects (or objects) have to be combined in one clause, for
the clause containing one of the subjects (or objects) to be completed, the other being attached
subsequently." Driver (1913:55).

Gad') and 1 Sam 17:13 ('Eliab the firstborn, and second to him Abinadab, and the third Shammah'). About Num 3:4, Morešet (1967:253) implies that Nadab is not the initiator. These examples show that, apart from 1 Sam 17:13, it is only the order which indicates who comes first chronologically.

Chronological order is also maintained in the context of genealogical lists.

And she bore ... Aaron and Moses (Exod 6:20; Num 26:59)

And she bore him Nadab and Abihu, Eleazar and Ithamar (Exod 6:22)

This is Aaron and Moses to whom the Lord said (Exod 6:26)

Aaron himself and Moses (Exod 6:27 Septuagint)

These are the generations of Aaron and Moses (Num 3:1)

The sons of Joseph ...: Manasseh and Ephraim (Num 26:28)

The sons of Amram: Aaron and Moses (1 Chron 23:13)

Exodus 6 and Numbers 3 and 26 contain the only compound constituents in the Pentateuch in which Aaron is mentioned before Moses. The aim of the genealogy in Exodus 6 is to show the position of Moses and Aaron in the tribe of Levi and was written specifically for the present narrative (Cassuto 1967:84). (This applies to Numbers 3 and 26:57-62 as well.) In the genealogy itself, however, the narrative is not developed further; the persons mentioned in it hardly function as participants. Any difference between major and minor participants thus does not apply here. This makes it possible to refer to Aaron, the elder brother, before Moses. The order in which they are mentioned is determined by the genealogical context and as such is not an implicit comment.

Exod 6:26 and 27 may well be a transition to the narrative which is resumed in 6:28. This may explain the variation in the text of 6:27: 'Moses and Aaron' in the Masoretic Text; 'Aaron himself and Moses', thus stressing the priestly tradition (Le Boulluec & Sandevoir 1989:116), in the Septuagint.

Aaron is the eldest brother outside the genealogy as well. In Exod 15:20, where he does not function as a participant, either, Miriam is introduced as Aaron's and not as Moses' sister, "in accordance with the system in which the eldest brother is recognized as the head of the family (fratriarchy)" (Cassuto 1967:181-182). Traces of this system of fratriarchy by which people are referred to in relation to their eldest brother are also to be found in Gen 10:21, 28:9, Exod 6:23 (Cassuto 1964:165,218).

Shem ... the brother of Japheth the elder[14] (Gen 10:21)

Gen 25:9 contains an example which illustrates that order of centrality of participants in the narrative context prevails over chronological order. Isaac is the central participant here and until v. 12.

And they buried him Isaac and Ishmael his sons (Gen 25:9)

In the corresponding clause in Gen 35:29, Esau and Jacob are mentioned in order of centrality as well as chronological order. It is the genealogy of Esau that follows.

2.2 Social conventions

The order of participants may be determined by the following hierarchies, which may overlap.
• master wife son daughter servant maidservant cattle alien: Gen 17:23; 19:16; Exod 3:22; 4:20; 10:9; 20:10 (// Deut 5:14); 20:17; 21:4,5; Deut 3:19. 1 Sam 15:3 contains a similar instance. In one constituent, sons are mentioned before the daughters even when the sons are actually grandsons, as in Gen 31:28 and 32:1. Compare also Gen 46:7: 'sons, sons' sons, daughters, sons' daughters, all his seed'. In respect of this hierarchy, Exod 20:17 is remarkable.

> You shall not covet your neighbour's house; you shall not covet
> your neighbour's wife or his servant or his maidservant or his ox
> or his ass or anything... (Exod 20:17)

In the verse as a whole, it is interesting that the neighbour's house is mentioned first. In the last clause as such, however, the hierarchy is observed. 'The neighbour's house' can be seen as "a general term", including "the house and all that is in it ... The general statement is followed by detailed examples" (Cassuto 1967:249). In the parallel clause in Deut 5:21, however, the hierarchy is not observed in the order of elements ('house, field, ...').

In Exod 4:20, 10:9, and 18:2-3,5-6, the hierarchy is observed in connection with the movement from one place to another.

> And took Moses his wife and his sons ... and he returned
> (Exod 4:20)

These examples are similar to examples in Genesis of the following stereotyped formula: 'And so-and-so (the head of the family) took so-and-so and so-and-so

---

[14] According to the Septuagint, Symmachus, Luther, KJV, Segond, Buber - Rosenzweig and NIV. If one translates 'Shem ... the eldest brother of Japheth' it is hard to see the use of such a statement. If Shem were the eldest brother, this would already have been clear from the order in which the brothers are mentioned, Shem coming first.

(members of his family) and this possession and that possession (his cattle, and his beasts and his wealth, and the like) and he went, etc.' Cassuto (1964:277; 1975:23-24) discusses this formula. He mentions Gen 11:31, 12:5, 36:6, 46:6, Exod 18:2-3, and similar formulas in Ugaritic texts to show that ''it belongs to the general Canaanite tradition of antiquity'' (Cassuto 1975:24). The order of participants and other elements in this formula is explained by the hierarchy.

Along the lines of the hierarchy, Num 16:27 contains a discontinuous subject, which is mentioned in Driver (1913:55).

> And Dathan and Abiram came out... and their wives and their sons
> and their little ones (Num 16:27)

The following can also be included in this hierarchy: son, son's son, daughter-in-law / son's wife (Gen 11:31); wife, brother's son (Gen 12:5).

In accordance with the hierarchy above, man and beast or cattle are mentioned in that order by convention. Examples are Exod 9:9,10,19,20,21,22,25; 11:7; 12:12; 13:2. When servants are mentioned with cattle and goods only, they may not always come first (cf. Gen 20:14, 24:35, 2 Kgs 5:26).

In Deut 28:54, the brother is mentioned before the wife and children. When starving, one is likely to grudge food to one's brother more than to one's wife and surviving children.
• father mother son daughter brother sister: Gen 2:24; 34:18,20,24,26; 47:5,11,12; Exod 20:12 // Deut 5:16; Lev 21:2-3; Num 6:7. In Genesis 34, Hamor is mentioned before his son Shechem except for 34:13. Here, just after Shechem's own request to Jacob and his sons in vv. 11-12, Shechem is more central to them. In Lev 19:3 and 21:2, where the relationship to the parents is involved, the mother is mentioned before the father.

> Everyone his mother and father you shall fear (Lev 19:3)[15]

The following may be included in this hierarchy: elder brother, younger brother (chronological order, see section 2.1).
• husband son daughter: one instance of this order occurs in Deut 28:56.
• man woman (a Cooper-Ross semantic principle, see O'Connor 1980:97): Gen 2:25, 3:8,21 ('Adam and his wife'); 18:11 ('Abraham and Sarah'); Exod 21:28,29; 35:29; 36:6.
• Levite alien orphan widow: Deut 14:29; 16:11,14; 24:17,19,20; 26:12,13; 27:19.
• maidservant's son, alien: Exod 23:12. Compare Gen 17:12,13,23,27: the one

---

[15] This commandment comes at the beginning of what may have been a children's decalogue (Lev 19:3-4,11-12). This might explain why the mother is mentioned first here. In this connection, it is interesting that prohibitions against killing and adultery are lacking (Vriezen - van der Woude 1973:44). Rashi says that since the natural tendency is to fear a father more than a mother, the mother is mentioned first to stress that she deserves as much respect as one's father. (The verb here is not כבד 'honour' as in Exod 20:12.)

born in the house, the one bought with money.
• son brother friend neighbour: Exod 32:27 (three consecutive objects, but not in the same constituent), 29.
• pharao servants people: Exod 7:10,20,28; 8:5,7,17,25,27. The order of servants and people may also be due to the fact that specific groups of participants are mentioned before the largest group (see above). The reverse, however, occurs in Exod 7:29. Perhaps כל 'all' makes the servants a less restricted and more all-embracing group.

> And on you and on your people and on all your servants shall the frogs come up (Exod 7:29)

• higher position, lower position: 'rulers of thousands, of hundreds, (of fifties, and of tens)': Exod 18:21,25, Num 31:14, Deut 1:15, 2 Sam 18:1; 'sons of the king and sons of the queen-mother (גבירה)': 2 Kgs 10:13; '... the king's mother (אם המלך) and the king's wives ...': 2 Kgs 24:15; 'Hilkiah, the high priest, and the priests of the second rank, and the keepers of the threshold': 2 Kgs 23:4 (cf. 2 Kgs 25:18).

2.3 Set phrases and variety
The following combinations of words are mentioned in that order by convention, preferring "to place short words before long ones" (Cassuto 1964:165). This phonological principle goes back to Panini's Law, which states "that other things being equal, the shorter of two items comes first in a compound" (O'Connor 1980:98).
• Zebah Zalmunna: Judg 8:5-21.
• sun moon stars: Gen 37:9 (cf. Gen 1:16 and 2 Kgs 23:5).
• (army) horse(s) chariot(s) rider(s) (army): Gen 50:9, Exod 14:9,17,18,23,28 (prose), 15:1,19,21 (poetry), Deut 11:4, 1 Kgs 1:5, 9:22, 10:26, 20:1,21, 2 Kgs 2:12, 6:15,17, 13:14, 18:24; chariot(s) horses: 2 Sam 15:1, 2 Kgs 7:6, 10:2. It does not make a difference to the order whether the context consists of prose or poetry. Where 'army' (חיל) occurs, it occurs either before or after these words.
• There appears to be variation between 'flock cattle' (Gen 47:1,17; Exod 10:9,24; 12:32,38; Deut 16:2; 1 Kgs 8:5) and 'cattle flock' (Deut 14:23,26; 15:19). Nevertheless, the stress unit of the first of the two is never longer than the second.

With regard to some terms and nations the order of participants in such "set phrases" (Levi 1987:58) can vary. In those few instances no order seems to be preferred.
• 'widow and orphan' (Exod 22:21,23) but 'orphan and widow' in Deuteronomy (10:18 and elsewhere).
• 'the alien and the native of the land' (Exod 12:19) but also 'the native and the alien living among you' (Exod 12:49). In both cases, the category which is described further is mentioned last.
• The peoples of Canaan in Exod 23:23, 23:28, 33:2, 34:11, Deut 7:1, 20:17, Judg

3:5 and 1 Kgs 9:20 are mentioned in a different order almost every time. They stand for the inhabitants of the land. In Exod 23:28 only three of these nations are mentioned; the author assumes that the reader knows the peoples who live in the land (Levi 1987:83).

• In the majority of instances, 'women' are mentioned before קט 'little ones'. In some cases, the order is the reverse. The order even varies in analogous contexts. This becomes clear when one compares Deut 29:10 with Josh 8:35, or Num 32:26 with Josh 1:14.

> Our little ones, our wives ... shall remain there ... (Num 32:26)

> Your wives, your little ones ... shall remain in the land ... beyond the Jordan (Josh 1:14)

The order in Num 32:26 could still be explained in terms of centrality: the little ones have already been mentioned in 32:17,24 and are thus more central. But the other instances where 'little ones' are mentioned before 'women' (e.g., Gen 34:29, 45:19, 46:5) cannot be explained in this way.

• In Ezra 3:2,8,9 the order of elements in the compound subject varies, "perhaps to give stylistic variety" (Morešet 1967:259). Jeshua and Zerubbabel seem to be equally important.

3. Rhetorical significance

The patterns discussed above can be explained by syntactic and conventional rules of the language and are not as such rhetorically significant. The rhetorically determined instances of participant order in the Pentateuch and Earlier Prophets are discussed in this section.

Considering Gen 10:21 ('Shem ... the brother of Japheth the elder', see section 2.1), the order of 'Shem, (Ham,) and Japheth' in 5:32, 6:10, 7:13 and 9:18,23 is not chronological, not even in the genealogical context of 10:1. Although Ham is the youngest (9:24), Japheth is mentioned last because of a preference "to place short words before long ones" (Cassuto 1964:165). Shem is mentioned first because he is the central one of the three in the context. Centrality thus overrules other factors. Shem, Ham, and Japheth are not mentioned in this order according to age but rather according to their relative importance to the nation of Israel (Cassuto 1964:198,217; Jacob 1934:273). Although the order in 10:1 according to relative centrality is in itself not rhetorically significant, it is made part of a chiastic, rhetorical structure. Once the sons are introduced in 10:1, their segmented genealogies are then dealt with in reverse order, beginning with Japheth (10:2-5), the least important to Israel's history, followed by Ham (10:6-20), who was rejected, and concluding with Shem, the ancestor of the Patriarchs and of Israel (10:21-31). Bailey (1994:274) describes the rhetorical significance of this order as follows.

> In this way the order of [these] three genealogies forms a chiasm to the opening
> title in 10:1, but in this case the chiasm should not be viewed as emphasizing
> Japheth in center position. Rather the chiasm occurs to make Shem, as the most
> important of the brothers, both first and last topics of discussion.[16]

In accordance with this, the most important descendants of Shem are not to be found in his first genealogy (10:21-31) but in his second (11:10-26) (Andersen 1994:261).

It is tempting to apply the rule of centrality to Gen 28:5 ('... Rebekah, the mother of Jacob and Esau') and say that Jacob is mentioned first because he has been a central participant in the context whereas Esau has not. In the sentence itself, however, they are hardly participants but only part of an extended description of Rebekah. In this light the order in which they are mentioned becomes significant and a reminder that Jacob is Rebekah's favourite (according to Gen 25:28).

Manasseh was born before Ephraim (Gen 41:50-52). Hence, they are mentioned in chronological order in Gen 46:20 and 48:1 (see section 2.1). When Jacob speaks to Joseph, however, he mentions Ephraim before Manasseh (48:5,20) even though Ephraim is not more central in the text than Manasseh. Jacob puts Ephraim before Manasseh (48:14,20) and so he refers to them in that order. This is already the case in v. 5, well before the text comes to the actual blessing.

A curious compound subject occurs in Gen 50:7-8.

> And went up Joseph to bury his father, and went with him (אתו)
> all the officials of Pharaoh, the senior members of his court and all
> of Egypt's dignitaries, and all of Joseph's household and his
> brothers and his father's household (Gen 50:7-8)

On the one hand, one could argue that Joseph's relatives, the bereaved, are central in the context (see vv. 12-14). Alternatively, one could argue that it is the Egyptians who are central here. Egyptians embalm and weep for Israel (vv. 2-3). Pharaoh gives permission for his burial in Canaan (v. 6). They play a central role in the mourning process, either as a display of honour to Joseph and respect for his father or, as Abarbanel suggested, because Pharaoh feared that Joseph and his brothers might be influenced to remain in Canaan. In any case, when the Egyptians are mentioned before the relatives in vv. 7-8 this is in striking contrast to the more usual order in v. 14 (see section 1.4).

> And Joseph returned..., he (הוא) and his brothers and all who had
> gone up with him... (Gen 50:14)

Here, the brothers are mentioned immediately after Joseph (van Selms

---

[16] Compare also the order of the promises in Gen 17:19-21 about Isaac and Ishmael where the most important promise, the one concerning Isaac, comes first and last.

1967b:288). The Egyptians are only mentioned at the end of the subject constituent and are not even referred to as such. Considering the preceding and following verses, and the end of Gen 49, the bereaved are central here. The burial is related to earlier family events ('the field ... which Abraham bought', 50:13).

In Exod 1:6 Joseph is mentioned separately. Joseph, rather than Jacob, has been the major participant in the final chapters of Genesis. The introductory verses in Exod 1, particularly vv. 6 and 8, seem to be influenced by this. Exod 1:6 does not say that the people born to Jacob (cf. v. 5) died but takes up the death of Joseph in Gen 50:26.

> And died Joseph and all his brothers and all that generation
> (Exod 1:6)

Joseph is singled out. Consequently, in the compound constituent, the other participant groups are referred to after him and in relation to him. What is rhetorically significant is that the beginning of Exodus is explicitly linked to Genesis in this way.

It is striking that, contrary to the family hierarchy, the narrator in Exod 18:5 mentions Moses' sons before his wife.

> And came *Jethro, Moses' father-in-law, and his sons and his wife*
> to Moses ... (Exod 18:5)

A chiasmus is formed by this order and the one in 18,2-4 where the wife is mentioned before the sons (Houtman 1989:364). The chiastic structure is rhetorically relevant.

This phenomenon also occurs in Gen 31:17 ('his sons and his wives') and 33:7 ('Joseph and Rachel',[17] also in the Samaritan Pentateuch). Joseph does not play a central role in the near context of 33:7 but this verse is a first indication of Joseph's importance later in Genesis (in the remote context). A translation should, if possible, also hint at Joseph's future role at this point. The translators of the Septuagint and Syriac Version, however, have deliberately changed the order into 'Rachel and Joseph' (van Selms 1967b:147), presumably to match it with v. 2.

In Gen 8:16, God mentions Noah's wife before his sons. In Gen 7:7,13 and 8:18, however, it is the narrator who mentions Noah's sons before his wife. For him, they are Noah's progeny and are important in the genealogies of Genesis.

> And came out Noah and his sons and his wife and the wives of his
> sons with him (אתו) (Gen 8:18)

In Exod 18:5 the narrator refers to the sons in terms of their relation to Moses as 'his [Moses'] sons'. On the other hand it is striking that v. 6 (Jethro) as well as v.

---

[17] According to Rashi, Joseph wanted to shield his mother from Esau's gaze.

3 (narrator) refer to them as 'her [Zipporah's] sons' after Zipporah. It is thus emphasized that they are primarily sons of hers and not of Moses's. This information should not be lost in translation. Unfortunately this has happened in the Willibrord Translation, even in the revised edition of 1995, in v. 6: "Your wife and sons are in my company." (English backtranslation mine).[18] Although the result is a very natural Dutch sentence, a translation which is not only natural but in which the rhetorical point is made as well, is to be preferred.

It is only in Lev 26:42 that Abraham, Isaac, and Jacob are mentioned in reverse order - in contrast with Exod 6:3-4; 32:13; Num 32:11 and Deut 34:4 - though not in one constituent.

> Then I will remember my covenant with Jacob, and also my covenant with Isaac, and also my covenant with Abraham will I remember, and the land I will remember. (Lev 26:42)

This reverse order may draw the reader's attention, stressing what is going to be said.[19] With the order 'Jacob ... Isaac ... Abraham' we go back into the past (Gispen 1950:390). This is the only time in Scripture that it says that God remembers the land (Levine 1989:191). The land was first promised to Abram (Gen 15:7,18; 17:8, based on 12:1). The covenants with Isaac and Jacob explicitly refer to this (Gen 26:3-4; 28:13; 35:12). Psa 105:42 interprets "Israel's saving history in light of God's remembering his promises to Abraham" (Hartley 1992:470). Lev 26:42 seems to mention the three Patriarchs in reverse order on purpose, so that it is the covenant with Abraham which is most closely connected with the possession of the land.

The variation in the order in which Joshua and Caleb are mentioned in the Pentateuch seems rhetorically significant.[20] Joshua and Caleb are mentioned in that order in Num 14:6,38 where it is added that they were among those who explored the land. But Caleb is mentioned before Joshua in v. 30 of the same chapter as well as in Num 26:65; 32:12 and (though not in one constituent) in Deut 1:36,38. In these instances, they are mentioned as the survivors, in contrast to the people, who will not see the land. Caleb is mentioned first, probably because it is to him that land is promised and given explicitly (Num 14:24; Deut 1:36; Josh 14-15; 21:12). In Num 13:30, it is Caleb who stands up against the ten spies (Gispen 1959:235).

According to Deut 13:7-9, even a close family-member or friend who entices somebody to worship other gods, is to be stoned to death. These people are mentioned in a very unusual order.

---

[18] This translation may well have followed the Septuagint and Vulgate (οἱ δύο υἱοί σου; *duo filii tui* *'your* two sons') at this particular point.

[19] See Beentjes' contribution to this volume, p. 37, note 26.

[20] Klaas Spronk, personal communication.

... your brother, [the son of your father or[21]] the son of your mother, or your son or your daughter or the wife of your bosom or your friend who is as your own soul (כנפשך)[22] ... (Deut 13:7)

In addition to the unusual order, note the extended descriptions of the brother, and of wife and friend. It is terrible to have to stone one's own brother, who is closer than a half-brother. But it is in fact impossible to stone the wife you love or your intimate friend. In this constituent, the most unlikely candidates for stoning are mentioned last. The more difficult it would be to stone someone, the later he is mentioned.

In Deut 27:12-13, the tribes named after the elder brothers (Leah's own eldest sons) are mentioned first, as the tribes for the blessing (v. 12), while those named after the younger brothers are mentioned last, as the tribes for the curse (v. 13). But there are two interesting deviations from this chronological classification. Joseph and Benjamin, the youngest, are mentioned among the tribes for the blessing, while Reuben, the eldest, is mentioned among the tribes for the curse. Joseph and Benjamin were the sons of Jacob's favourite wife, Rachel. Significantly, they are included in v. 12 among the tribes for the blessing, and mentioned at the end because they were the youngest. The remaining tribes are for the curse (v. 13). Their ancestors were the youngest, apart from Joseph and Benjamin, and Reuben. It is striking that, even though he was the first-born, Reuben is mentioned among the tribes for the curse. This is probably an implicit allusion to Gen 35:22 and 49:3-4.

2 Sam 5:13 deviates from social[23] and phonological convention by mentioning concubines before wives: 'And David took more concubines (פלגשים) and wives (נשים)[24] ...'. Nor are the concubines more central in the near context than the wives. But elsewhere in 2 Samuel, in the remote context, the concubines are mentioned again. See 15:16, 20:3, and especially 16:21-22 where Absalom lies with his father's concubines. It is at least plausible that the order in 2 Sam 5:13 alludes to what happens later in the book. Again, this piece of information should not be lost in translation.[25]

In 1 Kings 1, Zadok is always mentioned first; he is the one who anoints Solomon (v. 39, see section 1). However, in the rest of Samuel and Kings Zadok comes first as well, even though he usually does not play a part in the context. When Zadok and Abiathar are mentioned together, Zadok always comes first (see 2 Sam 15:29,35, 17:15, 19:11, 20:25, 1 Kgs 2:27,35, 4:4). It is unlikely that this order is determined by the length of the names as Abiathar is mentioned before

---

[21] According to the Samaritan Pentateuch and Septuagint.

[22] Compare 1 Sam 18:1.

[23] In 2 Sam 19:6 Joab mentions the lives of the wives before the lives of the concubines, in a context where the concubines matter least of all. In 1 Kgs 11:3 Solomon's wives are mentioned before his concubines.

[24] Interestingly, the parallel line in 1 Chr 14:3 only mentions נשים 'wives'.

[25] Unfortunately, the Willibrord Translation, including the revised edition, and Revidierte Lutherübersetzung mention the wives before the concubines at this point.

Joab in 1 Kgs 1:19 and 2:22. Rather, it seems to be caused by the fact that in 1 Kgs 2:27,35 Solomon makes Zadok the only high priest in Jerusalem whereas Abiathar is expelled (Goslinga 1962:179). It seems rhetorically significant that on the basis of this, Zadok is mentioned before Abiathar throughout the text.

In 1 Kgs 20:3,5 wives and sons are mentioned after silver and gold.

> Your silver and your gold and your wives and your sons give to me (1 Kgs 20:5)

This order is, of course, unconventional. Although servants are sometimes mentioned after goods (see section 2.2), wives and children are not. This order thus seems to emphasize the harshness of Ben-hadad's request to Ahab (who himself uses the conventional order in v. 7).

4. Implications for translation

The order of participants in compound clausal elements is thus rhetorically significant in specific instances only. The implications of this for translators are important. The syntactic and conventional rules of participant reference are likely to vary from language to language. So where there is no rhetorical significance in the order of participants in the source text, these rules of the receptor language are to be respected in translation, whether participants are mentioned in the same clausal element or not. This applies, for instance, to a language in which centrality in the context does not take precedence over conventional order. Thus in a language in which the father is always to be mentioned before the son,[26] 'Laban and Bethuel' (Gen 24:50) has to be translated differently, provided it somehow remains clear that Laban is more central in the context than Bethuel. And in a language in which the speaker will only mention himself last, like English, 'I and your mother and your brothers' (Gen 37:10) may have to be rendered 'Your mother, your brothers and I' (Gen 37:10 TEV) as long as it remains clear that the sun in v. 9 represents Jacob (Mundhenk 1979:432).

On the other hand, instances of participant reference that are rhetorically significant may well have to be treated differently from other cases. Where the order of participants is determined by rhetorical strategy, this rhetorical element has to be made clear in the translation or at least the order has to be left intact.

---

[26] E.g., Suriname Javanese (Janet Dyk, personal communication).

References

T.D. Andersen, "Genealogical Prominence and the Structure of Genesis," *Biblical Hebrew and Discourse Linguistics* (ed. R.D. Bergen; Dallas: Summer Institute of Linguistics, 1994) 242-266.

N.A. Bailey, "Some Literary and Grammatical Aspects of Genealogies in Genesis," *Biblical Hebrew and Discourse Linguistics* (ed. R.D. Bergen; Dallas: Summer Institute of Linguistics, 1994) 267-282.

A. Le Boulluec - P. Sandevoir, *La Bible d'Alexandrie: L'Exode - Traduction du texte grec de la Septante, Introduction et Notes* (Paris: Cerf, 1989).

H.A. Brongers, *II Koningen* (De prediking van het Oude Testament; Nijkerk, The Netherlands: Callenbach, 1970).

Die Schrift verdeutscht von Martin Buber gemeinsam mit Franz Rosenzweig, I: Die fünf Bücher der Weisung (Heidelberg: Lambert Schneider, ⁹1976).

U. Cassuto, "Biblical and Canaanite Literature," in: *Biblical and Oriental Studies, Vol. II: Bible and Ancient Oriental Texts* (Jerusalem: The Magnes Press, The Hebrew University, 1975) 16-59. Published before in *Tarbiz* 13 (1942) 197-212; *ibid.* 14 (1942), 1-10 [Translated from the Hebrew].

------, *A Commentary on the Book of Genesis, Part II: From Noah To Abraham* (Jerusalem: The Magnes Press, The Hebrew University, 1964).

------, *A Commentary on the Book of Exodus* (Jerusalem: The Magnes Press, The Hebrew University, 1967).

M. Cogan - H. Tadmor, *II Kings* (AB 11; Doubleday, 1988).

S. Creason, *Split Subjects and Participant Reference in Hebrew Narrative*, paper read at the Seminar on Discourse Linguistics and Biblical Hebrew, SIL Translation Department (Dallas, 1993).

S.J. De Vries, *1 Kings* (WBC 12; Waco, TX: Word Books, 1985).

S.R. Driver, *Notes on the Hebrew Text and the Topography of the Books of Samuel* (2nd ed.; Oxford: Clarendon, 1913).

W.H. Gispen, *Het boek Leviticus* (Commentaar op het Oude Testament; Kampen: Kok, 1950).

------, *Het boek Numeri, Deel I* (Commentaar op het Oude Testament; Kampen: Kok, 1959).

------, *Het boek Numeri, Deel II* (Commentaar op het Oude Testament; Kampen: Kok, 1964).

C.J. Goslinga, *Het tweede boek Samuel* (Commentaar op het Oude Testament; Kampen: Kok, 1962).

J.E. Hartley, *Leviticus* (Word Biblical Commentary 4; Dallas: Word Books, 1992).

C. Houtman, *Exodus vertaald en verklaard, Deel II: Exodus 7:14-19:25* (Commentaar op het Oude Testament; Kampen: Kok, 1989).

B. Jacob, *Genesis* (Berlin: Shocken, 1934).

P. Joüon - T. Muraoka, *A Grammar of Biblical Hebrew* (Roma: Editrice Pontificio Istituto Biblico, 1991).

J. Levi, *Die Inkongruenz im biblischen Hebräisch* (Wiesbaden: Harrassowitz, 1987).

B.A. Levine, *The JPS Torah Commentary: Leviticus* (Philadelphia [etc.]: Jewish Publication Society, 1989).

J. Mauchline, *1 and 2 Samuel* (NCB; London: Oliphants, 1971).

C.L. Miller, "Introducing Direct Discourse in Biblical Hebrew Narrative," *Biblical Hebrew and Discourse Linguistics* (ed. R.D. Bergen; Dallas: Summer Institute of Linguistics, 1994) 199-241.

M. Morešet, "The Predicate Preceding a Compound Subject in the Biblical Language" [Hebrew], *Lěšonénu* 31 (1967) 251-260.

N.A. Mundhenk, "Translating Lists," *BT* 30 (1979) 426-434.

T. Muraoka, *Emphatic Words and Structures in Biblical Hebrew* (Jerusalem: The Magnes Press, The Hebrew University / Leiden: Brill, 1985).

M. O'Connor, *Hebrew Verse Structure* (Winona Lake, IN: Eisenbrauns, 1980).

L.J. de Regt, "Participant Reference in Some Biblical Hebrew Texts," *Jaarbericht Ex Oriente Lux* 32 (1991-1992) 150-172.

A. van Selms, *Genesis deel I* (De prediking van het Oude Testament; Nijkerk, The Netherlands: Callenbach, 1967a).

A. van Selms, *Genesis deel II* (De prediking van het Oude Testament; Nijkerk, The Netherlands: Callenbach, 1967b).

Th.C. Vriezen - A.S. van der Woude, *De literatuur van Oud-Israël* (Wassenaar, The Netherlands: Servire, ⁴1973).

B.K. Waltke - M. O'Connor, *An Introduction to Biblical Hebrew Syntax* (Winona Lake, IN: Eisenbrauns, 1990).

Translations

Revidierte Lutherübersetzung (Stuttgart: Württembergische Bibelanstalt, 1973).

Willibrord Translation ('s-Hertogenbosch, The Netherlands: Katholieke Bijbelstichting, 1982, revised edition 1995.

THE DISCOURSE IMPLICATIONS OF RESUMPTION
IN HEBREW אֲשֶׁר CLAUSES:
A PRELIMINARY ASSESSMENT FROM GENESIS

H. VAN DYKE PARUNAK

Abstract

As described in introductory grammar books, languages are full of "optional" features whose appearance is considered either random or the result of vague factors such as "style."[1] One of the great contributions of discourse linguistics has been to identify clear communicative functions performed by such features. This study presents preliminary results for one such feature in biblical Hebrew, based on a survey of usage in Genesis. In Hebrew, unlike European languages, resumption of the antecedent of a relative clause[2] by a noun or pronoun in the relative clause itself is "optional." For some constructions resumption is usual, while for other constructions it is the exception. This study provides evidence that unusual resumption or nonresumption carries discourse meaning.

1. Basic Concepts

This paper draws its linguistic terminology from tagmemics, in which the fundamental unit of analysis is the tagmeme, the correlation of a functional slot with the class of items that can fill it.[3] The function associated with the functional slot is defined in the context of a sequence of tagmemes, or syntagmeme. For example (and greatly oversimplified), a clause is a syntagmeme with a Predicate slot (often filled by a verb), an optional Subject slot (usually filled by a noun or a noun phrase), and (depending on the Predicate) an optional Object slot (usually filled by a noun or a noun phrase). Frequently in this paper I need to discuss the various kinds of constructions that can perform the same grammatical or semantic function, so the notion of a slot (representing the function) with a class of candidate fillers is

---

[1]   For example, Davidson (*Hebrew Syntax*, Third Edition, Edinburgh: T. & T. Clark, 1901) repeatedly states that the usage of the Hebrew article "fluctuates" (p. 29), and that "it is a point of style" to vary word order (pp. 147,156).

[2]   This paper restricts its attention to relative clauses introduced by the particle אֲשֶׁר, and so speaks in terms of "אֲשֶׁר clauses" rather than "relative clauses" when referring to the Hebrew data.

[3]   W.A. Cook, *Introduction to Tagmemic Analysis*. Washington, DC: Georgetown University Press, 1969.

extremely useful. Often, it is useful to focus on the form of the filler rather than the function of the slot, leading to terms such as "substantive slot" (a slot whose filler must be a substantive). Following standard conventions of historical Semitic grammar, I use three terms, Nominative (for nouns that govern verbs or that appear in verbless clauses), Genitive (for nouns governed by prepositions or by other nouns), and Accusative (for nouns governed by verbs), to label slots whose fillers will be of the appropriate case.[4] For example, in the schema "He went to X," X marks a genitive slot, which might be filled by a noun ("He went to town") or by a relative clause ("He went to where he was before").

The Hebrew relative clause either fills or modifies a substantive slot in the main clause. It also contains a substantive slot with the same referent as the slot that it modifies. The slot in the relative clause may be filled by a separate noun or pronoun, in which case the relative clause is said to "resume" its antecedent. For example, consider Example 1.

> Example 1: *The boy hit the ball that was red.*

Example 1 has two slots that refer to the same object, "the ball." The first defines the object of the action "to hit," and the second the subject of the predication "to be red." Like the pin in a hinge, this object plays a role in both clauses, so I refer to it as the pivot. Strictly speaking, the pivot is the common referent of substantive slots in the main and relative clauses, not a slot. However, it is often convenient to use the term "pivot" as shorthand for "the slot that references the pivot."

In European languages, the relative particle is a pronoun, so relative clauses always resume their antecedents, and the resumptive element is always the relative pronoun. Because the relative marker is a pronoun, there can be neither nonresumption (Example 2)

> Example 2: **The boy hit the ball # was red.*

nor a resumption by a separate element (Examples 3 and 4)

> Example 3: **The boy hit the ball that it was red.*
> Example 4: **The boy hit the ball that the ball was red.*

These languages permit resumption only if the relative clause has multiple slots referring to the pivot, in which case one is filled by the relative pronoun and the others by other substantives (*it* in Example 5).

> Example 5: *The boy hit the ball that had dirt on it.*

---

[4]   These traditional categories are a convenient heuristic device to sort out the raw data, not a claim about the case structure of classical Hebrew, which was probably more complex and less Indoeuropean than these labels suggest (C. Rabin, "The Structure of the Semitic System of Case Endings," *Proceedings of the International Conference on Semitic Studies 1965*, Jerusalem, 1969, 190-204).

The relative marker in biblical Hebrew, אֲשֶׁר, is not a pronoun. Usually (in 309 of the 371 occurrences of אֲשֶׁר in Genesis) the pivot is not resumed explicitly in the relative clause, and אֲשֶׁר seems to take on the role of a relative pronoun. In other cases, however (62/371 in Genesis), the pivot is resumed by a pronoun, noun, or adverb (שָׁם or שָׁמָּה functioning as the pivot would if it were an adverbial accusative). Sixteen relative clauses in Genesis[5] offer multiple slots in which the pivot may be resumed (compare Example 5). The generalizations offered by the lexica and grammars are only approximate and do not explain the numerous exceptions. This paper explores explanations at the discourse level for some of this variation.

Not every clause introduced by אֲשֶׁר shares a pivot with another clause. אֲשֶׁר may serve as a conjunction with no pivot involved, either alone (30:18) or preceded by a preposition (39:9).[6] In 24:3a, the אֲשֶׁר clause serves as the object of direct discourse in the main clause, but there is no slot for resumption. Thus at least these eight clauses offer no slots for resumption, but some other cases are ambiguous. For now I count all occurrences of אֲשֶׁר in the statistics.

What happens to the pivot in cases of nonresumption? One might suggest that it is simply elided. Alternatively, there is evidence that אֲשֶׁר assumes its function. Specifically, resumption is very common when the slot is excluded from the initial position in the clause by other features, such as negative or existential particles or the governing noun in a genitive construction. One has the impression (which I shall take as a working hypothesis) that אֲשֶׁר is felt to represent the pivot in the relative clause when the pivot's slot can be clause-initial, but when the slot is forced later in the clause, אֲשֶׁר (which must itself be initial) can no longer fill that role.

Section 2 summarizes the occurrence of resumption or nonresumption. This analysis will show that patterns of resumption or nonresumption tend to cluster with the case of the slots in the relative clause. Section 3 discusses the significance of resumptive marking for Nominative slots, Section 4 for Genitive slots, and Section 5 for Accusative slots. Section 6 summarizes the various usages identified.

2. Master Matrix

While the ambiguity of the classical grammars concerning resumption strongly suggests that the phenomenon has discourse significance, there may be other factors that also affect whether the pivot is resumed. This section reviews resumption in all אֲשֶׁר clauses in Genesis, to identify broad overall patterns of resumption and highlight deviations that require further discussion.

Genesis includes both verbless and verbal relative clauses. Predicates attested in

---

[5]   1:11, 12, 29b; 2:3; 4:11; 11:6; 15:7; 24:7c, 14, 27; 36:24; 39:19; 42:21; 45:27b; 46:5; 49:28b. All references are to Genesis unless otherwise specified. A lower case 'a,' 'b,' 'c,' or 'd' distinguishes multiple clauses governed by אֲשֶׁר in the same verse; a lower case roman numeral distinguishes multiple slots in the same אֲשֶׁר clause.

[6]   Other clear conjunctions are 18:19a; 22:16, 18; 24:3; 26:5; 39:23a.

verbless clauses include nouns, prepositional phrases, and participles or adjectives. (Because participles and adjectives pattern similarly as predicates in verbless clauses, I treat them together, and loosely describe them both as "participles.") In verbal clauses, the verb may be in either prefix or suffix conjugation, and some embedded clauses have infinitive verbs. For each type of clause, I distinguish the case within the אֲשֶׁר clause (nominative, genitive, accusative) of any slots available for the pivot, and whether or not the pivot is resumed in this slot. Table 1 classifies the slots occupied by pivots in the אֲשֶׁר clauses in Genesis by case and type of clause.

Each cell contains three values, in the form "*A + B (C)*". (If *C* is not recorded, it is zero.) *A* gives the number of slots in clauses immediately governed by אֲשֶׁר, and *B* counts slots in embedded clauses, clauses subordinate to the אֲשֶׁר clause. *C* counts the number of slots in אֲשֶׁר clauses that directly fill the pivot's slot in the main clause (e.g., 1:31; 7:23b), rather than modifying an explicit noun phrase in the main clause (e.g., הַמַּיִם in 1:7; כָּל־הַיְקוּם in 7:23a). Shaded cells are not used. Unshaded cells with no entry have counts *0+0 (0)*. The table does not include the eight clear conjunctive uses (footnote 6), but do include uses that are probably conjunctive but where a case could be made for a pivot.

The distribution of data in this table does indeed suggest that there are some dominant trends of resumption or nonresumption, and that these trends differ on the basis of grammatical features below the discourse level. Overall, of 385 slots, 72 slots (19%) resume their pivots and 313 (81%) do not. In general, the ratios by type of predicates (recorded in rows) are comparable with this overall ratio. (For example, 16% of slots in verbal clauses with suffixed predicates resume their pivots, while 84% do not.) The exception, slots in verbless clauses with nouns as predicates, is based on only three occurrences for the category as a whole, and so does not represent a trend. The picture is quite different considering the ratios by case (recorded in columns), where resumptions are either much less common than the overall ratio (for nominative and accusatives), or more common (for genitives). These trends suggest that the presence or absence of resumption may be largely explained on the basis of the case of the slot in question, leading us to organize our further exploration along this feature. Along the way, I shall also discuss lesser trends that are suggested by predicate types.

The counts in parentheses in the table represent slots in אֲשֶׁר clauses that directly fill a noun slot in the main clause, rather than modifying an explicit noun phrase. Strictly speaking, these slots cannot "resume" the pivot, since it is not expressed outside of the אֲשֶׁר clause. However, the presence or absence of an explicit element in the clause representing the pivot is about as common in these cases as in others, and at this stage in the analysis appears to follow similar patterns.

		Nominative		Genitive		Accusative		Tally		% by Pred
		Res	Not	Res	Not	Res	Not	Res	Not	
Verbless:								32+0 (6)	125+0 (45)	
Noun	Res	3+0 (1)						3+0 (1)		75
	Not						1+0		1+0	25
Prep'l Phrase	Res	1+0		18+0 (3)				19+0 (3)		15
	Not		107+0 (35)						107+0 (35)	85
Participle	Res	5+0 (2)		4+0		1+0		10+0 (2)		37
	Not		1+0				16+0 (10)		17+0 (10)	63
Verbal:								36+4 (5)	178+10 (40)	
Prefix	Res			6+0 (3)		3+0 (1)		9+0 (4)		20
	Not		8+2 (2)		1+0 (1)		25+0 (14)		34+2 (17)	80
Suffix	Res			16 +1 (1)		11+0		27+1 (1)		16
	Not		27+1 (1)				117+0 (21)		144+1 (22)	84
Infinitive	Res			0+3				0+3		30
	Not				0+5		0+2 (1)		0+7 (1)	70
Tally	Res	9+0 (3)		44+4 (7)		15+0 (1)		68+4 (11)		19
	Not		143+3 (38)		1+5 (1)		159+2 (46)		303+10 (85)	81
% by Case		6	94	89	11	9	91	19	81	

Table 1: Slots Resumed and Not Resumed, by Case and Predicate Type

3. Nominative

Pivots are overwhelmingly not resumed in nominative slots. Nominative slots never resume their pivots in verbal clauses, and out of 117 verbless clauses, there are only 9 resumptions, representing all three verbless predicates. Most of the verbless clauses represent prepositional predicates, and only one of these is resumed. The other two predicate types (nouns and participles/adjectives) are dominated by resumption, and nonresumption is rare or nonexistent. These trends can be explained by grammatical considerations below the level of discourse. In particular, five out of the eight resumptions in nominative slots result from the use of a negative or existential particle.

3.1 Negative and Existential Verbless Clauses

Negation and existential meaning are marked in verbless clauses with the particles אֵין (or לֹא) and יֵשׁ, respectively, each of which must be clause-initial. In these cases, אֲשֶׁר cannot support the pivot, which must be resumed explicitly. All five verbless negative or existential clauses with nominative pivot slots resume their pivots. Four of these[7] have participial/adjectival predicates, while the fifth[8] is in a prepositional clause. The only other existential or negative verbless clause in the corpus is 45:6, which does not resume its pivot. The slot in 45:6 is an adverbial accusative of time, a category that will be discussed below under the accusative case. Eight verbal clauses are negated with לֹא, but none of them resumes its pivot, presumably because the verbal affix indicates the required slot. In sum, a nominative slot in an existential or negative verbless clause always resumes its pivot, as a result of word order constraints.

3.2 Nominal Predicates

There are only three אֲשֶׁר clauses with nominal predicates (2:11, 13:14, 21:17), and all three resume their pivots. In all cases, the slot into which the pivot is resumed is the predicate of the clause. That is, in the absence of resumption, there would be no noun to serve as the predicate of the אֲשֶׁר clause, and thus no clause at all.

3.3 Participial Predicates[9]

Five out of six nominal slots in participial clauses are resumed, but four of these resumptions result from the negative (7:2, 8b) or existential (7:8a; 30:33) syntax of their clauses. The only remaining nominative slots in participial predications are 9:3 (כָּל־רֶמֶשׂ אֲשֶׁר הוּא־חַי, which resumes its pivot) and 40:5b (describing Pharaoh's baker and butler אֲשֶׁר אֲסוּרִים בְּבֵית הַסֹּהַר, which does not).

From the discourse perspective, אֲשֶׁר clauses with participial predicates are interesting whether or not they resume their pivots. Compared with prepositional

---

[7] 7:2, 8b (negative); 7:8a; 30:33 (existential).
[8] 17:12 (negative).
[9] Recall that this category includes adjectival predicates. References in this section to "participles" include adjectives as well.

predicates, participial predicates (with or without resumption) are rare in אֲשֶׁר
clauses. It is much more common for participles to modify their governing nouns
directly in the attributive position than to form independent clauses subordinated by
אֲשֶׁר. Addition of negation or existential particles naturally precludes the attributive
position and requires a relative construction, but other cases invite us to ask not only
why the pivot is resumed or not, but also why the modifier is embedded in a relative
construction at all. While this study does not provide a detailed analysis of
differences in usage between attributive and relative syntax for participles, one may
hypothesize that the relative construction puts the modifier in focus[10]. Such a
hypothesis explains both of the residual participial אֲשֶׁר clauses in the corpus.

Consider first 40:5, which reports that Pharaoh's butler and baker, אֲשֶׁר אֲסוּרִים
בְּבֵית הַסֹּהַר, had dreams. Grammatically an attributive construction הָאֲסוּרִים וגו'
would certainly be possible, but their location is of more than passing interest to the
narrator. Only because they are bound in the prison can their dreams come to the
attention of Joseph, who interprets them and thus comes to the attention of Pharaoh.
The narrator marks the special importance of the statement about their imprisonment
by promoting it from attributive to relative position.

Focus through promotion is also reasonable in the case of 9:3, כָּל־רֶמֶשׂ אֲשֶׁר
הוּא־חַי לָכֶם יִהְיֶה לְאָכְלָה. The stipulation appears to adumbrate the Levitical
prohibition against consuming animals that are found already dead (Lev 17:15). The
point of the modifier is not just that creeping things are a class of living creatures,
but that they may be eaten if they are taken alive. "Every creeping thing will be your
food - that is, if it is alive." In this case, the modifier is the single word חַי, and
Genesis has no one-word אֲשֶׁר clauses. I hypothesize that the resumptive pronoun in
this case is needed for reasons of balance, but more examples are needed for
confirmation.

Thus resumption does not appear to serve a discourse function directly in
participial אֲשֶׁר clauses, but may be needed to permit single-word modifiers to be
promoted to relative clauses, and this promotion is a focusing mechanism in
comparison with attributive constructions.

3.4 Prepositional Predicates

Unlike participial modifiers, which commonly modify nouns through the attributive
construction and enter relative constructions only for discourse focus or under
negative or existential transforms, Hebrew prepositional phrases are almost always
adverbial in nature, and the unmarked way to apply them to nouns is through a
relative construction. Thus they are by far the most common verbless predicate in the
corpus, accounting for 107 of the 117 verbless nominative slots. In spite of their
overwhelming prominence, only one example resumes its pivot in a nominative slot,
and that instance (17:12) is explained by the negative construction.

---

[10]   I use the term in the sense defined by K. Callow, *Discourse Considerations in Translating the Word
       of God* (Grand Rapids: Zondervan, 1974) 52, a mechanism for drawing the reader's attention to a
       subject and insisting, "This is important. Pay attention."

3.5 Summary
Resumption of the pivot into a nominative slot is extremely rare. Most cases are examples of the negative or existential transform, and are consistent with the hypothesis that אֲשֶׁר indeed resumes the pivot except when some other element must be clause-initial. The other examples appear to be motivated by factors below the level of discourse grammar, although resumption may be a condition for promotion of a participial predicate to relative clause status in order to mark focus in contrast with the unmarked attributive construction.

4. Genitive

Although overall about 19% of all slots resume their pivots, for genitives resumption is the unmarked case, and only 11% of genitive slots (six out of 54) do not resume their pivots. Thus in genitive slots pivots that are not resumed, rather than those that are resumed, are prime candidates for discourse significance.

Resumption is natural for genitive pivots because the Hebrew genitive must follow the noun that governs it. Since אֲשֶׁר precedes the clause it introduces, it cannot represent a pivot that is genitive to a noun or preposition within the clause, as the English relative pronoun can in colloquial usage (Example 6):

Example 6: *the bat which the ball was hit with.*

At least for prepositional constructions, formal English permits the governing preposition to precede the relative pronoun, as in Example 7.

Example 7: *The bat with which the ball was hit.*

This "with which" construction is at best extremely rare in Hebrew.

Five of the six non-resumed genitive slots are subjects of infinitives in clauses subordinate to the אֲשֶׁר clause. The other case is a potential example of the "with which" construction, for which I offer an alternative explanation with discourse significance. Finally, I introduce a case where a resumed genitive may have discourse significance, a case that is more readily discussed after analysis of some evidence with resumed accusatives.

4.1 Subjects of Infinitives
The corpus includes seven embedded infinitive clauses with a total of eight genitive slots. In principle, each of the infinitives could govern a genitive suffix as its subject. In practice, only two do so, the two clauses in which the infinitive is itself governed by the preposition בְּ to form a temporal clause. In the other five cases, when the infinitive is governed by לְ either as a purpose clause or (24:7cii) in the citation formula לֵאמֹר, the subject is never resumed. Presence or lack of resumption appears to be determined by the construction in which the infinitive is used, but more study

is necessary to determine the frequency with which infinitives take explicit genitive subjects in different constructions.

4.2 The "With Which" Construction in 31:32

Genitive slots that are the objects of prepositions within the אֲשֶׁר clause almost always resume their pivots. The sole exception is 31:32. Laban accuses Jacob with the theft of his gods, and Jacob invites Laban to search the camp with the promise, עִם אֲשֶׁר תִּמְצָא אֶת־אֱלֹהֶיךָ לֹא יִחְיֶה. The expected pattern is *אֲשֶׁר תִּמְצָא עִמּוֹ אֶת־אֱלֹהֶיךָ לֹא יִחְיֶה. Proposed examples of this reversal elsewhere in the OT are very rare. In addition to 31:32, BDB lists only two, both of which are questionable. בַּאֲשֶׁר in Isa 47:12 could be a conjunction, "in that" or "because," rather than a prepositional adjunct within the אֲשֶׁר clause. לַאֲשֶׁר in Ezek 23:40 is commonly taken to refer to Israel's pagan allies, "for whom you washed yourself, painted your eyes, and put on your fine clothes," but could also refer to the adulterous woman herself: "behold, they came to you, you who washed yourself, painted your eyes, and put on your fine clothes." In the latter reading the introductory preposition belongs to the main clause, not the אֲשֶׁר clause. These alternative explanations make the construction in 31:32 all the more unusual, and invite us to consider explanations at the level of discourse grammar.

One clue is that the accentuation of this verse is tripartite, having a *segolta* clause in addition to the usual *atnax* and *sof pasuq* clauses of Hebrew narrative. Lode[11] argues that *segolta* clauses are a mark of high tension at the onset of narrative climax or complication. His suggestion certainly makes sense in this context. Jacob's manner of leaving Haran shows that he does not want to confront Laban over his departure, so Laban's successful pursuit puts him under considerable tension, a situation that is compounded with the accusation that Jacob has stolen Laban's gods. Jacob is completely unprepared for this accusation, but the reader, whose sympathies are with Jacob, has known since 31:19 that Rachel took the images, and Laban's discovery of the theft puts the reader under tension as well.

Longacre[12] has observed that heightened vividness, sometimes accompanied by unusual grammatical constructions, is a feature of episode climax. The unusual genitive syntax of the אֲשֶׁר clause in 31:32 appears to be an example of such confusion. Along with the *segolta* clause, it marks the climax of the episode. It is also completely understandable as a result of Jacob's tension. The construction is not an alternative legitimate genitive construction for אֲשֶׁר clauses, but the stuttering, stumbling words of a man whose hopes of escape have been frustrated, and who is faced with a completely unexpected accusation.

4.3 Significant Resumed Genitives

Resumption of genitives is driven by syntactical concerns, not discourse ones. However, most genitive slots (30/54) are objects of prepositions, and one may ask

---

[11] L. Lode, "A Discourse Perspective on the Significance of the Massoretic Accents," *Biblical Hebrew and Discourse Linguistics* (ed. R.D. Bergen; Dallas: Summer Institute of Linguistics, 1994) 155-72.
[12] R. Longacre, *Anatomy of Speech Notions* (Lisse: Peter de Ridder, 1976) 219-22.

whether the prepositional phrase itself is required. Five times in the corpus, a place or road is further identified with an אֲשֶׁר clause using the verb הלך. Three times הלך has no explicit locative modifier (בַּדֶּרֶךְ אֲשֶׁר הָלָכְתִּי 35:3; 28:15a, 20), while twice it is modified with a prepositional phrase governing the pivot (בַּדֶּרֶךְ 42:38 אֲשֶׁר תֵּלְכוּ־בָהּ; 24:42). The contrast between the three clauses without the prepositional phrase and the two clauses with it is not strong enough to serve as the foundation of a theory of resumption, but evidence from accusative slots will suggest a plausible theory that fits these cases as well, and they will be discussed in more detail in that context.

4.4 Summary

Genitive slots are overwhelmingly resumed, because of the positional constraints on the Hebrew genitive. The presence or lack of resumption for the subjects of infinitives appears to be conditioned by the construction in which the infinitive is used, and thus is not of significance at the discourse level. The lack of resumption in 31:32 is of discourse significance, as a marker of the climax in the episode of Jacob's flight from Haran.

Although a prepositional phrase embedded in an אֲשֶׁר clause requires an explicit object, sometimes the presence of the entire prepositional phrase appears to be optional. Some of these cases will be discussed in the next section with accusative slots that fill a similar semantic function. Further work is needed to evaluate whether the presence or absence of prepositional phrases in other examples may also be motivated by discourse considerations.

5. Accusative

Fifteen out of 176 accusative slots resume their pivots. Of these, two resume their pivots with nouns, four with pronouns, and nine with the particle, שָׁם, or שָׁמָּה, functioning as an adverbial accusative of place. The two cases with nouns are susceptible to alternative interpretations in which the pivot is not resumed. In some other cases, presence or absence of resumption appears to depend on semantic distinctions such as the use of the accusative or the identity of the governing verb. The remaining data suggest that אֲשֶׁר clauses that resume their pivots into accusative slots (or into other slots in cases where the resumption is not explained by the syntactical constraints discussed in the previous sections) function to define or restrict, rather than simply describe, the noun phrase they modify.

5.1 Nominal Resumptions

To avoid arbitrariness, I have analyzed אֲשֶׁר clauses as relative constructions rather than as conjunctions wherever possible, but sometimes the alternative interpretation as a conjunction is strong enough that the clause is not credible evidence for discourse hypotheses. The two cases in which a noun resumes the pivot fall into this category.

A relative .הָבָה נֵרְדָה וְנָבְלָה שָׁם שְׂפָתָם אֲשֶׁר לֹא יִשְׁמְעוּ אִישׁ שְׂפַת רֵעֵהוּ 11:7,

reading is possible. An English translation cannot follow the form of the Hebrew, but the sense would be, "Let us confuse their speech, which each will not be able to understand from his neighbor." However, the most natural interpretation of אֲשֶׁר is as a conjunction indicating purpose: "Let us confuse there their speech, so that no one will understand his neighbor."

13:16, וְשַׂמְתִּי אֶת־זַרְעֲךָ כַּעֲפַר הָאָרֶץ אֲשֶׁר אִם־יוּכַל אִישׁ לִמְנוֹת אֶת־עֲפַר הָאָרֶץ גַּם־זַרְעֲךָ יִמָּנֶה. Again, the relative reading is possible, and easier than in 11:7: "I will establish your seed as the dust of the earth, which if one can number, so can your seed be numbered." However, אֲשֶׁר is most likely a conjunction of purpose: "I will establish your seed as the dust of the earth, so that if one can number the dust of the earth, so your seed can be numbered."

Because of the strong possibility that these examples are conjunctive rather than relative, I will not draw discourse conclusions from these resumptions.

5.2 Semantic Selection
In some examples, resumption may depend on the semantics of the אֲשֶׁר clause. Some verbs appear to prefer or reject resumption, and at least one use of the accusative is uniformly not resumed.

The notion of deep structure cases is a convenient tool for exploring semantic differences.[13] This approach discerns a number of roles or "cases" that noun phrases and prepositional phrases can play toward the verb in a clause, roles that are not necessarily marked in the surface structure of the language. For example, in "The boy broke the window" and "The window broke," "boy" is the Subject in the first sentence, as is "window" in the second, but their relations to the verb are very different. In the first case, "boy" causes the action of the verb, and has the deep structure Agent case, while in both clauses, "window" receives the action of the verb and is said to have the Patient case. The term "case" is inspired by the surface-level markers used in many languages to mark nouns as subjects or objects of verbs or as filling other syntactic roles. The term "deep structure case" emphasizes that we are concerned with the underlying meaning of the noun in relation to the verb, not its surface position as subject or object.

The various accusative slots in the corpus represent a number of different (deep structure) cases. In some examples,[14] including Patient (10, 3), Place (16, 9), Discourse (31, 2), and Object of Transfer (34, 1), both resumed and nonresumed examples can be found. However, the 79 slots that represent deep structure cases of Percept (9, 0), Time (12, 0), Action (24, 0), or Product (34, 0) never resume their pivots. While these classifications are preliminary, they suggest a semantic constraint on resumption.

A similar constraint may be associated with some verbal stems or semantic fields.

---

[13] C.J. Fillmore, "The Case for Case," in E. Bach and R.T. Harms, eds, *Universals in Linguistic Theory*, New York: Holt, Rinehart and Winston, 1-88, 1968; W.A. Cook, *Case Grammar: Development of the Matrix Model (1970-1978)*, Washington, DC: Georgetown University Press, 1979.

[14] The counts after each case (A, B) indicate (A) the number of slots with the specified case and (B) the number of resumptions.

Of the five verbs that occur more than ten times in אֲשֶׁר clauses in the corpus, only one ever resumes its pivot into an accusative slot, and two of them never take an explicit accusative (or an explicit nominative, if passive), whether or not it resumes the pivot.[15] In at least one case (ילד "to bear a child"), this lack of resumption supports the hypothesis developed in the next section. The verbs ברך "to bless" (27:27, 41) and ארר "to curse" (5:29) always take explicit accusatives, and because of their semantic similarity one should be cautious about discerning any discourse significance when the accusative slot resumes the pivot, though I will discuss the two cases where this happens in the next section. A broader survey of how accusatives are expressed with various verbs is clearly needed.

5.3 Restrictive Clauses Resume Pivots
There remain several accusative resumptions that are not explained by these considerations. This section will argue that resumption in such cases marks the אֲשֶׁר clause as restrictive or defining (compare English "that" clauses), rather than descriptive (compare English "which" clauses). The distinction is clear in some "minimal pairs" of very similar constructions that differ in whether the pivot is resumed or not, and is also consistent with the relative infrequency of resumption in clauses that modify noun phrases whose identity is already clearly defined. This section also explores the applicability of the hypothesis to cases of resumption and lack of resumption for which the corpus does not offer minimal pairs.

5.3.1 Minimal Pairs
Perhaps the most striking "minimal pair" for resumption is 39:20 (unresumed) vs. 40:3 (resumed). In 39:20, Joseph is placed in the prison, מְקוֹם אֲשֶׁר אֲסוּרֵי הַמֶּלֶךְ אֲסוּרִים. In 40:3, he is joined by the king's baker and butler, who are placed in the prison, מְקוֹם אֲשֶׁר יוֹסֵף אָסוּר שָׁם. In the first case, the reader needs to understand simply that Joseph is being placed in a royal prison. Any royal prison will do. But in 40:3, the stories about the baker and butler depend on the fact that they are placed in the very same prison where Joseph is. Only this circumstance will enable him to interpret their visions, which in turn brings him out of prison to the position of Pharaoh's chief of staff. The resumption of the pivot in 40:3 has the same effect as would the English adjective "very." Joseph is brought to "a place [any place] where the king's prisoners were bound," but the baker and butler come to "the very place where Joseph was bound."[16] In terms of English grammar, relative clauses with resumption are restrictive (like English clauses introduced by "that"). They define

---

[15] The numbers (A, B) following each root indicate (A) the number of times it occurs and (B) the number of slots for accusative pivots in these instances: עשה (34, 32), ילד (18, 13), דבר (15, 14), אמר (14, 11), נתן (13, 10). דבר resumes its pivot into an accusative slot once, at 35:15, discussed below; אמר three times governs direct discourse in the accusative; נתן takes an object three times, but only as an embedded clause (15:7ii; 24:7ciii) or in a construction in which אֲשֶׁר is a conjunction (30:18). Other less frequent verbs are similarly consistent. For example, all five occurrences of רכש govern unresumed accusative pivots.

[16] The AV makes this very distinction in its use of the indefinite article in 39:20 and of the definite article in 40:3.

more closely the noun phrase that they modify, singling it out from a broader population of items. Clauses without resumption are descriptive (English "which"). They provide the reader with more information about the object named in the noun phrase, but do not define it.

Three times in 35:13-15, an אֲשֶׁר clause describes the site of Jacob's vision as מָקוֹם אֲשֶׁר דִּבֶּר אִתּוֹ [אֱלֹהִים]. It is this place from which God went up from him; where Jacob erected a pillar; and which he called by the name "Beth-El." The first two cases do not resume the pivot, but the third does, with שָׁם. During the course of Jacob's pilgrimage, he will encounter God again and erect other monuments, but this place alone merits the name "Beth-El," because it is "the very place where God spoke with him."

As noted in the discussion of genitive slots, in three cases, the verb הלך has no explicit locative modifier (35:3 בַּדֶּרֶךְ אֲשֶׁר הָלָכְתִּי; 28:15a, 20), while twice it is modified with a prepositional phrase governing the pivot (42:38 בַּדֶּרֶךְ אֲשֶׁר תֵּלְכוּ־בָהּ; 24:42). The unresumed cases describe Jacob's wanderings. He does not know where they will take him or what he will experience. Contrast the resumption in 24:42, in which Eliezer is asking God for help in the very specific mission that he is undertaking to find a wife for Isaac. In 42:38 Jacob refuses to let Benjamin return with the other brothers to Egypt, lest mischief befall him "in the very way in which you travel." The resumption indicates that Jacob fears danger in the specific road that the brothers are traveling. Jacob may harbor suspicions about the role that the brothers played in Joseph's earlier misfortune. "The very way in which [they] travel[ed]" proved disastrous for Joseph, and now he fears their association may also be dangerous to Benjamin.

5.3.2 Argument from Definiteness

Fifty-two of the accusative slots occur in clauses that modify a noun phrase that is already defined, either through a genitive suffix, a demonstrative pronoun, or as a proper noun. One would expect the אֲשֶׁר clause in such cases to be descriptive rather than restrictive, and in fact the majority of these cases (48) do not resume their pivots. This phenomenon may also explain why ילד does not resume its pivot in the accusative, and thus (according to the hypothesis) only appears in descriptive clauses. In every case, the person who has been born is named or otherwise identified in the narrative context, so that no further definition is needed.

The four cases in which otherwise definite noun phrases are modified by a clause with resumption are all proper names and can be explained on the hypothesis that the intended hearer or reader of the phrase might not be expected to recognize the proper name. Thus even in these cases resumption has a defining function.

When Joseph reveals himself to his brothers in 45:4, he says, "I am Joseph, your brother, אֲשֶׁר־מְכַרְתֶּם אֹתִי מִצְרָיְמָה." The reference to being sold into Egypt is hardly incidental or offhanded. Joseph knows they think him long dead, and does not assume that the mere name will suffice to identify him. Many expatriate Semites in Egypt might be able to say, "I am Joseph." This Joseph wants to narrow down the options, and so uses the restrictive construction: "I am Joseph, your brother, the very same one whom you sold into Egypt."

Resumption plays a similar role in 31:13a,b. Though Jacob asked God to bring him again to Canaan when he first left, after years of earning wives he appears to have forgotten the land of promise, to which he is the heir. Haran, originally a temporary destination to escape Esau's wrath, has become Jacob's permanent residence. God reminds him of his destiny by saying, "I am the God of Bethel, אֲשֶׁר מָשַׁחְתָּ שָּׁם מַצֵּבָה אֲשֶׁר נָדַרְתָּ לִּי שָׁם נֶדֶר." The resumption implies that Jacob has forgotten where Bethel is and what it means, so that God must define it for him. "Jacob, do you remember Bethel? You know, the place where you anointed the pillar and swore an oath to me."

In 35:27, after his wanderings, Jacob finally returns to see his father Isaac at Hebron, אֲשֶׁר־גָּר־שָׁם אַבְרָהָם וְיִצְחָק. Hebron is hardly unknown to the reader at this point. In fact, the narrator goes to special pains to point out when other geographical names refer to the same place as Hebron (13:18; 23:1,19), a degree of attention paid to few other places in Genesis. The resumption in this passage may be a clue as to why Hebron receives this special attention. Hebron is the place where Abraham settles after the Lord promises to give him and his descendants the land of Canaan (13:14-18). In spite of that promise, the descendants are prone to wander. Isaac, Abraham's son and heir to the promise, requires a special warning to keep him from abandoning the land for Egypt (26:2), and Jacob, who inherits the promise from Isaac, actually does leave the land for a prolonged sojourn in Haran that ends only by divine intervention (31:3, 11-13). The passage under consideration (35:27) finally resolves both of these tensions, for it finds Isaac back in Hebron and brings Jacob to meet him there. In fact, it is the only narrative verse in Genesis (as opposed to speeches in the mouths of characters) that brings together Abraham, Isaac, and Jacob. The effect of the resumption is to tell the reader in what sense the reference to Hebron is to be taken. Hebron is a place name, but the reader must not make the mistake of thinking that finding Hebron on a map will yield the message the writer wishes to convey. The importance of Jacob's journey to Hebron is not that he reaches a specific named place, but that he finally returns to the ancestral seat of Abraham and Isaac, the token of the larger promise of the land. Hebron is significant in the discourse not as a geographical coordinate, but as the place where Abraham and Isaac lived, and the resumption insists that the reader take this circumstance, and not the proper name, as defining the significance of the reference.

5.3.3 Other Examples of Resumption

This section reviews other examples of resumed accusatives in the light of the hypothesis that "optional" resumption marks an אֲשֶׁר clause as restrictive, defining rather than just describing the pivot. These cases by themselves are not strong enough to prove the thesis, and some of them may have other explanations, but they do show that in general the hypothesis fits well.

In 13:3, Abram returns from Egypt to the vicinity of Bethel, and in particular, to the place אֲשֶׁר־הָיָה שָׁם אָהֳלֹו בַּתְּחִלָּה. The restrictive use is entirely appropriate, singling out one place in terms of its history. Almost the same construction appears, with similar appropriateness, in 33:19, which defines the parcel of land that Jacob purchases from the children of Hamor as the specific field אֲשֶׁר נָטָה־שָׁם אָהֳלֹו.

The morning after the destruction of Sodom and Gomorrah, Abraham goes "to the place אֲשֶׁר־עָמַד שָׁם אֶת־פְּנֵי יְהוָה," that is, the place where he had pled for the city and its inhabitants, to survey the damage (19:27). Again, the restrictive use is completely appropriate, since it singles out the particular place from many in the vicinity of Mamre that Abraham might have visited.

In 20:13c, Abraham recounts to Abimelech how he elicited a promise from Sarah while they still lived in Haran. He asked her, "אֶל כָּל־הַמָּקוֹם אֲשֶׁר נָבוֹא שָׁמָּה say 'He is my brother.'" The resumption stands in contrast to 28:15, 20; 35:3, clauses describing Jacob's wanderings, all without resumption. An important clue is that Abraham's request refers not (as in AV) to "every place where we may come" (which would require that be plural) but to "the entire place to which we come." Jacob is fleeing Esau, and Haran is merely a temporary stop to wait out his brother's anger. Abraham is headed to a land that God has promised to show him, a specific destination (12:1) that is to become his inheritance. His request to Sarah concerns not just any place that they might happen to find themselves (which would be the sense given by a descriptive clause), but the specific place that God has promised them and to which he is leading them. In speaking of it as "the place where we are going," he is not merely describing it, but defining it.

Two readings are possible for 21:2, which tells how Sarah bore Abraham a son לַמּוֹעֵד אֲשֶׁר־דִּבֶּר אֹתוֹ אֱלֹהִים. The pivot is מוֹעֵד, the appointed time that was the substance of God's promise to Abraham in 17:21. In the conventional reading (BDB *sub voce* דָּבַר, 3d), the antecedent of אֹתוֹ is Abraham, the pivot is not resumed, and the hypothesis suggests a descriptive reading: "the appointed time, of which God spoke with him." But a restrictive sense is appropriate, and since דִּבֶּר can govern an accusative describing the substance of the speech, אֹתוֹ is better understood as resuming the pivot: "the particular appointed time of which God spoke."

The last two examples contain verbs of blessing and cursing. As noted above, such verbs in the corpus always take explicit accusatives, and in two cases these accusatives resume the pivot, so the resumption may be due to semantic selection rather than the role of the clause as restrictive, but it is interesting to see how far the hypothesis can be pressed in these cases.

When Lamech the father of Noah names his son in 5:29, he does so with reference to הָאֲדָמָה אֲשֶׁר אֵרְרָהּ יְהוָה. The resumption certainly could be understood restrictively: Noah will comfort his people with respect to the very same ground that has been under the divine curse since Gen 3:17.

In 27:27, Isaac describes the smell of Jacob, whom he takes to be Esau, as "the smell of a field אֲשֶׁר בֵּרֲכוֹ יְהוָה." Without resumption, the clause would be descriptive: "the smell of my son is like the smell of a field, which is a wonderful smell because God blesses fields." The resumption suggests that not just any field has the kind of smell he senses, but only fields under God's blessing, and he goes on to describe the fruitfulness that would result from such blessing. There may be an allusion to God's blessing on the earth, also motivated by a smell, in 8:21-22.

5.3.4 How about Unresumed Cases?
In each case of resumption in the corpus not otherwise explained by syntactical constraints, it is plausible to see the resumption as marking the אֲשֶׁר clause as restrictive rather than descriptive, defining rather than simply describing its antecedent. Table 1 shows that there are 161 - 46 = 115 nonresumed accusative slots in clauses that modify explicit noun phrases. The question naturally arises whether all these cases can be assumed to be descriptive and not restrictive.

The question is methodologically difficult, since no other mark of the restrictive/descriptive distinction has been proposed. Thus the question of whether a given unresumed clause is restrictive or descriptive must be largely subjective. A survey of these clauses yields 21 that might be considered restrictive. Of these, nine use verbs that never take explicit accusatives in the corpus (four instances each of עשה and אמר, and one of רכש). But twelve examples remain of unresumed אֲשֶׁר clauses that are probably restrictive (12:1; 13:15; 20:3; 24:44; 25:10; 26:3, 18b; 28:18; 29:27; 31:16a; 39:6b; 41:28). While some of these may be explained on other grounds, it seems best to understand unresumed cases as unmarked for the restrictive/descriptive opposition, while resumption marks its clause as restrictive.

6. Summary
This study is only a preliminary assessment, based on a limited corpus. Within these constraints, several tentative conclusions are possible.

There are syntactic or semantic explanations for resumption that must be taken into account before asking about the discourse relevance of a particular case. In particular:

• אֲשֶׁר in general represents the pivot when the pivot can be clause-initial. The pivot cannot be clause-initial as the subject of a negative or existential clause or as the *rectum* of a genitive construction, and in these cases resumption is purely syntactical and has no discourse function.

• Certain semantic conditions (adverbial accusatives of time, percept, action, or product; specific verbs or semantically related groups of verbs) appear to demand or reject resumption of accusative pivots consistently.

Independent of resumption, a participle or adjective can modify its noun either in the attributive position or (for greater focus) through an אֲשֶׁר clause. Apparently, single-word אֲשֶׁר clauses are not possible, so if the modifier is only a single word, resumption of the pivot into the nominative position is a prerequisite for this focusing transformation.

The "with which" construction is not clearly attested in biblical Hebrew. The example in 31:32 is better understood as a deliberate deviation from the usual construction to emphasize Jacob's mental tension and the climax of the discourse.

The most prominent conclusion is that otherwise unexplained resumption marks an אֲשֶׁר clause as restrictive, serving to define or single out rather than simply to describe the noun phrase it modifies. The unresumed case is unmarked for this distinction. The effect is most clearly attested in accusative slots, but appears also in the decision whether or not to include a prepositional phrase with locative force.

COORDINATION INTERRUPTED, OR LITERARY INSERTION AX&B PATTERN, IN THE BOOKS OF SAMUEL

DAVID TOSHIO TSUMURA

1. Introduction

Since 1980 I have worked on the theme of literary insertion AXB pattern in order to elucidate "unusual" word orders in Hebrew. The paper which I read at Jerusalem in 1981 was published in 1982 and again in a revised form in 1983. In 1986, *UF* 18, I explained this phenomenon in terms of adjacency and dependency in the syntactical structure of poetic parallelism of Hebrew and Ugaritic literatures. The basic principle of the AXB pattern was first supported by C.H. Gordon (1982:81*, n. 1). Since then the phenomenon has been noted by a number of scholars such as Watson (1984:169, n. 21; 1988:365, n. 3; 1994:133, n. 145), Olmo Lete (1984:423, n. 24), Kselman (1984:25, n. 11), Sekine (1985:15, n. 16), R.P. Gordon (1986:342), Waldman (1989:78), Waltke and O'Connor (1990:708), Haak (1992:68, n. 234) and Wonneberger (1992:85), and the designation "AXB pattern" seems to be accepted. In this paper I would like to discuss literary insertion with a special focus on the AX&B pattern, that is, cases of "interrupted coordination" (A ... &B) caused by the insertion of other material (X), in the Books of Samuel.

2. Definitions

First, let us define the AXB pattern more generally.

[AB] stands for a syntactical unit such as a genitive construction (construct chain), an appositional construction or an adjectival combination. [A & B] stands for a coordinate construction which constitutes a composite unit, such as a verbal hendiadys or a merismatic coordination (e.g. "heaven and earth" which refers to the whole creation). In the AXB Pattern, the two items A and B constitute a composite unit even after the insertion of X between them, thus violating the normal grammatical rule of adjacency. In this stylistic phenomenon, X is not simply interrupting the A-B linkage, but grammatically governs or is governed by the A-B complex as a whole.

In this pattern, the inserted material X can be not only a word but even a phrase or a clause. It can also be a colon inserted into a bicolon A // B.

Insertion, not inversion

It is important to note that the AXB pattern as defined above is a phenomenon of insertion, not of inversion or a simple break-up. While the inversion ACB is simply the switch of word order ABC, the AXB is the insertion of X between the A and B of a composite unit [AB]. Thus, AXB implies: while the adjacency of A and B is lost, A ... B is still recognized as a composite unit, in which A and B keep their grammatical relationship and which as a whole holds its dependency with X. Therefore, AXB does not signify that X holds its grammatical relationship with A and with B at the same time but X holds its grammatical relationship with the [A...B] composite unit as a whole.

For example, in Hos 6:9, דרך ירצחו־שכמה is certainly an ''impossible'' word order from the standpoint of ordinary prose grammar. It cannot be explained as an example of a normal inversion (ACB). However, we can say that the ירצחו (X) was inserted between elements of the construct chain for stylistic/rhetorical reasons, and the two elements דרך (A) and שכמה (B) still keep their grammatical relationship even after their loss of adjacency; and the verb ירצחו (X) holds its grammatical relationship with the phrase, דרך ... שכמה (A ... B), as a whole. Hence, the text means ''they commit murder on the way to Shechem''.

Isa 10:5

הוי אשור שבט אפי   ''Ah! Assyria is the rod of my anger,
ומטה־הוא בידם זעמו   and the staff of my fury is in their hand''

is usually translated with an emendation of the text. For example, RSV translates: ''Ah, Assyria, the rod of my anger, the staff of my fury!'' with a note: ''Heb: a staff it is in their hand my fury.'' However in our understanding, the grammatical relationship between מטה (A) and זעמי (B) as a construct chain like שבט אפי is kept even after the insertion of the element X: הוא בידם. Grammatically ''(it) is in their hand'' (X) functions as a predicate to the composite noun ''the staff of my fury'' (AB) which serves as a subject. Here the AXB pattern has the effect of slowing down the speed by polarizing the two elements (A ↔ B) of a composite unit in a colon, which is the minimum breathing unit of poetic parallelism.

Insertion, not ellipsis

X can be inserted also into the [A & B] composite unit. In other words, [A & B] is treated as a composite unit and keeps its internal grammatical relationship, i.e. coordination, even after X is inserted between A and B. And this X retains its grammatical relationship with the [A & B] complex as a whole. Hence this is not the same as the phenomenon of ellipsis, AX and B(X), where the second X is deleted on the surface structure for stylistic reasons.

To cite a new example,

Judg 5:8b

מגן אם־יראה ורמח   ''a shield, if it is seen, and a spear''

Here מגן (A), a defensive weapon, and רמח (B), an offensive weapon, still constitute a merismatic word pair, after a clause אסׁ־יראה "if it is seen" = "it is not seen" (X) was inserted between them. In this AX&B pattern the composite unit [A ... &B] as a whole has a grammatical relationship with X. Hence, its translation would be: "Neither a shield nor a spear is seen".

Inserted colon
The AXB pattern can be extended vertically to parallel structures, in which an X line that modifies a bicolon as a whole is inserted between the A and B lines, thus constituting A//X//B. And even after the X line is inserted between them, these two lines keep their grammatical relationship to each other. Watson (1984:169) explains this as a " 'split couplet' where a parallel bicolon encloses other material"; here the "other material" is same as the X of our A//X//B. This X can be further expanded to become a bicolon itself, creating an A//X//Y//B pattern. In other words, X//Y is an "inserted bicolon" (see Tsumura 1988) within a bicolon A//B.

Vertical grammar
This stylistic phenomenon of "insertion" can be recognized not only in poetic texts, but also in poetic prose. Since Biblical literature is essentially "aural" (Parunak 1982), virtually the whole Bible is subject to rhetorical analysis and has some of the characteristics of parallelism. Elsewhere I have demonstrated the "poetic" nature of the prose narrative of 1 Sam 2:12-17 (Tsumura 1993) through a vertical analysis of relationships among the elements, since, as R. Jakobson says, "the poetic function projects the principle of equivalence from the axis of selection into the axis of combination."[1] Poetry is thus characterized by its own grammar, which I call a *vertical* grammar in contrast to the usual *horizontal* one. It is no surprise that both Books of Samuel, both the poetic and the prose sections, utilize the technique of literary insertion AXB pattern for stylistic reasons.

Thus, the AXB pattern is an important phenomenon of Hebrew grammar and style. The existence of this seemingly ungrammatical or "unusual" word order pattern is another literary characteristic of the Bible. In the following examples we would like to focus on the AX&B pattern in the Books of Samuel.

---

[1]   R. Jakobson, "Linguistics and Poetics," in T. A. Sebeok (ed.), *Style in Language* (Cambridge, Mass.: M.I.T. Press, 1960) 358.

3. Interrupted coordination in the Books of Samuel: examples

3.1. [A & B] unit

A (NP) & B (NP), X (NP)

1 Sam 8:16

ואת־עבדיכם ואת־שפחותיכם

ואת־בחוריכם הטובים ואת־חמוריכם יקח

He will take your menservants and maidservants,

and the best of your cattle and your asses (RSV)

Since הטובים follows three nouns and precedes "and your asses", one might be tempted to excise the last item as a late addition. But, as McCarter (1980) notes, "no textual warrant exists" for such emendation.

Syntactically there have been two positions with regard to the function of הטובים. The first is that of RSV which takes the adjective as modifying only the immediately preceding noun בחוריכם, which is emended to mean "your cattle". The second position is that of McCarter, who takes the adjective as modifying the three preceding nouns and translates: "Your best slaves, maidservants, and cattle, and your asses he will take and use for his own work." However, this understanding still does not explain why the adjective modifies only the first three nouns but not the fourth.

Another possible position is to recognize the AX&B pattern here, in which הטובים (X) is inserted between a coordinate pair of words, i.e. "your young men" (A) and "your asses" (B), which is an example of "alternation of animal and man" like in v. 17 (Fokkelman 1993:351). In this stylistic phenomenon the adjective modifies the composite unit "your young men and asses" (A & B) as a whole, while the first two nouns remain as a merismatic word pair, i.e. male and female servants. Hence an improved translation would be:

He will take your male and female servants,

and the best of your young men and asses.

A (NP) & B (NP), X (VP)

2 Sam 3:34

ידך לא־אסרות ורגליך   3 (11)

לא־לנחשתים הגשו   2 (9)

Your hands were not bound,

your feet not fettered; (REB; also NIV)

Following 4QSam[a] *bzqym*, McCarter (1984:110-11) speculates with Freedman that the added expression "by manacles" provides "an excellent parallel" to "by fetters". He thus translates:

> Your hands were bound - though not by manacles!
> Your feet - though not by fetters - were confined!

However, the MT makes sense as it is, though the poetic structure should be a qinah-form with a scansion, 3 (11) // 2 (9), as BHS suggests. In this analysis, the first line can be taken as constituting the AX&B pattern, in which "your hands and feet" (A & B) is interrupted by the insertion of a verbal phrase "(be) not bound" (X) and A and B still hold as a composite unit governed by X. This is another example of polarization of two elements of a composite unit (A & B) in a colon with the effect of slowing down the tempo.

The improved translation would be:

> Your hands and feet were not bound;
> they were not put in fetters.

A (NP) & B (NP), X (AdvPh)

1 Sam 6:11

וישמו את־ארון יהוה אל־העגלה ואת הארגז

ואת עכברי הזהב ואת צלמי טחריהם

And they put the ark of the LORD on the cart, and the box
with the golden mice and the images of their tumors. (RSV)

Since the lists of the other items to be sent back with the ark vary on arrangement and completeness among MT, LXX[B] and LXX[L], McCarter (1980:130) does not think it likely that anything after "the ark" is original and translates simply as "and put the ark in the cart".

On the other hand, Fokkelman (1993:281) keeps MT as it is and observes the alliteration of *'ārōn* and *'argaz* which he thinks groups the many items into two series. According to him, the first series וישמו את־ארון יהוה אל־העגלה still has "a close-knit syntactic organization", while the second series "lapses into a continual adding on" ואת הארגז ואת עכברי הזהב ואת צלמי טחריהם. He thus translates:

> - they put the Ark of Yahweh onto the cart,
> and the chest, and the golden mice, and the
> representations of their haemorrhoids.

While keeping the MT as it is, Driver (1913:55) makes the significant observation that the type of sentence is one "not uncommon"in Hebrew as in Gen 12:17, 34:29, 43:15, Num 13:23b. He takes it as a feature of Hebrew style, "when two subjects (or objects) have to be combined in one clause, for the clause containing one of the

subjects (or objects) to be completed, the other being attached subsequently.''[2]
Hence he translates:

> And they set the ark of Yahweh upon the cart,
> *and also* the coffer,

Here Driver concludes that the second item, ''the coffer'', should go with the first,
while on the other hand Fokkelman divides the four items into one and three, i.e.
''the Ark'' and the other three items.

However, in v. 8 it was ordered that the Ark and the ''pouch'', which holds the
golden objects, be put ''on the cart''. Therefore, the text is better taken as having an
AX&B pattern in which ''the ark'' (A) and ''the pouch'' (B) are the items to be
placed ''on the cart'' (X), and the other two are the items which are to be put in the
pouch. Thus, an improved translation would be:

> and they put on the cart the Ark of Yahweh and the pouch,
> with the golden mice, *i.e.*[3] the images of their tumors, in it.

2 Sam 6:17c

ויעל דוד עלות לפני יהוה ושלמים

and David sacrificed burnt offerings and fellowship offerings before
the Lord. (NIV)

McCarter (1984:167) thinks that ושלמים ''and communion offerings'' is secondary,
for it comes at the end in MT and LXX: ''holocausts before Yahweh *and communion
offerings*'', while in Syr. it comes next to the last: ''holocausts *and communion
offerings* before Yahweh.'' He thus omits ''and communion offerings'' and
translates: ''and David offered holocausts before Yahweh''.

On the other hand, Fokkelman (1990:197, n. 98) explains that ''the final *lifnē yhwh*
in 17c has been placed prior to the peace offerings in order to get an epiphora on
šᵉlāmīm in 17c//18a'' (18a: ויכל דוד מהעלות העולה והשלמים). Here it is possible
to consider the phrase ''before the Lord'' as being inserted into a composite unit
''burnt offerings and fellowship offerings'' (A&B), thus forming AX&B pattern.

1 Sam 7:3

הסירו את־אלהי הנכר מתוככם והעשתרות

then put away the foreign gods and the Ashtaroth from among you (RSV)

---

[2] Driver cites the following examples:
   a) Gen 2:9b, 41:27a, Ex 35:22, Lev 22:4, Nu 16:2a, 18b, 27b, Jud 6:5a, 2Ki 6:15,
   b) Gen 1:16b, 12:17, 34:29, 43:15, 18, Ex 29:3, Jud 21:10b, 1Ki 5:9, Jer 27:7a, 32:29,
   c) (analogous examples with prepositions) Gen 28:14b, Ex 34:27b, Dt 7:14b, 28:46, 54a, 56a, Jer 25:12(MT), 40:9a.
[3] Taking *waw* as explicative.

Here "from among you" is the X of AX&B pattern, in which "the foreign gods and the Ashtaroth" (A&B) is interrupted by the insertion of "from among you" (X).

A (NP) & B (NP), X (clause)

2 Sam 1:21

הרי בגלבע אל־טל ואל־מטר עליכם ושדי תרומת

O mountains of Gilboa,
may you have neither dew nor rain,
nor fields that yield offerings of grain. (NIV)

The phrase ושדי תרומת is often emended to make it parallel with "dew" and "rain" and is taken as meaning "upsurging of the deep" (RSV) or "flowing of the deeps" (McCarter 1984:69-70). However, ושדי תרומת as it is probably means "fields of the heights" (Freedman), i.e. "uplands" and can be equivalent to מרומי שדה in Judg 5:18 (Fokkelman 1986:740), thus "fields" and "hills" make a word pair (Talmon, cited by Fokkelman 1986:662). Therefore, it is possible that "mountains in Gilboa and fields of the heights" (A&B) is interrupted by the insertion of a clause "let there be no dew and no rain upon you" (X), thus constituting the AX&B pattern. The improved translation would be:

> O mountains in Gilboa and fields of the heights,
> let there be no dew and no rain upon you!

1 Sam 26:11

ועתה קח־נא את־החנית אשר מראשתו [מראשתיו]
ואת־צפחת המים   ונלכה לנו

take the spear and water jar which are at his head

Here "the spear and the water jar" (A&B) is interrupted by the insertion of "which are at his head" (X). In this AX&B pattern, "which are at his head" modifies "the spear and the water jar" as a whole, as in vv. 12 and 16 where the order is A&BX. Here too the AX&B pattern has the effect of slowing down the tempo. Perhaps the narrator wants to mention the water jar "fairly inconspicuously" (Fokkelman 1986:537) after the spear.

A (VP) & B (VP), X (AdvPh)

1 Sam 7:16

והלך מדי שנה בשנה וסבב בית־אל והגלגל והמצפה

And he went on a circuit year by year to Bethel, Gilgal, and Mizpah; (RSV)

Here a verbal hendiadys, "to go" (A) and "to surround" (B), is interrupted by the insertion of a temporal phrase "year by year" (X).

2 Sam 12:11

ולקחתי את־נשיך לעיניך ונתתי לרעיך

And I will take your wives and give them to your friends before your eyes.

Here "before your eyes" is the X of the AX&B pattern; though it is inserted between two verbal phrases, i.e. "and I will take" (A) and "I will give" (B), the entire actions of taking and giving are to be held "before your eyes".

1 Sam 24:8

ושאול קם מהמערה וילך בדרך

McCarter (1980:382) translates as "and Saul got up and went on down the road." (AB), reading *wyqm š'wl wyrd bdrk* on the basis of LXX[B]. On the other hand, NIV translates קם מ as "he left" rather than "he arose from": "And Saul left the cave and went his way." However, by recognizing an AX&B pattern here, one can translate the passage as "and Saul arose and went from the cave on his way": lit. "and Saul arose from the cave and went on his way" (AX&B).

A (AdvPh) & B (AdvPh), X (AdvPh)

1 Sam 1:9

ותקם חנה אחרי אכלה בשלה ואחרי שתה

Hannah arose after eating and drinking at Shiloh.

Driver (1913:12) and others divide MT as *'hry 'kl hbšlh* "after eating *the boiled meat*" (cf. 2:13). McCarter (1980:53) emends to *bšly* "privately, quietly", for he also thinks that "the mention of Shiloh seems oddly repetitious here". However, a better solution would be to recognize an AX&B pattern here: "at Shiloh" (X) is inserted between two prepositional phrases which are usually combined as a unit (A & B).

3.2. [A//B] unit

A//X//B in poetry

1 Sam 2:2

There is none holy like the LORD,	אין־קדוש כיהוה
there is none besides thee;	כי אין בלתך
there is no rock like our God. (RSV)	ואין צור כאלהינו

McCarter (1980:68-69) takes the passage as an "original bicolon", since he thinks this verse is "conflate in all witnesses". However, the three lines constitute an A//X//B pattern, in which the first and the third correspond to each other while the second is inserted between them as a subordinate colon; this is supported grammatically by the fact that the A line and B line are 3p, while the X line is 2p. The "radical shift in the subject of a sentence" in parallelism is noted also by Sasson (1990:165) who translates the verse as follows:

> No god is holy like the Lord
> - none beside you;
> indeed, no rock is like our God.

Thus the well-balanced bicolon, A//B,

> There is no holy one like the Lord;
> there is no rock like our God.

is interrupted by the insertion of the "emphatic" *kî*-clause

> indeed there is none but you,

with a sudden change from the third to the second person. This is not a simple stylistic variation. The second person, which is used only twice (vv. 1 and 2) in this prayer, exhibits a sense of nearness and intimacy. This change or variation certainly creates excitement and sharp tension in the mind of the hearer too. While an ABA pattern would prepare him to come back to the beginning with variation, the AXB pattern creates in him an unexpected sense of suspense because of the interruption and the slowing down of the flow of discourse.

1 Sam 2:3a

Do not speak too much,	אל־תרבו תדברו
very haughtily,	גבהה גבהה
let arrogance not go out of your mouth!	יצא עתק מפיכם

Driver thinks that "the line is unduly long". Since McCarter (1980:69) considers MT to be "a conflation of it in correct and corrupt form", he takes this passage as constituting a bicolon: "Do not speak haughtily // Or let arrogance out of your mouth!" However, the parallelism follows the A//X//B pattern in which the bicolon, A//B, is interrupted by the insertion of the "other material" (X), which modifies the entire bicolon A//B. Sasson (1990:165) also takes this as a tricolon, translating:

> "Do not increase your words,
> inflating them enormously,
> your mouth pouring out insolence"

A//X//B in poetic prose

1 Sam 2:13

The younger priest would come,	ובא נער הכהן
while the meat was boiling,	בשל הבשר
with a three-pronged fork in his hand,	והמזלג שלש־השנים בידו

The second line, which is a temporal phrase meaning "while the meat was boiling", interrupts the flow of the sentence, since the third line refers directly back to נער הכהן in the first line through the pronominal suffix ־ו. While this can be explained simply as an inversion of the second line and the third, this may be an example of the AXB pattern (see Tsumura 1993:295-96), in which the second line (X) is inserted between the first (A) and the last (B) and yet holds a grammatical relationship with AB as a whole.

1 Sam 3:1

And the word of the Lord was rare	ודבר־יהוה היה יקר
in those days	בימים ההם
the vision was not frequent.	אין חזון נפרץ

Read as poetic prose, the third line is in parallel with the first, the second being inserted between the first and the third, thus constituting an A//X//B pattern.

1 Sam 28:19

ויתן יהוה גם את־ישראל עמך

ביד־פלשתים

ומהר אתה ובניך עמי

גם את־מחנה ישראל יתן יהוה

ביד־פלשתים

McCarter (1980:419) thinks that "this verse is corrupt in all witnesses, conflating two versions of one clause, viz.

(1) ויתן יהוה גם את־ישראל עמך ביד־פלשתים

"And Yahweh will give Israel, too, with you into the hand of the Philistines," and

(2) גם את־מחנה ישראל יתן יהוה ביד־פלשתים

"Indeed the camp of Israel will Yahweh give into the hand of the Philistines".

However, the passage follows the AXB pattern, where "in time to come you and your sons will be with me" ומחר אתה ובניך עמי (X) is inserted between a bicolon (A//B), which constitutes a chiastic parallelism: a-b-c // b-a-c. The passage would be better translated as follows:

> "so that the Lord may give even Israel with you
> in to the hand of Philistines
> - in time to come you and your sons will be with me;

even the camp of Israel the Lord may give
into the hand of Philistines!''

2 Sam 12:9

את אוריה החתי הכית בחרב
ואת־אשתו לקחת לך לאשה
ואתו הרגת בחרב בני עמון

The passage displays an AXB pattern, in which ''his wife you have taken as your
wife'' (X) is inserted between a perfectly balanced bicolon A//B,

> Uriah the Hittite you have struck down with the sword;
> him you have killed with the sword of the Ammonites.

In this bicolon the word order in each colon is exactly the same, and the shortness
of the pronominal expression ''him'' in B is balanced by the ballast variant,[4] ''the
sword of the Ammonites''.

It is clear from the macro-structure of the David-Bathsheba story that the second
line (X) expresses the purpose, i.e. to take Uriah's wife, while A and B express the
method, i.e. by killing him with the enemy's sword. Nathan begins by reproaching
David's cunning method of killing Uriah and then suddenly switches the topic to his
wife. This is not a simple device of ABA alternation; Nathan deliberately interrupted
the flow of discourse (AB) by inserting the new and major phrase X, thus creating
suspense in David's mind. The poetic structure exhibits that the main motive of
David was to ''take'' Uriah's wife, thus breaking the 10th (covet) commandment
which resulted in breaking the 7th (adultery), the 6th (murder) and the 8th (stealing)
commandments. The translation would be:

> Uriah the Hittite you have struck down with the sword;
> - his wife you have taken as your wife;
> him you have killed with the sword of the Ammonites.

A//X//Y//B

2 Sam 3:33b-34

33b	הכמות נבל ימות אבנר	4	(9)	A
34	ידך לא־אסרות ורגליך	3	(11)	X
	לא־לנחשתים הגשו	2	(8)	Y
	כנפול לפני בני־עולה נפלת	4	(11)	B

---

[4] See Gordon, C.H. (1965), §13.116; Watson (1984) 343-47.

McCarter (1984) emends the text and translates these verses as follows:

> Alas, as an outcast dies, Abiner died!
> Your hands were bound - though not by manacles!
> Your feet - though not by fetters - were confined!
> As a criminal falls, you fell!

However, the passage can be interpreted without emending the text as the A//X//Y//B pattern, i.e. a bicolon X//Y being inserted between a bicolon A//B (see Tsumura 1988). Hence, a better translation would be:

> "Like a death of a fool should Abner die?
>   Your hands and feet were not bound;[5]
>   they were not put in fetters.
> Like a falling before sons of injustice have you fallen?"

4. Summary and examples

[AB] unit

AB (NP: cstr chain), X (affix)
  Isa 9:2 (1983:471)
  Ps 92:13 (1983:471)
  2 Kgs 3:4 (1983:471)
  Hab 3:8 (1988a:33)

AB (NP: cstr chain), X (NP)
  Ps 24:6 (1982:2, 1983:471; Wonneberger 1992:85)
  Hab 3:9b (1988a:39)

AB (NP: cstr chain), X (VP)
  Hos 6:9 (1982:2, 1983:469, 1986:353)
  Hos 14:3 (1983:469)

AB (NP: cstr chain), X (AdvPh)
  Job 27:3 (1983:472)

AB (NP: cstr chain), X (clause)
  Isa 10:5 (1982:2, 1983:472, 1986:354)

---

[5] For this line, see above.

AB (NP), X (clause)
  Jer 41:9 (1982:2, 1983:473)

AB (VP: verbal idiom), X (NP)
  Jer 9:2 (1982:3, 1983:473)

AB (clause), X (VP)
  Ps 109:10 (1983:475)

AB (clause), X (NP)
  1 Sam 2:14 (1993:297)

AB (clause), X (clause)
  Gen 39:17 (1982:3)

[A & B] unit

A (NP) & B (NP), X (NP)
  Ps 46:2 (1982:3, 1983:475)

A (NP) & B (NP), X (VP)
  Deut 32:14 (1980:53, 1981:168, 1982:3, 1983:476)
  Ps 11:5 (1983:476, 1986:357)
  Ps 37:20 (1983:476)

A (NP) & B (NP), X (AdvPh)
  Jer 32:11 (1982:4, 1983:477)
  Judg 14:8 (1983:477)

A (NP) & B (NP), X (clause)
  Deut 12:26 (1982:4)

A (VP) & B (VP), X (NP)
  Hab 2:2 (1982a:295, 1983:477, 1986:358)

A (VP) & B (VP), X (AdvPh)
  Ps 50:20 (1983:478, 1986:357)
  Ps 37:20 (1983:478)

A (AdvPh) & B (AdvPh), X (AdvPh)
  Jer 32:20 (1982:4, 1983:478)
  Deut 1:33 (1983:479; Watson 1988:365, 1994:133)

A (AdvPh) & B (AdvPh), X (clause)
    Deut 1:36 (1983:479)

[A//B] unit

A//X//B
    Ps 6:11 (1982:5, 1983:480)
    Ps 5:7 (1983:480)
    Ps 9:15 (1983:481)
    Ps 86:12 (1983:481)
    Gen 49:8 (1982:5, 1983:481)
    Ps 40:7 (1986:359)
    Ps 51:21 (1991:39)
    Ps 51:16 (1991:40)
    Ps 51:18 (1991:40)
    Ps 22:3 (Inagaki 1993:57)
    Ps 49:15 (1994:18)

A//X//Y//B
    Amos 1:5 (1986:360, 1988:234)
    Ps 9:7 (1986:360, 1988:235)
    Hab 3:13b (1988a:43, SBL 1989)
    Hos 11:10 (SBL 1989)
    Isa 35:4 (SBL 1989)
    Ps 17:1 (SBL 1989)
    Mic 2:4 (SBL 1989)
    Job 12:24-25 (SBL 1989)

AXB in Discourse Structure

AB (discourse), X (discourse)
    Gen 37-39ff., Gen 38 (1982:5)
    Hos 1-3, Hos 2 (1982:5)

A (discourse) & B (discourse), X (discourse)
    Job 27 & 29f., Job 28 (1982:5)

Bibliography

Driver (1913): S.R. Driver, *Notes on the Hebrew Text and the Topography of the Books of Samuel* (Oxford: Clarendon, 1913).

Fokkelman (1981): J.P. Fokkelman, *Narrative Art and Poetry in the Books of Samuel: a full interpretation based on stylistic and structural analyses.* Vol. I: *King David (II Sam. 9-20 & I Kings 1-2)* (Assen: Van Gorcum, 1981).

Fokkelman (1986): J.P. Fokkelman, *Narrative Art and Poetry in the Books of Samuel: a full interpretation based on stylistic and structural analyses.* Vol. II: *The Crossing Fates (I Sam. 13-31 & II Sam. 1)* (Assen: Van Gorcum, 1986).

Fokkelman (1990): J.P. Fokkelman, *Narrative Art and Poetry in the Books of Samuel: a full interpretation based on stylistic and structural analyses.* Vol. III: *Throne and City (II Sam. 2-8 & 21-24)* (Assen: Van Gorcum, 1990).

Fokkelman (1993): J.P. Fokkelman, *Narrative Art and Poetry in the Books of Samuel: a full interpretation based on stylistic and structural analyses.* Vol. IV: *Vow and Desire (I Sam. 1-12)* (Assen: Van Gorcum, 1993).

Gordon, C.H. (1965): C.H. Gordon, *Ugaritic Textbook* (Rome: Pontificium Institutum Biblicum, 1965).

Gordon, C.H. (1982): C.H. Gordon, "Asymmetric Janus Parallelism," *Eretz-Israel* 16 [*Harry M. Orlinsky Volume*] (1982) 81*.

Gordon, R.P. (1986): R.P. Gordon, *1 & 2 Samuel: A Commentary* (Exeter: Paternoster, 1986).

Haak (1992): R.D. Haak, *Habakkuk* (SVT 44; Leiden: Brill, 1992).

Inagaki (1993): H. Inagaki, "The Literary Structure of Psalm 22:3," *Exegetica* 4 (1993) 51-60 [in Japanese with English summary].

Joüon-Muraoka (1991): P. Joüon & T. Muraoka, *A Grammar of Biblical Hebrew.* 2 vols. (Subsidia Biblica 14; Roma: Pontificio Istituto Biblico, 1991).

Kselman (1984): J.S. Kselman, "A Note on Psalm 85:9-10," *CBQ* 46 (1984) 23-27.

McCarter (1980): P.K. McCarter, Jr., *I Samuel: A New Translation with Introduction, Notes & Commentary* (AB 8; Garden City: Doubleday, 1980).

McCarter (1984): P.K. McCarter, Jr., *II Samuel: A New Translation with Introduction, Notes & Commentary* (AB 9; Garden City: Doubleday, 1984).

Olmo Lete (1984): G. del Olmo Lete, "David's Farewell Oracle (2 Samuel xxiii 1-7): A Literary Analysis," *VT* 34 (1984) 414-37.

Parunak (1982): H. Van Dyke Parunak, "Some Axioms for Literary Architecture," *Semitics* 8 (1982) 1-16.

Sasson (1990): J.M. Sasson, *Jonah: A New Translation with Introduction, Commentary, and Interpretation* (AB 24B; New York: Doubleday, 1990).

Sekine (1985): M. Sekine (1985): "Der 'Bruch' in der althebräischen Poesie," *Annual of the Japanese Biblical Institute* 11 (1985) 3-15.

Tsumura (1980): D.T. Tsumura, "Literary Structure of Psalm 46, 2-8," *Annual of the Japanese Biblical Institute* 6 (1980) 29-55.

Tsumura (1981): D.T. Tsumura, "Twofold Image of Wine in Psalm 46:4-5," *JQR* 71 (1981) 167-175.

Tsumura (1982): D.T. Tsumura, "Literary Insertion (AXB) Pattern in Biblical Hebrew," *Proceedings of the Eighth World Congress of Jewish Studies, 1981.* Division a: The Period of the Bible. (Jerusalem, 1982) 1-6.

Tsumura (1982a): D.T. Tsumura, "Hab 2,2 in the Light of Akkadian Legal Practice," *ZAW* 94 (1982) 294-295.

Tsumura (1983): D.T. Tsumura, "Literary Insertion (AXB Pattern) in Biblical Hebrew," *VT* 33 (1983) 468-82.

Tsumura (1986): D.T. Tsumura, "Literary Insertion, AXB Pattern, in Hebrew and Ugaritic: A Problem of Adjacency and Dependency in Poetic Parallelism," *UF* 18 (1986) 351-61.

Tsumura (1988): D.T. Tsumura, " 'Inserted Bicolon', the AXYB Pattern, in Amos I 5 and Psalm IX 7," *VT* 38 (1988) 234-36.

Tsumura (1988a): D.T. Tsumura, "Ugaritic Poetry and Habakkuk 3," *Tyndale Bulletin* 40 (1988) 24-48.

Tsumura (1991): D.T. Tsumura, "The Unity of Psalm 51," *Exegetica* 2 (1991) 35-48 [in Japanese with English summary].

Tsumura (1993): D.T. Tsumura, "Poetic Nature of the Hebrew Narrative Prose in I Samuel 2:12-17," in J.C. de Moor and W.G.E. Watson (eds.), *Verse in Ancient Near Eastern Prose* (AOAT 42; Neukirchen-Vluyn: Neukirchener, 1993) 293-304.

Tsumura (1994): D.T. Tsumura, "Psalm 49:15 - its Poetic Structure and Translation," *Exegetica* 5 (1994) 13-26 [in Japanese with English summary].

Tsumura (SBL 1989): " 'Inserted Bicolon', the AXYB Pattern, in Hebrew and Ugaritic" (Paper, read at SBL Anaheim, Nov. 19, 1989).

Waldman (1989): N.M. Waldman, *The Recent Study of Hebrew: A Survey of the Literature with Selected Bibliography* (Winona Lake: Eisenbrauns, 1989).

Waltke-O'Connor (1990): B.K. Waltke & M. O'Connor, *An Introduction to Biblical Hebrew Syntax.* (Winona Lake: Eisenbrauns, 1990).

Watson (1984): W.G.E. Watson, *Classical Hebrew Poetry* (Sheffield: JSOT Press, 1984).

Watson (1988): W.G.E. Watson, "Internal (Half-line) Parallelism in Ugaritic Once More," *UF* 20 (1988) 365-74.

Watson (1994): W.G.E. Watson, *Traditional Techniques in Classical Hebrew Verse* (Sheffield: Sheffield Academic Press, 1994).

Wonneberger (1992): R. Wonneberger, *Redaktion: Studien zur Textfortschreibung im Alten Testament, entwickelt am Beispiel der Samuel-Überlieferung.* (Göttingen: Vandenhoeck & Ruprecht, 1992).

II. STUDIES ON TEXTS

THE TEXT AS AN ELOQUENT GUIDE
RHETORICAL, LINGUISTIC AND LITERARY FEATURES
IN GENESIS 1

ELLEN VAN WOLDE

A text is like a guide who directs a reader on a journey. The reader starts travelling, but the text maps out the road along which the reader can walk and points out the direction. The text achieves this by providing specific information presented from different angles or points of view. One could even go so far as to say that the perspectives of narrator and characters are the reader's eyes and ears. The text also employs literary means and stylistic features to guide the reader and to focus the attention on one aspect rather than on another. But most of all, the text determines the main route on which the reader sets out through theme and content. All these factors contribute to the rhetorical equipment which a text uses to help a reader find its bearings. The exegete or text analyst studies the linguistic and literary aspects through which this rhetorical guiding works. For the translator it is good to be aware of these signposts in order to translate a text correctly.

This article is aimed at the study of narrative texts. It focuses on a number of linguistic and literary features which form the basis of rhetorical equipment of narrative texts in general and that of the creation story of Genesis 1:1-2:4a in particular.

Beginning and ending of the story: Gen 1:1 and 2:4a

A narrative text creates a beginning in time and through the ordering of time it breathes life into a possible reality. To this effect, the story links up a series of actions and situations in a coherent arrangement, presenting them as a development so that a certain line in the events materialises. Inspiring stories or true stories are not indeed inspiring or true because they happened exactly the way they are narrated. Life, after all, *is not* a story, and does not consist of a fixed line of events. However, events acquire meaning precisely because the story offers a context and gives coherence to events: in a narrative text there is a beginning which gradually develops into ever-changing situations resulting in a conclusion. In an analysis one should therefore start with a determination of the beginning and the ending of the story and of the transformation in between. One may use adjuncts of time and place, changes in (the names of) characters and in patterns of actions, together with stylistic and syntactic features as indicators of the demarcation of the story.

As for the story of the creation in Gen 1, determining the beginning is not a problem. Verse 1:1 is the beginning of Genesis and of the entire Bible. The very first word, בראשית, shows that a beginning is being made. Usually this word is translated as 'in the beginning', although there is no definite article in the Hebrew of the Masoretic text nor an indication for a *status constructus* (as is clear from the *qatal* form of the verb ברא).[1] The lack of a definite article and of a genitive nominal construction, as well as the masoretic accentuation of בראשית with a *tipha* (which is normal for words in the absolute state, while words in the construct state usually have a conjunctive accent), may lead to the conclusion that verse 1 is an independent clause in which בראשית is in the absolute state, indicating an indefinite beginning, to be translated as 'in *a* beginning'.[2] The function of this indefinite beginning is possibly to indicate that one cannot speak of 'the' beginning unless 'time' already exists. This is, actually, the moment that the phenomenon of 'time' originates. Creation does not happen at a particular moment *in* time: time is created *with* the cosmos.

In verse 1:1 the indication of time (בראשית) is followed by the verb which refers to the action of creating (ברא), the subject of the action (אלהים), and the object (את השמים ואת הארץ). The verb ברא, to create, refers to the origin of everything, but the question is whether this creation is realised in verse 1 or not. The second option is most plausible, since creation in Gen 1 is achieved through the speaking of God. God is, however, not speaking here, as verse 1 is a narrator's text. Another indication is the fact that God actually creates heaven in verse 6-8, 'God said: "Let there be a firmament in the midst of the waters (...)." And God made the firmament (...) and God called the firmament heaven'. In verse 9 God makes the earth appear, 'God said: "...let the dry land appear." And God called the dry land earth'. It follows, therefore, that the first verse as a narrator's text constitutes a kind of caption of the entire story, and expresses at the outset the main thought of Gen 1. Its great poetic and rhetoric power is originated in the alliteration of sounds, the rythm of the words, and the extreme brevity of the utterance.

The determination of the ending of the story appears to be more of a problem. At first sight there seem to be several possibilities for a precise demarcation of the ending of Gen 1. However, the story of Gen 2-3 cannot begin with 2:1, 2:2 or 2:3, because these verses are too closely linked to the preceding text; the seventh day forms a unit with the first six days. In determining the ending of the creation story,

---

[1] If one decides to change the Masoretic vocalisation, other explanations are possible. Firstly, the vocalisation of בראשית with *shewa* might be changed into בראשית with *qames*, which makes a translation of 'in the beginning' possible. Secondly, the vocalisation of ברא with two *qames* could be changed into ברא with a *shewa* and *holem*, to make a *status constructus* ('in the beginning of God's creation') possible. Perhaps there is another possibility to keep the vocals of the Masoretic Text and consider בראשית ברא as a noun construction, although rarely found with pure substantives, cf. Hos 1:2, Isa 29:1 and Jer 50:46 (See Joüon-Muraoka §129p).

[2] For a survey of the recent studies about v. 1 and בראשית, see: V. Hamilton, *The Book of Genesis. Chapters 1-17* (NICOT; Grand Rapids: Eerdmans 1990) 103-108.

the question is really whether it ends with verse 2:4a or 2:4b.[3] On the basis of the differences in, firstly, the naming of the main character God in Gen 1:1-2:4a as אלהים and in Gen 2:4b-3:24 as יהוה אלהים, and secondly, the description of the action of creating as ברא in 2:4a and as עשה in 2:4b, and, thirdly, the representation of the object of creation as השמים והארץ (with definite articles and in this order) in 2:4a and as ארץ ושמים (without definite articles and *nota accusativi*, and in a different order) in 2:4b, one may conclude that the story of creation ends in verse 2:4a. Two other features confirm this. The temporal adjunct ביום in 2:4b marks the beginning of a new episode or textual unit and indicates that a new story starts in 2:4b-6 with a new situation where neither plants and animals nor human beings exist on earth. Another indication is בהבראם, a *nif'al* infinitive of ברא with the suffix ם-, that describes the creation activities as completed. One may therefore conclude that the narrative of Gen 1 begins in 1:1 and ends in 2:4a.

A comparison of beginning and ending of the creation story proves to be instructive:

1:1	בראשית	ברא אלהים את השמים ואת הארץ	
2:4ᵃ	אלה תולדות	השמים והארץ	בהבראם

In both verses three components are central: time, creating, and heaven and earth. The first component, time, is described in verse 1:1 by the word בראשית that introduces the coming events; in verse 2:4a time is alluded to by the words אלה תולדות ('these were the begettings'), which situate the actions in the past. The second element, ברא, occurs in 1:1 in the active *qal qatal* form, whilst in 2:4a ברא is presented in the *nif'al* infinitive form, indicating that the creation has been accomplished. Excepting the *nota accusativi* את, the third component, the heaven and the earth, is the same in 1:1 and 2:4a. All components seem to have been used at the beginning and deliberately repeated at the end of the story to give the text an *inclusio* structure. Thus, small deflections show that the first verse indicates beforehand what is going to happen and the last verse afterwards summarises what has happened. One element which does occur in verse 1:1 but not in 2:4a (except the difference between בראשית and תולדות) is the word אלהים; in 2:4a occur, on the other hand, the word אלה and the suffix ם-, which are absent in 1:1. The similarity between these words אלהים and ם-, אלה is striking, as both have the same consonants. Could this possibly mean that the end of the story speaks implicitly of God's creation of heaven and earth, as the beginning did explicitly? If this is true, one might infer that אלהים in 2:4a is not mentioned *expressis verbis*, because in the cosmos only the created things are visible, while God is only indirectly perceptible.

---

[3] For a survey of the different positions of exegetes in the last century with regard to Gen 2:4, see T. Stordalen, "Genesis 2,4. Restudying a *locus classicus*," *ZAW* 104 (1992) 163-177.

Initial and final situation: Gen 1:2 and 2:1-3

The situation existing prior to creation, is described immediately following verse 1:

$$
\begin{array}{ll}
\text{והארץ היתה תהו ובהו} & \text{1:2a} \\
\text{וחשך על־פני תהום} & \text{1:2b} \\
\text{ורוח אלהים מרחפת על־פני המים} & \text{1:2c}
\end{array}
$$

The initial situation is characterised by the earth being תהו ובהו (1:2a). The term תהו occurs twenty times in the Hebrew Bible with the meaning of 'desert', a 'desert-like place' or 'emptiness'.[4] Here it refers to the empty earth without any vegetation. The term בהו only occurs three times in the Hebrew Bible, always in combination with תהו, and it also refers to emptiness and void.[5] These words together describe here the earth in its bare state: without vegetation and without animals or human beings. This not-yet productive earth becomes productive at the moment that God says: 'Let the earth bring forth plants' (1:11). And the empty earth becomes inhabited at the moment that God says: 'Let the earth bring forth living creatures' (1:24), and: 'Let us make man' (1:26). The order of these creative actions is inspired by the fact that first vegetation must grow in order that it may serve as food for animals and human beings. Through God's *fiat* alone, the barren earth may become productive and inhabited. The situation that precedes, described as תהו ובהו, has therefore nothing to do with chaos but only refers to the unproductive and uninhabited state of the earth.

The initial situation is not only characterised by an earth without vegetation and devoid of living creatures, but also by a תהום wrapped in darkness (1:2b). The word תהום (related to the general Semitic term *tiham*, primeval ocean) refers to unspecified waters or ocean.[6] It is the abyss or void, the immeasurable expanse of water that existed before the creation of heaven made a division between the waters above and the waters below.[7] תהום here refers to the waters that stretch out in all directions (especially in a vertical direction) and it describes the situation before the

---

[4] 'Desert': Deut 32:10; Jb 6:18, 12:24; Ps 107:40. 'A desert-like place': Isa 24:10, 34:11, 40:23, 45:18; Jer 4:23; Jb 26:7. 'Emptiness' or 'nothingness': 1 Sam 12:21 (twice); Isa 29:21, 40:17, 41:29, 44:9; 45:19; 49:4, 59:4. And it occurs in Gen 1:2, of course. For a discussion see: C. Westermann, *Genesis* (BKAT I,1; Neukirchen Vluyn: Neukirchener Verlag, 1976) 142ff, and D. Tsumura, *The Earth and the Waters in Genesis 1 and 2. A Linguistic Investigation* (JSOTS 83; Sheffield: JSOT Press 1989) 30-43.

[5] Gen 1:2; Is 34:11; Jr 4:23.

[6] For ample descriptions see: Westermann (1976: 146), *THAT* II 1030; *HAL* 1558; *BDB* 1062-1063.

[7] Cf. T.A. Perry, "A Poetics of Absence: The Structure and Meaning of Genesis 1.2," *JSOT* 58 (1993) 2-11, esp. 5: "As regards the synonymy of תהום and מים, it is quite likely that the waters of statement c (= verse 1.2b) are not 'the deep' but rather those waters that will soon be separated (vv. 6-7) into higher and lower by the firmament and which thus originally occupied all of vertical space. (...) From Gen 7.11 there is the further suggestion that the תהום itself is not horizontal, as we currently observe the ocean to be, but vertical, the 'cosmic abyssal water' that occupies both upper and lower regions."

creation of heaven, שמים.[8] When in verse 6 God makes a firmament or solid expanse, רקיע,[9] that establishes a division between the waters above and the waters below, he calls this in verse 1:8 שמים, a plural form that shows great resemblance to מים waters. The first syllable of שמים might even point to -ש (as an abridged form of אשר) or 'that which relates to' the מים. Thus, word and text express the same motion: the שמים separates the מים above from the מים below.[10] Before this שמים existed, there was only a vertical mass of water, the תהום. This תהום is characterised by a lack of light. As the earth is devoid of life, the תהום is devoid of light; this lack will be removed in verse 3. In other words, in 1:2b a description is given of the situation before heaven came into being.

The third factor that characterises the initial situation is described in 1:2c. There, רוח אלהים, the spirit of God, is moving over the waters. But what is the spirit of God? The words רוח אלהים refer to God before he appears as creator. This spirit of God is situated facing the waters, and the word על־פני, 'upon the face of' shows that, apart from water (both the horizontal waters that cover the earth and the vertical תהום waters that exist before heaven emerges) there is nothing, only God's spirit. In this initial situation, the רוח אלהים alludes to God as he is before he begins to create, and to God who does not yet have a relationship with 'beings' because they do not yet exist. From the moment that God begins to speak, he is no longer אלהים רוח, but אלהים.

In short, the creation story in Gen 1:2 shows us the initial situation as a 'not-yet' situation: the earth is not yet productive (without vegetation) and not yet inhabited (lacking animals and human beings); there is no heaven, only תהום or mass of water lacking light; God is merely active as רוח אלהים, not yet as a speaking, seeing, dividing, creating, generating or name-giving אלהים. Gradually the reader comes to realise how skilfully the first two verses of Gen 1 have been structured.

1.	in a beginning	God created	the heaven and the earth
2.	the earth	was	not-yet distinct
	the heaven	was	not-yet distinct
	God	was	not-yet creating

All elements in the first verse recur in the second verse as phenomena that do not yet exist: God does not yet create, there is no heaven, but only תהום, and the earth is תהו ובהו. The analogy in the description of the earth and of the not-yet-existing heaven is striking, for תהום and תהו ובהו express iconically a massive undistinctiveness. This is the primeval situation: no 'nothing', nor a chaos that needs

---

[8] See also Tsumura, *The Earth and the Waters in Genesis 1 and 2*, 45-83.

[9] רקיע (according to *BDB* and *HAL* √ רקע, 'to spread', and to *TWAT* √ רקק, 'to be thin', 'to make thin') refers to the "extended surface, (solid) expanse (as if beaten out)" (*BDB*), "das Breitgeschalene (Metall-) Platte; Firmament, das feste Himmelsgewölbe" (*HAL*), "eine festgefügte stabile Größe, die sich oberhalb der Erde befindet und die Lebenswelt gegen den Einbruch des chaotischen Wassers sichert." (*TWAT*).

[10] This also explains why שמים cannot be translated with 'heavens': it is a singular word referring to the רקיע between the waters.

sorting out, but a situation of 'before' or 'not-yet' in view of what is coming. Even God is not yet the creator God, but moves upon the face of the waters as an indefinable spirit of God.

From verse 3 onwards the story proper develops. The Hebrew syntax presents this clearly, as 1:3 contains the very first *wayyiqtol* form. The three nominal phrases in verse 2 point at the previous static situation, while verse 1 (*x-qatal*) is no part of the narration itself, but a kind of title. In 1:3 the chain of *wayyiqtol* forms starts that presents the narrative chain or series of actions by which the initial situation is transformed into the end situation in 2:1-3. The intervening text narrates about God's creation of heaven and earth and about God's equipment of the heaven with heavenly bodies and of the earth with plants, animals and human beings. As one whole, the cosmos, represented by the word combination of השמים והארץ, only occurs in 1:1, 2:1 and 2:4a, that is to say, in the initial and end situations of the story in order to announce or conclude the whole.

This end situation (2:1-3) begins with the announcement that 'the heaven and the earth and all the things with which they were fitted out, were completed'. God 'completes (כלה) everything (כל), he completes (כלה) his work, he ceases (שבת) from all (כל) his work (twice)'. Repeatedly there are statements such as 'his work which he had made', 'all his work which he had made', 'all his work which God created and made'. Making, that is what this work is all about; making what not yet is. On the seventh day God rested from all his work and therefore God blessed and sanctified that seventh day. On that day he ended his work, the creation of heaven and earth. The final verse (2:4a) concludes with 'these are the תולדות of the heaven and the earth when they were created'.

One particular thing becomes very clear in this sketch of the transformation between the initial and final situation in the creation story of Gen 1. This story is not solely about the creation of humankind, nor about the creation of the earth, nor even about the way human beings should behave on the earth. Gen 1 is primarily focused at God's creation of heaven and earth, at the population and continuation of the 'inhabitants' of heaven (sun, moon and stars, water above the firmament) and the inhabitants of earth (plants, animals and human beings).

Syntactic analysis, embeddedness of discourses and perspectives

The description of a narrative text as a text in which actions accomplish the transformation of the initial situation towards the final situation and in which possibilities of reality have been actualised, only partially explains what makes a text an absorbing story that grips the reader. The reader's involvement with the characters in a story can only be understood if the significance of another crucial characteristic of a narrative text is recognised, namely that the narrator does not merely tell about actions of characters or about situations, but also looks through the eyes of the characters and speaks through their mouths. The narrator then surrenders the observation or narrative point of view to those characters in the narrative, so that character texts or discourses emerge that are embedded in the narrator's text.

Through this embedding of discourses in the narrator's text, the reader is guided in a particular way, since the information that the reader obtains is always determined, per embedded text unit, by the textual perspective or point of view of the narrator and/or the character. Therefore a study of the rhetorical devices of *embeddedness* and *textual perspective* is needed, that is based both on linguistic markings[11] in the text and on its literary characteristics.[12]

In order to get a clearer picture of this process of guiding, the text is analysed in syntactic units or clauses, each consisting of a subject and predicate and not more than one finite verb form. Thus, a distinction can be made between the clauses in which the narrator tells about events or actions (narrative) and the clauses representing speech by a character (embedded discourses). Within the spoken text, a character may let himself/herself or another person speak. Consider Gen 3:2-3:

> 3:2   The woman said to the serpent:
>   We may eat from the fruit of the trees in the garden,
> 3:3   but of the fruit of the tree in the centre of the garden God said:
>   You may not eat from it
>   and you may not touch it
>   lest you die.

In this example, the clause 'The woman said to the serpent' belongs to the narrative and the clauses 'We may eat ... God said' form an embedded discourse, connected to the woman, in which another discourse, connected to God, is embedded: 'You may

---

[11] Linguistic studies are, generally spoken, less known in the field of Bible exegesis than literary narratological studies. Important (text-)linguistic studies of perspective are: A. Banfield, *Unspeakable Sentences. Narration and Representation in the Language of Fiction* (Boston: Routledge, 1982); D. Cohn, *Transparent Minds. Narrative Modes for Presenting Consciousness in Fiction* (Princeton: Princeton University Press, 1978); J. Dinsmore, *Partitioned Representations* (Dordrecht: Kluwer, 1991); S. Ehrlich, *Point of View: A Linguistic Analysis of Literary Style* (London: Routledge, 1990); S. Ehrlich, "Referential Linking and the Interpretation of Tense," *Journal of Pragmatics* 14 (1990) 57-75; M. Fludernik, *The Fictions of Language and the Languages of Fiction. The Linguistic Representation of Speech and Consciousness* (London: Routledge, 1993); C. Graumann and C. Sommer, "Perspective Structure in Language Production and Comprehension," *Journal of Language and Social Psychology* 7 (1988) 193-212; M. Jahn, "Contextualizing Represented Speech and Thought," *Journal of Pragmatics* 17 (1992) 347-367; J. Sanders, *Perspective in Narrative Discourse*. (Tilburg: Diss. Tilburg University, 1994); J. Sanders and G. Redeker, "Perspective and the Representation of Speech and Thought in Narrative Discourse," in *Spaces, Grammar and Discourse* (ed. G. Fauconnier and E. Sweetser; Chicago: Univ. of Chicago Press. In press).

[12] The best known studies in the field of literary-narratological Bible research are: R. Alter, *The Art of Biblical Narrative* (New York: Basic Books, 1981); M. Bal, *Femmes imaginaires. L'Ancien Testament au risque d'une narratologie critique* (Utrecht: Hes, 1986); M. Bal, *Lethal Love: Feminist Literary Readings of Biblical Love Stories* (Bloomington: Indiana Univ. Press, 1987); S. Bar-Efrat, *Narrative Art in the Bible* (JSOTS 70, Sheffield: Almond Press, 1989); A. Berlin, *Poetics and Interpretation of Biblical Narrative* (Sheffield: Sheffield Univ. Press, 1983); A. Berlin, "Point of View in Biblical Narrative," *A Sense of Text. The Art of Language in the Study of Biblical Literature* (ed. S.A. Geller; Winona Lake: Eisenbrauns, 1983) 71-113; M. Sternberg, *The Poetics of Biblical Narrative. Ideological Literature and the Drama of Reading* (Bloomington: Indiana Univ., 1987); H.C. Brichto, *Toward a Grammar of Biblical Poetics. Tales of Prophets* (Oxford/New York: Oxford Univ. Press, 1992).

not eat ... lest you die'. Thus, the woman is responsible for both embedded discourses, although she herself attributes the responsibility for the second part to God. The clauses of a story may thus be arranged in a hierarchical structure of one or more embedded discourses in a narrative.

The textual perspectives, which are related to this embeddedness of textual units, can be analysed on the basis of the following three gauging points.[13]

1. The story's *referential point of departure (R)*. This point of departure relates to the finite form of the verb (person, aspect and tense). If the referential point of departure lies with the narrator, the character will be referred to in the third person and the verb will (as a rule) describe the action as perfective or as a fact. If the referential point of departure lies with the embedded speaker (character), the character will speak in the first person and address the other characters in the second person; the standard aspect is non-perfective or progressive. For example, the sentence 'Of his wife Sarai Abram said that she was his sister' is told by the narrator, and the aspect of the verb refers to the fact of Sara's being Abram's sister, while in Gen 12:13 'Tell them: "You are my sister" ' the character Abram is speaking and the accent lies on the progressive aspect.

2. The story's *deictic point of departure (D)*. This point of departure relates to locative and temporal adjuncts. These are actually speaker-oriented. One becomes aware of the deictic point of departure by asking oneself from whose orientation 'here' or 'there', 'this' or 'that', and 'now' and 'when' is spoken. For instance, compare 'Abraham's servant stood near the well and he saw a woman coming towards him' and Gen 24:15: 'Abraham's servant stood near the well and he saw that Rebekah came out to draw water'. In the first case the servant is the deictic point of departure of the observation ('him' and 'come *towards*'); in the second case (Gen. 24:15) the narrator is the deictic point of departure, not the servant, as appears from the verb 'come *out*' and the name Rebekah, known to the narrator but not to the servant.

3. the *propositional content (P)* of the speech: who is responsible for the content? What is represented, is connected with, holds for or is factual for the person who speaks, observes or thinks it. Take for example Ruth 1:6, ''Naomi returned from the fields of Moab, because she had *heard* in the country of Moab that YHWH had visited his people by giving them bread'; the first two clauses are narrator's texts and the third clause ('that YHWH had visited his people') represents Naomi's observation: the narrator is responsible for the form (*R* and *D*), and Naomi is responsible for the content of this observation (*P*).[14] In short, the way in which a narrator represents actions, statements, observations or the mental awareness of himself/herself and of

---

[13] For literature see Sanders (1994); see also Banfield (1982), Cohn (1978) and Ehrlich (1990).

[14] Note that the narrator does not say that YHWH is responsible for ending the famine; nor does he say in verse 1:1 that YHWH was responsible for bringing about the famine. However, Naomi apparently supposes it. Thus in my view, Hubbard makes a mistake in his comment on Ruth when he states that: "This is the first report of God's direct action in the book. (...) Here his (= God's) gift marks a hopeful turning point in Naomi's tragic story." (R. Hubbard, *The Book of Ruth* (NICOT, Grand Rapids: Eerdmans, 1988) 100.)

the characters, determines the reader's view of a text. The reader is guided to look through the eyes of the narrator or of a character, whilst the responsability for form and content now lies with the narrator and then with the character.

Depending on the language, perspectives and embedded texts are presented in a particular way. As regards this presentation, Biblical Hebrew often, but not always, parallels modern Indo-European languages.[15] One of the biggest differences is that in Biblical Hebrew the distinction between the narrator's text and the embedded discourse is linguistically marked. These markers are based on the syntax of Hebrew verb forms as well as on certain words for direct speech and direct observation.

First of all, embedded clauses and perspectives are indicated by Hebrew verb forms. Recent text-syntactic research shows that these do not only indicate tense or aspect within the clause, but fulfil also certain functions within the narrative and the embedded discourses.[16] A *wayyiqtol* form, for instance, indicates a narrative: after starting off with a tense indicator containing a *qatal* form, the narrator uses the *wayyiqtol* form to represent the character's actions. In addition the narrator may freeze the action and interrupt the narrative to give background information. The narrator describes the circumstances that form the backdrop of the events by means of a non-*wayyiqtol* form, usually a nominal clause or a verbal clause with a *qatal* form. In an embedded discourse, a character is speaking; verbs are (mostly) in *yiqtol* form, imperative, cohortative or iussive. In addition, a character may freeze the action and interrupt his or her report about events to give background information. He/she then mostly uses non-*yiqtol* forms, a nominal clause or a verbal clause containing a *qatal* form. Summarising, narrator and character are differentiated in their presentation of actions or foreground information by the use of different verb forms; in the presentation of background information, narrator and character use the same verb forms that relate to the circumstances.

Secondly, discourses that are embedded in a narrative and the resulting effects for the representation of perspective in Biblical Hebrew, are determined by one word that marks the embedded direct speech: the verb אמר 'to say' will always introduce direct speech.[17] That the direct discourse requires אמר 'to say' and would not be

---

[15] For an extensive description of perspectives in Biblical Hebrew see: E. van Wolde, "Who guides whom? Embeddedness and Perspective in Biblical Hebrew and in 1 Kings 3:18-26." *Journal of Biblical Literature* 114/4 (1995) 623-642.

[16] In particular I refer to the study of H. Weinrich, *Tempus. besprochene und erzählte Welt* (Stuttgart: Kohlhammer, 1964¹, 1985⁴); W. Schneider, *Grammatik des Biblischen Hebräisch* (München: Claudius Verlag, 1974¹, 1985⁶); E. Talstra, "Text Grammar and Hebrew Bible. I: Elements of a Theory," *BiOr* 35 (1978) 169-174; E. Talstra, "Text Grammar and Hebrew Bible. II. Syntax and Semantics," *BiOr* 39 (1982) 26-38; E. Talstra, "Text Grammar and Biblical Hebrew: The Viewpoint of Wolfgang Schneider," *Journal of Translation and Textlinguistics* 5.4 (1992) 269-297; A. Niccacci, *The Syntax of the Verb in Classical Hebrew Prose*, (JSOTS 86; Sheffield: Academic Press, 1990); A. Niccacci, *Lettura Sintattica della Prosa Ebraico-Biblica. Principi e Applicazioni* (Jerusalem: Franciscan Printing Press, 1991).

[17] See: G. Goldenberg, "On Direct Speech and the Hebrew Bible," in *Studies in Hebrew and Aramaic Syntax. Festschrift J. Hoftijzer* (ed. K. Jongeling et all; Leiden: Brill, 1991) 79-96, esp. 85-86. The survey which S. Meier (*Speaking of Speaking. Marking Direct Discourse in the Hebrew Bible* (Supplements to Vetus Testamentum XLVI; Leiden: Brill, 1992) 324-337) made of all the verbs of

presented by any other *verbum dicendi*, is evident from the fact that some form of אמר, especially the infinitive לאמור, is required to be added after another verb of saying.[18] In the use of this marking of direct speech by means of the verb אמר, Biblical Hebrew differs from the modern Indo-European languages in which the syndetic or asyndetic connection determines the difference between direct and indirect speech ('that', 'dat', 'dass', 'que', 'che'). If sentences in the Hebrew Bible start with *verba dicendi* other than אמר (נגד, ענה, and the like) or with *verba sentiendi* (ראה, שמע and the like), then it is done by means of a narrator's text, as is shown by the *wayyiqtol* forms.[19] The classical distinction between direct and indirect speech (as exists in Indo-European languages) must therefore be abandoned for Biblical Hebrew.

The presentation of contents in syntactic structures and embedded textual units affects the reader's involvement in the text. The reader of a Hebrew Bible text is either directly involved in the perspective (the observation, the words or the awareness) of the narrator, or in that of the character. This has important consequences for the translation of a Bible text. When a translator chooses to translate a narrator's text or a direct speech in the Hebrew source text into an indirect speech, he/she will alter the reader's involvement in the text. In many Biblical stories a Hebrew direct speech is usually translated as an indirect speech, as for example in the translation of the *Jewish Publication Society* (1985) of Gen 12:13: 'say: you are my sister' (אמרי-נא אחותי את) as: 'please say that you are my sister.' The possessive pronoun 'my' and the personal pronoun 'you' show that in both texts Abram's perspective is shared, but the reader of the Hebrew source text is more directly involved in Abram's words than the one of the *JPS* translation.

Summarising, for a translation of Hebrew, i.e. a language with only directly represented narrator's texts or character texts, into a language with directly as well as indirectly represented text forms (as e.g. English), it is necessary that one is aware of the perspectives in the source text so that they may be preserved in the translation as much as possible.

---

speaking before a direct discourse could be read as a confirmation of Goldenberg's position. G. Fischer (*Jahwe unser Gott. Sprache, Aufbau und Erzähltechnik in der Berufung des Mose (Ex 3-4)* (Orbis Biblicus et Orientalis 91; Göttingen: Vandenhoeck & Ruprecht, 1989) 40-42) gives a list of introductions of direct speech ('Redeeinführungen') in the books of the Pentateuch and this description confirms Goldenberg's theory as well.

[18] There are, however, elliptic texts in which the verb אמר is assumed. An example is Ex 16:28-29 in which the direct speech of YHWH is followed by a direct speech by Moses without any indication to that effect. Here, a clause such as ויאמר משה is missing. In such a case the switches in referential point of departure are the linguistic indication that a change took place from one speaker to another: thus in Ex 16:28-29, the change from the first person ('my commandments') to the third person (he, YHWH) shows that the speaking person has changed.

[19] Goldenberg, who very convincingly described אמר as a marker for direct speech in Biblical Hebrew, unfortunately failed to abandon the classical distinction between direct and indirect speech (as exists in the Indo-European languages) for Biblical Hebrew. If he had done so, it would have become clear that clauses introduced by *verba dicendi* other than אמר or by *verba sentiendi*, do not in fact introduce indirect speeches, but belong to the narrator's text. This is demonstrated by the *wayyiqtol* forms in the examples of indirect discourses mentioned by Goldenberg (for instance in his note 17).

Syntactic structure, embeddedness and perspective in Genesis 1

Gen 1 is characterised by a great number of embedded discourses in which God is the speaking-subject. The narrator represents God's speech acts, as is visible in the *wayyiqtol*-forms of ויאמר. In these embedded discourses the character God is responsible for the propositional content; the referential and deictic points of departure are related to God as well. In his discourses God calls everything into being. All eleven times that God speaks in Gen 1 (ten times, in 1:3.6.9.11.14.20. 24.26.28.29, preceded by ויאמר אלהים, and once, in 1:22, by ויברך לאמר), this speaking constitutes something new. At the same time the used verb forms point at God as referential point of departure. The first three times God creates something by using the verb 'to be' in the *iussive*, יהי, 'let there be': for the light, the firmament and the lights in the firmament. When populating the earth, the sky and the waters, God uses four times a *iussive*, but here it concerns verbs of procreation: 'let the earth bring forth (תדשא) young plants' (1:11), 'let the water bring forth (ישרצו) living creatures abundantly' (1:20), 'let birds fly (יעופף) in the firmament of the heaven' (1:20) and 'let the earth bring forth (תוצא) animals' (1:24). Subsequently, God addresses in six *imperatives* the animals (פרו ורבו ומלאו) and the human beings (פרו ורבו ומלאו): they must become productive, multiply and fill the waters (1:22) and the earth (1:28). While in the *iussives* God calls things into being, he concentrates in the *imperatives* on the continuation of life by the inhabitants of the waters, the earth and the sky. The only time that God speaks in a *cohortative* (1:26) is when he speaks to himself: 'let us make' (נעשה). These verb forms, be it in first (*cohortative*), second (*imperative*) or third (*iussive*) person, function on the basis of a direct referential relationship between God and the addressant or addressant in a nascent stage.

In a text or story it is usually the narrator who introduces the characters: he or she presents the information and represents the words, thoughts and emotions of the character, be this character a human or a divine persona. Similarily the narrator of Gen 1 introduces God as a character and makes him say things. As creation story, however, Gen 1 pretends something more: its value and function are based on the assumption of a transcendence of the border between fictional and real world. In the communication process between text and readers, God not only functions as a character locked up in the world of the text. His speech acts are not considered to be actions that only take place in the inner textual world, but as actions that are considered to have been constitutive for the outertextual world as well. Gen 1 expresses this iconically. The narrator regularly confirms, classifies or evaluates what happened previously in God's speech. In doing so, he often echoes God's words. God's utterance 'let there be light', for example, is a performative speech act: the clause constitutes the coming into being of light. Only after God has said 'let there be light', the narrator states 'there is light', as if the instance of speech is God's, not the narrator's. In this sense the speech acts of God turn out to be constitutive for the speech acts of the narrator. Another feature confirms this special position of the divine character. The other characters are created by the words of God, although he is a character *in* the text. The narrator can only speak about these characters and can only let them speak in embedded discourses *after* God's creation.[20] On the other hand it is the narrator who represents the divine speeches and who describes (in 1:1-2) what is going to happen and what the situation before God's creation looks like. It is the narrator who introduces God as character and who presents the creatures, made by God, as *characters* and who represents their speeches.

One might conclude that this complex relationship between the narrator and the divine character makes it possible for readers to consider the text as an incomplete sign that asks for multiple signification. First, the reader gives meaning to language forms in order to create a textual world or story-world presented by the narrator. Second, he or she might consider the performative divine speech acts in the text to be signs of God's creative power in the world outside the text, and thus makes this meaningful sign function in the transgression of the borderline between text and extratextual world. In another stage, the reader still continues to acknowledge that it is the narrator's representation which makes this border transgression between character's world and narrator's world possible. Simultaneously the reader might consider these textual signs to be referential signs refering to an external world in which the speaking of the narrator is made possible by the initial speech acts of God. Nevertheless, the reader is still aware of the fact that it is all depending on the narrator's power to present this in a text. This reading process of assigning meaning in interaction with the intratextual and the extratextual world could be called *unlimited semiosis.*[21]

Only once (1:29) God's speech is not a performative speech act. Here he speaks in an *indicative* in the first person, not in the plural as in the *cohortative* of 1:26, but in the singular: הנה נתתי לכם. Through the word הנה he explicitly enters into contact with the addressees and calls on them to join his perspective. After he has made everything and has ensured the continuance of everything through *iussives* and *imperatives*, God gives something to his creatures: 'See, I give you *every* seed-bearing plant that is upon *all* the earth, and *every* tree that has seed-bearing fruit; they shall be yours for food. And to *all* the animals on the land, to *all* the birds of the sky, and to *everything* that creeps on the earth, in which there is the breath of life, I give *all* the green plants for food' (1:29-30). Thus he not only ensures the beginning of all creatures but their continuance as well. In order to underline the completeness of this gift, God seven times uses the word כל, 'every' or 'all'. In his speech God puts great emphasis on his gift, which is indicated by the use of הנה, the indicative, the gift itself, as well as by the sevenfold use of כל. This gift concludes God's speaking.

---

[20] H.C. White, *Narration and Discourse in the Book of Genesis* (Cambridge: Cambridge University Press, 1991) 102, describes this as follows: "The initial, pivotal Biblical characters are presented by the narrator as creatures of the Word; they are personages who appear in the narrative as recipients of an inward address by the divine Word, and their personal being in the narrative is thus formed from the outset by the divine Word. (...) The divine Voice thus occurs midway between the effaced author's instance of speech, and that of his characters, and mediates the opposition between them."

[21] See E.J. van Wolde, *Words Become Worlds. Semantic Studies of Genesis 1-11* (Biblical Interpretation Series, vol.6; Leiden: Brill, 1994) 113-148.

During the first six days God speaks and creates, on the seventh he stops speaking and therefore also creating. At that point only the narrator has the floor. This narrator puts the emphasis on the seventh day, as is clear from the three times occurring יום השביעי. The readers learn of God's blessing and sanctification of the seventh day only through the words and observation of the narrator. And his words do not read: 'God blessed the seventh day saying (לאמר): "This day is blessed".' It says, however, 'God blessed the seventh day and sanctified it' (2:3a). The narrator's perspective is therefore reflected in this direct narrator's text: where God emphasises the gift of everything, the narrator emphasises the conclusion of all God's work and the day on which this comes to pass.

Text-semantic analysis and Genesis 1

After the study of the syntactic structure and the linguistically marked perspectives in a text, a text-semantic analysis is aimed at patterns of meaning which a text offers the reader. In a text-semantic study the elements of meaning (words) are studied in relation to their place and function in the lexicon of the Hebrew language, in relation to their actualisation in the concrete text and in their internal relationships in the text. In clarification of this text-semantic approach I present the following considerations.

Every language, including the Hebrew language, has various functions.[22] It has the ability to refer to empirical reality and therefore possesses a referential function.[23] However, language is not merely a tool to refer to reality, not simply a transparency or a window through which one looks out at the world, but also an instrument which people use to communicate. As a result, every language is an activity, an act of speech to affect, to convince or to manipulate. Equally important is the capability of a language to generate new meanings through conscious literary or linguistic composition. This poetic function is particularly important for text-semantic research, in which one studies a text as a phenomenon that draws attention to the language, as a phenomenon that orders the reader's perception and focuses his

---

[22] Since R. Jakobson ("Linguistics and Poetics," in *Style in Language* (T.A. Sebeok, ed., Cambridge, M.I.T. Press 1960) 350-377) six functions of language are generally distinguished: the emotive function, i.e. the abilities of a language to express the attitude of the sender; the conative function, i.e. the ability to enter into communication with a receiver: to move, to touch emotionally, to insult, to activate or to badger into buying a product, etc.; the phatic function, i.e. the ability of a language to install and keep contact; the referential function, i.e. the ability of a language to refer to the real world; the metalinguistic function, i.e. the ability to speak in a language about language; and, last but not least, the poetic function, i.e. the ability of a language to ask attention for the sounds, words and texts itself and to create new meanings through conscious composition.

[23] From an information theory point of view, the perfect language would be a language which can perform this function unimpededly. A maximum of non-interference would exist if the language were completely subservient to the referential function. For that purpose, a language would need to be imperceptible, an entirely transparent medium, so that our perception could completely focus on the empirical reality to which a language utterance refers. See for an extensive description: W. Bronzwaer, *Lessen in Lyriek. Nieuwe Nederlandse poëtica* (Nijmegen: Sun, 1993) 11-29.

or her attention through its creation of meanings. The way in which a text creates meanings through language is multiform.

In the first place a language, as for example Biblical Hebrew, determines meanings of words on the basis of conventions. In these conventions the relations between a particular form and a particular content have been defined. The definitions are laid down in a language system, also called primary code or paradigm. This primary code consists of carefully distinguished rules and elements that constitute the potential of possibilities from which selections for utterances can be made. A concrete text or syntagm is the result of a selection procedure and consists of a specific combination of selected elements. The relationship between the language system (paradigm) and the realisation of the system in the concrete text (syntagm) may be compared to the relationship between the menu in a restaurant and the meal you select from it. The menu gives the paradigm: you can choose a starter, a main course, and a dessert. The combination of the selected dishes forms the actual meal, the syntagm.[24]

Through intensive use in daily life, the primary code wears away; people start using the language 'automatically'. Therefore, an author does not merely use the primary code for a (literary) text, but adds a secondary code to counteract the wear and tear of the language system.[25] This secondary code provides a separate layer of meaning that de-automatises the conventional meanings of the primary code. 'De-automatisation' or 'de-familiarisation' is to make perception which is usually automatic a new experience. Sklovsky[26] describes this process of de-familiarisation as follows:

> Art exists that one may recover the sense of life; it exists to make one feel things, to make the stone stony. The purpose of art is to impart the sensation of things as they are perceived and not as they are known. The technique of art is to make objects 'unfamiliar', to make forms difficult, to increase the difficulty and the length of perception because the process of perception is an aesthetic end in itself and must be prolonged.

What Sklovsky argues about art or literary texts, also holds for texts in the Hebrew Bible. These have likewise been carefully composed and are aimed at adding a religious dimension to the perception of reality, to intensify perception and to reveal the unfamiliar in a familiar reality. The text-internal structure enables readers to discover these new meanings. The linguistic and literary forms of a text therefore have a very important function: by being elaborate and complicated, they seem to push the content into the background, in order to precisely reveal the content all the more articulately and surprisingly in the end. It is essential in this context that the

---

[24] See: E. van Wolde, "A Text-Semantic Study of the Hebrew Bible, Illustrated with Noah and Job," *Journal of Biblical Literature* 113/1 (1994) 19-35.

[25] J. Lotman (*Die Struktur literarischer Texte*. München: Fink, 1981; originally published in Russian in 1972) calls this the 'secondary modelling (= meaning generating) system'.

[26] V. Sklovsky, "Art as Technique" (L.T. Lemon & M.J. Reis eds., *Russian Formalist Criticism. Four Essays*. Lincoln/London: University of Nebraska Press, 1965: 3-24) 12. This article was written in Russian in 1917; after its translation into English in 1965 it influenced strongly western literary theory.

content thus revealed should prove to possess certain characteristics of the form. This explains why a text is not simply a realisation of a language system based on conventions, but also possesses a secondary structure that is iconic in nature and carries connotations of its own. This form language or iconic language of the secondary code shows that every element in a text matters, that every element might be the carrier of a poetical function and an image of the content. The periodical repetition in Gen 1 might for instance reflect the order of creation and the order of the days that follow. Here, the language of form in itself generates meaning: it creates a sense of consecration, of structure and correlation, of a hidden order of all things. Thus, the organisation of a text functions as an icon of its content. Iconicity is our use of language when we strive to escape from the arbitrariness or predictabil-ity of the language signs, when we do not wish the language to refer to an already existing reality, but use it to call up new meanings and to bring about new realities as a result.

These two aspects of language, the primary or conventional code and the secondary or iconic code of a language and their mutual relations, form the object of text-semantic analysis. They are means by which a text may guide or persuade readers or coax them towards new meanings. (In addition, particularly the referential function of the language in a text would have to be analysed in an extensional semantic study).[27] Summarizing, on the one hand a text-semantic analysis studies words as references to their conventional relations in the primary code, and on the other hand as representatives or icons of newly created meanings. The exegete will therefore have to analyse the conventional as well as the iconic character of a text, and explain that language signs are not just a direct reflection of reality, but also a creation of meaning and of meaning structure. A translation will have to communi-cate the primary as well as secondary code of the source text. In addition to an extensive knowledge of the conventions of the Hebrew language system, the translator is required to possess great feeling for the form of a text and the ability to transpose the iconic network of meanings of the source text into a corresponding iconic network in the target text, in order that the latter, too, may challenge the reader to an intensified and de-automatised form of generation of meaning.

If we apply these insights in a text-semantic analysis of Genesis 1, many words, word orders and lines of meaning have a particular significance. Various elements have been elucidated in the numerous studies about Gen 1. I can (and must) accordingly restrict myself to one particular line of meaning, formed by a repetition of the words למינו, למינהו, למינהם, למינה, 'according to her/their/his kind', and בצלמנו, בצלמו, בצלם, 'after the/ his/our image'.

In the creation of the plants and the inhabitants of the earth, both God and the narrator reveal what counts most in the creation of a living being. God makes the creatures, and always adds that they bear seed '(each) according to their kind'. God first states this in verse 11 of the trees of the earth (עץ פרי עשה פרי למינו), after

---

27   Usually a distinction is made between intensional semantics and extensional semantics. In the first, language-internal structures of meaning are studied, in the second the relationship between the referring aspects of language and (conceptualised) reality is the object of research.

which the narrator twice confirms it regarding the plants (עשב מזריע זרע למינהו)
(דשא) and the trees of the earth (ועץ עשה פרי אשר זרע־בו למינהו) (v.12). Later,
in 1:21, the narrator mentions twice that the animals move and swarm in the waters
'according to their kind' (למינהם) and the birds fill the sky 'according to their kind'
(למינהו). Further on, God himself says twice that the earth must bring forth living
creatures 'after his kind' (למינה) (1:24). In the following evaluative text (v.25), the
narrator confirms this with a triple 'according to its kind', למינה two times and once
למינהו.

The conventional meaning of the word מין is 'kind' or 'species',[28] where this
species itself brings forth living beings after its own kind: מין is therefore the species
'with genetic potential'. The reference is shown by the description of the green plants
and trees in 1:11-12: מין there refers to the plants and trees in reality, where trees
are distinct from plants because they reproduce by means of seed-bearing fruit. The
referential function reveals language as a window through which the reader looks out,
at real vegetation. The window itself, the word מין, is the convention that enables
you to look at this reality.

At the same time, the window of a language draws attention to itself. The tenfold
repetition of מין with the preposition -ל and the prenominal suffix of the third person
is a very clear indication of its importance. Also, an increase in the use of this word
can be observed in the narrator's texts as well as in God's speeches (once and twice;
twice; and twice and three times, respectively). This word may therefore start to
function as a secondary code, in which words develop an iconic charge. Through
their statements both God and the narrator show that plants and animals are primarily
interested in their own kind and its survival: their point of reference is their own
kind, both at the time of creation and in the period following it. Subsequently it may
become clear that things are different where humankind is concerned.

ויאמר אלהים   1:26
נעשה אדם בצלמנו כדמותנו
ויברא אלהים את־האדם בצלמו   1:27
בצלם אלהים ברא אתו

The human being is the only creature which God does *not* make למינו, 'after its own
kind', but בצלמנו, 'in our image' and כדמותנו, 'after our likeness'. The possessive
pronouns belonging to מין ('his', 'their', 'her') which with other living beings refer
back to those creatures themselves, are distinct from the possessive pronouns
belonging to צלם and דמות, for they do not refer to humankind but to God. This
contrast in possessive pronouns is an iconic indication that the human being, unlike
the other creatures, does not find a point of reference in him- or herself, but in God.

God's direct speeches speak volumes. In the process of creating plants and
animals, God speaks in the third person; creating human beings, however, God
speaks in the first person and three times uses pronouns relating to the first person

---

[28] *BDB* 568; *HAL* 547; *TWAT* IV, 867-69.

plural: 'let us make', 'in our image', 'in our likeness'. God speaks and addresses himself, in his other speeches he addresses creatures in the second person. The plural in this internal monologue corresponds with the plural 'they' with which God refers to the human being. In both cases ('let us make' and 'that they rule') God or the human being in the singular is linked up with a verb in the plural. God who defines the other creatures in relation to the earth, the sky and the sea, defines humankind in relation to God. We as readers are so closely involved in this creation that we experience it from God's perspective. Joining his viewpoint, we see that the human being is a creature, made to refer to God.

In addition to possessive pronouns and perspectives, the word צלם also plays an important role. In 1:26 God himself speaks of בצלמנו, and in 1:27 the narrator summarises with בצלמו, 'in his image', and בצלם אלהים, 'in the image of God'. Moreover, God also says כדמותנו, 'after our likeness', which is not repeated in the narrator's text. In determining the conventional content of צלם in the Hebrew language system, one may consult a dictionary or a lexicon. Barr proposes an accurate way to execute a semantic analysis of the conventional contents (or primary code) of words in Biblical Hebrew:[29]

> Rather than concentrating on the one word *selem* 'image' and trying to squeeze from it alone a decisive oracle about its meaning (...), we look at a whole group of words and hope that meaning may be indicated by the choice of one word rather than another within this group. The basis for procedure, then, is an approach to meanings not as direct relations between one word and the referent which it indicates, but as functions of choices within the lexical stock of a given language at a given time; it is the choice, rather than the word itself, which signifies.

Barr describes the words *pesel, masseka, demut, mar'e, temuna, semel* and *tabnit* in the same semantic field as צלם as 'transparant' with regard to their meanings, because of their relationships with concrete verb forms.[30] So the word *pesel* not only means 'graven image' (of a god) but is immediately transparant because of its relationship with the verb *pasal* 'to cut or carve stone'. *Masseka* means 'statue made by casting' and is connected with the verb *nasak* 'to pour'. The word *d'mut* is transparently connected with *dama* 'to be like', *mar'e* with *ra'a* 'to see' and *tabnit* with *bana* 'to build'. But the term צלם has no analogy with verbs like this (although

---

[29] J. Barr ("The Image of God in the Book of Genesis - A Study of Terminology," *Bulletin of the John Rylands Library of Manchester* 51 (1968) 11-26, esp. 14-15) gives a linguistic analysis of the term צלם. He discusses a group of Hebrew words which may be said to lie in the semantic field of 'image, likeness, similarity'. These are: *selem* ('image'), *d'mut* ('likeness'), *mar'e* ('appearance'), *t'muna* ('shape'), *tabnit* ('design'), *pesel* ('graven idol'), *masseka* ('cast idol') and *semel* ('statue').

[30] "Transparency, very roughly, means that the user feels not only that the word has a meaning but that you can see through it to some kind of reason why it has that meaning. When this condition is absent, the word is opaque. English *glove* is opaque; the speaker knows what it is, but not why. German *Handschuh* is transparent because it is made up from elements which appear to explain why it is called what it is called. (...) I am not speaking about the sense of the 'root' of the word; the question is not what is meant by the root, but what is meant by the words in actual usage which suggest themselves as sources of derivational transparency." Barr, "The Image of God," 17-18.

dictionaries sometimes suppose that it is derived from a verb which, if it existed in Hebrew (which is not the case) would be *salam* 'to cut'). The term צלם is therefore opaque, not linked with a verb denoting statue, sculpture or cutting. 'This is important, because certain of the words in the same semantic field may well have been unacceptable to the Genesis writer precisely because of these associations with verbs. *Dᵉmut*, the one easily transparent word which he did use, was related to the straightforward verb *dama* 'to be like' and created no serious obstacle. But *mar'e* was unsuitable because it clearly suggested that God might be *seen*.'[31] The word צלם may refer to a physical representation (without a carving, cutting or graving aspect) or to a non-physical representation; depending on its context it might be defined more closely as a statue, a picture, or as a figurative image.[32] צלם represents something that is not present and may therefore be described by the word 'sign'. A sign is something that refers to something or somebody which/who is absent. On the basis of this conventional analysis one could conclude that according to Gen 1:26-27, the human being was put on earth to be a sign of God.

The conventional content of צלם is reinforced by the secondary code of Gen 1, because the creation of the human being בצלם אליהם functions in parallelism with the creations of the inhabitants of the earth למינו. In the creation of the plants and animals the word מין refers to the individual species and the continuation of that species. On the moment the human being is created, the word מין is not used but the term צלם. This indicates that the human being is not made to refer to the own species, but to point away from itself: humankind is made to be a sign of God, to represent the creator who is not directly perceptible in the created world. The possessive pronouns confirm this. Animals and plants have their point of reference in themselves, the human's point of reference is in God. In humankind and his and her descendants, being an image of God is essential. This condition of being an image of God holds for all people: every human being, black or white or yellow, male or female, hetero or homo, rich or poor is made as image of God. As words are composed in a text to be the icons of the newly presented meanings, human beings are created in the world to be icons of God.

---

[31] Barr, "The Image of God," 18-19.

[32] D. Clines ("The Image of God in Man," *Tyndale Bulletin* 19 (1967) 53-103, esp. 87-88) argues along literary lines, but arrives at the same conclusion as Barr: 'Reference has already been made to the function of the image as representative of one who is really or spiritually present, though physically absent. The king puts his statue in a conquered land to signify his real, though not physical, presence there. The god has his statue set up in the temple to signify his real presence there, though he may be in heaven, on the mountain of the gods, or located in some natural phenomenon, and so not physically present in the temple. According to Genesis 1:26ff, man is set on earth in order to be the representative there of the absent God who is nevertheless present by His image.'

GENESIS 37 AND 38 AT THE INTERFACE OF STRUCTURAL ANALYSIS AND HERMENEUTICS

JAN P. FOKKELMAN

Introduction

The stories that together offer the overture of the narrative cycle on Joseph and his brothers fill chapters 37 and 38 of the book of Genesis. Chapter 37 contains an initial group of three literary units and ends with Joseph being sold to an Egyptian official. For a very long time nobody in Canaan will hear or know anything about the boy. This breaking off at the very moment when Joseph has disappeared behind the southern horizon, seemingly for good, creates a considerable amount of temporal space, so that the narrator grabs the opportunity to launch his excursus on Judah in ch.38, with its long and time-consuming exposition (vv.1-11). After this apparent diversion he picks up the thread on Joseph: the opening verse of ch.39 exactly reflects the last verse of ch.37, not only by repeating the name and position at court of Potiphar who has bought Joseph as a slave, but also by mentioning the caravan journey and its goal. This resumption shows a careful inclusion, varying active and passive stems (the hiph'il and the hoph'al) of the verb of movement, *yrd*. My translation retains the word order of the Hebrew:

> "Now Joseph had been taken down [*hurad*] to Egypt; and Potiphar,
> a courtier of Pharaoh and his chief steward, an Egyptian man, had
> bought him from the Ishmaelites who had taken him [*horiduhu*]
> there."

The syntax of the start, w^e + subject + qtl-form, signals a flashback. Joseph is the grammatical subject but can derive no illusion from that. Semantically he is the object; this is his real status, as the ending - another flashback - discloses by giving the position of subject to the Arab caravan drivers. As we will see, the differences between subject and object status are characteristic of Gen 37. The two occurrences of *yrd* complete a trio, as they are the sequel and the realization of the goal *l^ehorid* (the hiph'il infinitive at the end of 37:25). The connection suggests how Joseph, "transported to Egypt" like gum, balm and ladanum, has become a mere commodity.

From the start of ch.39 on, the reader's attention will mainly be focused on Egypt and Joseph's further destiny (chapters 39-41, 44-45 and 47-50, with an intermezzo in chs.42-43 reporting the discussions in Jacob's household, and his journey to Egypt plus genealogy in ch.46). Accordingly, the stories of chs.37-38 set in Canaan may indeed be called the overture to the cycle as a whole.

In this article I intend a) to study some remarkable but neglected features of style and structure that help us to achieve a more precise understanding of the text, and b) to publish and discuss the concentric patterns of composition governing "Joseph in Dothan" and "Judah and Tamar", in order to c) further corroborate the position that Gen 38 forms an essential and integral part of the entire narrative.[1] At the back of this article the reader will find the Hebrew text of the two larger units in a colometrical layout.

Background and Programme: Genesis 37:2-11

The first literary unit comprises three sequences, vv.2-4/5-8/9-11. Their boundaries are marked by a double-barreled refrain, 'hatred' plus *dbr* (4bc // 8d // 11ab), so that these paragraphs are regulated by an overall parallelism at sequence level.[2] This outline is fleshed out by the obvious similarity between the nuclei of the second and third paragraphs. Both show the pattern of a dream told by Joseph plus the shocked and angry reactions of his addressees.

In both cases Joseph starts his speech with an introductory line asking his brothers' attention. The dreams are marked by the lively and deictic *hinneh*. The initial lines are based on the same paronomasia, as the verb *hlm* is doubled by its internal object. In this way v.9d is equal to v.6b, and in his turn the father prolongs the stylistic device when he vents his indignation in v.10c with: "What is this dream that you've dreamt?" And this is not all. The paronomastic usage of *hlm* ties in with the forceful and conspicuous appearance of the absolute infinitive, as part of a new paronomasia in v.8bc // 10e which founds a strong parallelism between the two angry speeches.

The responses, by the brothers (in v.8) and the father (in v.10) respectively, show a neat balance, as they each consist of two sentences.[3] These lines are all rhetorical questions and their content is basically identical: the fear of being dominated by the pretentious dreamer. This applies to the situation within the story, to the world-in-words. What the speakers are not and cannot be aware of is the message conveyed by these dreams at the higher level of communication between text and reader. In conjunction with the result of the first sequence (the brothers' hatred), they

---

[1] This position has been eloquently explored by Robert Alter in ch.1 of *The Art of Biblical Narrative*, New York 1981, and by James S. Ackerman, "Joseph, Judah, and Jacob", in Kenneth R.R. Gros Louis (editor, with James S. Ackerman), *Literary Interpretations of Biblical Narratives*, Vol. 2, Abingdon 1982, pp.85-113.

[2] The letters after the verse numbers refer to the clauses the masoretic verses consist of. Thus v.10e denotes the fifth clause of Gen 37:10, and 38:4c refers to the third clause of verse 4 in the next chapter. How this arrangement of the text works out may be seen at the end of this article, where 38:18-36 and ch.38 are printed in 'colometrical' Hebrew.

[3] Moreover, this balance of two plus two rhetorical questions (8bc // 10de) ties in with v.9de: another pair of lines starting with the paronomasia of חלם. Note how lines 9e//10e are transformations of each other: 9e contains the image of three celestial figures which in v.10e is interpreted by the father in a spontaneous and immediate reaction, as if the three characters father/mother/brothers form the one and only true explanation. The connection 9e-10e is also made by a kind of epiphora, as the key verb השתחוה is repeated at the end of the speeches.

reveal a veritable programme for the entire cycle.

The brothers' negative feelings can only deepen when they hear the content of Joseph's visions and realize that these images have the power of providential revelation. And so an explosive combination of hatred and dreams is formed. This fusion of two powerful factors is reflected by the composition of the first unit, 37:2-11, which consists of two parts. The first one coincides with the first paragraph (vv.2-4) and has the function of background proper. The second part (vv.5-11) is covered by sequences two and three; its programmatic function and its rôle in the plot of the cycle can hardly be overestimated.

The dangerous interaction of hatred and dreams forms the fountainhead of the macroplot that governs Gen 37-45 and again emerges in ch.50, when the brothers still cannot believe that their relationship with Joseph has become secure and positive. In terms of the reader's experience, it shapes a pattern of expectations and helps us to formulate questions such as: will Joseph indeed become a ruler? Will his next of kin really get in a position of having to bow before him? How can this happen to someone who is a slave in Egypt, a despised Semite at that? In this sense the dream sequences embody a veritable narrative program for the fourth and final section of the book of Genesis.

Most clauses in Gen 37 are very short, which is not unusual at all. If we count words, we discover that there are three clauses of a rather disproportionate length. They have ten words each, and are strategically positioned at the boundaries of the chapter.[4] The very last line, v.36, has ten words, and the two nominal clauses with which the cycle opens have exactly the same size. My rendering of the syntax in v.2bc is as follows:[5]

> "At seventeen years of age, Joseph tended the flocks with his brothers,
> he was a helper to the sons of his father's wives Bilhah and Zilpah."

Its counterpart, the boundary line v.36, tells us how this brand-new career will prove to be abortive.

---

[4] I disregard v.2a here, "these are the engenderings [= this is the family history] of Jacob". This short nominal clause is an epigraphic line and as such belongs to the entire cycle, not to the chapter or the first unit. The clause is very important, though, as the key word *tol'doth* is used in two sets of five occurrences (one set offering four headings plus one postscript [i.e. Gen 2:4a!] for narrative blocks, the other containing five headings of genealogical lists) which serve to organize and articulate the first book of the Bible as "the Book of Engenderings" and effectively intertwine the genres of story-telling and genealogy - see my contribution on Genesis in R. Alter & F. Kermode (eds.), *The Literary Guide to the Bible*, Harvard University Press 1987.

[5] I concur with the JPS translation and copy its rendering of v.2b here. However, a better translation of the combination *hayah ro'eh* is possible. I prefer to see *hayah* as a descriptive and static perfect form, followed by a substantivized participle denoting the profession of shepherd. As a consequence, the phrase does not denote an action, however durative it may be, but the job of the hero who is being introduced by verse 2.

The first sequence is a carefully composed series of three times three clauses. The central trio deals with the father, with his attitude (love, v.3a) and its motivation (v.3b, a nominal *ki*-clause), plus the action that makes his preference for Joseph concrete (v.3c, purchase of a costly tunic) and painfully visible.[6]

The first trio, v.2bcd, was obviously designed to introduce the hero, his tender age, and his profession. In view of the fact that the cycle as a whole deals with "Joseph and his brothers" (as a provisional title might say), the long nominal clauses 2bc right at the start are remarkably effective in situating Joseph in the midst of his siblings. For a short while we are under the illusion that he really shares something important with them: his profession. The third clause, v.2d, is still about their relationship, but quickly undermines the idea of any harmony. The narrator has applied a surplus of stylistic finesse in order to foreground this line. Its importance is heightened even more as two wordplays work together here.

The regular flow of wyqtl clauses is the backbone of Hebrew narration.[7] In most stories it gets under way very soon, after one or two static lines introducing the hero or providing information about time or space. In our case the whole series of nine lines (vv.2b-4, the first sequence) serves as background. Between the many data that fill in the picture of vv.2b-3, line 2d sticks out as action, and as a wyqtl clause that looks lonely amidst so much nominal information.[8] This is what it says:

ויבא יוסף את דבתם רעה אל אביהם

By telling us that he went back home, this report severs Joseph's contact with his brothers. The very last word denotes the single character who is the goal of his journey and represents the norm or authority in this patriarchal world: the father

---

[6] Here we meet our first linguistic obstacle. How can we explain the verb form שהעו which cannot possibly be a perfectum consecutivum and surely is a kind of preterite? Why did not the writer choose the narrative form *wayya'as* to open the third line of v.3? First of all, I propose to take this perfect as a flashback, because it still belongs to the background information. True, the pluperfect in Gen 39:1 (another kind of flashback) is continued by a wyqtl form; *wyqnhw* denotes an action in the same time sphere as its predecessor, "Potiphar *had* bought him." In 37:3 we can only take שהעו as a so-called perfectum copulativum, i.e. as a preterite introduced by the normal conjunction "and" instead of the waw *hippuk* (waw inversum). I think this verb, as a qal perfect in nearly complete assonance with הבא, is intended as counterpart and continuation of the qal perfect in v.3a. Indeed, Jacob's purchase of the tunic is the material proof of his love. - A different explanation of שהעו is given by Robert E. Longacre, *Weqatal* forms in Biblical Hebrew Prose, pp.50-98 of Robert D. Bergen (ed.), *Biblical Hebrew and Discourse Linguistics*, Winona Lake, Indiana 1994. On p.84 he argues for a climactic function.

[7] Gen 37 contains 86 lines of narrator text (in a colometrical typography that gives each predicate its own line). No less than 68 of these are wyqtl clauses straight and simple. In addition there are several lines that show equivalent preterites following a word such as *ki*, the negation, etc.

[8] Verse 3 has two verbal clauses, but the first verb denotes attitude and emotion, not action, and the perfect form in v.3c, whether it is a flashback or not, is no consecutive form. It is no link in the characteristic chain of wyqtl forms. As regards verse 4, one could even argue that in the strictest sense this trio has no action either, as it tells us of visual reception (4a) and an emotional reaction (4b) that leads to being blocked (4c). Verse 4 functions as conclusion and result of the first sequence as a whole. We are still waiting for a plot to emerge.

figure. We note how this word touches the next one that opens verse 3; they have the same referent. In this way the word "father" prepares for the central verse of the sequence, which is totally given to "Israel".

The line on Joseph's journey back home reports action on the part of the young man. This implies that the narrator has decided to give the initiative to his hero as soon as possible, despite the fact that he needs considerable space to set out the whole of the background paragraph.

The words that Joseph chooses to bring home and the journey itself are also a form of anticipation. Line 2d foreshadows the entire unit comprising vv.12-17, which is about the next journey, Jacob sending his favourite son on a mission to visit his brothers in the field near Shechem and expecting him back in due time. As we shall see, the relation between this unit and v.2d is peculiar, to say the least.

Most translations of v.2d recognize that *dibbatam* has an objective genitive, "the rumours about them". Unfortunately, what is lost in the modern versions I know of - twenty or so, in five languages - is the syntactical status of the succeeding adjective רעה. This noun is used as a predicative element; it is not attributive, as it lacks the article, which would in that case be necessary.[9] As a consequence, the text does not say that there is ugly gossip around, which subsequently is brought to Jacob by a sedulous recorder. That the talk about the brothers is bad is not an objective fact. Instead, the text says: "Joseph brought the rumours about them to their father as bad", which is unpretty English for: he brought this gossip to his father [and presented it] as bad. This means that the text leaves open the possibility, if it does not say so unequivocally, that Joseph himself is the source of, and is responsible for, the negative import of his message. And this makes Joseph and his less than brotherly performance as downright informer the first cause of the venomous family conflict which quickly develops. The first cause, that is, in a series of exactly three causes or reasons; the next two being Jacob's favouritism - bad policy from the pater familias! - and the conspicuous cloak that is bound to make the brothers' blood curdle.

The ominous adjective *r'h* forms a nexus of two wordplays. The first one connects the phrase *DBtm R'h* through a maximum amount of alliteration - threefold

---

[9] Of the usual reference grammars, Gesenius-Kautzsch, Beer-Meyer, Bauer & Leander, Brockelmann, *Hebräische Syntax* (which has got it wrong, see § 103a), Waltke & O'Connor, and Joüon-Muraoka (the second edition of Joüon 1923 and 1947, thoroughly revised, updated and translated), only the last mentions Gen 38:2d and this predicative function, see § 126a (= p.455-456). The word "bad" functions in the same way as the word "red" in: "Rosie dyed her hair red." The point of this kind of predicating is the colour of the hair, not the action of the dyeing.

The word *dibbah* returns in Num.14:37; how striking that this noun, made definite by the construct state combination, is succeeded by another *ra'ah* which is also predicative! Compare I Sam.2:23c and NAPS IV *ad loc.*

Robert E. Longacre, *Joseph, a Story of Divine Providence*, Winona Lake, Indiana, 1989, has overlooked the objective genitive as well as the predicative usage of *r'h* in v.2. At the end of his book he gives a full transliteration of Gen 37 and 39-45. Forms like 'ăněyī and kᵉšāmě'ō (instead of 'onyī and kᵉšom'ō), or 'akālātěhū, 'ārěṣā and ḥālāmětā show that the shewa sign and the qames hatuf are total mysteries to this author.

alliteration, the umpteenth instance of the ternary principle![10] - to the refrain word *dbr* and its various meanings in v.4c // 8d // 11b: "speaking to him", "his words", and "the whole matter" (a sign of the father being intrigued and trying to be objective towards the significance of the dreams). In passing, I note here that exactly the same pattern, in inverse order, is used by the poet Jeremiah in one of his most personal and poignant laments, Jer 20:7-18.[11]

The pun forges a strong link between v.2d and 4c, with explanatory power. The suggestion is that the brothers "would not speak to him in a friendly way" any more (דברו לשלם) because their hatred partly springs from Joseph choosing to bring back an ugly report on them. There is an aspect of measure for measure here, as the initial discourse (from A about B) leads to the non-discourse (back from B to A) of deadly and telling silence.

Would Joseph, whom we will not see any more among the cattle, have ever become a competent shepherd? I doubt it, as he himself darkens his status of *ro'eh* by an evil, *ra'ah*, that is of his own making and is brought to his father as an objective fact. Soon Joseph will be a slightly ridiculous *to'eh*, in unit vv.12-17 which forms a bridge unit between the first story and "Joseph in Dothan", the latter text being the real start of the action and the fountainhead of the cycle's macroplot. Losing his bearings, the wandering Joseph needs an anonymous passer-by to find the way to his brothers. The catastrophe in Dothan is bracketed by the words חיה רעה אכלתהו. This clause from v.20 is repeated without any change in v.33. It completes another trio and intimates another measure for measure, because the evil of 2d (*ra'ah*) is answered by the redoubled *ra'ah* of a wild animal bringing death. This is supported by another form of balance, which again constitutes a trio. What Joseph did in v.2d was "bringing back (..) evil to their father," a hiph'il of the root בוא. His deed is mirrored (read: avenged) by the brothers in v.32b, when they send the bloodied cloak to their father - the same narrative form in the plural. In v.28d we find this ויביאו once more; by selling Joseph as a slave to tradesmen, the group makes sure the boy is taken to Egypt.

The third trio of lines, v.4abc, presents the result of the initial sequence. All the clauses fall to the brothers, they get the full status of subject. This is an ominous preparation for the unit where they conspire and, celebrating their subject position, decide to act with violence, vv.18-33.

A terrible chasm cuts right through the family, as the father's love is countered by the hatred of the brothers. The line of fracture starts with אהב, passes three

---

[10] Many instances of this principle, which refers to the narrator ordering his elements (sounds, words, phrases, words, clauses, motifs, etc.) in threesomes, can be found in the subject index of *Vow and Desire*, = vol. IV (1993) of my *Narrative Art and Poetry in the Books of Samuel*, Assen 1981-1993. This index covers all the Samuel material. Another series of ternary phenomena will emerge shortly in Gen 38.

[11] This poem has three stanzas (vv.7-10/11-13/14-17) which are forcefully integrated by the sounds and meanings of a brilliant chain connecting many nominal and verbal forms of the roots *ykl, kll, kwl, kly, škl, kšl,* etc. The first stanza is delineated clearly by inclusion (פתה and יכל in its first and last verses). Strophes #2 and 3 both use אדבר for Jeremiah's preaching and the friction with the דבר יהוה (vv.8 and 9), the fourth strophe (v.10) uses *DBt Rbym* to represent the enemies and their enormous pressure.

occurrences of שׂנא (the first in v.4b, next 5c = 8d), and culminates in the final קנא of v.11a, as if punning on the synonymity of *sin'ah // qin'ah*. Usually the root *qn'* denotes jealousy, and that emotion is certainly part of the brothers' position. But here it also forms the climax of the *sn' leitmotiv*, so that it laces the hatred with a certain venom and leads the family to the brink of disaster.[12] The singular form *yosef* (a jussive hiph'il, if we may believe Gen 30:24) occurring in 2b, 2d and 5a in a way engenders the plural *yosifu* on the brothers' side, vv.5c and 8.

Going from the one "eating" which refers to the devouring animal, to the other (v.20d // 33d), we pass a third occurrence of אכל in between. In v.25a the brothers sit down to eat, right after having treated Joseph with physical violence. This shows them to be callous and without remorse. The connection made by the triplet suggests they do not differ much, morally speaking, from the beast they have invented themselves.

The last word of the background paragraph, immediately after the keyword *dbr*, is *shalom*. Both words return in the order Jacob gives in v.14bcd: "Go, find out if your brothers are well and the cattle is well, and bring back word to me." The double use of the noun שׁלום again makes for a trio. The word is at the basis of one more wordplay that traverses the whole unit: *shalom*, everybody's well-being, is shattered by *chalom*, the word for dream(ing)[13] and deliberately frequent here, a clash which leads to the conspicuous infinitives spicing the angry speeches in vv.8 and 10. This expressive style device marks the acme of indignation; the narrator uses the absolute infinitives *mašol* and *malok* that link up with *shalom* via alliteration and assonance.

---

[12] Note how the contrast of hate and love is used in Ps.109:5 and II Sam.13:15 (where it is the pivot of the plot!). It is striking to see how Qohelet brings love, hate and envy together in one string. Eccl. 9:6 reads, in a context of death and oblivion: "Their love, their hatred, their jealousy have long since perished; and they have no more share till the end of time."

[13] Our second linguistic obstacle is the form תסבינה in v.7c (in the third הנה line): how to explain the choice of the imperfect? In his revision of Joüon's grammar, § 113f, Muraoka suggests that it is a durative form, but casts some doubt on this reading in § 118n. A possible solution dawns when we realize that this case of dream-telling does not quite follow the book. As a rule, such *hinneh* lines have participles as predicates. Their descriptive and durative potential then represents the present of the spectator (dreamer). The three הנה lines of Jacob's dream in Gen 28 are a telling example. Here in ch.37, the situation is different. It is not the narrator but a character who tells the dream. His first line (v.7a with *m'lmym*) still obeys the rule, but after that the participial style is abandoned. Verse 7b has two perfect forms, 7c contains the imperfect under discussion and 7d uses the narrative form which is so well known outside direct discourse. Therefore, the imperfect form of 7c can have no other function than that of a preterite between the adjacent preterites. Here, then, we have the narrative yqtl form we know better from poetry, like *yṣb* in Deut.32:8 or *ybhr* and *yr'h* in Jud.5:8, or *y'hz* and *ydmw* in Ex.15:15-16. All these forms are matched by adjacent perfect forms. We also know this narrative yqtl from Ugaritic and Akkadian. Finally, we should consider the style factor. The choice for תסבינה might have been influenced by the rhyme connecting this verb of movement with the (consecutive) imperfect ותשתחוינה (another verb of movement).

The Shift from Subject to Object: the Bridge Unit 37:12-17

In the first unit it was Joseph who took the initiative in each of the three sequences. In the second unit, vv.12-17, his status as hero is confirmed by his father. Here, Jacob acts as sender who provides Joseph with a quest, assigning him a visit to the brothers.[14] These are actantial positions: the father is the *destinateur*, the son is the subject who travels along the axis of desire and action; and the object is clear: a report on the well-being of the brothers and the flock.

Most of vv.12-14 speaks for itself, which makes the surprise of v.15-17 all the greater. What is the point of this enigmatic meeting? Why is this stranger brought in? We will find the answer by confidently following the structural leads.

This intermediate unit, containing 75 words, is divided in two halves. Vv.12-14 and vv.15-17 show a neat balance, not only as regards length (39 versus 36 words), but also as regards their structure. Both parts are marked by precise frames which are based mainly on the ordering of space. These flank two dialogues of exactly the same length (three speeches and 19 words each):

v.12	his brothers went (...)	. . . . .	near Shechem בשכם
	Jacob + Joseph: dialogue, three speeches		
v.14d	he arrived	. . . . .	מעמק חברון in Shechem
v.15ab	a man found him (...)		in the field איפה הם
	dialogue: man + Joseph three speeches		
v.17f	he found them	. . . . .	דתינה in Dothan

One comment should suffice with respect to vv.12-14. What on earth drives Jacob to give the job of inspection to this son? He appears not to be aware of the tensions

---

[14] The obvious word to reflect a quest is to search, to seek. It does indeed occur in the text: twice, in v.15d // 16b.

in the family, or he would have understood that a boy who thinks fit to speak ill of his own brothers and in this way contributes to demolishing *shalom* is the last person who should find out about their *shalom*. This young man is hardly credible as a trustworthy source, when it comes to bringing back word on his brothers' well-being! The clash between v.2d and 14cd is marked by key words. In his blindness Jacob fails to realize that a visit by Joseph to his hateful brothers could become a very unpleasant experience. And it is at this very juncture that the reader realizes how the strange meeting in the field links up with the clear orders from the father. It is good psychology on the narrator's side to show how Joseph loses track as soon as he approaches the area where he can expect the others. Joseph is not as blind as his father about his brothers' state of mind.

And so we come to understand that this unit is a bridge. In the first unit (vv.2-11) the initiative was on Joseph's side and he was not impeded by modesty or nerves either. In the third unit he does not speak at all and becomes the target and the victim of his conspiring brothers. Accordingly, what is left for him in vv.18-36 is no more than the status of grammatical object. The point of the short and intermediate unit vv.12-17 is to mould the transition: how the proud subject is sent away, loses his certainty on this outward journey and shifts to the object position. An anonymous "man found him", not the other way round!

What is worse, still, is that this man discovers for us how Joseph, the would-be *ro'eh*, has become a *to'eh* in the field, somebody lost. The narrator slows the pace of narration, when he depicts the slight wonder of this man, in v.15b. He respects the stranger's physical point of view (or focalisation) by choosing the characteristic *hinneh* + participle syntax which covers the present of the spectator.

Joseph is not the one who dares to speak first. It is only after being questioned that he discloses what he is looking for, v.16. Then it is his turn to ask for information, "tell me please where they are tending the flock!" The man and the information that is his to give ("they went to Dothan") are indispensable to the progress of the story. Without them, Joseph would not have found his brothers, they could not have stripped and sold him, and Joseph would not have been taken to Egypt. The contrast between being found (15a) and finding (17f) is a highly effective reversal and an instance of irony at the expense of the rapidly shrinking hero. Joseph is a boy, hardly able to cope with the challenges he faces in the world of grown-ups: uncertainty and hatred.

Joseph in Dothan: Violence and Deception, Gen 37:18-36

This full-scale story can only be interpreted correctly after its structure has been established. As long as the composition is unclear as a result of a lack in narratological understanding on the reader's part, exegesis is in danger of producing disastrous statements like this one: "Von V.18 an bis zum Schluss des Kapitels ist die Handlung und das Gespräch der Brüder sehr unruhig und überladen und deshalb unübersichtlich erzählt." This is what Gerhard von Rad, a German exegete of great repute, says in his Genesis commentary.[15] Passing three negative value judgments (restive, overloaded, disorderly), he has projected his own confusion on the text and asserts that it is the story which is confused.

We are able to find the structure only when we take the means of articulation seriously. The terms of space were prominent enough in the previous unit. Here they become crucial and will guide us to the correct division of the text into nine members. The narrator wastes no time in drawing our attention to the space. He flaunts his handling of movement and spatiality by establishing the opposition far/near in the very first couple of clauses (רחק vs. קרב, v.18ab). The conspiracy and Reuben's counterproposal cannot be heard by Joseph, who is still at a distance, vv.18-22. In v.23, however, he arrives at the scene. This approach is conspicuously marked by the introductory sentence 23a and its coordinates, terms relating to time and space alike. Moreover, the verb form ויהי signals the start of a new paragraph; and so line 23a is the threshold of the decisive and ugly meeting:

ויהי כאשר בא יוסף אל אחיו

Violence will erupt shortly.

Reuben's proposal is defeated by Judah. Of all the words spoken in Dothan, Judah's speech carries the day. His proposal to sell Joseph instead of letting him rot in the pit is approved by his brothers; "they listened" in v.27d means that they complied.[16]

The decisive option is flanked by two long verses which both mention a caravan and end with a hiph'il verb of movement plus the locative "to Egypt", vv.25 and 28. Along the linear axis they complement each other: in 25 the brothers see the caravan, its many commodities and the direction it takes, in v.28 they use the passing of the traders to turn Joseph into another commodity by selling him. Judah's proposal is in an intermediary position and provides the connection 25 > 28.

Space gets even more dramatic in vv.24 and 29, where the nominal negation אין twice points to the empty pit. Emptiness first means "no water" and is metonymically connected with death, the second time emptiness is what Reuben discovers to his great dismay. Shocked, he sees that Joseph is gone, and his gestures of mourning

---

[15] G. von Rad, *Genesis*, ATD (1972) p.288. Such a prejudiced beginning leads, as is to be expected, to diachronical speculations and even impels the author to substitute the character Judah for Reuben in v.21; he is not the only one doing so, see e.g. the KBS version (in Dutch). We will see how this 'improvement' totally ruins the composition and the portraits of both Reuben and Judah.

On the same page 288 we find von Rad's judgment on the bridge unit: "*Merkwürdig umständlich* ist erzählt, wie es dazu kam, das Joseph nach anfänglichem Verirren seine Brüder dann noch gefunden hat, - im Fortgang der Ereignisse eigentlich ein *ganz nebensächlicher* Zug." (Italics mine, JF.) Again, von Rad has completely missed the point.

[16] Note how this וישמעו at the end of v.27 is a counterpart of Reuben's וישמע at the beginning of vv.21-22 (segment B, as we will see). Complying with Judah implies disregarding Reuben's proposal. Note how Reuben's speech to the father in ch.42:37 is once more overruled by Judah (speaking to Jacob in the beginning of ch.43). Judah is the only one who manages to wrench consent from the desperate old man.

once more signify death. A week or less later, his father assumes the same
hypothesis. What Jacob does not know is that he is being flagrantly manipulated by
his sons from a great distance. Note how this spatial separation is presupposed by
32ab (sending). The brothers simply do not dare to hand over the bloodied cloth
themselves and in this way to come face to face with their old man.

The composition of vv.18-33 is a concentric symmetry of nine members. Judah
occupies the pivot. The outer flanks are marked strikingly by the killing animal; the
repetition of this clause is the double cornerstone of the structure.

A	brothers' conspiracy	חיה רעה אכלתהו	vv.18-20
B	Reuben proposes to throw Joseph into a pit		vv.21-22
C	the brothers strip Joseph and throw him		
	into the empty pit		vv.23-24
D	a caravan approaches (description via הנה)		v.25
X	Judah proposes to sell Joseph		vv.26-27
D'	Joseph sold to the caravan traders		v.28
C'	Reuben finds *the pit empty*		v.29
B'	Reuben expresses despair		v.30
A'	cover-up by the brothers,		vv.31-33
	'recognition' by the father	חיה רעה אכלתהו	

This pattern opens new windows and so helps us to find new meanings and
correspondences. Inversely, the correspondences I now wish to discuss corroborate
the concentric pattern and its validity.

The most substantial speeches are found in the centre and at the boundaries; thus
in A + X + A':
- 19 words in vv.19-20, said by the conspiring brothers (six lines),
- 20 words by Judah, vv.26-27 (six lines),
- 17 words in vv.32-33: the heart-rending remote exchange between the manipulative
brothers and Jacob (five lines).

The speech by Reuben sub B has a counterpart in his disconsolate outcry sub B'
(v.30). The correspondence BB' implies that Reuben gets thoroughly outmanoeuvred.
In vv.21-22 he may have harboured the illusion that he could save Joseph, but soon
after that he is outflanked by what happens. The writer goes out of his way to honour
the good intentions on the part of Reuben who, in his position as firstborn, clearly
feels responsible for the youngest brother present. The narrator takes up Reuben's
speech in 22bcd in a rare move: he resumes talking, i.e. lines 22ef are again the
narrator's words, but he does not introduce a new predicate in his own text. Instead,
he forges a *parallelismus membrorum* that is based on a double hiph'il[17] and can

---

[17] An interesting parallel is to be found in II Sam.3:10: the end of Abner's angry speech to Ishboshet
contains another pair of infinitival clauses both using the hiph'il. See the colometrical representation
of the text at the back of my *Throne and City*, = NAPS III, and my discussion on pp.76-77.

easily be scanned as a bicolon:

למען הציל אתו מידם // להשיבו אל אביו

This pair is not a report and depicts no action. The nature and import of these cola are those of commentary arising from narratorial omniscience. This look into Reuben's mind, however, only serves to highlight his powerlessness in vv.29-30. Reuben is the victim of irony when he is dramatically robbed of all means to turn back the clock. Worse still, he did not even know about the transaction with the tradesmen. After complaining (v.30) to his brothers, the only thing left to him is to find out how Joseph got out of the pit, and this kind of quest is not something the narrator wants to cover. Instead, he has created a triplet to show how helpless the position of the eldest brother is. Reuben's illusion earned a hiph'il of the root *$\check{s}wb$ in v.22f, his desperate movements towards and away from the pit in vv.29a and 30a are presented by a double qal narrative, *wayyašob*.[18]

Reuben's discovery represents a gap for the reader. In v.29 we suddenly realize that Reuben cannot have been a participant in the transaction. We should, however, not flee into diachronical speculations precipitately. We might first try to deal with the gap in a synchronic way and remain true to a sound narratology. The first productive question to be asked is this: what would the alternative have been to the narrator? If Reuben had been present at the selling, he would have had no choice but to come into the open with his good intentions, and he would have felt it necessary to protest against the sale, etc. But this is not what suits the narrator!

The narrator has manoeuvred himself into a difficult position by revealing the inner life of Jacob's firstborn in v.22ef. He now solves his problem with v.29 and creates a gap. This device is, in this text, an iconic sign which connects our embarrassment when we read v.29 with Reuben's. Our shock as we stumble over the gap is analogous to Reuben's shock when he stares into the empty pit and feels helpless.

The segments B and B' of the compositional pattern had Reuben speaking. As a contrast, segments CD and D'C' have no spoken word at all. They only report action and movement, and here the narrator is the only voice. He uses exactly seventy words to do his job. This number is exactly the sum total of the words used in the

---

[18] In a fine touch, the narrator shows that Reuben has not given up on his role and responsibility. Much later, in 42:37, when the brothers have returned home from their first journey to Egypt, and are speechless with embarrassment because they just found back their money in the sacks with grain, Reuben says to his trembling father who has just heard the vizier's demand to send Benjamin down to Egypt: "You may kill my two sons if I do not bring him [i.e. Benjamin] back to you. Put him in my care, and *I will return him* to you." Jacob answers with words that are carefully attuned to his lament at the conclusion of ch.37: "My son must not go down with you, for his brother is dead and he alone is left. If he meets with disaster on the journey you are taking, you will send my white head down to Sheol in grief." Note how the author has put the verb אשיבנו into Reuben's mouth, and see the situational irony of the sequel in 43:21, ונשב אתי.

outer pair, segments A + A'.[19]

Segments D and D' focus on two collectives and confront them with one another; they end up by looking beyond the horizon and having the end station Egypt as rhyme words (both times in the locative form).[20] The segments C and C' form a pair on the basis of a mixture of similarity and difference. The difference is that in verse 23 Joseph is thrown into the pit, and in v.29 he is missing from it. The similarity is not only provided by the notion of emptiness (as indicated by אֵין), but also by the attribute of clothing and the violence factor. In v.23 we witnessed the brutal stripping of Joseph, and we felt the rage of the brothers who vent this heat on the tunic. Note how explicit the narrator is on this attribute at the end of v.23 - but, surprisingly, in v.29 another piece of cloth is torn, this time by Reuben who is in mourning. Tearing up his own clothing puts him beside the victim from a semiotic viewpoint and puts him in a sympathetic light. A few days later a third person will join him in tearing his clothes: it is Jacob himself, when he has received the bloodstained tunic (v.34). This gets the firstborn, who in vain had been considerate of his father's perspective in v.22, to a position very close to Jacob after all.[21] Surveying the many references to textile in this story, we find that not one piece has remained intact. As the first one was the costly tunic of the boy, the eldest son and his father follow him in a certain sense. They perform a gesture of metonymical-metaphorical relevance by rending their own clothes, and in this way they reveal how they participate in his (supposedly) gruesome fate.

Symmetries such as the parallel pattern ABC ABC, or the concentric ABC CBA, or AB.. N X N' .. BA, can only claim to be valid if the correspondences between their components are relevant and verifiable. These connections (A-A', B-B', etc.) are either based on identity or on opposition. In practice, however, when we look into the matter more closely, they always turn out to be a mixture of similarity and difference.

---

[19] Segment A, vv.18-20, contains 32 words, exactly the same amount as the adjacent segment B = vv.21-22. Segment A' has 38 words, while the closing verses 34-36, outside the concentric symmetry, have a similar number of words (39).

[20] The relation between the names Ishmaelites and Midianites is not necessarily problematic. Either we fill the blank on the caravan traders by assuming there were two different groups in the caravan: drivers who were Arabs versus tradesmen who were Midianites, or we choose a solution with the help of Jud.6-8, where the invading Midianites are also called Ishmaelites by the writer (8:24). I take Midianites as a precise ethnic term referring to a tribe, while the name Ishmaelites is vague; it refers to the life style of the desert and approximately means "Arabs" (as e.g. the Gesenius-Buhl lexicon has it). After v.28a there is an unmarked shift of subject, something which is not rare at all in Hebrew narration. It is unnatural to assign the second and third narrative forms to other persons than the brothers, one reason being that v.28 clearly is the fulfilment of what Judah had just proposed to his brothers. Note how vv.28a + 28d form an inclusion, in the sense that the traders are the subject of the first and last verb forms in the verse. See also Longacre, *Joseph*, p.31, on the device of participant introduction.

[21] Reuben being outflanked in ch.37 is no surprise to a reader who is aware that the cycle also deserves a political reading. Reuben had violated his father's privacy and sexual pride in 35:22, and Jacob does not forget this incident. It partly turns his blessing (in that chapter full of poetry, Gen 49) into a curse, 49:3-4.

Absolute identity does not exist. The striking repetition of the devouring animal is an illuminating proof of this. The words remain exactly the same, and so do their meanings. The function of the clause in v.20, however, is different in many respects from that in v.33. Just before receiving Joseph in their midst, the brothers' clause חיה רעה אכלתהו is a plan, a deliberate lie which they discuss and intend to use later to their father. It indicates a possible line of future conduct. How different this line sounds as direct discourse in v.33! Here it is a speech by the father, who unawares is being manipulated. From his lips the clause is a conclusion, a wrong inference at the sight of the bloodied cloth; it triggers deep mourning for more than twenty years. During this whole period having lost his beloved son will be a cruel reality for Jacob.

Everybody around him knows better. The brothers see his grief and do not speak up. Outside the story, i.e. beyond the narrated world, the narrator and the reader know that Jacob is being deceived. The old man's 'knowledge' of Joseph's demise puts him in a chilling isolation. Functioning in its second immediate context, the clause about the killing beast marks a horrifying exacerbation, because deception by the brothers for Jacob has become self-deception, as a result of manipulation from the far distance. The words and meanings remain the same, but the trajectory from A through A', and from plan to denouement, has changed considerably. Even the correspondence 20d=33d does not mean complete identity. The literal repetition is an example of what I call the dialectic of identity and difference.

How much this story belongs to the brothers can be seen from the fact that the selling of Joseph does not constitute the denouement. The actual denouement comes with the shocking and tragic delusion of the father who does not realize the difference between recognizing the tunic and inferring violent death. In his mouth the two clauses are united in a perfect balance, as a full poetic line, a bicolon of 3 + 3 beats:

חיה רעה אכלתהו // טרף טרף יוסף

For the second time, Jacob uses the absolute infinitive, this time to establish a truth that he cannot handle or digest.

The superior knowledge of the brothers undermines and poisons their ability to relate to Jacob as true sons. They try to comfort him but their inner life has become divided, following rules of its own that they underestimate dramatically. Two decades later their bad conscience will become the pressure-cooker cleverly used by the vizier of Egypt to turn them around. Here, in ch.37, their vibrations cannot be honest and true. Accordingly, the consolation they offer does not work. This is reflected at the level of a sequence in another concentric pattern:

A		Jacob rent his clothes
B		and put sackcloth on his loins.
	C	He observed *mourning* ...
		D ... *for his son* many days.
		E All his sons and daughters sought to *comfort* him,
		E' but he refused to be *comforted*,
		D' saying, "No, I will go down *to my son* ...
	C'	*mourning* ...
B'		... in Sheol."
A'		Thus his father bewailed him.

Here in vv.34-35, death, rituals of grief and attributes of mourning form the iron rings that make good intentions powerless.

At the same time, the temporal phrase *yamim rabbim* carries a surplus of meaning.[22] At the level of communication between text and reader it is a signal from the narrator that opens a vast temporal space. This space is covered by the temporal clause *wayyirbu hayyamim* in Gen 38:12a, and accordingly coincides with most of the long period of narrative time taken up by Gen 38 and Judah's marriage to Shua's daughter.

Looking ahead and back: antecedents and sequels
The number of Joseph's years, seventeen, leads us back to Genesis 31, when Rachel was delivered of her first child. This birth made her husband Jacob decide he should end his long stay in Haran and return to Canaan, together with his family and flock. The cover-up by the brothers in ch.37 and its reverse, the 'recognition' by Jacob, have at least two important literary antecedents.

In Gen 31 Rachel deceived her own father by stealing his house-gods, the *t*ᵉ*rafim*, and hiding them in her camel saddle. When things came to a head and father Laban started a thorough search of Jacob's retinue, she alleged that she could not dismount because of her menstruation. Ignorant of her scheme, Jacob himself swore to his uncle that the person with whom the sacred objects would turn up would be executed, and so without realizing introduced the dimension of life and death with his own words.[23] In a certain sense, then, Jacob was deceived there as well. The

---

[22] In OTS xxv I have demonstrated the importance of the *yamim rabbim* at the very end of ch.21. In the underlying time schedule that organizes the entire structure of the Abraham cycle, this time marker is strategically important, being the exact counterpart of the temporal hiatus between 16:16 and 17:1 which covers a period of 13 years. Together these time designations form an inclusion and so delineate the huge and central text of Gen 17-21 which is completely devoted to the hundredth year of the hero's lifetime. See J.P. Fokkelman, Time and the Structure of the Abraham Cycle, OTS xxv (1989) pp.96-109.

[23] A short while later, when Laban's search has ended in failure, Jacob complains of his long and hard term of service with his uncle, in a long speech to Laban himself (31:36-42). It is no coincidence that the poignant word *trf*, chosen and underlined by another paronomasia in 37:33, is found here as well: "That which *was torn by beasts* I never brought to you," 31:39. The verb joins the *trf* of the idols in the saddlebag by force of alliteration.

formal link with ch.37 is established by the keyword **nkr*. Jacob uses it in 31:32. Moreover, the elements of a scheming daughter, sacred objects, hiding them, and the challenge of recognition will all return, in the Tamar story we will study shortly.

The same verb 'to recognize' leads us further back. The goat whose blood was an indispensable part of the brothers' scheme and led to "recognition" by Jacob, has a predecessor in Gen 27. At that time Jacob, a young man himself, deceived his blind father and robbed his brother of the blessing. Creating a huge problem of recognition for Isaac, he used the skin and meat of a kid, to give himself a hairy appearance and bring his father the dish he longed for. What was at stake for the old man was the identity of his son, and this is again aptly denoted by *nkr*, 27:23.

The link between this scene and ch.37 is another instance of measure-for-measure. Jacob has now become a father and is deceived by his sons in turn. In ch.27 he exploited Isaac's inability to see. In ch.37 his sons first avoid eye contact, then use their father's sight in a very paradoxical and malicious way: they have the tunic put before him, and yet they manage to obscure Jacob's vision because they tempt him into an erroneous inference.

This karmic link between past and present leads through Gen 31. I remind the reader that Jacob served Laban for twenty years, as the patriarch himself twice says to his uncle. Perhaps we should connect this with the number the author decided to put in the text of ch.37, where Joseph is sold for twenty pieces of silver. The references to his age in 37:2 and in 41:46 (he is thirty years old when he is appointed vizier by Pharaoh) help us in our calculations. Adding the seven years of abundance, we conclude that Joseph is at least 37 years old when he sees his brothers again, at the start of the seven years of drought. And so we discover that the great reversal - Joseph making himself known to the remorseful brothers and inviting his father to live in Goshen - takes place some twenty years after the pit incident. This dramatic moment is explicitly marked by several occurrences of the verb *nkr*.

It will be no surprise to the readers that this same root forms a crucial link between chapters 37 and 38. Let us therefore look ahead to the Judah-Tamar story.

Opening Eyes: the Judah and Tamar Story, Genesis 38

The spectacular story about a woman's taboo-breaking conduct has a solid construction. The linear axis is carefully articulated by thresholds, time designations which mark the beginning of new paragraphs:

ויהי בעת ההוא	1a
וירבו הימים	12a
ויהי כמשלש חדשים	24a
ויהי לעת לדתה	27a

This series yields a provisional division of the text along the syntagmatic axis.[24] First we have an exceptionally long run-up, vv.1-11.[25] This textual unit is a kind of prelude or exposition, and covers many years of narrative time, in which Judah's marriage produces three sons and two of them reach marriageable age themselves.[26]

The hero, this time actually a heroine, appears very late.[27] It is not until verse 13 that she comes to the fore as an actor in her own right, but as from that moment she will take audacious initiatives and develop a firm hold on the situation. In this way, the solid middle part is all hers: vv.12-23. A plot analysis confirms this delineation.

What is the initial problem which bedevils Tamar? How does the heroine's trajectory run? And what prize is she after? These questions are central to a proper plot analysis, and as soon as we have answered them, we realize that the main plot[28] also starts as late as verse 13. Like most plots, it springs from a deficiency: there is no husband; what is more important, there is no male offspring, and Judah has 'forgotten' to give Tamar as a sexual partner or wife to the second *levir* (*yabam*), Shelah. He has experienced two deaths and does not want to risk a third. Hence his soliloquy in v.11de, brought to us by the omniscient narrator who can read minds. Deliberately, he tries to push Tamar into oblivion. And so the exposition ends on a note of inactivity and stagnation, "she lived [and waited for years] in her father's house."

Tamar is not the person to accept passivity and oblivion. She establishes her problem in v.14ef - the narrator covers her point of view - and counters the powerless 'sitting' (*wtšb*) in v.11g with a very different sitting in v.14d (*wtšb*). Again, she is waiting for Judah's move, this time "along the road to Timnah". She knows exactly what she wants: seed from that male who is the closest kinsman to her deceased husband Er, in order to secure a form of social and psychological survival for him, or "not to have his name blotted out from the face of the earth", as the Hebrew Bible has it elsewhere.

The central part is dedicated to the central event, Tamar's stunning performance as a whore, and is also delineated by terms of space. The crucial meeting between Judah and Tamar in disguise, and their negotiations, take place in the vicinity of Timnah. This textual unit is framed by movements back and forth (in vv.12-13 and 20-21). First we see Judah and his friend travelling towards Timnah, for a

---

[24] The last time designation (27a) is echoed by v.28a, ויהי בלדתה, and 29a, ויהי כמשיב ידו. The series 27a-28a-29a shows an increasing precision, focusing on the details of the delivery. Therefore, the time designations of 28a and 29a stay within the last sequence, in subordinate positions.

[25] Long, that is, in terms of the number of lines; put in other words, the narration time is long.

[26] Shelah, the youngest, does not reach that age until later: during the narrative time covered by v.12 and indicated by Judah as speaker in v.11bc. Note that the long unit vv.1-11 is divided into two halves by another temporal clause, which this time is positioned as an ending: v.5d, והיה בכזיב בלדתה אתי.

[27] I here disregard her presence in verses 6-11, where she is hardly more than an object of her father-in-law's care and manipulation. This humble position is exactly what she decides to abandon from v.13 on.

[28] A subplot may be assigned to the exposition. Judah would then be the hero/subject who strives for survival or genealogical continuity, and therefore takes measures with respect to marriage and levirate, to ensure a next generation.

celebration in connection with sheep shearing. The journey back home is skipped, but Hirah gets a paragraph on his own in vv.20-23. He is sent from Adullam (if that is where Judah lives, cf. verse 1c) to Petach Enaim, to deliver the goat to the prostitute as a reward. This time she is called a קדשה, perhaps a euphemism for the straight word זונה as it has a cultic ring. Hirah looks in vain for the woman. This result, his "not finding her", is shaped and distributed as a trio, with a nice variation in verb forms covering all the grammatical persons.[29] The narrative time needed for the central event and the amusing failure to pay the price is less than a week.

The dramatic climax of the story is a paragraph about life and death. Tamar is about to be burnt alive by order of her indignant father-in-law, when she suddenly produces the objects - three of them! - that he had given her as a pledge and Hirah had not been able to retrieve. These verses 24-26 obviously are the denouement. Carefully dated and linked to the central event by v.24a, this clash consumes only an hour of narrative time or so. In much the same way as the central event and Hirah's excursus, this sequence mainly consists of direct discourse.

Once more we skip a lot of narrative time and arrive at the aftermath (vv.27-30). This is about half a year later, when we become witnesses to the birth. It needs no more than a day, presumably. If we call all verses after v.12 the Tamar story proper, the total narrative time in vv.13-30 is less than one year, while the exposition required at least some fifteen to twenty years. It is quite productive to realize the amount of time required by Gen 38 as an excursus on Judah. Measuring the story time enables us to assert that the Judah who appeared before the vizier of Egypt and had to achieve his rhetorical best on behalf of Jacob and Benjamin as spokesman for the group, had become a different man after the painful lesson on his double standard of morals. A transformed and remorseful Judah, who unawares had stood in for Shelah as *levir*, is the only person who can credibly say that he wants to stand in for Benjamin.[30] Joseph, still not recognized, senses this, is moved by the urgent plea and makes himself known.

I leave the syntagmatic axis and Tamar's successful plot. The paradigmatic axis and the principle of selection are even more productive. The composition of Gen 38 appears to be a concentric symmetry of eleven members:

---

[29] The preterite forms of מצא are in the third, first and second persons masc., in vv.20b//22c//23e respectively. Much the same spreading of grammatical persons can be observed for בוא, the verb denoting intercourse here, in vv.16d, 16h, and 18f (a threesome).

[30] As we will see, the idea of substitution and the connection between chs.38 and 44 are marked by the root ערב.

A	Judah marries outside the tribe >	
	his wife bears three sons	vv.1-5
B	a) death rampant: two sons are killed	vv.6-10
	b) Judah's speech to Tamar: Shelah is left.	
	Tamar put on a side track?	v.11
C	feast after mourning, Judah goes to Timnah	
	with his friend Hirah	vv.12-13
D	Tamar takes off her widow's dress,	
	and puts on a veil	v.14
E	Judah spots whore (he thinks),	
	sexual appetite	v.15
X	central dialogue: six speeches	
	on whore's reward and pledge (עברון)	vv.16-18d
	(speakers: he-she-he / she-he-she)	
E'	intercourse > Tamar conceives	v.18efg
D'	Tamar takes off the veil,	
	and puts on her widow's dress	v.19
C'	Judah sends Hirah after the prostitute,	
	he searches in vain, brings back report	vv.20-23
B'	a') death threat: Tamar to be killed by fire?	
	She plays her trumps >	
	b') Judah recognizes: she is right;	
	he mentions Shelah	vv.24-26
A'	life prevails: Tamar bears twins	
	(in a very 'Jacobean' delivery)	vv.27-30

Once more, many windows have popped up, inviting us to look through them. The new meanings we then see are controlled by the correspondences which create the pairs. The correspondences build and support the structure; the structure supports the correspondences. This is one of the most concrete ways in which the nature of the hermeneutic circle - that never-ending movement from the parts to the whole and from the whole to the parts - can be demonstrated. In my account of the pairs that constitute the concentric structure, I would like first to concentrate on those features which led me to the symmetrical pattern, simply because they were so conspicuous.

To begin with, there is the precision, almost like stage directions, with which the narrator has Tamar put textile on and off. The appearance of mourning garb is in itself a sequel to the violent incident of the previous chapter, and can be used here because the motif of recognition appears next. Here, the handling of the widow's weeds is accompanied by, and contrasted to, using the veil. The veil is probably a sign of the profession which for an hour or so will be Tamar's new role and ruse.

The juxtaposition of the widow's dress and the veil makes for a double change of clothes, in vv.14 and 19, and takes the shape of a simple but very effective device of mirroring, a chiasmus. One more opposition is added, Tamar's ישב in v.14d versus her קום in 19a:

She took off her widow's garb,	14a
and covered her face with a veil.	b
She sat down (...) along the road (...)	d

. . . .

She stood up and left.	19a
She took off her veil	b
and again put on her widow's garb.	c

The full figure is an instance of neat inclusion that sets apart the central meeting between Judah and the whore. Tamar's disguise makes the series DEXE'D' into the central part of the chapter. Segments DE and E'D' do not contain any spoken word, whereas the pivotal segment with its rounds of negotiation is essentially dialogue. Exactly the same contrast was at work in and around the centre of "Joseph in Dothan", where the turning point was Judah's proposal and the flanks (CD and D'C') did not contain any character text at all.

Our next step in exploring the structure of Gen 38 moves outwards and brings us to the ring around the centre, C-C'. Here we meet Judah's long-time friend, Hirah. This man seemed an insignificant neighbour under A, and no more than pleasant (macho) company under C, where the two men want to go on a spree. However, Hirah's two appearances are upgraded as soon as we notice from the concentric pattern that element C' is the counterpart of C. Suddenly, Hirah has grown into an indispensable helper, and accordingly is allowed to occupy his own full paragraph (vv.20-23). Judah wants to pay the agreed price for the whore's services, all the more so as he needs to get back the very personal objects that are symbols of his identity. He sends his friend on a very delicate mission. Hirah tries hard enough, but can not trace the lady any more. The number of words spoken is divided evenly: sixteen words are spoken to Hirah, sixteen words come from his own lips.

Hirah's failure to find the woman is one thing, to allocate an entire sequence to this incident is another and takes place at a different level, where the narrator is in control. This decision on the writer's part reminds us of Reuben and his return to the pit, which he found empty. His failure to find Joseph also happened immediately after the decisive and centrally placed transaction, which in Gen 37 also was of a commercial nature.

The next ring is B-B'. The first parts of both segments show the ugly faces of death. Because of the structure, that is the paradigmatic choices made by the composer, the threat to Tamar of being executed by fire has become the fatal counterpart to the deaths of Er and Onan, which also had the character of punishment. This figure of correspondence is continued and underlined by the relation between b-b' (= v.11 versus v.26). Both times Judah is the speaker, and his subject is the same: the levirate marriage to Shelah which is a family interest and should bring Tamar the offspring she is entitled to. His speech in v.11 is split in two. First we have the part which is of a more or less public nature, because it is addressed to Tamar herself. Here, in v.11b, Judah speaks of delay and sounds reasonable. The second part, however, is set apart by its own quotation formula v.11d which does not mention any address. The content of clause 11e proves that the line is a soliloquy and puts Judah in an awful light by revealing his real purpose: he is stalling for time, hoping that tomorrow will never come. He is frightened and wants nothing more to do with the lady who seems to bring death. This tactic of deliberate misleading is radically exposed by Tamar; years may go by, but her memory does not give up. And so, her father-in-law finds himself compelled in v.26 to speak up once more on the time delay, to admit guilt and fully recognize that Tamar is right. The correct rendering of the preposition *min* in the forensic clause צדקה ממני should be forceful and produce a black and white picture: "she is in the right, I am not."[31] However, it is not unequivocally in Judah's favour that for this speech there is no addressee mentioned either in its quotation formula v.26b. Thus, the narrator leaves open the possibility that this speech of recognition is another soliloquy, so that Judah in his moment of utter shame seems to dodge a face to face confrontation with the injured but vindicated Tamar.

The number of words spoken by Judah in v.11 (segment B, part b) is thirteen. How many words does his speech in v.26 (segment B', part b') contain? This raises a very delicate question. Until now, nobody has ever questioned the status of the clause in v.26e: ולא יסף עוד לדעתה. It is simply taken for granted that this line is part of the narrator's text, so that we have to consider it a piece of information, referring to Judah's behaviour and given to us by the author. I wish to challenge this assumption.

First things first. We should begin with the fundamental question whether v.26e is narrator text or character text. In the latter case, the clause consists of words spoken by Judah and the subject of the verb "to go on, to continue" (יסף) changes into Shelah. Before defending this option, I will consider the traditional view, and I must confess I am glad that I do not need to defend it, because there is no justification for it.

Whenever we read a story, we start from the assumption that a sentence from the author or narrator is there because it makes sense to be there. The line should be relevant or useful, in one way or another. But what could be the relevance of the information that Judah "had no intercourse with Tamar any more"? Giving this information carries the logical implication of the possibility, or rather the conceivability, of such sexual contact. Now this implication seems to me outrageous as well as absurd. It is simply inconceivable that this father-in-law would sexually approach the very woman who has triumphantly disclosed the double standard of his morals, who, moreover, is his own daughter-in-law and finally is three months pregnant by him. The fact that Tamar had broken the taboo on this kind of intercourse when she was near Timnah can only be assessed within the framework

---

[31] The JPS translation and many others are disappointing here, reading rather lamely: "She is more in the right than I." Judah is not right at all, and the preposition has full exclusive force, just as in Gen 27:1 or 29:30 (Jacob loved Rachel, he did not love Leah!) and elsewhere; no comparison more/less is being made. The same construction with the same צדק occurs in I Sam.24:18. See NAG p.129 (plus note 10 there) and NAPS II, p.469. The preposition *min* is correctly rendered by H.-J. Boecker, *Redeformen des israelitischen Rechtslebens*, Bonn 1959, pp.130-132, and Thomas Krüger (in OBO 126, see below note 38).

of the ploy she was using. Therefore, her breaking of the taboo does not diminish
the force and validity of it; on the contrary, being an exception, it can only confirm
and underline the rule. Tamar's proceeding to play her game and turn Judah into a
one-time sexual partner was based on an ethical decision, the decision that
life/progeny for her husband carries more weight than the sexual taboo. Which
means that her decision does not address the taboo as such, and that her disguise
aims at circumventing it.

Once more, what could be the use or sense of saying that Judah had no intercourse
with Tamar from now on? I do not see what such a statement could add to the
drama, now that the story has already got past the denouement. Nor does the line
have any impact in terms of information any more.

The levirate construction presupposed by this chapter requires that Tamar's first
husband, Er, should be honoured after his death and in the genealogical sense live
on through male progeny, which was to be fathered by the next available brother.
And so it fell to Onan to make Tamar conceive. We know how he violated this
sacred duty by committing coitus interruptus, and worse, that he abused and
humiliated Tamar by doing so repeatedly. The two verbs of the wqtl type in v.9
explicitly signify past iterativity; in a different terminology, *whyh* and *wšht* are
frequentatives. Enraged by this ignominious behaviour, the deity eliminates Onan, as
he refused to continue intercourse in the decent, non-selfish sense which is in line
with the family interest. There is, however, one more brother, Shelah. He is not yet
of marriageable age, but that is no problem. Judah's speech in v.11 clearly
presupposes that in due time it will be this youngest brother's duty to have
intercourse with Tamar, on behalf of Er. What Er did not achieve by means of
intercourse, can and should be continued by Onan or eventually by Shelah. This kind
of continuation is covered and denoted by the verb *yasaf* in v.26e.

How many words does Judah's speech in v.26 contain? When we assign the last
clause to his voice, the number is thirteen, exactly the same as in the counterpart,
v.11. The reader who feels tempted to dismiss this identity as a case of coincidence
might like to try another count. Judah's speech in v.26 is the answer to Tamar's
words in vv.25c and 25e. The number of words she uses to present the disclosure
that is the hard core of the denouement is again thirteen.

Adopting my answer to the question of the actual status of v.26e actually is, the
text of verse 26 now reads:

> Judah recognized [the objects],
> and said:
>> "She is in the right, not I,
>> because I did not give her to my son Shelah
>> and he did not go on to have further intercourse with her."

Now that the last line belongs to the speaker Judah, the syntax has changed too. The
male subject of the verb *yasaf* is Shelah and the last line has turned into a
subordinate clause governed by 'because'. The motivating conjunction *ki* opens the
first dependent clause (v.26d) and does double duty so that it also governs the line

on Shelah's possible contribution. The relation between 26d and 26e is more than consecutive: "I did not give her to my son Shelah *so that* he had no chance in his turn to have intercourse with her." The order of the persons in 26d (giving "her" to "him"), is mirrored in 26e by "he ... her". We also note a modest parallelism based on semantics (both lines referring to sexual partnership) and the repetition of לא plus perfect form. The two lines 26cd rhyme on the long vowel of the first-person suffix, while the motivational pair 26de twice contains the suffix for "her".

The balance of 13 + 13 words of dialogue in the denouement is not an isolated figure. We have seen already that the number of words spoken to Hirah tallies with that spoken by Hirah (16 + 16) in the paragraph he occupies. But there is more. The elements B and B' also contain equal amounts of words spoken. Both contain three speeches and the total number of words in either case is twenty-two. When we finally scrutinize the centre (segment X, vv.16-18d), we find another perfect match. During their negotiations Tamar and Judah each speak three times, and the balance of their words is 15 + 15.[32]

From ch.37 we recall how important is the subject/object difference. Tamar was in full control of the central event, and now, three months later, she is the triumphant producer of the denouement, the moment that is dramatically and morally the crucial disclosure. Tamar is a subject in the best sense of the word. She has overcome the sloppy morals and sluggish delay tactics of her father-in-law. She has defeated oblivion. Finally, by giving birth to twins, she overcomes death.

The two sons of this proud and courageous woman are the obvious substitutes for the two sons of her fallible father-in-law. They more than compensate for the loss of Er and Onan, who "were bad in the eyes of YHWH." This correspondence, which forms the basis of the pair A-A' in the concentric pattern, is indicated by the repetition of the keyword *yld* and of the element of name-giving by the mother.[33]

Although the story of the delivery is full of amusing details, the point is not the humour. It is the fact that this complicated birth is a highly Jacobean achievement. The struggle of the two male foetuses to come out first reminds us strongly of the bickering in Rebeccah's womb (Gen 25:22-26). She, too, was pregnant with twins, and when the red and hairy one appeared first, his heel was held by his brother's hand. Here we have another baby's hand, popping out for a moment but then disappearing, ribbon and all. The boy who then appears refuses to be in second position, just like Jacob. He is called Peres, and his true contribution to the national history appears, not in the Book of *Tolᵉdoth* that is Genesis, but elsewhere: in that

---

[32] If we take elements B and C together (or even ABCDE) and count the numbers of spoken words in ABCDE, X, C' and B', we get an ascending series of 28 - 30 - 32 - 34 words respectively. This points to B' as the climax (A' contains no more than seven spoken words); no surprise to the reader, as B' is the denouement and the moment of Tamar's triumph.

[33] I mention two details with respect to the balance of A and A'. In segment A there is a chain of three times *wtld*, ending with בלדתה. Segment A' starts with two times בלדתה and then has a nicely variant piʻel form referring to the midwife, *myldt*. In the Masoretic text, the two elements are unexpectedly complementary. Under A the name-giving is twice assigned to the mother, in vv.4-5 (after one masc. form of קרא in v.3), but in A' the verb denoting name-giving both times has a masculine form: vv.29e//30b.

singular *tol*ᵉ*doth* list which constitutes the ending of the book of Ruth. Counting down from Judah via his son Peres, and much later passing Boaz amongst others, there are ten generations to Israel's most famous king, the Judahite David. And this genealogical distance or number of generations is exactly the same as the distance from Adam to Noah (Genesis 5) and after that, the number of generations from Noah to Abraham.

Just as Rebeccah's confinement is the main precedent to Tamar's, so the birth of the competing Peres and Zerah is the main antecedent of another genealogical surprise in ch.48:12-20. Just before dying, the father of the nation gives his blessing to Ephraim and Manasseh, the sons of his beloved Joseph, but is still vital enough to play his last Jacobean trick. He crosses his hands, so that the order of the two grandsons is reversed. A shocked witness, Joseph starts to protest, to no avail. These scenes may be very familiar to the reader, but they deserve to be mentioned here because their connections with ch.38 are one set among many links that helps to integrate the Judah-Tamar story which has been misconceived by historical-critical scholarship as an interpolation so tenaciously for so long.

In the last section of this article I propose to discuss four topics of increasing importance. First I would like to study the workings of the ternary principle here. Secondly, I will return to the recognition scene and show how far is the reach, and consequently the integrating power, of the keyword **nkr*. Thirdly, on our way to the heart of the matter we will need to pay attention to the isotopy of seeing and not-seeing, of knowing and not-knowing, and assess the emblematic aspects of several names. Finally, the purpose of the story and its functioning in the cycle as a whole can be indicated. We will meet the key word *'rb*, study its relation to Judah, and recognize his growth and unique contribution.

1. *The ternary principle* does not allow itself to remain hidden. It hits the eye at the start and at the centre of the story, when three sons are born to Judah and three objects of value are handed to Tamar as a pledge. The use of "three" as an ordering device is so pervasive that we would actually be able to retell most of the story by simply stepping from one triplet to another along the linear axis. The three births in the exposition are supported by the threefold use of *wtld*, which is followed three times by the act of name-giving. The word "seed" forms a cluster in vv.8d + 9ac. At the start of the exposition, and at the beginning and in the first and last paragraphs of the central section (v.1c, 12d and 20a), Hirah's position is defined in relation to Judah: he is "a man/his friend from Adullam".

Defining somebody in relation to Judah is a technique the author also applies to Tamar. She first receives an accurate family term when she is called his "daughter-in-law" (*kallah*) three times, in vv.11a, 16d, 24c. This status of hers proves not quite permanent as soon as Judah decides to be negligent about the postponed contact between his third son and Tamar. Her being a daughter-in-law is almost lost from sight and is in danger of being obscured by her new state of widowhood: she is called *'almanah* by Judah himself (which in retrospect, and in view of the soliloquy the narrator offers us in v.11e, is sneaky). Later, however, she deals sovereignly with "her widowhood" (vv.14a + 19c, the ring on clothing) and is able to put it on and off as she would a piece of textile.

These labels for Tamar are two triplets taken from familial vocabulary. But there are two more triplets in store for her that are more or less judgmental, and refer to sexual behaviour. Three times she is called a q^edeshah, and three times the root *znh* is applied to her. The one triplet compares to the other as a euphemism to a four-letter word. The less offensive term is used consistently in direct discourse, and its trio sticks together, in the sequence on Hirah's unsuccessful search. The word 'whore' is each time related (vv.15b, 24cd) to the perspective of Judah and his milieu; a usage which is not exactly flattering to the father-in-law. Note how *zonah*, in v.15b Judah's (wrong) assessment of the woman along the road, becomes *zan^etah*, the preterite form of what could for one moment be seen as a merely neutral piece of information, and finally hardens into a noun form that is a downright accusation: z^enunim, a plurale tantum. - All in all, Tamar now has received, or shall we say endured, four times three = twelve (!) labels, and immediately after the twelfth one, Judah explodes, v.24ef: burn the whore! From that moment on, there is no label left for Tamar any more.

Narrated space gets two triplets too, in the central part. The name of the town Timnah is used three times in the specific form of the locative, *timnátah*, vv.12d, 13b, 14d. (Below, I will discuss its alliterative connections with the key words '*alm^enutah* and *ntn*.) This town marks the direction in which three people go: the two friends for a celebration, and the woman in disguise. The latter, who is our heroine of course, is positioned "along the road" three times: vv.14d, 16a, 21b.

As soon as Judah has sighted the harlot, he demands intercourse. The verb for it is the hollow root בוא, and it appears in a singular form that refers to Judah, in the neat order of first, second and third person.[34] The three occurrences are in vv.16d, 16h, 18f. Judah offers the harlot a kid in payment, and this g^edi (*ha'izzim*) is mentioned three times, each time as the object of the verb "to send", *šlh*; see vv.17b, 20a, 23d.

Because Judah has no goat on a leash, Tamar demands a pledge. This word '*erabon* will turn out to be the spearhead of the key word technique (*Leitwortstil*, to quote Martin Buber). It is the focal point of the pivotal sequence X (the negotiations, three plus three speeches), in line with the fact that this pledge quickly eclipses the goat and becomes the stakes of the deal. It occurs in vv.17d, 18b, and 20a.[35] Its prime importance is definitively established in the denouement, of course. In passing, I note that the narrator has studiously avoided to use the word itself in that paragraph, in order not to spoil its crucial contribution to the total network of triplets. Instead, what we find in v.25e are the three objects - another trio, v.25e, summed up by the heroine herself, as a direct reminder of v.18d, where she was the person to bring them to our attention in the first place.

After Hirah's failure to trace the woman and retrieve the pledge - three times 'to find' cancelled by the negation, as we saw - the narrator takes a special measure in

---

[34] See also note 29 above, on the verb מצא, which is used in a similar way.

[35] The pledge is part of a chiasmus with the verb 'to give' in vv.17d + 18b (question and answer), and becomes the object of the verb 'to take' in v.20a.

his ternary fabric. He brings the numeral "three" itself into play and puts it in a conspicuous place, as the crucial word of the threshold (v.24a) which provides the date for the climax. In the aftermath (vv.27-30) we find the verb ילד three times (vv.27a//28a, 28c), as well as the root פרץ (a tight cluster, v.29de), and the verb יצא (vv.28e, 29b, 30a). Earlier, the conception that was the object of Tamar's stunning move and therefore crucial to the central event, was denoted by a threefold הרה, in vv.18g, 24d, and 25c.

2. *The recognition motif.* What exactly is the offence that can be held against Judah? It is the neglect consisting of wilful "not giving" [Tamar to Shelah]. The importance of this definition can be shown only when we consider one more triplet, that of "not giving". First, I have to distinguish between the occurrences of the verb "to give" within and those outside the central event (vv.16-18). The verb occurs three times in the central exchange of direct discourse, and its implementation (the pledge being given to her) is the fourth occurrence, which, coming from the narrator, clinches the deal.[35] However, the triplet of not giving outside the centre is much more interesting. It enables the reader to discover an ugly juxtaposition that can do Judah's reputation no good. His admission in v.26 to having failed to give Tamar to his youngest son, לא נתתיה, covers what the heroine had established for herself in v.14: "she saw that Shelah had grown up, yet she had not been given to him as a wife (לא נתנה)." This realization exposes Judah's neglect, as the words of v.14ef - almost a free indirect speech by Tamar - mirror the words "until my son Shelah grows up" which Judah himself had spoken with Tamar as his addressee. Rereading the whole of verse 11, we find another instance of studious avoidance. Sending Tamar away, Judah seems to speak reassuringly. He suggests that he will not forget her, but will pursue the levirate business and accordingly give her to Shelah, but he does not say so explicitly! He seems to make a promise to his daughter-in-law, but the appropriate text is simply not there, and consequently he has not really committed himself. The true extent of this kind of misleading, however, emerges when we trace the third occurrence of "not giving". It is the line that defines the original sense of onanism, v.9c. Onan is so heartless to repeatedly "spoil his seed on the ground, so as not to give offspring to his brother." His object is marked by the exceptional form of the infinitive (n^e*ton* instead of the usual *tet*). The triplet on *ntn* invites the reader to make the connection: this criminal act of withholding seed is to a certain degree committed by Onan's father as well. The main difference is that Judah thinks he looks much less callous than his second son and is very skilful in covering his tracks. Fortunately, the only person whom he makes a fool of is himself. His is a blatant underestimation of his daughter-in-law's awareness and family loyalty.

Such is the lesson of the recognition scene. Through this climax, the entire story of disguise and disclosure appears as a bridge between Gen 31 and 37 on the one hand, and Gen 44-45 on the other. The link between Gen 31 and Tamar's revelation is even stronger than the link with "Joseph in Dothan". The confrontations Laban has to go through with Rachel and Jacob are caused by a woman, focus on multiple and tangible objects (compare these idols with the prestigious three objects constituting Judah's pledge), turn on recognition (which does not materialize in Gen

31, surely to Laban's great frustration) and are a matter of life and death. Death is
a serious threat and carries the legal connotation of punishment in chs.31 and 38
equally.

The points of comparison between 37:31-34 and the central event plus denouement
in ch.38 are by now obvious: deception by means of clothing, recognition, the death
aspect (real to Jacob, a threat to Tamar, imposed as a verdict by Judah). Note how
Jacob and Judah shift to parallel positions of powerless fathers as they both stare at
material objects, are tremendously shocked and can do nothing but speak words of
recognition.

   Perhaps the most weighty point of comparison lies in identity being at stake.
Joseph's identity seems an obvious conclusion to Jacob, with the bloody tunic in his
hands. Judah's identity is at stake in various ways. It is referred to by the three
objects that to a great extent are simple means of identification. But having
apparently lost them for three long and perhaps unnerving months, Judah finally gets
to a position where he can no longer avoid to raise the question of his spiritual
identity. Is he really a father-in-law? Is his fear of death more important than loyalty
to his family, Tamar included? Can he claim to be mature and humane? Such is the
moral and spiritual lesson of the circumstances which emerge and, by their nature,
metonymically and symbolically point to Judah's heart.

   Just after having received this spectacular lesson, Judah is the main speaker in
chs.43 and 44. In 43:8-10 he is the only one of the brothers who is able to convince
Jacob to send Benjamin to Egypt and its formidable vizier. One of the most salient
words he uses is the root *'rb*. In ch.44 he delivers the speech and achieves the,
desired, effect on the supposed Egyptian. This long stretch of direct discourse
together with the beginning of ch.45 constitutes the well-known and touching
denouement of the cycle and its macroplot. Several occurrences of **nkr* mark this
turning point. They show the dialectical skill of the author, as they explore the
semantic field that separates and unites various meanings of the root, such as 'being
a stranger', i.e. 'being unrecognized' (the hitpa'el of *nkr*) versus 'making oneself
known'. The dynamics of this is anticipated in 42:8, with its yes/no structure: "For
though Joseph recognized his brothers, they did not recognize him."

   3. In all these cases, from Gen 27 (of blind father Isaac) all the way down to
ch.45, recognition and non-recognition are bound up with seeing. This brings me to
the isotopy of seeing and knowing which pervades all of Gen 38 as a network. Its
most surprising point is that the story is about opening people's eyes; opening
Judah's eyes, that is, as Tamar has chosen to take up a strategical position at Petach
Enaim. A prig might say that this place can not be found on the map of ancient
Israel, and pride himself on being so learned. The sensitive reader understands that
the name is an emblem, having its place on the map of human growth and morals.
It is the signpost meant for Judah so that he can reassess his place on the map.

   Until now, I have studiously avoided to say that the writer is brilliant, but the time
has come to recognize his art - one aspect of which is his consummate handling of
alliteration. It is no coincidence that *timnátah* (a triplet) is connected to all the
consonants of *ntn* (the triplet concerning the refusal to give) and that its own
consonants, all of them, recur in the word *'almᵉnut*, widowhood (part of a third

triplet). We come to understand that Timnah marks the area where Judah

a) gives his seed to Tamar and
b) does not know it is the widow Tamar who is his partner in sex;
a') is seduced because he failed to give his son to Tamar, and
b') is asked to give as a pledge three objects that represent his identity.
Elements a-a' represent the truth, elements b-b' function at the level of ignorance.

The author/narrator has exploited the phonological possibilities of the two geographical names and expanded their range of effects greatly by opening up emblematic and metaphorical meanings. This creative play at several levels (sounds, words, motifs, structure) is supported by a network of terms relating to vision. It is not for nothing that the eyes of the Lord are present in the text as early as the exposition. It will not do to dismiss them in a reductionistic gesture by saying they are just part of hackneyed formulaic language (vv.7a // 10a). In this way the first spot where morality and judgment become explicit, i.e. are verbalized, belongs to the deity and his vision. His eyes are related to the very behaviour which triggers Tamar's daunting enterprise, and which much later will be fiercely criticized by her in deeds rather than words.

The next application of the isotopy of seeing is in verse 14, at the Door of Perception (freely translating Petach Enaim, with a wink in the direction of Huxley). Covering herself with a veil, Tamar prevents any seeing. Her sitting in Petach Enaim is directly linked to her own seeing: she has seen that Shelah had grown up and that Judah had neglected the follow-up. This kind of seeing can not be separated from insight, that is, knowledge. Comes verse 15, segment E of the concentric pattern. This trio of very short clauses even puts seeing in front, and ends with "her face" and another occurrence of "covering" = hiding. This time, however, the terms of vision demonstrate Judah's ignorance. Seeing is here the opposite of knowing.

Hirah's search also becomes part of the unfolding network of seeing and knowing versus not-knowing. He looks in vain for the woman. This now becomes, in a kind of metonymical or metaphorical way, a parallel to Judah's particular kind of perception: seeing yes, knowing no. In the paragraph containing the climax, the pregnant Tamar plays the rôle of a midwife (in the Socratic sense) to Judah: she helps him to see after many years of blindness. Finally he sees the map, his place on it, the truth. Recognizing is seeing is understanding. The opposition 'seeing' versus 'knowing' is cancelled.

Judah was in Kezib, when Shelah was born. Perhaps this place name is another emblem. The root *kzb* means 'lie', and the lie in Judah's life that launches this whole affair is connected with his (failure in) handling the third son. Elsewhere in Canaanite territory, a woman with a veil will lay the foundation of the truth in him. The spot is honoured by receiving its own name, Petach Enaim, and so becomes the opposite to Kezib.

4. *The pledge, standing in for somebody, substitution.* From the concordance on the Hebrew Bible we learn that the one word that unites the three personal objects, *'erabon*, the word that refers to the crucial attributes and occurs a triplet, does not

occur anywhere else in the Hebrew Bible. Next, we discover that the verb *'rb* occurs two more times in the cycle of the three J's, and nowhere else in the Torah. Moreover, the verb is used both times by Judah as a speaker, and in each text, 43:9 and 44:32, refers to the same act: Judah standing in for Benjamin, the youngest sibling and Joseph's only full brother. The first addressee is Jacob, the second is Joseph (still unrecognized):

> 43:9   I myself will be surety for him;   אנכי אערבנו
>   you may hold me responsible: מידי תבקשנו
>   if I do not bring him back to you and set him before you,
>   I shall stand guilty before you forever.
> 44:32f Your servant has pledged himself for the boy to the father,
>   saying, 'If I do not bring him back to you,
>   I shall stand guilty before my father forever.'
>   Therefore, please let your servant remain as a slave to my
>   lord instead of the boy,
>   and let the boy go back with his brothers.

To bring back the boy to his father: that is what Reuben had wanted, but failed to accomplish.[36] The writer allows Judah to bring it off. It is a time of *ra'abon*, famine; the solution, Judah says and knows from personal experiences with substitution, is *'erabon*, and *re'uben* is not important any more.[37]

Genesis 38 is filled to the brim with substitutions. The three objects for identification are substitutes for the kid, which is the substitute for paying, which is the commercial exchange and substitute for the visit to a whore, which is the substitute for intercourse between Shelah and Tamar, which should have been the legal substitute for Onan giving his seed to her, which was the legal substitute for Tamar conceiving from her husband. The searching Hirah replaces Judah, and the twins are also involved in a struggle of substitution (who will be the firstborn?).

The inner side of substitution is beyond Judah, until he has gone through this whole chain of substitutions and learns from it that people ought to be their brother's keeper. At the root of his negligence towards Tamar is his fear of death

---

[36] Note that Reuben is there in 42:37, in vain trying to convince Jacob he will return his son. The word for hunger and drought, *ra'"bon*, is frequent from 41:27 on, when Joseph explains the seven lean/empty cows/ears as seven years of famine.

[37] Under the entry *z'qunim*, a plurale tantum that is chillingly similar to *z'nunim*, the concordance tells us that this substantive for "old age" occurs as two pairs in Genesis, and is not found anywhere else in the entire Bible. The first pair occurs in one short unit, the birth of Isaac (who is Abraham's son of old age), and the second pair is split between Joseph (who apparently drops out) and his younger brother, Benjamin. I invite the reader to think through the semantic consequences of this pairing of pairs, Gen 21:2 and 7, and 37:3 (narrator) plus 44:20 (Judah speaking!), about Benjamin being Jacob's son of old age - an obvious substitute for 37:3). Here, I only want to stress that this touch is one more indication that Judah belongs firmly to the final cycle of Genesis and that the composition of this book is integrated much more solidly than so often is assumed (concordance in the teeth of so much discordance).

which prevents him from standing in for family members. The outcome is that Tamar represents life instead of death, and bears him two children as substitutes for Er and Onan.[38]

Judah's speech in ch.44 is the longest of the cycle. Judah is the spokesman of the group, he has become the most important brother. He already was the decisive speaker in Dothan. In ch.38 he goes through a growth process that prepares and equips him for the difficult task ahead, when Joseph turns up, many years after the pit incident. This hard-won maturity lends authority to Judah's speeches to his father in ch.43 and to Joseph in ch.44. His offer to stand in for Benjamin is entirely credible. The poetry of Gen 49 underlines the prominent positions of Joseph and Judah amongst the brothers. Each brother gets one strophe (one to three full poetic lines) from the father who distributes blessings, except Judah and Joseph. They both get an entire stanza: vv.8-12 (three strophes) is the eight-verse stanza for Judah, vv.22-26 is the nine-line stanza for Joseph (again three strophes).[39]

The many plays on sounds and words, the use of key words, the isotopies of disguise and deception, of crime and recognition, of ignorance and identity which link Gen 38 to its immediate and wider contexts firmly keep this chapter in place. It stands where it belongs and where it was put by a brilliant artist, right from the genesis of Genesis on.

Short bibliography

H. Bauer & P. Leander, *Historische Grammatik der Hebräischen Sprache*, Halle 1922 (= Hildesheim 1965).

G.Beer & R.Meyer, *Hebräische Grammatik*, Berlin 1972.

C. Brockelmann, *Hebräische Syntax*, Neukirchen 1956.

W. Gesenius & E. Kautzsch, *Hebräische Grammatik*, 28th edition, Leipzig 1909.

P.Joüon & T. Muraoka, *A Grammar of Biblical Hebrew*, Roma 1991 (2nd edition, translated from the French: Joüon, *Grammaire de l'Hébreu biblique*, Rome 1928 and 1947).

NAG: J.P. Fokkelman, *Narrative Art in Genesis*, Assen 1975 (reprinted, 2nd edition, Sheffield 1991).

NAPS: J.P. Fokkelman, *Narrative Art and Poetry in the Books of Samuel, a full interpretation based on stylistic and structural analyses*, Assen 1981-1993, four volumes.

B.K. Waltke & M. O'Connor, *An Introduction to biblical Hebrew Syntax*, Winona Lake Indiana, 1990.

---

[38] The ethical aspects presupposed and/or raised by Gen 38 are covered well by Thomas Krüger, Genesis 38 - ein "Lehrstück" alttestamentlicher Ethik, pp.205-226 of: *Konsequente Traditionsgeschichte*, Festschrift für Klaus Baltzer zum 65. Geburtstag, = OBO 126, herausgegeben von Rüdiger Bartelmus, Thomas Krüger und Helmut Utzschneider.

[39] My last exercise in the ternary technique: Judah gets three times three speeches from the author: three in the exposition, three in the pivotal sequence, and three afterwards (vv.23-26).

"Joseph in Dothan" (Gen 37:18-36) in a colometrical typography

18	a	ויראו אתו מרחק
	b	ובטרם יקרב אליהם
	c	ויתנכלו אתו להמיתו
19	a	ויאמרו איש אל אחיו
	b	הנה בעל החלמות הלזה בא
20	a	ועתה לכו ונהרגהו
	b	ונשלכהו באחד הברות
	c	ואמרנו
	d	חיה רעה אכלתהו
	e	ונראה מה יהיו חלמתיו
21	a	וישמע ראובן
	b	ויצלהו מידם
	c	ויאמר
	d	לא נכנו נפש
22	a	ויאמר אלהם ראובן
	b	אל תשפכו דם
	c	השליכו אתו אל הבור הזה אשר במדבר
	d	ויד אל תשלחו בו
	e	למען הציל אתו מידם
	f	להשיבו אל אביו
23	a	ויהי כאשר בא יוסף אל אחיו
	b	ויפשיטו את יוסף את כתנתו
	c	את כתנת הפסים אשר עליו
24	a	ויקחהו וישלכו אתו הברה
	b	והבור רק
	c	אין בו מים
25	a	וישבו לאכל לחם
	b	וישאו עיניהם ויראו
	c	והנה ארחת ישמעאלים באה מגלעד
	d	וגמליהם נשאים נכאת וצרי ולט
	e	הולכים להוריד מצרימה

26 a ויאמר יהודה אל אחיו
b מה בצע
c כי נהרג את אחינו
d וכסינו את דמו
27 a לכו ונמכרנו לישמעאלים
b וידנו אל תהי בו
c כי אחינו בשרנו הוא
d וישמעו אחיו
28 a ויעברו אנשים מדינים סחרים
b וימשכו ויעלו את יוסף מן הבור
c וימכרו את יוסף לישמעאלים בעשרים כסף
d ויביאו את יוסף מצרימה

29 a וישב ראובן אל הבור
b והנה אין יוסף בבור
c ויקרע את בגדיו
30 a וישב אל אחיו
b ויאמר
c הילד איננו
d ואני אנה אני בא

31 a ויקחו את כתנת יוסף
b וישחטו שעיר עזים
c ויטבלו את הכתנת בדם
32 a וישלחו את כתנת הפסים
b ויביאו אל אביהם
c ויאמרו
d זאת מצאנו
e הכר נא הכתנת בנך הוא אם לא
33 a ויכירה
b ויאמר
c כתנת בני
d חיה רעה אכלתהו
e טרף טרף יוסף
34 a ויקרע יעקב שמלתיו
b וישם שק במתניו
c ויתאבל על בנו ימים רבים
35 a ויקמו כל בניו וכל בנתיו לנחמו
b וימאן להתנחם
c ויאמר
d כי ארד אל בני אבל שאלה
e ויבך אתו אביו
36 a והמדנים מכרו אתו אל מצרים לפוטיפר סריס פרעה שר הטבחים

The text of Genesis 38 in a colometrical typography

ויהי בעת ההוא	a	1
וירד יהודה מאת אחיו	b	
ויט עד איש עדלמי ושמו חירה	c	
וירא שם יהודה בת איש כנעני ושמו שוע	a	2
ויקחה ויבא אליה	b	
ותהר ותלד בן	a	3
ויקרא את שמו ער	b	
ותהר עוד ותלד בן	a	4
ותקרא את שמו אונן	b	
ותסף עוד ותלד בן	a	5
ותקרא את שמו שלה	b	
והיה בכזיב בלדתה אתו	c	
ויקח יהודה אשה לער בכורו ושמה תמר	a	6
ויהי ער בכור יהודה רע בעיני יהוה	a	7
וימתהו יהוה	b	
ויאמר יהודה לאונן	a	8
בא אל אשת אחיך	b	
ויבם אתה	c	
והקם זרע לאחיך	d	
וידע אונן כי לא לו יהיה הזרע	a	9
והיה אם בא אל אשת אחיו	b	
ושחת ארצה לבלתי נתן זרע לאחיו	c	
וירע בעיני יהוה אשר עשה	a	10
וימת גם אתו	b	
ויאמר יהודה לתמר כלתו	a	11
שבי אלמנה בית אביך	b	
עד יגדל שלה בני	c	
כי אמר	d	
פן ימות גם הוא כאחיו	e	
ותלך תמר	f	
ותשב בית אביה	g	

12 a וירבו הימים
b ותמת בת שוע אשת יהודה
c וינחם יהודה
d ויעל על גזזי צאנו הוא וחירה רעהו העדלמי תמנתה
13 a ויגד לתמר לאמר
b הנה חמיך עלה תמנתה לגז צאנו
14 a ותסר בגדי אלמנותה מעליה
b ותכס בצעיף
c ותתעלף
d ותשב בפתח עינים אשר על דרך תמנתה
e כי ראתה כי גדל שלה
f והוא לא נתנה לו לאשה
15 a וירא יהודה
b ויחשבה לזונה
c כי כסתה פניה

16 a ויט אליה אל הדרך
b ויאמר
c הבה נא
d אבוא אליך
e כי לא ידע כי כלתו הוא
f ותאמר
g מה תתן לי
h כי תבוא אלי
17 a ויאמר
b אנכי אשלח גדי עזים מן הצאן
c ותאמר
d אם תתן ערבון עד שלחך
18 a ויאמר
b מה הערבון אשר אתן לך
c ותאמר
d חתמך ופתילך ומטך אשר בידך

e ויתן לה
f ויבא אליה
g ותהר לו
19 a ותקם ותלך
b ותסר צעיפה מעליה
c ותלבש בגדי אלמנותה

20 a   וישלח יהודה את גדי העזים ביד רעהו העדלמי לקחת הערבון מיד האשה
   b   ולא מצאה
21 a   וישאל את אנשי מקמה לאמר
   b   איה הקדשה הוא בעינים על הדרך
   c   ויאמרו
   d   לא היתה בזה קדשה
22 a   וישב אל יהודה
   b   ויאמר
   c   לא מצאתיה
   d   וגם אנשי המקום אמרו
   e   לא היתה בזה קדשה
23 a   ויאמר יהודה
   b   תקח לה
   c   פן נהיה לבוז
   d   הנה שלחתי הגדי הזה
   e   ואתה לא מצאתה

24 a   ויהי כמשלש חדשים
   b   ויגד ליהודה לאמר
   c   זנתה תמר כלתך
   d   וגם הנם הרה לזנונים
   e   ויאמר יהודה
   f   הוציאוה ותשרף
25 a   הוא מוצאת
   b   והיא שלחה אל חמיה לאמר
   c   לאיש אשר אלה לו אנכי הרה
   d   ותאמר
   e   הכר נא למי החתמת והפתילים והמטה האלה
26 a   ויכר יהודה
   b   ויאמר
   c   צדקה ממני
   d   כי על כן לא נתתיה לשלה בני
   e   ולא יסף עוד לדעתה

27 a ויהי בעת לדתה
   b והנה תאומים בבטנה
28 a ויהי בלדתה
   b ויתן יד
   c ותקח המילדת
   d ותקשר על ידו שני לאמר
   e זה יצא ראשונה
29 a ויהי כמשיב ידו
   b והנה יצא אחיו
   c ותאמר
   d מה פרצת עליך פרץ
   e ויקרא שמו פרץ
30 a ואחר יצא אחיו אשר על ידו השני
   b ויקרא שמו זרח

KNOWING YAHWEH
EXOD 6:3 IN THE CONTEXT OF GENESIS 1–EXODUS 15

LYLE ESLINGER

1. The history of the phrase & the problem

A. Zimmerli's work

The phrase "and you shall know that I am Yahweh" is a direct divine utterance that seems to reveal a great deal about the biblical God's intentions for the human experience of history. The phrase is only common in two biblical texts, in the exodus narrative in the book of Exodus and throughout the book of Ezekiel.[1] These recollections of exodus and exile, the two axial events in biblical Israel's history, explore the manner and significance of God's intervention in human history and how he is revealed through these cataclysmic historical events. Consistently, the human existential context in which the phrase is significant is one of violence and disaster. Human suffering, both Israel's and that of its captors, is an inseparable element of the numinous events. The Israelites are the historical focal point of these interventions, either surrendered to the clutches of the nations or rescued from them. In this setting of national and personal existential crisis it is Yahweh's hope that he may be "known" through his miraculous interventions involving Israel in history. The deity thinks that these experiences of disaster will bring all concerned, Israel and the nations alike, to "know Yahweh."

In the early 1950's, Walther Zimmerli did the basic work on this motif, primarily in regard to the book of Ezekiel, but also considering the book of Exodus.[2] Zimmerli thought that he had discovered an Israelite historiography that found only relative value in the events of Israel's history. "God's acts do not occur for their own sake, but rather are directed at human beings; they mean to influence human beings and to create knowledge in them — and that also means, as we shall later see more clearly, to elicit from them acknowledgement of Yahweh. Yahweh acts because he wants to effect this acknowledgement among human beings."[3] Historical events, even

---

[1] Occurrences in other books are comparatively rare: Deut 29:5 (6 Eng.); 1 Kgs 20:13, 28; Isa 45:3; 49:23, 26; 60:16; Hos 2:22 (20 Eng.); Joel 2:27; 4:17 (3:17 Eng.).

[2] W. Zimmerli, "Ich bin Yahweh," *Geschichte und Altes Testament. Beiträge zur historischen Theologie 16. Albrecht Alt zum 70. Geburtstag dargebracht* (J.C.B. Mohr (Paul Siebeck): Tübingen, 1953) 179–209; *Erkenntnis Gottes nach dem Buch Ezechiel* (Zwingli Ver.: Zürich, 1954)..

[3] "Knowledge of God According to the Book of Ezekiel," p. 37. References are according to the English translation of D.W. Stott in the collection of Zimmerli's essays entitled *I Am Yahweh* (Atlanta: John Knox Press, 1982).

crucial ones like the exile and exodus, are means to an end — what Zimmerli calls the real dynamic behind the story, the revelation of Yahweh's name. Zimmerli's work uncovered a neglected element in biblical historiography, a gnostic sub-theme that would find its strongest echo only much later (and through the rather distant channel of the philosophical traditions in Islam, Judaism, and Christianity) in Western thought on transcendence and the meaning of immanence. Even where Israel's history had risen to the level of a peak experience, it is not the particular course of history that is significant on this view. Rather, it is the experience of divinity in that hour. It is, nevertheless, traditional to construe the tale so that it is the historical consequence, liberation from Egypt or return from Exile, that occupies our attention, thus distracting our attention from the transcendental implications of these divine interventions.

By way of a close reading of the exodus story (Exod 1–15), I have explored some of the implications of this emphasis on revelation through catastrophe (Eslinger 1991). God delays delivering his people so that he can display his might (and himself) through the miracles. Freeing Israel from Egypt's power seems the point of the whole affair, but a careful look at the overall shape of these events, as we know them from the text, leads me to believe that liberation is subordinate to the manifestation of the divine name through the miraculous interventions. Traditionally, the miracles serve a dual purpose, but it becomes obvious that Yahweh controls the Pharaoh's response to the miracles and that he means to delay the departure in order to extend the historical revelation. To mention but one illustration of this intent, Yahweh, at least in private conversation between himself, Moses, and the Egyptian Pharaoh (Exod 10:1–2), is shameless about his apparent egotistic exhibitionism at the expense of a defenseless and suffering client. But such shamelessness is grounded in a divine purpose, which is precisely the revelation. To that end, the liberation of Israel is necessary but ancillary material, the 'potter's clay' (Jer 18:6). Something must indeed happen and it does; but all that does take place does so in order that the human participants, Egypt no less than Israel, "may know that I am Yahweh."[4]

B. The problem of Exod 6:3

The phrase — "that you may know that I am Yahweh"[5] — is the key to Exodus 6:3, itself a key for traditional historical-critical pentateuchal criticism. The verse has become difficult for translators, if only because of their unavoidable consciousness of the issues in pentateuchal criticism.[6] In Exod 6:3, we find the first biblical instance of the collocation of the verb "to know" (yd') with the name Yahweh or the accusative clause "that I am Yahweh" ($k\hat{\imath}$ $^{a}n\hat{\imath}$ $Yahweh$) as object. There is no need, here, to review the rich debate regarding this verse, which has played an important

---

[4] Exod 6:3, 7; 7:5, 17; 8:10, 22; 10:2; 14:4, 18. These trans-national revelations, along with those in the book of Ezekiel, are as expansive as any expression of universalism in the Bible.

[5] Zimmerli, as form critic, labeled the phrase with the nondescript form-critical tag "statement of recognition."

[6] Were it not for the issues of pentateuchal criticism, Exod 6:3 would pose little difficulty for translators, since its grammar and diction are only slightly unusual.

part in shaping the history of pentateuchal source criticism. R.W.L. Moberly (1992) has traced it well enough as a preface to his own novel solution to the source-critical analysis of the verse. But briefly stated, the problem that Exod 6:3 presents is that Yahweh's apparent attempt to unveil his name here ("by my name Yahweh I wasn't known to them") is gainsaid by many prior occurrences of the divine name in the book of Genesis. The contradiction can be sharpened with a little narrative analysis. Of the 148 individual uses of the name in Genesis, the majority belong to the narrator (96 instances), whose posterior, unconditioned knowledge need not be taken to undermine the validity of the statement exclaimed at any particular point in the unfolding history of the story world. But the contradiction, as commentators ought to have seen for a long time, exists even on the epistemological plane of the story world itself. In Exod 6:3 Yahweh says that the divine name proper, Yahweh, was not known before the historical moment of the exodus. But already in Gen 4:26, to take the stock example, one reads "at that time, men began to call on the name of Yahweh" (*'āz hûhal liqrō' bᵉšēm Yahweh*). For most readers, though the passage permits a contrary reading,[7] Gen 4:26 says that people at that point in history invoked the divine name. In fact, this business of human characters uttering the name of Yahweh can be traced back even further, to the very beginnings of human history. In Gen 4:1, Eve herself said, "I have created a man with Yahweh" (Gen 4:1, *qānîtî 'îš 'et-Yahweh*). A crucial assumption underlying the recognition of these obvious contradictions is that to use the name requires that one "know" the name. This seemingly innocent axiom has initiated many a tree's fall to the source critic's pen.

C. The two solutions

Two main pathways have been beaten round the riddle of Exod 6:3 and the question of how to translate it: a.) the conservative confessional solution, primarily harmonistic reading; and b.) the modern critical solution, which uses the discrepancy as an entry point into the literary history of the Pentateuch. The contradiction is resolved, in the latter solution, by taking it as evidence of the diverse compositional forces that created the existing biblical text. In the simple terms of pentateuchal source analysis, Gen 4:26 is J and Exod 6:3 is P. In the former, the most common tactic in support of harmonistic readings is to offer a nuanced translation and understanding of the key phrase, "but by my name Yahweh I was not known to them" (*ûšᵉmî Yahweh lō' nôdaʿtî lāhem*). Such translators assume that there is no real contradiction and then try to reform their initial response to the verse so as to convey a veiled complementarity between it and the book of Genesis. According to Moberly, the plain sense of the uncomplicated Hebrew in Exod 6:3 is the biggest obstacle to harmonistic readings of the passage. "... if it means what it says — or appears to say — the harmonizing approach is doomed" (p. 55). "The necessary strategy, therefore, is to retranslate and/or reinterpret the Hebrew so that it says something else. The difficulty, however, is that the Hebrew presents no serious difficulty. This has meant

---

[7] That is, that Gen 4:26 expresses a narratorial assessment of what humans were actually doing, however ignorant they may have been of whom it was they addressed in their prayers.

that, although several ingenious retranslations[8] have been offered, there is no
unanimity that any particular rendering has pinpointed the matter of grammar, syntax,
or vocabulary that has been supposedly misconstrued in the conventional rendering"
(pp. 55-56).

Since the source critical solution to Exod 6:3 would not even exist if there were
no contradiction, the logical beginning for any new approach to the verse or its
translation is harmonistic interpretation. Moberly summarizes the logic of harmonistic
readings as follows: "The essence of the approach is to argue that what is new in
Exodus 3 and 6 is not the name YAHWEH as such but rather the meaning of the
name. If it is the giving of a new and distinctive content to an already familiar name
that is the meaning of Exodus 3 and 6, then the apparent contradiction with Gen.
4:26, etc., is resolved" (Moberly 1992:53). Moberly traces the history of this
interpretive avenue back to Targum Ps-Jonathan and applauds it as "the most obvious
way of reading the text" (p. 53). But in the end, he thinks that such harmonistic
readings have two fatal weaknesses: i) one must suppose that though the patriarchs
knew and used the name Yahweh, it was "meaningless to them, a mere sound
without significance" (p. 65); ii) a survey of the usage of Yahweh in the book of
Genesis indicates no difference in significance from that following Exod 6:3. We
shall see that the context of the collocation *yd'* + *Yahweh* in the book of Exodus
makes point one significant, though not as Moberly thinks; so far as point two is
concerned, the equation between the collocated use of Yahweh and its non-collocated
use in Genesis will prove incommensurable.

Moberly's new solution
Though his critique might seem to force us to a source-critical solution, Moberly
spins another twist on the harmonistic yarn. His new solution combines aspects of
traditional harmonistic reading with the historical concerns of traditional pentateuchal
criticism. The glue that holds these two contraries together is an insight implicitly
relying on narrative ontology. Moberly, however, does not explicitly draw on
narrative theory. Though he rejects conservative harmonistic solutions, his new
solution respects the fundamental attitude in this approach, which "represents the
most obvious way of reading the text" (Moberly 1992:53). He summarizes his thesis:
"in principle the use of YAHWEH in Genesis 12–50 conveys the perspective of the
Yahwistic storytellers, who are retelling originally non-Yahwistic traditions in a
Yahwistic context, and as they appropriate the stories for Yahwism, so they tend to

---

[8] Moberly supplies the following samples: "I am Jehovah; and I appeared to Abraham, Isaac, and Jacob
as God Almighty; and did I not (or, of course I did) let myself be known to them as to my name
Jehovah (?)" (G.R. Driver); "I showed myself to Abraham, Israel and Jacob ... I made myself known
to them" (F.I. Andersen, who claims that we must recognize the negative particle, *lō'*, as assertative
[*The Sentence in Biblical Hebrew* (Mouton: The Hague, 1974), p. 102]); "And I showed myself to
Abraham, to Isaac, and to Jacob in the character of El Shaddai, but in the character expressed by my
name Yahweh I did not make myself known to them" (J.A. Motyer). Moberly rejects all such nuances
because they suggest only the possibility of a distinction between acquaintance with the name and
knowledge of its significance (p. 58). It is equally possible, he says, to read the text as affirming that
neither the name nor its meaning were conveyed to the patriarchs.

use the familiar name of their God" (p. 70). The pentateuchal record is, by his reckoning, consistent: Yahweh is first revealed in the exodus events (Exodus 3, a revelation reaffirmed in Exodus 6); instances of the name prior to the revelation in Exodus 3:14–15 should be understood as the anachronistic perspective of Yahwistic tradents.[9]

2. Building on Moberly

Moberly's suggestion opens an avenue to the problem of Exodus 6:3 that requires further exploration. The key insight depends on an essential characteristic of all narrative literature, mediacy of presentation.[10] Mediacy of presentation includes the possibility that a narrator (tradent, in the jargon of tradition history) may codify a biblical character's words or thoughts in language appropriate to the world view of the narrator, but not that of the character. Moberly's suggestion is that the name Yahweh is anachronistic in the patriarchal narratives. The voice invoking the name Yahweh in the book of Genesis may be the voice of Abraham, but the authorial hands that record the dialogue are the hands of the Yahwist. The analogy illustrates Moberly's suggestion, but it also reveals a weakness from the perspective of narrative theory. The voices that utter the name in the book of Genesis are often precisely those of the characters speaking in direct discourse. It is Eve, for example, who says, "I have created a man with [the help of] Yahweh" (Gen 4:1) and there is no clear contextual warrant to deny her, the character in the story world, this usage. Of the 199 instances of the divine name from Genesis 1:1 to Exodus 6:3, 39 are explicitly attributed to a human character.[11] It is, of course, possible to assume that these represent the diction and mindset of the narrator/editor speaking through the characters. But one could as well assume, without methodological principle, the same for the other divine names or any other concept or idea conveyed in character speech. The issue requires a refined literary discernment and is not liable to be settled by apodictic assertions. Simply to assume that expressions containing the name Yahweh represent exclusive authorial perspective is too weak to withstand any amount of scrutiny. Only a careful and sensitive analysis of the pertinent passages can begin to define when we face the narrator speaking through a character and when not. So Moberly's suggestion needs refinement. Is the selection of characters who use the name Yahweh in direct discourse systematic? Is there some pattern of development from the first instance (Eve in Gen 4:1) to the last (Jacob in Gen 49:18)? How do those instances of the name relate to instances in which the narrating voice uses the

---

[9] I have simplified Moberly's argument to those aspects that concern the text of Exodus 6:3. He goes on to support it with extensive discussions of other texts and their place, along with Exod 6:3, in the history of Israelite religion.

[10] "Whenever a piece of news is conveyed, whenever something is reported, there is a mediator — the voice of a narrator is audible. I term this phenomenon 'mediacy' (*Mittelbarkeit*)" (Stanzel 1984:4).

[11] Abram/Abraham (5 x); Eliezer (8 x); Eve (1 x); Hagar (1 x); Isaac (3 x); Jacob (6 x); Laban (5 x); Lamech (1 x); Leah (3 x); Lot (1 x); messengers of Yahweh (1 x); Noah (1 x); Rachel (1 x); Sarai (2 x).

name, both on its own behalf and on behalf of a character in the mixed voicing known as free indirect discourse? Last, how do such categorizations of the data correspond to source-critical discriminations?

A. The need to study the collocation: yd' + Yahweh
The questions of voicing and perspective are important and need precise treatment if we want to make sense of usage patterns regarding the name Yahweh in Genesis and Exodus. The necessary reflection requires painstaking analysis of all occurrences in context. Such careful analysis is well suited to the dissertation genre, but not to the article length piece underway here.

Fortunately, so far as the particular problem of how to interpret and thus translate Exod 6:3 is concerned, there is a rather simple bit of work that can be done first and which, once accomplished, seems to bridge most of the quagmire that has developed around this verse. We need not first solve the complex matter of ultimate attribution in the possible cases of mixed character/narratorial voice. When reading straightforward narrative literature, it is only normal reading practise to assume, unless the narrative supplies clear counter-indications, that characters are given their due and allowed to speak for themselves. We do not usually suppose dramatic irony in a character voice unless there are contextual indicators to suggest unwittingly accurate irony. So assuming that the cast of Genesis characters are in possession, though not to say "knowledge," of the name of Yahweh, how may this rather large body of counter-evidence be squared with what Yahweh says about his name in Exodus 6:3?

The solution that I propose paves the way to a straightforward translation of Exod 6:3 and connects strongly to the marked thematic emphasis on "knowing Yahweh" in the exodus story. The key lies in the insufficiently attended lexical collocation *yd' + Yahweh*. The collocation is familiar, in the book of Exodus, in the phrase, "you shall know that I am Yahweh," of which "by my name Yahweh I was not known" (Exod 6:3) is a variant. A careful examination of all pentateuchal instances of the name Yahweh, looking at the epistemic or discourse contexts in which it occurs and particularly for prior instances of the collocation of the verb *yd'* followed by the name "Yahweh" or the phrase "that I am Yahweh" as object, has not been done. In such a review, one must take care to maintain whatever distinctions the text implies between the collocation and related terms. Given the technical nature of the phrase "knowing Yahweh" in Exodus and especially Ezekiel, we should refrain from assuming that it means the same as "calling on the name of Yahweh." Translators must ensure that assumptions about a supposed common significance of these phrases do not lead them to blur distinctions in translations based on the dynamic equivalence model.

My study of the books of Genesis and Exodus uncovers no occurrence of the collocation prior to Exod 5:2,[12] where the Egyptian pharaoh disclaims such knowledge.[13] In fact, a search for the collocation in the entire Hebrew Bible only discovers eight instances of near consummation, that is, wherein the act of knowing Yahweh is accomplished (see fn. 14). In none of these is there ever a positive assertion, on the part of the narrator or any character in the story world, that so-and-so actually knows or knew Yahweh. There are only denials and negations of such knowledge, statements that it had not yet been acquired, or wishful hopes, mostly on the part of Yahweh or his representative, that Israel or the nations will gain this knowledge. The implication for the interpretation of Exod 6:3 is obvious: there is no contradiction between what Yahweh claims here, that he has not hitherto been "known," and anything in the book of Genesis.

The translation of Exod 6:3 can proceed quite literally: "I appeared to Abraham, to Isaac, and to Jacob as El Shaddai, but by my name Yahweh I was not known to them." The logical basis for the source critical identification of this verse as a key P-passage — that it is contradicted by all those J-passages in the book of Genesis — is dissolved. What Yahweh claims is not that no one used the name, but that no one has ever known him by the name Yahweh. This simple solution to the crux of Exod 6:3 might be demeaned as lexical sleight of hand, were it not for the immense thematic and lexical importance attached to the collocation in the exodus story, a story that is just unfurling when Yahweh makes this pronouncement in ch. 6.

B. The collocation in context: knowing Yahweh through the exodus events
The knowledge of Yahweh is the fundamental purpose of all that occurs in the exodus story (Exod 6:7; 7:5, 17; 8:10, 22; 9:14, 29; 10:2; 11:7; 14:4, 18).[14] All else, even the supposedly central act of liberation, is subordinate to that purpose. Though there are many supports for such an opinion, especially those offered by the action

---

[12] The three graphs in the appendix show: 1) a steep rise in the number of occurrences of the name Yahweh in the exodus story; 2) the absence of the collocation *yd' + yhwh* in the book of Genesis; and 3) a significant clustering of occurrences of the collocation in the exodus story within the book of Exodus.

[13] Though there is not the least suggestion in the entire exodus theology of Genesis–Exodus that the pharaoh's effrontery in Exod 5:2 is the spark that provokes the miraculous *débâcle* unleashed against him (the whole affair is too well contrived for any such accident), it is a fitting bit of irony, presaging the lesson that he'll be taught (e.g., Exod 9:14–16). The first biblical incidence of the collocation is found in Exodus, precisely in the context where the motif becomes central to the biblical story. In Exod 5:2, Pharaoh says, "Who is Yahweh, that I should heed his voice and let Israel go? I do not know Yahweh (*lō' yāda'tî 'et-yhwh*), and moreover I will not let Israel go" (modified RSV). Here we have the first biblical character to deny knowledge of Yahweh. His remark is dramatically ironic, seen retrospectively by the reader when the business of "knowing Yahweh" is brought to centre stage in the devastating miracles to follow. The absence of any collocation of *yd' + yhwh* in the book of Genesis shows that there is no contradiction between what Yahweh says in Exod 6:3 and anything in the book of Genesis. Yahweh was, in fact, unknown by the patriarchs. As the following events in the exodus story make clear, and as many commentators have observed regarding occurrences of the collocation, one comes to know Yahweh only through his awesome interventions in human affairs.

[14] For the defence of this reading I refer the reader to a previous article (Eslinger 1991). The new reading requires article length treatment because it contradicts the traditional reading, on which confessional readers and critical scholarship have long found themselves in agreement.

sequences of Exodus 1–15, it will suffice to recall the logical possibility that Yahweh might have imposed the last, most severe plague first, curtailing the whole process and preventing much suffering and loss of human life. That he did not do so suggests that the salvation of Israel was not his primary purpose. The logic of the divine intervention is that knowledge of Yahweh comes before liberation from Egypt, both in fact and in priority.[15] If that is true, then we need be most attentive when trying to come to grips with this initial statement, made by none other than Yahweh himself, about the history of this distinct form of human knowledge. According to Yahweh, it has not yet existed in the Israelite lineage. In the exodus events, the knowledge of Yahweh is supposed to be obtained, as Zimmerli has noted for the occurrences in the book of Ezekiel, through awesome divine interventions in historical events. Recalling the book of Genesis, the potential for such revelation is there: the expulsion from the garden, the flood, the reaction to the tower of Babel, the attacks on the patriarchal rivals (Gen 12, 20, 26) prefiguring the exodus plagues, and possibly through the dreams of Joseph. But nowhere does Yahweh proclaim his name in association with these events. For whatever reason, and there are no obvious ones, Yahweh does not choose to begin the significant interventions until the exodus event. One detects the vague outline of the usual Israelite focus on the foundational nature of the exodus events hidden behind this motif; beyond this suspicion I shall not venture here.

Regarding the matter of possible revelation through historical interventions in Genesis, I shall examine a single example from the book of Genesis and conclude with some general deliberations. Though Eve does use the divine name, in a piece of direct discourse in Gen 4:1, Yahweh had not proclaimed, either in the expulsion or at any time prior, 'through X you shall know that I am Yahweh.' Regarding Eve's statement in Gen 4:1, Yahweh did not say, 'through bearing children you shall know that I am Yahweh,' though it was a perfect opportunity to do so, given the implicit reforming value of her penal experience of childbirth.[16] So Eve can use the name, but her experience does not lead her to know that "I am Yahweh." Might humans not come to know Yahweh without him making any announcements about the significance of a historical event? Perhaps, but not in the biblical narratives

---

[15] I am careful to qualify that this is Yahweh's view for two reasons. First, the narrator does not obviously agree (or disagree) with this priority. Second, and more startling, there is nowhere in the entire exodus story, or even the entire Bible, where Yahweh's hope for recognition is fulfilled. There is no confirming, 'and X knew that he was Yahweh' — either for 'Jew or Greek' — anywhere in the Old Testament. The nearest we get are the eight passages denying such knowledge or expressing renewed hope for it (Exod 5:2; Judg 2:10; 1 Sam 2:12; 3:7; Isa 19:21; Jer 31:34; Hos 2:22; 6:3). Ezek 20 is a carefully constructed meditation on the various ways, all failures, by which Yahweh has sought to bring Israel to such knowledge. To his own time, according to this prophet of Yahweh, Yahweh had no success in imparting this special knowledge. The chapter concludes with yet another scheme, planned but not implemented, to use the return from exile as a spectacular occasion by which to evoke this knowledge (Ezek 20:38, 42, 44).

[16] Eve's misfortunes in labour might be seen as parallel to those of the nation labouring through exodus and exile. But the cognitive consequence of Eve's sexuality is limited to physical pain, with a dose of desire and subjugation (Gen 3:16) — a far cry from the knowledge of the transcendent implicit in "knowing (that I am) Yahweh."

concerned with historical experience. Might humans come to know Yahweh without any spectacular historical interventions? Not according to the biblical narrative of world history from creation to exile. The only vehicles for such knowledge are always and exclusively provided by specific, interpreted divine interventions. Might not humans who can use the name reasonably be said to "know Yahweh"? Well Pharaoh certainly uses the name in Exod 5:2, but his is an ironic disclaimer of such knowledge in the same breath with which he utters the name. To use the name is not necessarily to know "I am Yahweh" according to the theological conventions at work here. The collocation *yd'* + *Yahweh* has, in biblical literature, an inflexible reference. It describes a unique cognitive state borne of a particular experience derived from special intervention by Yahweh in human affairs. So the statement made by Yahweh seems true for the patriarchal period that he describes in Exod 6:3.

Unfortunately, for divine purposes, the same truth persists for the remainder of biblical history (cf. Ezek 20). We may speculate on Yahweh's reasons for delaying such revelation for so long—such reckoning is an important part of trying to grasp the overall shape and meaning of the book of Genesis—but the simple fact of the biblical record is that it is delayed until the exodus event. The delay is, in a certain sense, prophetic: just as Israel's ancestors do not know Yahweh before the exodus, neither do the descendants of the exodus survivors. The supreme irony of this key motif, far more ironic than Pharaoh's ripe-for-punishment dramatic irony in Exod 5:2, is that nobody ever explicitly attains this crucial knowledge through the numinous events in Israel's history. In the knowledge "that I am Yahweh," we touch on one of the keys to the gradual diminishment of historical concern and revelation that is apparent in the overall shape of the Jewish or Christian canons of the Hebrew Bible/Old Testament.[17]

C. Appendix: Data analysis of the collocation
yd' + Yahweh in the books of Genesis and Exodus[18]

The three tables illustrate: 1) a steep rise in the number of occurrences of the name Yahweh in the exodus story; 2) the absence of the collocation *yd'* + *yhwh* in the book of Genesis; and 3) a significant clustering of occurrences of the collocation in the exodus story within the book of Exodus.

---

[17] On the gradual withdrawal of divinity from immanent activity, see R. E. Friedman, "The Hiding of the Face: An Essay on the Literary Unity of Biblical Narrative," *Judaic Perspectives on Ancient Israel* (Eds. J. Neusner, B.A. Levine and E.S. Frerichs; Fortress Press: Philadelphia, 1987) 207–22.

[18] All tables show occurrences per 1000 words.

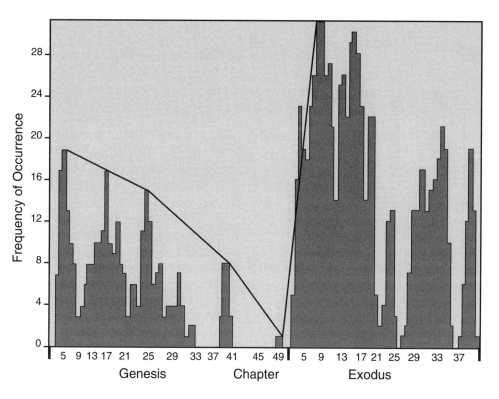

Table 1: Occurrences of Yahweh in the books of Genesis and Exodus

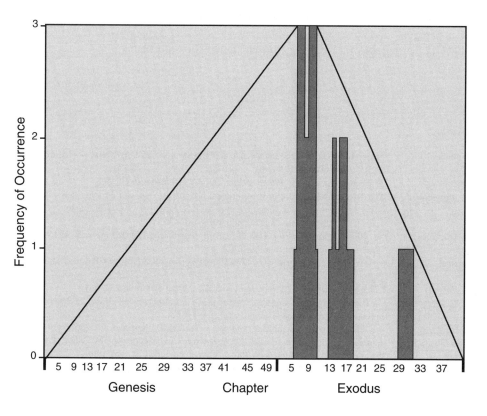

Table 2: "Knowing Yahweh" in the books of Genesis and Exodus

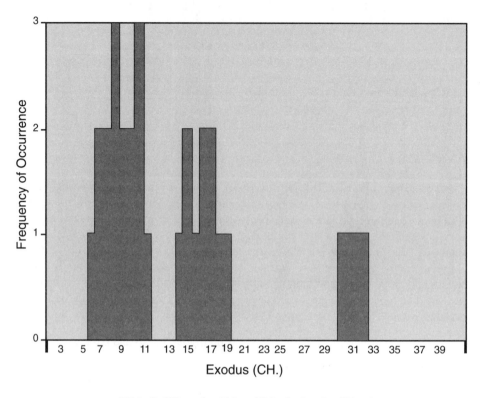

Table 3: "Knowing Yahweh" in the book of Exodus

Bibliography

L. Eslinger   "Freedom or Knowledge? Perspective & Purpose in the Exodus Narrative (Exodus 1–15)," *JSOT* 52 (1991) 43–60.

B. Jacob   *The Second Book of the Bible: EXODUS* (KTAV: Hoboken, NJ, 1992).

G.E. Mendenhall   "The Nature and Purpose of the Abraham Narratives," *Ancient Israelite Religion. Essays in Honor of Frank Moore Cross* (Eds. P.D. Miller, Jr., P.D. Hanson and S.D. McBride; Fortress Press: Philadelphia, 1987) 337–56.

R.W.L. Moberly   *The Old Testament of the Old Testament. Patriarchal Narratives and Mosaic Yahwism* (Fortress: Minneapolis, 1992).

R. Pascal   *Kafka's Narrators. A Study of His Stories and Sketches* (Cambridge UP: Cambridge, 1982).

F.K. Stanzel   *A Theory of Narrative* (Cambridge University Press: Cambridge, 1984).

M. Sternberg   *The Poetics of Biblical Narrative. Ideological Literature and the Drama of Reading* (Indiana University Press: Bloomington, IN, 1985).

W. Zimmerli   "Ich bin Yahweh," *Geschichte und Altes Testament. Beiträge zur historischen Theologie 16. Albrecht Alt zum 70. Geburtstag dargebracht* (J.C.B. Mohr (Paul Siebeck): Tübingen, 1953) 179–209.

W. Zimmerli   *Erkenntnis Gottes nach dem Buch Ezechiel* (Zwingli Ver.: Zürich, 1954).

LA STRUCTURE DU CORTEGE D'ISRAEL AUTOUR DE JERICHO D'APRES JOSUE 6

JEAN-CLAUDE MARGOT

Introduction

Dans leur ouvrage intitulé *La traduction: théorie et méthode,* Taber et Nida consacrent un paragraphe à la structure en tant que porteuse de signification. Ils font remarquer très justement que, contrairement à une opinion courante, ce ne sont pas seulement les mots et expressions particulières qui sont porteurs de sens, mais que "la grammaire par elle-même est chargée de signification" (1971:31). Depuis l'époque où ce livre est paru, la recherche s'est activement poursuivie dans le domaine de la traduction biblique, et l'on s'est attaché entre autres à démontrer comment la mise en valeur de certains éléments par un auteur (ce qu'on peut appeler d'une façon générale la fonction expressive du texte) joue un rôle déterminant pour la bonne compréhension et la bonne traduction du texte original ou texte source. En conséquence, le traducteur ne doit pas seulement se demander: "Qu'a dit l'auteur?", mais encore: "Comment l'a-t-il dit? Pourquoi l'a-t-il dit ainsi et pas autrement?" Cela implique que, dans la pratique de la traduction dite à équivalence fonctionnelle, si l'on doit respecter assurément "la fonction informative du texte à traduire", on ne doit pas négliger pour autant "sa fonction expressive" (voir J. Cl. Margot 1979/1990:336,339). De ce point de vue, il est indispensable d'être mieux renseigné sur les procédés d'ordre rhétorique auxquels les auteurs bibliques ont pu recourir en vue de la mise en valeur de certains éléments (cf. par exemple de Waard et Nida 1986:78-120, "Rhetorical Functions" et "Rhetorical Processes").

Dans les pages qui suivent, je me propose d'illustrer à l'aide d'une péricope de Josué 6 l'erreur qu'on risque de commettre dans la traduction en négligeant cet aspect de l'analyse du texte source. Il s'agira plus précisément d'examiner la façon dont l'auteur, ou le rédacteur final, de Josué 6 présente les divers éléments du cortège des Israélites en marche autour de Jéricho avant la prise de la ville. Mais, tout d'abord, il convient de situer d'une façon générale le chapitre en cause.

Quelques remarques générales sur Josué 6

a. Le caractère liturgique du récit
D'après R. Boling, le chapitre 6 de Josué est placé au début d'une importante partie du livre (6:1 - 10:43), relatant trois victoires dues à l'intervention de

Yahweh: à Jéricho (chap. 6), à Aï (chap. 7-8) et à Gabaon (chap. 9-10) (1984:204). Cependant, même une lecture rapide de ces textes révèle une différence frappante entre le chapitre 6 et les chapitres suivants. En effet, si dans le cas d'Aï et de Gabaon, l'élément militaire, stratégique ou tactique, joue un rôle sensible, tel n'est pas le cas en ce qui concerne la prise de Jéricho: elle n'est pas précédée d'aucune bataille. C'est en particulier ce qui incite la plupart des commentateurs à relever le caractère liturgique du récit de Josué 6.

Voici par exemple ce qu'en dit A. Soggin: "Ici est célébrée la conquête, dans une cérémonie ... qui comprend, entre autres, une action symbolique représentant l'événement fêté" (1970:67). De son côté, R. Boling souligne également cet aspect symbolique du récit en déclarant: "The first victory of the Yahweh army west of the Jordan had symbolic importance out of all proportion of the size of the actual enterprise. Tell es Sultan, the site of the Bronze Age and Iron Age Jericho, dominated an extensive oasis, but it was not a large city at any time in the biblical era. Given the incommensurability of the military achievement and its theological import, it is not surprising that *the bulk of the action in the chapter appears to be liturgical*" (1984:204-205; c'est moi qui souligne). De son côté, M. Görg fait remarquer, après d'autres commentateurs, que les fouilles archéologiques n'ont décelé aucune trace d'une conquête israélite de Jéricho telle que celle relatée en Josué 6 (1991:27; cf. A. Soggin 1970:68s.), argument qui donne du poids à l'interprétation liturgique du texte. C'est donc avec de bonnes raisons qu'on a pu considérer que le cortège des Israélites autour de Jéricho avait le caractère d'une "procession de l'arche" (A. Boudart, 1987:686) plutôt que d'une manoeuvre proprement militaire d'encerclement de la ville. A cela s'ajoute la valeur symbolique du chiffre sept, revenant à plusieurs reprises dans le texte (quatre fois dans le seul v. 4!), qui est également un trait typique de la présentation d'une "liturgie processionnelle" (M. Görg 1991:27).

Par conséquent, on peut souscrire sans grande hésitation à l'opinion souvent avancée selon laquelle on aurait dans le récit de Josué 6 le reflet d'une célébration rituelle de l'occupation de la Terre promise. Plusieurs auteurs relient cette célébration au sanctuaire de Guilgal, proche de Jéricho. Notons cependant l'hypothèse différente d'O. Kaiser qui, d'après 9:27, met cette cérémonie plutôt en rapport avec Gabaon et en dernier ressort avec Jérusalem (cité par M. Woudstra 1981:7). Quoi qu'il en soit de cette opinion divergente sur ce point, elle ne contredit en rien l'interprétation liturgique du récit.

b. Unité et sources du récit
Il est chaudement recommandé aux traducteurs bibliques de consulter de bons commentaires avant de traduire un texte. Cependant, s'ils le font dans le cas qui nous occupe, ils risquent d'être bien embarrassés en prenant connaissance des diverses hypothèses concernant les sources de Josué 6, ainsi que de certaines incohérences relevées par plusieurs auteurs dans le texte tel qu'il se présente à nous aujourd'hui. Il est donc nécessaire de relever les principaux aspects de ce double problème pour voir en quoi il concerne le travail de traduction.

Si l'on examine attentivement *la surface* du texte de Josué 6 dans une édition récente de la Bible hébraïque, il est possible d'y relever des tensions qui sont comme autant de traces d'une construction composite. Par exemple, selon A. Soggin, ''on ne voit pas du tout clairement qui doit sonner de la trompe: dans les v. 4, 6, 8, 13, 16, ce sont les prêtres, mais en 9b et 13b l'arrière-garde, formée d'on ne sait trop qui, doit en sonner elle aussi;[1] de même la relation entre le son de la trompe et le cri de guerre du peuple n'est pas claire: au v. 5 le second doit suivre le premier sans ordres spéciaux et précéder l'assaut, cf. cependant le v. 20 où l'enchaînement est: des cris - le son de la trompe - une clameur; en 8ss les trompes sonnent mais le peuple doit se taire jusqu'à ce qu'il reçoive l'ordre de crier, donné ensuite en 16ss, tandis qu'ailleurs cet ordre est transmis par un coup de trompe plus prolongé; et au v. 16, Josué donne effectivement l'ordre de crier, puis continue à parler quand le peuple aurait dû crier ...'' (1970.67; voir aussi J. Gray 1986:80). Si l'on admet un tel regard jeté sur le texte, il y a évidemment de quoi rester perplexe, d'autant plus que le passage que nous venons de citer n'est pas lui-même des plus clairs!

En fait, des remarques comme celles de Soggin, ou d'autres commentateurs, sont sans aucun doute étroitement liées à la question des *sources* du récit: si celui-ci repose sur plusieurs sources, on s'explique mieux pourquoi il comporte certaines incohérences. Que peut-on dire alors sur la manière dont le texte a été formé petit à petit? Remarquons tout d'abord que si la plupart des commentateurs actuels situent le livre de Josué dans la perspective deutéronomiste, ils sont loin de s'entendre quant à leur façon de concevoir les éventuelles étapes de la formation du texte de ce livre. Pour illustrer ce fait, il me suffira de citer deux positions foncièrement opposées.

Dans une étude sur la conquête de Jéricho, L. Schwienhorst croit pouvoir discerner une série de couches successives dans l'élaboration du texte de Josué 6: une ''Grundschicht'' (1986:39ss), une ''jahwistische Erweiterung'' (p. 73ss), une première, une deuxième et une troisième ''deuteronomistische Erweiterung'' (p. 85ss, 99ss, 105ss), une ''priesterliche Erweiterung'' (p. 113ss), ainsi qu'une ''spätchronistische Erweiterung'' (p. 125ss), à quoi il ajoute encore des traces de développement ultérieur dans le Rouleau de la guerre de Qumrân, 1 QM (p. 137ss).

Si l'on reste impressionné par l'ingéniosité avec laquelle Schwienhorst décortique le texte, on sera d'autant plus frappé par le point de vue opposé qu'avance M. Woudstra, dans une perspective conservatrice. En effet, cet auteur défend l'unité de composition du récit (1981:13ss). Il conclut son argumentation en ces termes: ''In light of the evidence presented above, it appears that a strong case can be made for unity of composition, not to the exclusion of the one of diverse sources, but by means of them'' (p. 16). Il n'exclut même pas que les données du récit datent de l'époque de Josué et des anciens qui lui ont succédé.

---

[1] Cette remarque est en relation avec la façon dont Soggin traduit 13b: ''... et l'arrière-garde suivait l'Arche de YHWH, sonnant de la trompe, elle aussi, tout en marchant'' (mais voir TOB par exemple: ''... et l'arrière-garde suivait l'arche du Seigneur: on marchait en sonnant du cor.'').

A lire tout ce qui s'est écrit sur le sujet, on ne peut qu'approuver le point de vue d'A. Boudart quand il déclare que le livre de Josué laisse "transparaître les traces d'une longue histoire que les critiques s'efforcent de démêler, depuis un siècle, sans qu'on puisse, à ce jour, parler d'un accord" (1987:686). Ce qu'il dit du livre de Josué en général se vérifie pour le chapitre 6. Toutefois, il suffira pour notre propos de relever un double fait: le récit actuel de la prise de Jéricho repose fort vraisemblablement sur des traditions orales ou écrites qui l'ont précédé; mais cela n'empêche pas que, considéré dans l'ensemble de sa forme finale, il ait une "unité réelle", comme le reconnaît A. Soggin lui-même (1970:67).[2] D'ailleurs, malgré tout ce que L. Schwienhorst a pu écrire sur les nombreux développements qui, selon lui, sont à la base de la formation de Josué 6, cet auteur tient à affirmer d'emblée que le texte canonique est celui qui correspond au stade ultime de sa rédaction; par conséquent, il doit être pris au sérieux "gerade in der letzten Phase seiner Entstehungsgeschichte" (1986:13). Et c'est précisément cela qui compte pour le traducteur: il n'a pas à se soucier de donner dans sa traduction des "points de repère" des éventuelles sources du texte; en revanche, il est essentiel qu'il détermine, à l'aide d'études appropriées, les point saillants qui ressortent du texte actuel, les données ou les constantes mises au service de sa fonction expressive. C'est de ce point de vue que je vais analyser maintenant la structure du cortège (ou de la procession) d'Israël dans sa marche autour de la ville de Jéricho, en commençant par la situer dans l'ensemble du passage.

Plan du passage

Le plan du passage ne présente pas de difficulté particulière, car la ligne générale en est claire. C'est ainsi qu'une note de la TOB (Traduction oecuménique de la Bible) peut affirmer que "malgré les répétitions et les surcharges, la structure du récit est assez facile à percevoir" (1988:434, note *i* à 6:2).

On remarquera tout d'abord que la péricope qui nous intéresse peut être aisément délimitée. En effet, il saute aux yeux du lecteur que les v. 1-2 du chapitre 6 lui servent d'introduction, en présentant la situation au moment où le peuple d'Israël arrive devant les murs de la ville de Jéricho: bien que la cité semble imprenable,[3] elle est déjà en fait livrée à Josué, selon la promesse du Seigneur. Quant à la conclusion de la péricope, elle est tout naturellement

---

[2] Je laisse de côté la comparaison entre le texte massorétique et le texte plus court de la LXX dont R. Boling estime qu'il repose sur une source moins "liturgique" (1984:206). Voir aussi la note *h* de la TOB à 6:1 ("Pour ce ch., le texte grec est nettement plus court que l'hébr.; les divergences, trop nombreuses entre les deux textes, n'omt pas été notées.").

[3] Notons que la façon dont la TOB rend le début du v. 1 ("Jéricho était fermée et enfermée") est un littéralisme qui ne rend pas le sens de la forme hébraïque. Contrairement à ce que dit la note *g* de cette version, il ne s'agit pas là d'un "jeu de mots", mais d'une tournure idiomatique. On a successivement le participe qal et le participe pual du verbe *sgr*, "fermer"; le second participe accentue la force du premier, de sorte qu'une traduction comme "solidement barricadée" serait plus justifiée (voir J. Cl. Margot 1979/1990:275s.).

apportée par les v. 20-21 qui décrivent en quelques mots la chute de la ville, ainsi que la mise à l'interdit de sa population et du bétail qui s'y trouvait.[4]

Cela précisé, je propose le plan suivant de notre passage:

v. 1-2   Introduction
v. 3-5   L'ordre que le Seigneur adresse à Josué
v. 6-10   L'ordre est transmis par Josué aux prêtres, puis à tout le peuple. Mise en place du cortège
v. 11-14 L'exécution de l'ordre du Seigneur durant les six premiers jours
v. 15-19 L'exécution de l'ordre du Seigneur le septième jour, avec mention de l'interdit frappant la ville
v. 20-21 Prise de la ville et exécution de l'interdit.

Dans le cadre de ce récit, nous allons, comme prévu, nous attacher spécialement aux données concernant l'ordonnance du cortège (ou de la procession) des Israélites.

La présentation des divers éléments du cortège

Décrivant la procession liturgique, à propos des v. 6-10, A. Soggin mentionne les éléments suivants du cortège: "La procession est ouverte par un détachement d'hommes en armes, suivis par des prêtres portant des trompes; puis vient un objet, identifié par la suite avec l'Arche ... Une arrière-garde fermait la procession." (1970:70). Il ajoute que "la participation du peuple à la cérémonie s'exprimait à travers le 'cri de guerre' lancé soit à un signal déterminé des trompes, soit suivant l'ordre explicite de celui qui dirigeait la cérémonie ..." (ibid.). On voit ainsi qu'il est aisé de se faire une idée générale de la composition du cortège et de la place de chacun de ses éléments.

Cependant, si l'on compare l'ordre logique de la procession tel que Soggin le présente et la façon dont les divers éléments du cortège sont disposés dans le texte, on constate que cette disposition s'écarte constamment de cet ordre logique. C'est précisément ce fait qui doit retenir toute notre attention, ainsi que celle du traducteur. Afin de procéder à une analyse méthodique de cet aspect de la question, nous allons définir maintenant les diverses catégories de participants à la procession, en leur attribuant successivement un repère à l'aide des lettres *A* à *E*. Cette classification, fondée sur la terminologie de la TOB, nous permettra

---

[4] Bien que les v. 22-27 soient en relation directe avec les ordres donnés par Josué (comparer par exemple les v. 23 et 17b, ainsi que les v. 24 et 17a), je les laisse de côté, car ils ne jouent pas de rôle par rapport à la structure du cortège d'Israël autour de Jéricho. Ils peuvent être traités comme une péricope à part, centrés qu'ils sont sur l'accomplissement de la promesse faite à Rahab d'après 2:12-14 (voir le sous-titre de la TOB, "Le salut pour la maison de Rahab", ou celui de la BFC, "Josué laisse la vie à Rahab"). Notons aussi cette remarque de Bratcher et Newman: "Since there is something of a transition in the narrative at this point (v. 22), it may be important to introduce a new section heading ..." (1983:81).

d'établir ensuite un tableau caractérisant le "désordre" apparent du texte, avant d'en évaluer la signification.[5]

A. Le premier élément du cortège est *l'avant-garde*, selon le sens le plus probable que le terme hébreu *hâlûṣ* (litt. "équipé" ou "prêt à combattre") possède dans ce contexte. En effet, comme le note justement E. Dhorme, "dans ce chapitre le mot s'oppose à *me'assêph* qui représente l'arrière-garde aux versets 9 et 13 ... C'est donc l'avant-garde" (1956:640).

B. Le deuxième élément est representé par les *sept prêtres portant sept cors de béliers*. L'instrument en cause est désigné soit par *šôphar hayyôbel*, au v. 4, soit par *qèrèn hayyôbel*, à considérer comme l'équivalent de *šôphar* au v. 5 (cf. Ex 19:13, 16 et 19, avec la même équivalence). Son rôle dans la liturgie est apparent dans des textes comme Lv 25:9; 2 S 6:15; 1 R 1:34-41; 2 R 9:13; 2 Ch 15:14.

C. Le troisième élément est *l'arche de l'alliance du Seigneur*, portée par des prêtres (v. 6).

D. Le quatrième élément est *l'arrière-garde* (voir plus haut, à propos de A).

E. Enfin, il faut relever une catégorie à valeur plus générale ("les hommes de guerre", v. 3; "le peuple", v. 7) ou indéfinie (qu'on peut rendre par "on", v. 9 et 13, ou par "ils", v. 11). Cette catégorie englobant apparemment tout ou partie des participants ne joue en fait guère de rôle dans notre classification.

Voyons maintenant comment ces divers éléments sont disposés dans le texte, en particulier dans les v. 4-14:

1. au v. 4, nous avons *B* (les sept prêtres portant les sept cors de bélier) précédant *C* (l'arche de l'alliance);

2. le v. 5 mentionne *E*, c'est à dire le peuple en général, mention qu'on peut mettre entre parenthèses pour la raison énoncée ci-dessus, à propos de *E* précisément;

3. le v. 6 nous présente l'ordre *C - B - C*;

4. au v. 7, il y a *E*, mais surtout *A* et *C*;

5. aux v. 8 et 9, on relève l'ordre *B - C - A* (en relation avec B) - *D* (l'arrière-garde, en relation avec *C*) + *E* ("on", indéfini);

6. v. 10, *E*, le peuple, à mettre entre parenthèses;

7. v. 11, *C* + *E* ("ils", à valeur générale);

8. v. 12, *C*;

9. v. 13, *B* en relation avec *C - A* (en relation avec *B*) - *D* (en relation avec *C*) + *E* ("on");

10. v. 14, *E* ("ils", à valeur générale).

Que faut-il déduire de ce rapide inventaire? A première vue, on est frappé par le fait que les lettres ont l'air d'être disposées au hasard, et non dans la séquence *A - B - C - D* (+ *E* englobant en quelque sorte le tout). Incontestablement, donc, les éléments ne sont pas présentés dans l'ordre logique. Mais une analyse plus approfondie de la situation nous amène à formuler une seconde constatation, dont

---

[5] Je laisse de côté la personne de Josué, dont le rôle essentiel consiste à faire exécuter les ordres du Seigneur (v. 6, 7, 8, 10 et 16) ou à "se lever de bon matin" (v. 12)!

on ne saurait sous-estimer l'importance: la présence de l'arche, au centre du cortège, est sans cesse mise en évidence. En effet, si l'on examine de près le tableau esquissé ci-dessus, on remarque les caractéristiques suivantes: le texte donne la priorité à quatre reprises au couple *C - B* (v. 4, 6, 8 et 13). Ailleurs on a *C* en relation avec *A* (v. 7), avec *D* (v. 9 et 13), avec *E* au sens général ou indéfini (v. 11), ou même tout seul (v. 12). Certes, je ne suis pas le premier à relever cet aspect du texte. Pour ne donner qu'un exemple, on peut citer le commentaire de M. Woudstra: à propos des v. 6-7, il déclare qu'en relation avec la signification essentielle de l'arche, celle-ci est mentionnée en premier; de même, indique-t-il plus loin, le rôle important de l'arche dans la procession ressort du v. 8, bien que le v. 7 rapporte que les hommes en armes sont en tête de la colonne; enfin, toujours d'après lui, l'accent mis sur ce rôle de l'arche est de nouveau évident au v. 11 (1981:111s). Néanmoins, il me semble que les traducteurs n'ont pas été suffisamment attentifs à de telles remarques, comme nous le verrons dans le paragraphe suivant.

Pour le moment, il convient de souligner le fait suivant: bien que le texte dispose les divers éléments du cortège dans un ''désordre'' apparent, sa structure (à première vue surprenante) se fonde en réalité sur une logique certaine. Si l'on admet l'hypothèse d'A. Soggin selon laquelle la mention de l'arche n'appartenait pas à la tradition primitive, on est d'autant plus frappé de découvrir que, dans la dernière étape de la rédaction du texte, on l'a introduite de manière à en faire incontestablement le centre de gravité ou le centre théologique du récit. Comme le déclare M. Görg, ''die Lade hat hier wie im dtr Bestand von Jos 3f die Funktion eines Zeichens der machtvollen Präsenz Jahwes, die im Kult- und Kriegsgeschehen manifest wird'' (1991:28). Et l'on doit constater que la présentation des autres éléments du cortège reflète la même logique, car elle est établie constamment en fonction du rapport de ces éléments avec le rôle central de l'arche: ainsi, la présence de *B* (les sept prêtres portant sept cors de bélier) est destinée à attirer l'attention, liturgiquement parlant, sur l'arche, *C*, qu'elle précède (v. 4, 6, 8, 13; cf. le rapport semblable entre le son du cor et l'arche, amenée triomphalement à Jérusalem, dans le texte déjà cité de 2 S 6:15); par ailleurs, l'avant-garde, *A*, et l'arrière-garde, *D*, ne sont mentionnées que dans la mesure où elles encadrent le noyau central du cortège, et non pour en faire ressortir l'aspect militaire (v. 7, 9 , 13). Il faut mettre à part *E* qui, comme nous l'avons vu, a un caractère général ou indéfini sans incidence notable sur l'ordre du cortège.

On ne peut donc en douter: la structure du texte est mise au service de la conviction que l'arche du Seigneur - autrement dit le Seigneur lui-même (voir 6:27) - est le facteur fondamental et décisif ayant permis la prise de Jéricho (cf. K. Gutbrod 1985:54).

La structure du cortège de Josué 6 et sa traduction

Les théoriciens de la traduction ont souvent relevé que, dans diverses langues, la présentation des éléments d'un récit dans un autre ordre que celui de leur succession logique, pouvait susciter de réelles difficultés de compréhension pour le lecteur ou l'auditeur d'une version biblique. J'ai donné moi-même ailleurs des exemples de ces difficultés, à propos de la chaîne des participants et des événements, en analysant des textes comme Mc 6:14-29; Lc 1:1-4 et Ac 1:1-5 (J. Cl. Margot 1979/1990:187ss). C'est la raison pour laquelle on peut légitimement se demander comment traiter ou présenter dans de telles langues l'ordre du cortège de Josué 6. En effet, si l'on se contente de rendre la structure du texte hébreu selon le principe de l'équivalence formelle (le calque de la forme du texte source), on risque non seulement de causer quelque perplexité dans l'esprit des destinataires de la traduction, mais encore et surtout d'empêcher ceux-ci de saisir correctement la pointe du texte. Afin de parer à ce danger, on a cru bon d'adopter la solution suivante dans des traduction à équivalence fonctionnelle, destinées entre autres à servir de modèles à des traducteurs élaborant des versions dans d'autres parties du monde: on a choisi de rétablir l'ordre logique du cortège, en pensant favoriser ainsi une bonne compréhension de la situation pour le lecteur ou l'auditeur. Nous allons voir ce qu'il faut penser de cette solution à l'aide d'un double exemple.

a. Dans la *Good News Bible* (GNB, *The Bible in Today's English Version*, 1976), le traducteur de Josué a volontairement disposé les éléments du cortège dans leur ordre logique, sans aucun doute pour la raison mentionnée ci-dessus. C'est ainsi qu'il vaut la peine pour notre propos de voir comment il a combiné les v. 8-9:

> So, just as Joshua had ordered, an advance guard started out ahead of the priests who were blowig trumpets; behind these came the priests who were carrying the Covenant Box, followed by a rear guard. All this time the trumpets were sounding. ("Ainsi, comme Josué l'avait ordonné, une avant-garde (*A*) se mit en marche devant les prêtres qui sonnaient de la trompette (*B*); derrière ceux-ci venaient les prêtres qui portaient le coffre de l'alliance (*C*), suivis par l'arrière-garde (*D*). Durant tout ce temps les trompettes résonnaient.")

Les éléments du cortège sont donc rétablis dans l'ordre *A - B - C - D*, comme l'indiquent les lettres que j'ai introduites dans la traduction française.

Dans cette version, le traducteur a également combiné les v. 12-13:

> Joshua got up early the next morning, and for the second time the priests and soldiers marched around the city in the same order as the day before: first, the advanced guard; next, the seven priests blowing the seven trumpets; then, the priests carrying the Lord's Covenant Box; and finally, the rear guard. All this time the trumpets were sounding. ("Josué se leva tôt le lendemain matin, et, pour la seconde fois, les prêtres et soldats marchèrent autour de la ville, dans le même ordre que le jour précédent: tout d'abord, l'avant-garde (*A*); ensuite, les sept prêtres sonnant des sept trompettes (*B*); puis les prêtres portant le coffre de l'alliance du Seigneur (*C*); et, finalement, l'arrière-garde (*D*). Durant tout ce temps les trompettes résonnaient.")

De nouveau, l'ordre *A - B - C - D* est présenté d'une façon cohérente. Mais cela donne l'impression de la description d'un simple défilé (tout comme on ferait le reportage d'un cortège de fête avec, dans l'ordre, drapeaux, fanfare, autorités, sociétés locales et foule suivant le cortège!). L'arche y figure comme un élément parmi d'autres, sans importance particulière.[6]

b. Une même impression se dégage du commentaire de Josué, dû à Bratcher et Newman, qui suit étroitement le texte de la GNB. En effet, les choses sont présentées d'une manière tout à fait conforme à la restructuration que le traducteur a adoptée dans cette version. Tout d'abord, dans l'introduction aux v. 8-9, l'ordre du cortège est présenté ainsi: avant-garde - les sept prêtres qui sonnent de leurs trompettes - les prêtres qui portent l'arche de l'alliance - l'arrière-garde (1983:73). Plus loin, il est dit que, pour la clarté de l'exposé, il vaudrait mieux consacrer une phrase particulière pour chacun des groupes compris dans la procession, ce qui donnerait: "A select group of fighting men went first. They were followed by the seven priests who constantly blew the trumpets. The priests who carried the Covenant Box came next. A second group of fighting men marched behind the Covenant Box." (p. 74; on remarquera que la terminologie diffère ici quelque peu de celle donnée juste avant). Cette disposition en courtes phrases distinctes a de nouveau le caractère d'une simple juxtaposition des divers éléments du cortège, placés au même niveau, sans accent apparent sur l'un ou l'autre. Certes, les auteurs du commentaire déconseillent de combiner les v. 12-13 comme le fait la GNB; mais ils n'en restituent pas moins l'ordre "logique" du cortège au v. 13: avant-garde - les sept prêtres soufflant dans les sept trompettes - les prêtres portant l'arche de l'alliance du Seigneur - l'arrière-garde (p. 75).

Au début du chap. 6, le commentaire indique bien que la prise de Jéricho n'a pas été due à la puissance militaire des Israélites, mais au pouvoir de Dieu, maître de toutes choses (p. 68). Cependant, par la suite, aucune indication n'y est donnée sur la mise en évidence, dans la structure du texte, de l'arche de l'alliance, signe de la présence décisive du Seigneur dans l'événement relaté.

Evidemment, une première analyse générale du texte se justifie, et l'on peut donc reconnaître une certaine valeur à la présentation de l'ordre logique du cortège, telle qu'elle ressort de la GNB et du commentaire de Bratcher et Newman. Toutefois, il est nécessaire d'aller plus loin dans l'examen des particularités du texte, afin qu'au moment où l'on en arrive au niveau de la traduction proprement dite, on n'en reste pas au nivellement que nous avons constaté, qui porte atteinte à la fonction expressive de la narration et émousse sa pointe théologique. Si on aligne A - B - C - D dans cet ordre, on reproduit assurément la signification dénotative des divers éléments; mais du point de vue de la mise en évidence de certains de ces éléments dans le texte original, il y a là une lacune évidente.

---

[6] Voir aussi le v. 11, où la GNB a "So he had this group of men take the Lord's Covenant Box around the city one time ..." (cf. la traduction plus littérale de la TOB: "L'arche du Seigneur tourna autour de la ville pour en faire le tour une fois ..."). Il est évident que l'arche du Seigneur ne s'est pas déplacée toute seule autour de la ville, d'où l'explicitation formulée dans la GNB. Toutefois, en procédant ainsi, le traducteur atténue l'acent mis sur l'arche dans le texte original, ou même le déplace sur "this ghroup of men".

A titre de comparaison, on peut citer la version en français courant (BFC). Pour les raisons que je viens de relever, on y a suivi de plus près la structure du texte original, en se refusant consciemment à lui donner un ordre plus "logique". Voici, par exemple, comment s'y présentent les v. 8 et 9:

> 8 Tout se déroula comme Josué l'avait ordonné. Les sept prêtres porteurs de trompettes[7] avançaient en sonnant de leur instrument devant le coffre sacré. 9 L'avant-garde les précédait, et l'arrière-garde suivait le coffre. Pendant qu'ils marchaient, le son des trompettes ne cessait de retentir.

Quant aux v. 12 et 13, ils sont traduits ainsi:

> 12 Josué se leva tôt le lendemain matin, et les prêtres chargèrent de nouveau le coffre sacré sur leurs épaules. 13 Les sept prêtres porteurs de trompettes se remirent en marche devant le coffre en sonnant de leur instrument. L'avant-garde les précédait et l'arrière-garde suivait le coffre. Pendant qu'ils marchaient, le son des trompettes ne cessait de retentir.

La seule suggestion que l'on pourrait faire aux auteurs de cette version serait d'ajouter une note de bas de page attirant l'attention du lecteur sur la mise en évidence constante de l'arche de l'alliance et sur la raison d'être de ce fait.

Conclusion

En traitant un texte biblique, le traducteur doit se garder d'une double erreur. D'une part, il ne saurait se contenter d'une imitation formelle, ou d'un calque, du texte original. En effet, contrairement à ce que beaucoup pensent, en particulier dans le domaine biblique, la traduction littérale, bien loin d'être la plus fidèle au texte source, est un moyen assuré de produire des maladresses stylistiques, des incorrections et des contresens dans la langue d'arrivée. Mais, d'autre part, le traducteur doit se garder de dissocier la forme et le sens, en pensant que "peu importe la forme pourvu que le sens y soit". En réalité, la forme est au service du sens, elle fait partie du sens (voir J. Cl. Margot 1979/1990:335s). Il en résulte qu'une bonne compréhension du texte de base implique une bonne connaissance des procédés littéraires ou rhétoriques utilisés par un auteur pour mettre en valeur les éléments essentiels de la pensée ou du message qu'il veut communiquer. Il est donc indispensable qu'on tienne compte de cet aspect de la question dans des commentaires pour traducteurs, du type de celui de Bratcher et Newman, cité plus haut.

---

[7] Dans cette version, les traducteurs ont gardé le terme traditionnel "trompette", tout en étant conscients du fait qu'il ne s'agissait pas "de trompettes métalliques, mais de trompes en corne de bélier" (cf. note *k* de la TOB, à 6:4). Leur choix, dans ce cas, a été déterminé par la constatation qu'à la lecture à haute voix "cors de bélier" pouvait être confondu par des auditeurs non avertis avec "corps de bélier"! Il leur est donc apparu que l'essentiel était de suggérer l'idée d'un instrument au son retentissant, en évitant ainsi tout risque de malentendu.

En ce qui concerne le problème posé par la structure du cortège dans Josué 6, il n'est pas possible de donner une solution toute faite, valable dans toutes les langues du monde, car leur façon d'organiser ou de structurer un message peut varier grandement de l'une à l'autre. Toutefois, ce que l'on peut recommander en tout cas, c'est de procéder en premier lieu à une analyse précise de la structure du texte original, pour en découvrir les traits caractéristiques. Ensuite, il s'agira de découvrir dans chaque langue les procédés de mise en valeur qui lui sont propres afin de les appliquer à bon escient. Pour bien préciser la situation, on aura aussi la possibilité d'ajouter une note de bas de page relevant l'importance de tel ou tel détail de la péricope en cause. En bref, il convient tout d'abord de détecter la fonction des formes du texte source, puis de repérer dans la langue d'arrivée non pas des formes semblables, mais les formes (peut-être fort différentes) susceptibles de remplir la même fonction. C'est là ce qu'on appelle le principe de ''l'équivalence fonctionnelle'', qui concerne aussi bien la fonction informative que la fonction expressive du texte que l'on traduit.[8]

Bibliographie

R.G. Boling, *Joshua* (The Anchor Bible 6; New York: Doubleday, 1984).
A. Boudart, ''Josué'', in: *Dictionnaire encyclopédique de la Bible* (DEB) (Maredsous: Brepols, 1987) 684-687.
R.G. Bratcher et B.M. Newman, *A Translator's Handbook on the Book of Joshua* (London, New York, Stuttgart: United Bible Societies, 1983).
E. Dhorme, ''Josué'' (in: *La Bible, Ancien Testament I*; Paris: Gallimard, 1956) 625-714.
M. Görg, *Josua* (Die neue Echter Bibel; Würzburg: Echter Verlag, 1991).
J. Gray, *Joshua, Judges, Ruth* (The New Century Bible Commentary; Grand Rapids: Eerdmans, 1986).
K. Gutbrod, *Das Buch vom Lande Gottes, Josua und Richter* (Die Botschaft des Alten Testaments 10; Neu bearbeitete Auflage; Stuttgart: Calwer Verlag, 1985).
J. Cl. Margot, *Traduire sans trahir* (Lausanne: L'Age d'homme, 1979, nouveau tirage 1990).
L. Schwienhorst, *Die Eroberung Jerichos, Exegetische Untersuchung zu Josua 6* (Stuttgart: Verlag Katholisches Bibelwerk, 1986).
J.A. Soggin, *Josué* (Commentaire de l'Ancien Testament Va; Neuchâtel: Delachaux et Niestlé, 1970).
Ch.R. Taber et E.A. Nida, *La traduction: théorie et méthode* (Londres: Alliance biblique universelle, 1971).
J. de Waard et E.A. Nida, *From One Language to Another, Functional Equivalence in Bible Translating* (Nashville, Camden, New York: Thomas Nelson, 1986).
M.H. Woudstra, *The Book of Joshua* (The New International Commentary on the Old Testament; Grand Rapids: Eerdmans, 1981, nouveau tirage 1991).

Versions citées
La Bible en français courant (BFC; Paris: Alliance biblique universelle, 1982).
La Bible de la Pléiade (voir ci-dessus à E. Dhorme).

---

[8] Je tiens à remercier le Dr René Péter-Contesse, de Neuchâtel (Suisse), ainsi que les responsables de l'édition du présent ouvrage, qui, par leurs remarques pertinentes, ont contribué à améliorer mon texte.

La Bible, traduction oecuménique (TOB; Paris: Les éditions du Cerf/Société biblique française, 2e édition 1988).

Good News Bible, The Bible in Today's English Version (GNB; New York: American Bible Society, 1976).

MYTHOLOGICAL THEMES AND THE UNITY OF EZEKIEL

LAWRENCE BOADT, C.S.P.

Introduction

Ezekiel studies have shifted dramatically from a century ago when Richard Kraetzschmar held that the vast majority of the text, including the numerous duplications, were from Ezekiel himself, since the editors wanted to save every scrap of his sayings.[1] The first half of the century saw a shift toward severe skepticism to the point where Gustav Hölscher in 1924 considered only some 180 verses of poetry out of the book's nearly 1200 verses came from the original prophet.[2] Shortly after, Charles Torrey proposed the entire book was a pseudepigraph of the second century.[3] But by the middle of the century, the tide was already moving towards a more moderate estimation that a solid core from the prophet had grown over many decades by accretion,[4] and this was established as the near universal consensus with the magisterial commentary by Walther Zimmerli in 1969.[5] Zimmerli organized his study from a form-critical analysis of the units in the book,[6] and since then commentators have moved in two different directions. One, largely a German form-critical school, has pushed the *Nachgeschichte* (Zimmerli's term) far more extensively than did Zimmerli and sees even less of the text as from Ezekiel;[7] the other, based more on literary and rhetorical critical approaches, considers the text throughout to be much more unified and more likely to stem directly from the prophet's insights, even if completed by close disciples, and much more likely to

---

[1] Richard Kraetzschmar, *Das Buch Ezechiel* (HKAT; Göttingen: Vandenhoeck und Ruprecht, 1900).

[2] Gustav Hölscher, *Hesekiel: Der Dichter und das Buch. Eine Literarkritische Untersuchung* (BZAW 39; Giessen: Töpelmann, 1924).

[3] Charles Cutler Torrey, *Pseudo-Ezekiel and the Original Prophecy* (New Haven: Yale University Press, 1930).

[4] Carl Gordon Howie, *The Date and Composition of Ezekiel* (JBL Monograph Series 4; Philadelphia: Society of Biblical Literature, 1950).

[5] Walther Zimmerli, *Ezechiel I und II* (BKAT 13; Neukirchen-Vluyn, 1969), translated into English as *Ezekiel 1 and 2* (Hermeneia; Philadelphia: Fortress Press, 1979 and 1983).

[6] See my remarks on the strengths and limits of Zimmerli's approach in a review of the English translation in *CBQ* 43 (1981) 632-35; *CBQ* 47 (1985) 721-22.

[7] J. Garscha, *Studien zum Ezechielbuch: Eine Redaktionskritische Untersuchung von Ez 1-39* (Bern: Peter Lang, 1974); F. Hossfeld, *Untersuchungen zu Komposition und Theologie des Ezechielbuches* (FzB 20; Würzburg: Echter Verlag, 1977). See the helpful survey of Johan Lust, "Introduction: Ezekiel and his Book," in *Ezekiel and His Book: Textual and Literary Criticism and their Interrelation* (BETL LXXIV; Leuven: Leuven University Press, 1986)1-3.

have been brought to completion within the period of exile.[8] Since radical scholars such as Frank Hossfeld still argue forcefully for a much larger editorial component in the final book than Moshe Greenberg, for example, or myself would, it will be crucial to lay out some of the reasons for pursuing a search for the integral reading of the text as a work from the prophet himself and his close disciples. Since the most controverted material in the book is found in chaps. 38-48, I will focus attention on the important role these chapters play in the possible unity of the book. The specific viewpoint will be the use of mythological themes in 38-48 that are part of an overarching development throughout the book as a whole. The connections established suggest that these chapters do belong to a fundamental plan of the book that cannot be separated from the original delivery of Ezekiel's oracles.

Ezekiel 38-48 and the Problem of Unity

Ezekiel research in the twentieth century has largely focussed on the divisions in chapters 33-48 between 33-39 and 40-48. It has been generally accepted that the final bloc of materials in Ezekiel which includes the vision of the new temple in chapters 40-43, the new priestly ministry of the restored people in chapters 44-46, and the new division of the land in chapters 47-48 represent mostly a late elaboration by a school of disciples.[9] Although most historical-critical exegetes admit the presence of a core of Ezekiel's own prophetic proclamation, it is usually considered to be quite minimal.[10] The reason for this scholarly stance is clear enough: the situation supposed by the vision is a groundplan or program for the postexilic restoration and reflects the triumph of the priestly point of view that comports far better with the period from 539 to 450 than it does with the much more charismatic message of say a Second Isaiah in the last years of the Exile.[11]

Many other scholars have questioned the originality of chapters 38-39 and their place in the ministry of Ezekiel.[12] This extends to doubts whether they were even in the first edition of the redacted book since, e.g., the final summary of 37:24-28 seems to presuppose that the vision of the temple in 40-43 will follow immediately and no hint is given of the intervening cosmic disaster of chapters 38-39. Moreover, the language of chapters 38-39 has often been labeled ''apocalyptic'' and so has been

---

[8] Representative of this approach is Moshe Greenberg. *Ezekiel 1-20* (AB 22; New York: Doubleday; 1983. See also L. Boadt, ''Ezekiel,'' *ABD*, vol. 2, pp. 711-22.

[9] See, e.g. G. Hölscher, *Hesekiel, Der Dichter und das Buch* (BZAW 39; Giessen: Töpelmann, 1924) 208; and John Wevers, *Ezekiel* (The Century Bible, New Series; London: Nelson, 1969) 295-298.

[10] Thus, G.A. Cooke, *The Book of Ezekiel* ICC; Edinburgh: T. & T. Clark, 1936) xxv-xxvi; and W. Zimmerli, *Ezekiel 1*; Hermeneia; Philadelphia: Fortress Press, 1979) 68-72.

[11] Paul Hanson, *The Dawn of Apocalyptic: The Historical and Sociological Roots of Jewish Apocalyptic Eschatology* (Philadelphia: Fortress Press, 1979) is perhaps the most important and thorough delineation of the two points of view as they are found in exilic and postexilic biblical literature.

[12] Thus, e.g., J. Herrmann, *Ezechielstudien* (BWAT 2; Leipzig, 1908), generally held the two chapters were products of a later redactor, as did Hölscher, *op. cit.* W. Zimmerli, *Ezekiel 2*, 302-303, reviews the history of criticism up to 1969.

situated closer to the time of the Maccabees and the language of the Book of Daniel rather than to the Exilic period.[13] At best, these two chapters seem to be redundant to the message already found in chapters 33-37.[14] These observations, however, raise a serious methodological question about interpreting the book of Ezekiel as a whole since they import a criterion of comparison from outside the text without making a serious attempt to understand the relationship of the final bloc in chapters 40-48 to the previous bloc of salvation oracles in chapters 33-39. In turn, this forces the reader to ask structural questions about the relationship between chapters 1-24, 25-32, 33-37, 38-39, and 40-48 as an integrated sequence.

Preliminary Considerations on the Unity of Ezekiel

After years of study of Ezekiel, I am still most impressed with the normal and non-mythological arguments for the unity of the book based on stylistic characteristics that reappear consistently in section after section. These include the use of the title *ben-'adam*, ''Son of Man,'' to address the prophet in every section of the book;[15] the persistent first-person references to the prophet himself as the ''me'' that is being acted on—so strikingly different from either the Isaiah or Jeremiah traditions.[16] The recurrence of the ''Recognition Formula,'' *wᵉyadᵉ 'û kî-ᵃnî yhwh*, ''And they will know that I am Yahweh,'' at the end of nearly every oracle;[17] the occurrence of striking vocabulary, unique to this prophet, throughout the book;[18] and the discursive and repetitious prose that often includes substantial allegories, proverbial sayings or parables.[19] The combination of all these elements creates a unique style in the Bible. It is not closely paralleled by any other book or tradition, although various individual elements show some affinities to the Priestly source of the Pentateuch, especially in Leviticus 17-26, to Jeremiah's images and topics of individual oracles, and to descriptions of some earlier prophets in the Deuteronomic

---

[13] C.C. Torrey, *Pseudo-Ezekiel and the Original Prophecy* (New Haven: Yale University, 1930).

[14] See the comments in my article, "The Function of the Salvation Oracles in Ezekiel 33-37," *Hebrew Annual Review* 12 (1990) 1-22.

[15] This occurs less frequently in the disputed bloc of chaps. 40-48 because of the nature of the material as an extended discourse.

[16] The first-person reference to the prophet as a participant in his own oracles is found occasionally in earlier books. Thus Amos, Hosea, Micah and Habakkuk all have one or two self-referential oracles, but the only book that is similar to Ezekiel in the pervasive use of this first-person is Zechariah 1-8, a postexilic book with striking similarities to, and likely dependence on, Ezekiel.

[17] See the exhaustive treatment of W. Zimmerli, *I Am Yahweh* (Atlanta: John Knox, 1982; translated from the German original of 1953 by Douglas Scott), esp. ch. 2 "Knowledge of God according to the Book of Ezekiel," pp. 29-98.

[18] See L. Boadt, *Ezekiel's Oracles Against Egypt: A Literary and Philological Study of Ezekiel 29-32* (BibOr 37; Rome: Biblical Institute Press, 1980) 176-79.

[19] Cf. Claus Westermann, *Basic Forms of Prophetic Speech* (Philadelphia: Westminster, 1967) 205-209, where he notes Ezekiel's extensive literary extravagance while maintaining the basic elements of the judgment oracle—he calls it the dissolution of the basic form.

History.[20] No "school" seems to have developed from Ezekiel, and its legislation is never brought into conformity with the canonized Pentateuch under Ezra so that one should reasonably conclude that it was edited before 450. But this could be pushed back probably before 520, since even its vision of the temple does not match that of the postexilic reconstruction of the temple known from later sources and completed in 516 BCE.[21] Indeed, Donna Stephenson in a paper delivered to the SBL Annual Meeting in 1994, argued that the temple description in 40-42 does not even attempt to show the full dimensions of the temple building and courtyards, but measures instead the boundaries of access and the proper roles for personnel in the restored cultic life of the returned exiles.[22]

Certain other observations might suggest that the book was essentially complete at an even earlier date, perhaps no later than the death of Nebuchadnezzar in 562, or shortly thereafter. For one thing, there is no mention of a fate of Babylon as God's enemy that must be put down if God is to triumph. This would be surprising if the editors or disciples of Ezekiel had known of Babylon's disgraceful collapse and the overwhelming victory of Cyrus (as Second Isaiah clearly did between 548-540).[23] In fact, this lack has led some commentators to wonder whether the oracles against Gog are a hidden attack on Babylon.[24] A second consideration is that the carefully controlled series of dates in the book does not extend beyond 571 and the imminent invasion of Egypt by Babylonian forces.[25] The perspective of the book and its dating does not envision a weakened or failed Babylon (or oppositely, an exalted Persia) but apparently proposes a mythic or divinely commissioned cosmic overthrow of the present world order (Tyre in chap. 28:1-19; Egypt in 29:1-6 and 32:1-32; Gog in 38-39) since no other major world power is in sight that would be able to challenge Babylon's hegemony in the West. A third consideration is the (apparent) number of incorrect prophecies that are left in place—about Tyre in chapters 26-28; about Egypt in 30:20-26; about Sodom's restoration in 16:53-55. Taken together, these all suggest that the authors in the editorial process did not know anything

---

[20] See Zimmerli, *Ezekiel 1*, 44-52.

[21] Walther Zimmerli, "Ezechieltempel und Salomostadt," *Hebraïsche Wortforschung* (SVT 16; Leiden; Brill, 1967) 389-414.

[22] See Zimmerli, *Ezekiel 1*, 343-44, for similar observations. Stephenson titled her paper, "The Territorial Rhetoric of Ezekiel 40-48."

[23] See Isa 41:2-5; 44:24-45:7. Cyrus' impact must have been earthshaking for the biblical author to attribute to him the role of Israel's messiah in 45:1. For similar reactions to Cyrus in the Ancient Near East see ANET 312-315, "The Verse Account of Nabonidus," and ANET 315-16, "The Cyrus Cylinder."

[24] G.A. Cooke, *The Book of Ezekiel*, 408.

[25] See Gösta Ahlström, *The History of Palestine from the Paleolithic Period to Alexander's Conquest* (JSOTS 146; Sheffield: JSOT Press, 1993) 140-152. A Babylonian fragment mentions a campaign against Egypt in Nebuchadnezzar's 37th year, but what was the outcome is unknown. See also H.W.F. Saggs, *The Greatness that was Babylon* (New York: Hawthorn Books, 1962) 140-53.

concrete about the end of the Babylonian empire, as dramatic as it was, and as crucial as it turned out to be for Israel's changed state of existence afterwards.[26]

This is not to say that the book as a written whole stems directly from the hand of Ezekiel himself, but it is not a loose arrangement of theological reflections from many hands, either. As I have argued forcefully elsewhere, we cannot escape the conclusion that many of the prophet's oracles against nations in 25-32, and a number of other oracles scattered throughout chapters 1-24 were delivered on specific historical occasions and directed to definable and recoverable events.[27] And yet even these were then embedded in a vision structure, a carefully orchestrated drama that dominates the book and includes highly convoluted and elaborate *meshalim* whose topics and developments are inextricably woven together literarily. A good example would be the structural unity of chapters 4 to 7. It opens with a series of three symbolic actions: 4:1-8 (the prophet lies on his side facing a map); 4:9-17 (he eats bread cooked on dung); 5:1-4 (He cuts his hair and destroys it). These are presented as parables, not as oracles, but are balanced by three complex judgment oracles that follow. The first is addressed to Jerusalem alone (5:5-17); the second to the mountains of Israel (6:1-14); and the last to the four corners of the whole land (7:1-27). The purpose of arranging a three for three balance is to create a sense of ascending intensity and widening condemnation.[28] Ellen Davis has made a persuasive case for the careful literary composition of Ezekiel as the first truly designed ''prophetic book.''[29] Her treatment of the relationship between oral elements present in the oracles and the nature of the whole as a crafted literary production confirms my own conviction that, at a stage behind the present text, the prophet delivered a substantial number of the oracles in roughly the shape we find them, and then committed them to writing for a primarily paradigmatic purpose to teach or to stand as a model for understanding God's ''new'' ways as a result of the Exile and captivity in Babylon. The whole was composed so as to be proclaimed aloud, as ancient reading was done,[30] but its carefully spaced references to themes such as the mountains of Israel, or the purification of the land and people for the sake of divine holiness, invited further literary study.[31]

Ezekiel did not have to complete this book in his lifetime, but it seems most reasonable to presume that such a formal structure linking together concrete messages which had been geared to particular situations would have been developed personally

---

[26] Some commentators raise this possibility but usually are reluctant to support it. See Joseph Blenkinsopp, *Ezekiel* (Interpretation; Louisville: John Knox, 1990) 131, for an evaluation of the admission in Ezek 29:17-21 that the predictions against Tyre had failed to materialize.

[27] Boadt, *Ezekiel's Oracles Against Egypt*, 9-12.

[28] For a detailed treatment of this literary sequence, see Boadt, ''Rhetorical Strategies in Ezekiel's Oracles of Judgment,'' *BETL* LXXIV (1986) 182-200.

[29] Ellen Davis, *Swallowing the Scroll: Textuality and the Dynamics of Discourse in Ezekiel's Prophecy* (JSOTS 78; Sheffield, JSOT Press, 1989).

[30] Esp. note the scene in Jeremiah 36 on the proclamation of a scroll of prophetic oracles, and the scene envisioned by 1 Kings 18-19 in which the decrees of the Assyrian king are read so all the people can hear.

[31] See Boadt, ''Rhetorical Strategies,'' 190-93.

and directed by the prophet in accord with his visionary outlook.[32] Disciples, that always anonymous and indeterminate band of geniuses responsible for unifying, theologizing and envisioning larger wholes than the original master, cannot easily be imagined constructing such a unique and pervasively discordant style of prophecy unlike anything found in earlier prophetic collections. At best, disciples round out and expand the applications in accord with the developing priestly theology that will also structure the Pentateuch.[33]

The Place of Myth in Israelite Thinking

The discussion of myth in the Hebrew Bible has had a mixed history among western interpreters, but it has been largely negative, especially among Christian readers. A good example is the warning given by the author of 1 Timothy to the first Christians: "Charge certain persons not to teach a different doctrine nor to be concerned with myths..." (1 Tim 1:4). The letter goes on to contrast such speculation with sound teaching of faith, and characterizes such teachers with vain discussions that lead to distortion of what the Scriptures are about. There is also the implication throughout the letter that such concern with "myths" leads to immoral behavior. The author concludes with the command, "Have nothing to do with godless and silly myths. Train yourself instead in godliness!" (1 Tim 4:7). The same attitude recurs often at the end of the first century: 2 Tim 4:4; Tit 1:14; 2 Peter 1:16. Such a view largely corresponded to the prevailing one of the philosophical schools concerning the Homeric myths of the Greek gods.[34] These were judged to be either fictional stories for edification or warning, or else poetic metaphors of life. In a recent study, Bernard Batto has given an excellent overview of the different attitudes towards myth up to the twentieth century.[35] It is a history which continued to emphasize that biblical events were "historical" rather than fictional or metaphorical "myth." This concern to defend the bible against the false claims of pagan religions was all the more fiercely taken up when the discovery and decipherment of Babylonian and Egyptian literature in the late nineteenth century introduced hundreds of references to Ancient

---

[32] This by no means negates the likelihood of editorial seams that are added to sum up and link sections in the prophet's thought at a stage after the basic collection and its ordering were in place. Passages such as 11:18-21 or 37:24-28, which sound major motifs of the prophet proleptically, may well be positioned by the hands of editors.

[33] Note, e.g., that the widely-maintained opinion that 16:59-63 is a postexilic expansion of the priestly school that produced the P source of the Pentateuch, since these verses are an echo of Genesis 17. P is at latest, exilic, as I argue in *Reading the Old Testament: An Introduction* (New York: Paulist, 1984) 398-404.

[34] See the discussion of classical skepticism about the Homeric myths in C.K. Barrett, "Myth and the New Testament: the Greek word nudos," *Expository Times* 68 (1957) 345-48.

[35] Bernard F. Batto, *Slaying the Dragon: Mythmaking in the Biblical Tradition* (Louisville: Westminster/John Knox, 1992).

Near Eastern myths parallel to biblical texts.[36] Biblical defenders largely shifted from attacks on the myths of ancient religions as misguided imaginings towards viewing them as the pre-critical worldview of polytheism, i.e., a kind of pre-logical "scientific" observation of how the world can be explained.[37] They believed Israelite tradition had eviscerated this worldview by reinterpreting creation and human relationship to the divine through the lens of its monotheism. Although Israel kept the stories and the language of their neighbors' myths, they transformed them into "countermyths," rooted firmly in history, that illustrated how all the powers and attributes for god that were claimed for pagan deities properly belong to Yahweh, God of Israel, and how all the baneful and perverted views of creation are eliminated by such a monotheistic understanding.[38] This approach to myth in the Hebrew Bible tends to view any use of mythological language, or even allusion to it, as propaganda for the supremacy of the God of Israel, and therefore as almost entirely metaphorical in intent. Certainly, Israel itself did not "believe in" the actual truth of mythical stories since these are almost totally dependent on a polytheistic religious system to make sense as explanations of the world we live in.[39]

However, a more positive approach to the role of myth in religious thinking, including that of Jews and Christians and their sacred texts, has gradually emerged in this century. Psychology, through Freud and Jung;[40] anthropology, through Levy-Bruhl and others;[41] comparative religion through Mircea Eliade,[42] and the "Myth and Ritual" school of Sidney Hooke,[43] as well as sociology and philosophy[44] have

---

[36] See the discussion on reactions to the mythological in Hans Frei, *The Eclipse of Biblical Narrative: A Study in Eighteenth and Nineteenth Century Hermeneutics* (New Haven: Yale University, 1974), chap. 14 "Myth and Narrative Meaning," pp. 267-81. For the practical discussion among fundamentalists, see Kathleen Boone, *The Bible Tells Them So: The Discourse of Protestant Fundamentalism* (Albany; State University of New York, 1989) 23-60.

[37] William Foxwell Albright, *History, Archaeology and Christian Humanism* (New York: McGraw-Hill, 1964) 83-102, "The Place of the Old Testament in the History of Thought;" Lucien Lévy-Bruhl, *Primitive Mentality* (London: George Allen & Unwin, 1923); and Peter Ellis, *Men and Message of the Old Testament* (Collegeville, MN; Liturgical press, 1963) 75. James Frazer, *The Golden Bough: A Study in Magic and Religion* (London: MacMillan, 1911-1915) in 12 volumes.

[38] See James Barr, *Old and New in Interpretation* (New York: Harper & Row, 1966) 15-33; also the wide-ranging discussion in Lynn Clapham, "Mythopoeic Antecedents of the Biblical World View and their Transformation in Early Israelite Thought." *Magnalia Dei* (ed. F.M. Cross, W. Lemke and P.D. Miller, Jr.; New York: Doubleday, 1976) 108-119.

[39] See Brevard Childs, *Myth and Reality in the Old Testament* (Studies in Biblical Theology 27; London: SCM Press, 1960); also George Ernest Wright, *God Who Acts: Biblical Theology as Recital* (Studies in Biblical Theology 8; London: SCM Press, 1952).

[40] Sigmund Freud, *The Interpretation of Dreams* (first published in 1900; found in J. Strachey, *Standard Editions of the Complete Psychological Works*; London, 1953); C.J. Jung and C. Kerényi, *Essays on a Science of Mythology* (Bollingen Series XXII; New York: Pantheon, 1949).

[41] Lévy-Bruhl, *op. cit.*, and Bronislaw Malinowski, *Magic, Science and Religion and Other Essays* (Garden City, N.Y.: Doubleday, 1926, 1954) 72-124.

[42] Mircea Eliade, *The Sacred and the Profane: The Nature of Religion* (New York: Harper & Row, 1957); *Cosmos and History: The Myth of the Eternal Return* (New York: Harper & Row, 1959).

[43] Sidney H. Hooke, editor, *Myth and Ritual: Essays on the Myth and Ritual of the Hebrews in Relation to the Cultic Pattern of the Ancient East* (Oxford: Oxford University, 1933).

all contributed to understanding the significant role that mythopoeic thinking plays in human comprehension of the meaning of the world and our place in it. To be "mythopoeic" means to be devising stories that forge opposing human experiences of the immanent and transcendent, the natural and the supernatural, the explainable and unexplainable, into a coherent relationship with each other. It bridges the fundamental polarity found in the deepest structures of that experience like death and life, male and female, change and stability, order and chaos.[45] It doesn't have to be logical or scientific, it has to connect and in some way heal the gap in coherence of our experience of life. These "stories" touch foundational patterns of experience—the who, what, why and how of the origins of life's present realities. They must, as definers of myth make clear, be social in nature, i.e., they must be shared by the community as a whole; they must suggest reasons for behavior to the community; they must connect easily to ritual and acts of worship (even if they do not have to be the actual scripts of ritual celebrations); and they must be reflective and intentional (i.e., they are constructed to explain some aspect of reality, and can be taught and interpreted). As Batto points out very cogently, myths are *symbols* of a society, they set the patterns for the community's structures, religious practice and personal relationships and behaviors.[46]

I dwell on this understanding of myth in order to insist that Israel itself was quite conscious of its need for myths about Yahweh in order to undergird its faith and make sense over the centuries of its ever-more-refined monotheism. This mythopoeic process was operative throughout Israelite thinking and literary production down to the basic canonization of both the Pentateuch and Prophetic corpus in the fifth century.[47] And it lived on even into New Testament and early rabbinic times in the composition of apocalyptic works.[48]

Batto makes two other important observations in his book that are worth emphasizing. The first is that the study of myths from the ancient world reveals that almost all of them are carefully written compositions rather than reports of oral recitation.[49] Indeed, when we do see the myth recited, as appears in the broken record of the Babylonian Akitu festival, the priest *reads* the Enuma Elish to the god Marduk.[50] This does not deny that myths may have been told orally in hundreds of variant forms, or even that established oral versions were widely known, but it does

---

[44] Henri Frankfort, *Before Philosophy* (or earlier, *The Intellectual Adventure of Ancient Man*; Chicago: University of Chicago, 1946) 3-27, "Myth and Reality." For Philosophy, Ernst Cassirer, *Philosophie der symbolischen Formen* (Berlin: B. Cassirer; 2 vols., 1923, 1931. English edition: The Philosophy of Symbolic Forms, translated by B. Manheim; 3 vols. New Haven: Yale University, 1953).

[45] Claude Levi-Strauss, *Structural Anthropology* (New York: Basic Books, 1976); Edmund Leach and D.A. Aycock, *Structuralist Interpretations of Biblical Myth* (Cambridge: Cambridge University, 1983).

[46] Batto, *Slaying the Dragon*, p. 11.

[47] See John W. Miller, *The Origins of the Bible: Rethinking Canon History* (New York: Paulist Press, 1994), who argues forcefully for the completed canonization of the Hebrew Bible from Genesis through the Major Prophets by the fifth century.

[48] See Hermann Gunkel, *Schöpfung und Chaos in Urzeit und Endzeit: Eine religionsgeschichtliche Untersuchung über Gen 1 und Ap Joh 12* (Göttingen: Vandenhoeck und Ruprecht, 1985).

[49] Batto, *Slaying the Dragon*, 13-14.

[50] ANET 332.

suggest that the myths were carefully composed and studied, and that they often served important educational or socio-religious functions within ancient society.[51] There is ample evidence that Ezekiel differs from earlier prophetic books because of its insistent literary character. It is structured and ordered to move from one point to another as modern books might.[52] It takes the reader from impending judgment to destruction to restoration in stages, and the editorial connections are clear.

Batto's second point is stated thus, "The Combat Myth, whether in its Babylonian or Canaanite form, undergirds to some extent virtually every aspect of Israel's supposedly historically based faith."[53] He presents detailed studies of Genesis 2-8 (J source); Genesis 1 (P source); the Exodus Narrative; Ezekiel 38-39; and assorted Psalms and passages from the Deuteronomic History to prove its pervasiveness in Israel's understanding of Yahweh. Each new written attempt, however, also enlarged, adapted and transformed the traditional elements in the common semitic Combat Myth to make a new point or more developed point about how the God of Israel was to be understood. Thus mythmaking was not a matter of repeating ancient stories, but a lively process of growth. Batto's work is especially important because he convincingly illustrates how biblical authors consciously used the myth's basic patterns to interpret an active role for God in the changing historical situation of the nation. It seems to me that of all the examples, none stands forth more sharply than the thorough-going use of the Combat Myth in the final section of Ezekiel, chapters 38-48. And yet, this is only one piece in the mythmaking found throughout the book.[54]

At this point, we should distinguish between "mythopoetic" language which uses as metaphors and allusions well-known images or words from the popular myths, and "mythopoeic" activity that seeks to describe or portray *new* divine activity in categories with which the primordial divine activity of creating and originating has always been described. The mythopoetic remains a literary ornament, while a truly mythopoeic text attempts to persuade the audience that God is indeed creating something new just as in the day of primeval creation. Both are found throughout the Hebrew Scriptures, and Ezekiel makes use of the mythopoetic frequently, as, for example, in allusions to the cherubim throne (chaps. 1, 10; cf. the tree of life in chapter 32; or the description of Sheol in chapter 32). But if we examine the overall shape of the book, a larger mythopoeic purpose will become evident that moves far beyond simple mythopoetic allusion. It is our purpose to sketch that larger intent, and to suggest the reason for it. To do this, we will move backward through the text.

---

[51] Thorkild Jacobsen, *Treasures of Darkness: A History of Mesopotamian Religion* (New Haven: Yale University Press, 1976).
[52] See Ellen Davis, *Swallowing the Scroll*, 12.
[53] Batto, *Slaying The Dragon*, 3.
[54] L. Boadt, "Rhetorical Strategies," 186-87.

The Place of Ezekiel 40-48

Some of these concerns have been expressed by recent studies on Ezekiel 40-48. Thus, Jon Levenson, writing in 1976, traces several important themes that play a prominent role in these chapters: the mountain of God, the role of the king or prince, and the role of the priests in the new land.[55] Ezekiel employs all three of these themes in order to stress his rejection of the current ideologies of his day. Instead, the prophet hearkens back to ideals of an earlier period, at least as expressed in the Priestly traditions, that emphasized the holiness of God's name and a fidelity to the divine covenant that demanded total loyalty on the part of Israel.

Thus Ezek 45:7-17, 21-25 and 46:1-18, on the role of the prince, is modeled on the *nasî'* of each tribe in Numbers 2 and 7, who represent the leaders of faithful Israel on the march in the desert.[56] So, too, the diatribe against the levitical priests and the exaltation of the Zadokites, found in Ezek 44:6-16 and 48:11, recalls the story of Beth Peor in Numbers 25 where the criterion of loyalty was the rejection of all foreigners in the worshipping assembly. Ezekiel evidently believed that the priesthood of his day had allowed foreign idolatry into the temple (Ezek 8-11), and compared them unfavorably with the ancestor of Zadok, Phinehas, who had proven the archetype of a loyal priest at Beth Peor. Both for the prince and the priesthood, it was the ideal of the Exodus period that must prevail.[57]

But for my purposes, Levenson's treatment of the mountain of God is more important. He connects the mountain of Ezekiel's vision in chap. 40:2 (*har gaboah m^e'od*) on which there was a structure or form like a city (*k^emibneh 'îr*), with four separate traditions: the Mount Zion tradition, the Garden of Eden, Mount Sinai, and Mount Abarim. He notes about the Zion tradition that it often speaks of how high Mt. Zion is, and closely connects the ascent of the mountain with worship of God. Zion is called the holy mountain in this tradition (cf. Ps 48:2), and links fresh water to the temple (Ps 46:4), both themes that appear in Ezekiel 40-48. He points to a very strong connection between these nine chapters in Ezekiel and Psalm 48 in particular.[58]

He also notes a link between this mountain in Ezekiel and the image of Eden.[59] Ezek 28:14 tells the myth of the king of Tyre on the "holy mountain" as a figure of Eden, and Ezekiel uses the edenic theme elsewhere, notably in chapter 31 on the king of Egypt's pretensions. Themes such as water in the garden (Gen 2:10-14) or the tree of life (Gen 2:9) are reflected in Ezekiel's references to the river in chapter 47 or the tree of life in chapter 31. Levenson, however, understands the Zion tradition to be the primary vehicle through which such edenic motifs are brought to bear in Ezekiel's visions. Levenson sees the possibility that Ezekiel intended to

---

[55] Jon Levenson, *Theology of the Program of Restoration of Ezekiel 40-48* (Harvard Semitic Monographs 10; Decatur, GA: Scholar's Press, 1976).

[56] Ibid. pp. 57-107.

[57] Ibid. pp. 129-158.

[58] Ibid. pp. 7-24.

[59] Ibid. pp. 25-36.

identify Eden with the Jordan valley around the Dead Sea (as perhaps suggested in the description of Sodom and Gomorrah in Genesis 13) as part of a plan to reorient Israel in exile away from Mesopotamia and towards their homeland. In any case, the link between a mountain of God and a paradisal setting is present in the Ugaritic ideas of the mountain of El or Mount Saphon for Baal.[60]

The Mountain in Ezekiel is also associated with Mount Sinai.[61] First of all, Ezekiel 40-48 is the only body of Law in the Old Testament not in Moses' mouth, so Ezekiel plays the role. Secondly, the prophet is shown the blueprint of the temple as Moses was shown the plan of the sanctuary in the desert in Exod 25:9, 40. Thirdly, the whole vision and law giving are oriented to proper worship and community ordering as in the P strands in the books of Exodus through Numbers.

Finally, Levenson shows a linkage between the structure of Ezekiel 40-48 and the materials of the final chapters of the P narrative in Numbers 27-36.[62] It begins with Moses climbing Mt. Abarim to view the Holy Land which he may not enter. Then follows the definition of the liturgical calendar in Numbers 28-29 (cf. Ezek 45:18-25, 46:1-13); the distribution of the land in Numbers 32-33 (cf. Ezekiel 47-48); setting the boundaries of the land in Numbers 34 (cf. Ezek 47:13-20); allotting territory to the Levites in Numbers 35 (cf. Ezek 45:1-6, 48:13-14); and giving the rights of inheritance in Numbers 36 (cf. Ezek 46:16-18). Although the order is not identical, the programs in both are very close to one another.

Levenson has pointed to some very significant aspects of Ezekiel 40-48, above all the clear use of mythical traditions of the sacred mountain and the ideal pattern of the Exodus period, as well as the very similar visionary aims of both the P strands of the Pentateuch and the author of Ezekiel 40-48. But although he affirms that this bloc of material builds on Ezek 33-37, he does not attempt to develop a systematic inter-connection among chapters 33-37, 38-39 and 40-48.

Another important recent study is the sketch of the theology of Ezekiel 40-48 by Moshe Greenberg in *Interpretation*.[63] It is a preview of a more indepth treatment in his promised second volume of the Anchor Bible Commentary on Ezekiel. Greenberg sees 40-48 from the hand of the prophet, building on the promised restoration of Ezek 20:40 and 37:24-28. He especially sees the strong connection between the themes in these chapters 40-48 and the priestly style of the Pentateuch. The combination of law-giving and temple-building matches the role of Moses, the varied styles of lists and regulations are much like those of the Pentateuchal Book of Leviticus, and the concern with purification of people and land matches that of P. Greenberg also points to thematic links of Ezekiel 40-48 with the Jubilee theme of Lev 25 and the curses and blessings in Leviticus 26 which form the pattern for the structure of Ezekiel as a whole divided into chapters 1-24 and 33-48. Greenberg identifies three divisions of Ezekiel's program: (1) the building of a new temple

---

[60] CTA, texts 1-6. See the English translation available in *ANET* 129-142.

[61] Levenson, Theology of the Program of Restoration, pp. 37-42.

[62] Ibid. pp. 42-44.

[63] Moshe Greenberg, "The Design and Theme of Ezekiel's Program of Restoration," *Interpretation* 38 (1984) 181-208.

(40:1-43:12); The giving of law for personnel of the temple (44:1-46:24); and apportioning the land among the people (47:13-48:35). Two transition passages bridge the three: first the late description of the altar in 43:13-27, and second, the living water in 47:1-11. All three themes stress the separation of the holy from the profane, the gradations and division of roles, and the boundaries and who may enter and exit.

Greenberg builds on Levenson and Zimmerli's commentary to specify even further the close programmatic association of 40-48 with the Priestly ideal of Israel. Above all, he denies that it could be postexilic since it shows no realistic matching of the true temple dimensions or legal practices based on the Pentateuch which governed Israel at that time. And he emphasizes the very close linkage to the rest of Ezekiel to the point that without 40-48, the book would not be complete.

A third important study has been done by Susan Niditch in 1986.[64] She compares the visionary structure of chapters 40-48 with the Buddhist mandala tradition and notes the typical link between a visionary mystical vision and practical instruction that are found in both. The tour of the prophet through the temple is much like the shaman's journey around the mandala. The temple is the symbol of the cosmos and there are very strong creation and re-creation themes present in both Ezekiel and mandala thought. She offers several detailed analyses that link the concern with boundaries and limits in Ezekiel to the pattern of Genesis 1-11, esp. chapters 1-3, where the concern focusses primarily on the limits for human beings and the proper order of the world. But other themes, such as proper clothing, the purity of the participants and the difference between the people of Israel and the foreigners that play such a prominent role in Ezekiel are also found in Genesis 3, 9 and 11, and 10.

Niditch also sees a strong bond of unity centered on creation mythology for chapters 38-39 and 40-48, largely borrowed from Canaanite sources.[65] The pattern present in the Ugaritic myth of Baal and the Enuma Elish describes a cosmic battle of the warrior god who is to be king followed by the building of a new temple in his honor after the victory is achieved. She sees a series of six steps common to both the ANE myth and Ezekiel's development in these chapters: (1) the challenge to the deity; (2) the battle; (3) the victory of the god; (4) the triumphal procession; (5) the enthronement and building of the palace; (6) the feast. Most of these occur in chapters 38-39 with the building last in 40-48. Ezekiel 37 can be added to these as the vision of a new creation.

Like Greenberg and Levenson, Niditch sees these insights as compelling reason to link the writing of 40-48 to the same hand that composed 1-39.

---

[64] Susan Niditch, "Ezekiel 40-48 in a Visionary Context," *CBQ* 48 (1986) 208-224.
[65] See Michael Coogan, *Stories from Ancient Canaan* (Westminster Press, 1975) 75-115. See also Paul Hanson, "Zechariah 9 and the Recapitulation of an Ancient Ritual Pattern," *JBL* 92 (1973) 37-59.

The Mythological Aspects of Chapters 38-39

Once it seems possible that chapters 40-48 depend heavily on the mythopoetic patterns of ANE divine warrior creation and kingship myths, the same pattern should be sought in chapters 38-39. Niditch has briefly proposed such a course of action, but the relationship needs to be more thoroughly studied. Of course, hers is not the first suggestion along this line. It has long been noted by commentators that Ezekiel 38-39 has connections to well-known cosmic battle myths and to such biblical passages as Isaiah 24-27 and Isa 14:24-27.[66] Indeed, many scholars have posited that these chapters are a later proto-apocalyptic addition from the postexilic period.[67] Zimmerli's work, however, has changed the focus dramatically, emphasizing instead the prophetic reuse of older materials, especially the traditions of the foe from the north in Jeremiah 4-6, the defeat of the enemies on the mountains of Israel in Isaiah 14, and the defeat of enemies attacking Mt. Zion in Pss. 46, 48, 76. He also alludes briefly to the idea of a sacrificial feast behind the strange banquet of the slain in Ezek 39:17-20 that is found in Zeph 1:7 and Jer 12:9-13 and 46:10. Zimmerli, however, like most of the earlier commentators, is more interested in the historical referent to Gog and Magog and contents himself with understanding the mythical references as merely helpful to expressing the danger from a threatening foe from the north. He concedes there is a bare possibility that most of the two chapters stem from Ezekiel.[68]

Richard Clifford brings out several more interconnections with both the Ugaritic myths and the corresponding biblical chapters, but cautiously refrains from seeing a consistent mythic pattern behind Ezekiel 38-39 from the scattered traditions from Canaan and Israel. He does suggest there may be a single theme that is partially reflected in various places: that of a victory banquet of the king of the gods on a mountain while the enemies are made the victims of a slaughter feast.[69] The strongest support for this occurs in two texts from Isaiah: 25:6-8 and 34:5-8.

Indeed there should be a connection. First of all, in 1976, Michael Astour published his study of the Cuthean Legend of Naram Sin[70] in which he found the basic pattern of: (1) the summoning of an enormous army from the wilds of the North massed against Naram Sin; (2) a long invasion southwards in which the king suffered several defeats because of his hubris; (3) finally, his turning to the gods and gaining divine help for a total victory in the mountain country. But he was not to slaughter the enemy, Enlil himself would do so! Thus the Naram Sin Legend ends as does Ezekiel's vision, with the defeat of the barbarian hordes by Yahweh and not by any strength or might of Israel's armies.

---

[66] Thus Hugo Gressmann, *Der Ursprung der israelitisch-jüdischen Eschatologie* (FRLANT 6; Göttingen, 1905); Sigmund Mowinckel, *Psalmenstudien II* (Oslo: 1922).

[67] See the survey of authors who doubt the authenticity of these chapters in Zimmerli, *Ezekiel 2*, p. 302.

[68] Zimmerli, *Ezekiel 2*, pp. 296-304.

[69] Richard Clifford, *The Cosmic Mountain in Canaan and the Old Testament* (Harvard Semitic Monographs 4; Cambridge, MA: Harvard University, 1972) 173-177.

[70] Michael Astour, "Ezekiel's Prophecy of Gog and the Cuthewan Legend of Naram Sin," *JBL* 95 (1976) 567-79.

Ezekiel has adapted this mythological paradigm and diverges from the basic plot only in eliminating the central drama of Naram Sin's proud attempts to fight the hordes alone without the help of the gods. Only when he repented, offered sacrifices, and consulted the divine omens, did the gods intervene and destroy the hordes by plague and fire and natural disasters.[71] As Astour noted, this theme of royal hubris was unnecessary to Ezekiel's plan at this point in the book, since divine punishment had already been completed against both Judah's kings and the kings of foreign nations for hubris by chapter 32, and Ezekiel now needed a new purpose for the mythological story, namely its emphasis on the ability of Yahweh to maintain his holy land against all powers of the earth, and to insure peace and security for Israel forever.

The crucial points that need to be stressed are that Gog and his fellow kings are clearly symbolic of the vast hordes that live at the far edges of the known world and have some supernatural power deriving from being suckled by the chaos goddess Tiamat, but are human nevertheless.[72] Since the legend insists on this connection to Tiamat and even calls them "birdlike" (a quality that is seen in many mythological themes for ancient gods),[73] we can see the echoes of the primeval battle for order still threatening in their advance as an army, and the need for decisive battle of God against primeval evil (Tiamat) one more time. We might apply here Gunkel's principle of *Urzeit ist Endzeit*, to note how the final cataclysm to end this world and return to creation of a new world shares the same theme of divine combat against evil and chaos.[74] It can be noted that Ezek 38:9, *'alîtâ kasso'â tabô' kᵉ'anan*, "You (Gog) will advance like the storm, you will come like the thundercloud," echoes both the Naram Sin Legend and such ancient lamentations over destruction by enemies as the "Lamentation over the Destruction of Ur" (ANET 458) in which the Gutians are described as an evil storm unleashed by Enlil.

---

[71] Astour, p. 576, lists the following points in common between Ezekiel 38-39 and Naram-Sin: (1) a huge horde is set apart by the gods in the far north; (2) this area is Anatolia; (3) there are several kings under one supreme ruler; (4) this ruler bears an historical king's name but is used symbolically; (5) both accounts have the hordes go on a long march of plunder and devastation; (6) the hordes consist of many different nations; (7) these hordes are joined by southern hordes as they march; (8) they were destroyed by the gods not by human armies; (9) in both Ezekiel and Naram Sin, the anger of the chief god was paramount.

[72] The text explicitly says that they were created by the mother-goddess Belit-Ili, but nursed by Tiamat. That this refers to their demonic character can be seen in Ashurbanipal's charge that the chief of the Cimmerians was "the king of the ummanmanda, creature of Tiamat, likeness of the evil-demon" (D.D. Luckenbill, *Records of Assyria and Babylonia*; Chicago: University of Chicago, 1927; vol. 2, #1001). See Astour, p. 573.

[73] For the significance of icthyphallic and birdheaded creatures as symbolic of divine powers, see the discussion of Egyptian Religion, *Encyclopaedia Britannica* (Chicago: University of Chicago, 1973) vol. 8, pp. 52-53. Excellent illustrations are found in ANEP 564, 565, 567, 573.

[74] See note 48.

Astour was impressed enough with the similarities between the two works to insist that Ezekiel both knew the Naram Sin Legend and readapted it for his own uses.[75] If one accepts this, and I do, then suddenly the question is no longer primarily whether we can identify Ezekiel himself as the original author who intended Gog to be the fulfillment of Jeremiah's "foe from the North" oracles (Jeremiah 4-6).[76] At the same time, it is less important to wonder whether the obscure claim in 38:17-18 that Gog is "the one of whom the former prophets spoke," refers to some other earlier prophetic text which Ezekiel thought still had to be fulfilled.[77] The question whether these two chapters are a substantial composition of the prophet or have extensive interpolations by the editors of the book may be partially answered when we recognize that the striking similarities to the Naram Sin story clearly point to the author or authors' mythopoeic (and not merely mythopoetic!) intent from the start.

M. Nobile in 1986 has also pointed to the close ties of chapters 38-39 with the mythic patterns of (1) divine theophany, 92) battle with the forces of chaos, and (3) the establishment of the divine temple (palace).[78] But he would encompass the entire plan of the Book of Ezekiel in this pattern so that the theophany of the god is seen in chapter 1 (as well as 8-11 and 43); the battle against enemies is tied to all the Oracles Against Nations in chapters 25-32, 38-39, and to a certain extent in 8-11, which would include Israel; and finally the building of the temple in chapters 40-48. Indeed, he emphasizes the role of chapters 38-39 as fulfilling the destruction of the enemy nations, the seven nations of Deut 7:1, which Ezekiel alludes to.[79] 39:6-16 adds a note about seven years of fuel and seven months of burning to bring to completion this destruction of the seven nations. These final two chapters have been separated from 25-32 in order to insert 33-37 so that the present destruction and restoration of historical Israel might be connected to the future cosmic war for Yahweh's final domination. Thus the entire second half of Ezekiel is built on a careful interplay between the mythopoetic language of the creation pattern and the actual analysis of historical events in the sixth century.

Nobile is onto something in this. Margulis has already developed the strong role of mythic imagery in the oracles against foreign leaders in Ezekiel 26-32.[80] To

---

[75] The work itself was apparently very well-known in the ancient world. Four copies have been located in Ashurbanipal's Library at Nineveh, and a fifth copy was found in Sultantepe, totally 175 lines of text. See Astour, pp. 572-73, for original sources.

[76] Or less likely, Ezekiel may have intended to model Gog on the king of Babylon in Isaiah 14:1. Since Jeremiah's "foe from the North" would also presumably be widely understood to refer to Babylon, any use of these texts as sources for the portrayal of Gog would be only by way of borrowing their mythological power to apply to an even greater symbol of chaotic evil.

[77] See a full discussion of this issue in Daniel Block, "Gog in Prophetic Tradition: A New Look at Ezekiel XXXVIII:17," *VT* XLII (1992) 154-172.

[78] M. Nobile, "Beziehung zwischen Ez 32, 17-32 und der Gog-Perikope (Ez 38-39) im Lichte der Endredaktion," BETL LXXIV (1986) 255-259.

[79] See the discussion of the significance of "7" in the OAN of Ezekiel in L. Boadt, *Ezekiel's Oracles Against Egypt*, 9-11. See also note 88.

[80] B. Margulis, *Studies in the Oracles Against the Nations* (unpublished dissertation available through University Microfilms: Ann Arbor, MI, 1967).

connect this intent with a similar intent in chapters 38-39 leaves less room for arguing that the Gog pericopes are later insertions.

Do Chapters 38-39 Function Parallel to Chapters 25-32?

Nobile's suggestion that there was an original connection between chapters 25-32 and 38-39 points in the right direction. B. Margulis has already developed at length the importance of a subcategory of the Oracles Against Nations in chapters 25-32 which he terms "Oracles Against Foreign Rulers".[81] These are found employed against the king of Tyre in chapters 27-28, against the pharaoh in chapters 29, 31, and 32, and against Gog in chapters 38-39. They all share an intense use of mythological language connected in some way to the fundamental combat myth of chaos versus the god of order. At this point, we need to ask whether chapters 38-39 are intended to be parallel to the oracles against Egypt and Tyre earlier in the book which would suggest that they are part of a single overall plan.

Two recent studies offer some support to this approach. Robert Wilson's analysis of the editorial history of Ezekiel 28 sees a systematic series of references to the situation of the Jerusalem priesthood and temple, as well as the king of Judah, hidden under the primal royal myth of the king of Tyre.[82] Many of the mythological images in 28:11-19 are associated with the temple and its worship, including the use of cherubim in the holy place (28:16), gem stones on the priestly vestment (28:13), and the exaltation of the temple on a "holy mountain" (*har qodeš*) in 28:14 (cf. Pss 2:6; 48:2; Ezek 20:40). Wilson sees the underlying meaning to be tied to the destruction of the high priest and the temple in order to purify the land from those who defiled its sanctuaries (see Ezek 5:11; 23:38). He concludes that 28:11-19, at least, was really aimed at the high priest and not the king of Tyre, and the allusions "could not possibly have been missed by Ezekiel's audience."[83] Although Wilson has trouble identifying how such an oracle got included editorially alongside real attacks against Tyre in chaps. 26:1-28:10, the point can be drawn from his examples that mythological allusions attached to oracles against foreign powers often hint at God's designs for the land of Israel.

However, it seems to me that the double level of meaning against both Tyre and Israel stems from past history in which Tyre itself was the home base for the inroads of the cult of Baal into official Israel (see 1 Kings 17-21). Ezekiel's direct assault on the divine pretensions of the king of Tyre is really an attack on the claims of Baalism as an equal challenger to the divine authority of Yahweh over the land. This possibility gains strength when we note that a major accusation against the pharaoh of Egypt in the next bloc of oracles (chapters 29-32) is how he pollutes his streams

---

[81] *Ibid.* pp. 290-98.

[82] Robert Wilson, "The Death of the King of Tyre: The Editorial History of Ezekiel 28," *Love and Death in the Ancient Near East*, ed. John Marks and Robert Good (Guilford, CT: Four Quarters Press, 1987) 211-18.

[83] Wilson, "The Death of the King of Tyre," 217.

(Ezek 32:2) and how his punishment will require a purification of the land for forty years (29:9-13). The fate of the Egyptians thus becomes identical with that planned for the people of Judah in chaps. 1-24: exile and becoming small and powerless (29:14-15). Even the next step is the same: Yahweh will intervene after a time and restore Egypt as a purified land, still small and whose king will be without any divine or human glory (32:13-14, 17-32; cf. 20:40-44). Thus, this series of oracles can also be read as speaking both of the historical fate of Egypt as an enemy and at the same time of its paradigmatic value for understanding God's intention in allowing Judah to be devastated by its enemies. Nor would Ezekiel's audience forget that Egypt's pharaoh, too, like the king of Tyre, represented divine claims that challenged Yahweh's sovereign authority.

In the second study, Bernard Batto offers a particularly helpful analysis of the parallel roles played by the Oracles against Egypt and the Gog episode.[84] From chapters 25 to 48, he identifies a carefully structured double pattern of (1) 25-32 condemning Israel's historical enemies to (2) prepare for the establishment of the actual revived Israel in its land in 33-37; and (3) chapters 38-39 condemning a mythological foe to prepare for the (4) "advent of the eschatological era" in 40-48.[85] The main point is that the book intends this double series as two different levels of destruction and restoration, one on the historical level and one on the metahistorical level.[86] Batto amply surveys the mythic connections in the Gog oracles to the traditional creation/combat myths and concludes, "it is pointless to identify Gog and Magog with known historical entities from the ancient world."[87] Gog represents chaos, and Ezekiel's language employs the clear symbols of the conflict between creation and non-existence, cosmos and chaos.

One final consideration centers on the use of the symbolic number "7" in both blocs of 25-32 and 38-39. There are seven nations named in 25-32, and the final object of condemnation, Egypt, has seven oracles directed against it.[88] Many commentators also recognize that chapters 38-39 can be divided into seven oracles, each introduced by the messenger formula (38:3, 10, 14, 17, 39:1, 17, 25).[89] Even if we take the messenger formula to be only a seven-time drumbeat of judgment, and not strictly as the dividing line of independent oracles,[90] its role parallel to the Egyptian oracles is striking. At the very least, it reinforces the impression that chapters 38-39 are intended to stand in a function that matches that of chapters 25-32. Simply speaking, that function is that prior to any decisive action for restoring Israel as the people among whom God's universal glory and sovereignty is made

---

[84] B. Batto, "Egypt and Gog as Mythic Symbols in Ezekiel," chap. 5 of *Slaying the Dragon*, pp. 153-67. See note 35.

[85] *Ibid.* p. 157.

[86] See Greenberg, *Ezekiel 1-20*, pp. 309-24 on Ezekiel 17.

[87] *Slaying the Dragon*, 159.

[88] See Boadt, *Ezekiel's Oracles Against Egypt*, p. 9.

[89] See J.B. Taylor, *Ezekiel: An Introduction and Commentary* (Tyndale Old Testament Commentaries; Downer's Grove, IL: Intervarsity Press, 1969) 242 and Douglas Staurt, *Ezekiel* (Communicator's Commentary; Dallas, TX Word, 1989) 352.

[90] Leslie Allen, *Ezekiel 20-48* (Word Biblical Commentary; Dallas, TX, Word, 1990) 202.

manifest, there must be a manifestation of divine subjection of the nations with their rival pretensions to that glory made on behalf of their gods.[91]

The Function of Chapters 33-37

Many themes that were sounded in judgment against Israel in chapters 1-24 are "redeemed" in God's reversal of that condemnation in chapters 33-37. Thus the land that had become impure will be purified; the idolatry that was rampant will be forever ended; the glory of the Lord that was shamed will be again revealed; the people who had to be punished by exile will be restored; the mountains that had been defiled will be holy once again.[92] The program set forth in these chapters includes the people's acknowledgment of Yahweh as the true king over them and the submission of their human leaders to divine rule; the purification of the land; the restoration of the people to their homes; the renewal of the covenant and a full return to the blessing of the days of king David. It is a picture of a nation living by its covenantal obligations and according to the demands of holiness (*torah*). It fulfills the vision of chapter 20 which is rooted in the historical experience of Israel and foresees a revitalized historical nation not unlike what God desired in the time of the Exodus but did not get.[93]

At the same time, chapters 33-37 sound the themes that form the basis for what will be described in chapters 38-39, 40-48. Thus the Israel of chapters 33-37 with its obedient people and humble rulers who live in and keep holy the mountains of Yahweh, will be the basis for a universal kingdom of God described in chapters 38-48 that will reveal Yahweh's sovereignty over all the mountains of the earth, and over all the foes that would attack Israel as Edom did in chapter 35. It will also foreshadow with its purified mountains the glory of the true residence of God on Mount Zion, a city and temple that emerges in chapters 40-48 far different than the polluted and idolatrous Jerusalem of the time before Exile. What is developed in 38 to 48 is built upon the covenantal integrity brought about in the oracle series of chapters 33-37.

In sum, there is a conscious unity sought in the sequence of chapters 33-37, 38-39, 40-48. This is programmatic and sets forth a vision of what the restored Israel is to become. Lastly, they stand as a whole in a counterpoint relationship to chapters 1-24, reversing what Israel's sin had brought about.

How Chapters 25-32 Link 1-24 to 33-48

It is commonly held that the O.A.N. as found in the major prophetic collections such as Isaiah 13-23, Jeremiah 46-51 and Ezekiel 25-32 function to bridge between divine

---

[91] See Boadt, "The Function of the Salvation Oracles," p. 4.

[92] *Ibid.* pp. 9-14.

[93] *Ibid.* pp. 19-21.

judgment and divine salvation for Israel itself by reversing the power of foreign nations whom Yahweh had used as instruments of punishment but who had gone on to claim divine control over Israel for themselves. Certainly this is true of Ezekiel 25-32.[94] I have indicated elsewhere that there are special vocabulary uses, found nowhere else in the Hebrew Scriptures, that tie the language of chapters 25-32 to chapters 1-24 and then forward to chapters 38-39.[95] The strong use of mythological language when identifying the enemy as a king of foreign nations, whether He be the king of Tyre, the pharaoh, or Gog of Magog, further suggests that Ezekiel's purpose in organizing the book as a whole involves establishing a counter "myth" for Israel. It rejects the claims of Babylon and of Israel's immediate small neighbors that their gods are stronger than Israel's god, who was humiliated and shown to be powerless by the defeat and exile of 587.

As a prophet in the Exile, and acutely aware of the dangers that life in Babylon creates for a dejected people who complain to him, "the way of the Lord is not just" (33:17), Ezekiel views himself in the middle of a conflict between Yahweh's exclusive call and claim on this people and the attraction of the gods (idols) of other nations. In a preeminent way, the foreign oracles of chapters 25-32 deal with this question of the power and the divine pretensions of foreign gods.

The Judgment Oracles of Chapters 1-24

Ezekiel's reconstruction of the divine "myth" of Yahweh as God of the universe does not employ merely the victory phases or the enthronement phases of the traditional Ancient Near Eastern myth about the annual renewal of divine kingship, but includes as well the prior stages of the war against the gods of order by the forces of chaos and disorder (or "uncreation"). Some elements of this assault have been placed in the O.A.N. and in the Gog episode, as well as in the setting of the oracle against Edom's mountains in chapter 35. But these all represent for Ezekiel stage two of the battle, when foreign enemies join the attack. Stage one is Israel's idolatry itself as a war against Yahweh. This is signalled at the very beginning of chapters 1-24 when God addresses the prophet's task as a mission to "the people of Israel, to a rebel (*hammôrᵉdîm*) nation, who have rebelled (*marᵉdû*) against me; they and their ancestors have transgressed (*pašᵉû*) against me up to this very day!" (Ezek 2:3). The theme of rebellion and stubbornness is sounded throughout these first twenty-four chapters, climaxing in 24:1-14 in which the pot is so encrusted with filth and rust that even fire cannot seem to cleanse it; and 24:15-24, in which even as their own funeral procession is being symbolically enacted out, the people are still asking, "Won't you tell us what these things mean?" (Ezek 24:19).

At key places throughout this first half of the book, the oracles proleptically prepare for the divine victory that will be accomplished in steps throughout chapters 25-48. Certain themes are sounded that will find their reversal or completion only

---

[94] See *Zimmerli 2*, pp. 3-5.
[95] Boadt, *Ezekiel's Oracles Against Egypt*, 176-77.

in the second half of the book. Thus, the theme of the glory of God who must depart the city and the temple in order to destroy it (chapters 8-11) prepares for the return in 43:1-6 to a renewed and rebuilt house of God. At the same moment the prophet announces the day when that victory shall include a new covenant, a new heart and a new spirit which will be fulfilled in 36:26-28 (cf. 11:14-21). Another major theme is "the mountains of Israel" used as a symbol for the whole land, but representing as well the holy mountain of Zion. It is employed throughout the book to emphasize the need for holiness among God's people. The oracle against the mountains in chapter six stresses the need for purification from idolatrous practices; and its use again in chapter 17 focusses on the need for political loyalty to God on the part of kings; its appearance as promise in 20:40 follows the description of the purging of Israel from its rebellious and idolatrous past. At all key points it points ahead to the climactic description of the holy mountain in chapters 40-48.[96] Still other connections between 1-24 and the later half of the book can be made: the comparison of the cosmic trees in chapters 17 and 31; the use of the lamentation to announce the death of the old order in chapters 19 and 24 which prefigures the lamentation over Tyre in chapter 27 and over Egypt in chapter 32, but (shockingly?) *not* over Gog in the day of Yahweh's final victory in chapter 39.

Thus, the allusions to mythological themes in chapters 1-24 are more than simple rhetorical embellishments. They are part of the prophet's elaborate and sustained condemnation of the policies and attitudes of Judah. The nation had not only opposed Babylon's power, which Ezekiel believed was exercised as an instrument of divine rebuke and correction, but embraced alliances with Egypt and Tyre, the two nations that represented the epitome of idolatry, especially in the claims implicit in the divine titulary of their rulers. To combat this rebellious and stubborn rejection of their own God, Ezekiel summons up all the myth-making powers at his disposal to counter their claims and establish the divine kingship of Yahweh. This is readily detected when we realize that nearly every mythological reference can be associated with the annual New Year's rituals of Ancient Near Eastern nations in which the kingship of the chief god was reconfirmed over the universe.[97]

Conclusions

Since the early part of this century, a shift has taken place in Ezekiel studies away from reluctance to attribute any mythological or apocalyptic passages to Ezekiel's own ministry.[98] Most commentators now acknowledge a place for such imagery in Ezekiel's prophecy is likely because of his social location as an exile in Babylon.

---

[96] Boadt, "Rhetorical Strategies," pp. 190-93.

[97] See Sigmund Mowinckel, *The Psalms in Israel's Worship* (Nashville: Abingdon Press, 1962) 106-92; H.J. Kraus, *Theology of the Psalms* (Minneapolis: Augsburg, 1986) 134-36.

[98] See the remarks on the intrusive nature of the language of the OAN and Gog chapters in Walther Eichrodt, *Ezekiel: A Commentary* (OTL; Philadelphia: Westminster Press, 1970) and even more recently in Reuven Ahroni, "The Gog Prophecy and the Book of Ezekiel," *HUCA* 1 (1977) 1-27.

Modern prophetic study has largely also moved past the position that Israel's classical prophets only spoke judgement, to a general acceptance that salvation preaching may have played a secondary but important role as well. What has caused this shift? Two factors stand out: the first is the recovery of so many ancient parallels to the possible cultic occasions in which prophecy may have been exercised. And secondly, there has been extensive assimilation of the work of psalms study which revealed how extensive cosmic, mythological and "protopocalyptic" language was in Israel's cult.[99] Both cultic language and prophecy shared the conviction that there can be no judgment against the forces of evil without victory for the god. Ezekiel's books stands as the example par excellence of this integration.

Ezekiel draws on many other strands of renewal that are not treated here. For example, the book employs typological patterns based on the Exodus and Conquest traditions to formulate Israel's cycle of obedience and disobedience; it ties in to the torah-theology of the Priestly source and the Holiness Code in the Pentateuch; it has many close ties to the ritual psalmody of the Korah collection (Pss. 42-49); and it surely interacts with Jeremiah and the Deuteronomic tradition.[100]

Nevertheless, the mythopoeic elements alone are enough to insist that the book be read as a single, planned whole; that it represents an early exilic attempt to explain the reasons for the destruction of Israel's institutions and to directly counter any claims that Yahweh was therefore powerless against the stronger deities of Babylon, Egypt, Tyre, or any other nation. It seems reasonable to conclude that either this was the vision of the prophet himself, or it was the work of those around him following out the implications of his vision. It is not the result of a long redaction process because it was never adopted by the main tradents of Israel's faith from 540 onwards; it is, instead, a single glorious moment of insight that energized Israel to rebound from despair. It influenced Second Isaiah, it influenced Zechariah, and perhaps Haggai and Third Isaiah as well. But they went off in their own directions, leaving Ezekiel a lonely beacon light in the Exile, always seen brightly against the horizon but never gotten close to again.

---

[99] Thus Aubrey Johnson, *The Cultic Prophet in Ancient Israel* (Cardiff: University of Wales, 1944) and W. H. Bellinger, *Psalmody and Prophecy* (JSOTS 27; Sheffield: JSOT Press, 1984).

[100] Zimmerli, *Ezekiel 1* treats most of these themes in his introductory sections. Work has yet to be done on the links between Ezekiel's mythic patterns and the Exodus, Conquest and cultic festal patterns found in the Psalter.

PSALM 1 AND THE RHETORIC
OF RELIGIOUS ARGUMENTATION

YEHOSHUA GITAY

The first psalm, placed as it is at the start of the great lyrical collection of Hebrew religious poetry is expected to stimulate the reader's religious experience. However, this psalm may perplex the experienced reader with its routine proclamation of what might be summarized by the cliche: "The righteous prosper while the wicked suffer". The various repetitions of this theme throughout the wisdom literature demonstrate its repetitiveness:

> Think now, who that was innocent ever perished?
> Or where were the upright cut off? (Job 4:7)
> But the wicked will be cut off from the land,
> and the treacherous will be rooted out of it.[1] (Prov 2:22)
> The way of the wicked is like deep darkness;
> they do not know what they stumble over. (Prov 4:19)[2]

Nonetheless, this habitual theme of the reward of the righteous versus the fate of the wicked, is not conveyed by the poet of Psalm 1 in its condensed formulaic state. The psalmist confronts the audience with a specific vivid literary structure, creating a monumental poem, which is "more than introduction to the psalter; it is rather a *precis* to the book of Psalms".[3]

From a literary point of view Psalm 1 signifies a specific design of a series of three repeated negatives (v. 1) and a descriptive metaphor (vv. 3-4). The stress on the negatives לא, "no", (*antimachus*) already in the first verse underlines and strengthens the poet's decisive negation of a specific view.[4] The "no" sentences use rhetorical awareness to express a concept which might otherwise be misconstrued. The affirmation demands a sharp rejection of its contradictory view. Furthermore, the employment of figurative language indicates a need to give concrete form to the affirmative view, otherwise the message might elude the

---

[1] The niphal of סחה, "be swept away", is rare. For the piel see Ezek 26:4.
[2] Also compare Prov 10:29 and 15:29 and consult P. Auvray, "Le Psaume 1: Notes de grammaire et d'exégèse," *Revue Biblique* 53 (1946) 365-371.
[3] M. Dahood, *Psalms 1* (Garden City, N.Y.: Doubleday, 1966) 1.
[4] Compare Isa 1:3, 42:2-3, 43:22-24. For the impact of the negative consult Aristotle, *Rhetoric*, 1408a.

addressees. Thus the use of metaphor shows a tendency to demonstrate, that is, to make a certain abstract idea tangible.

This sensitivity to the audience's perception raises the need to explore two fundamental issues, which derive from the psalmist's rhetorical orientation: (1) *why* a known religious theme still requires a complex rhetorical technique of delivery, and (2) *how* this rhetorical strategy is designed to appeal.

The poem's sensitivity to its audience, and its employment of specific rhetorical strategies in order to affect the listeners should not surprise us. The biblical discourse, especially the poetic literature, is furnished with ample illustrations of rhetorical means like figurations, repetitions, sound effects and unconventional patterns designed to attract the reader's (or listener's) attention.[5] It is sufficient for the sake of demonstration to call attention to the song of the vineyard of Isa 5:1-7. The theme of the song is characteristic: the wicked betray, hence they are destroyed: God punishes them. This conventional biblical theme, proclaiming the fundamental prophetic concept of divine judgment, is not plainly recited. Rather, a remarkable parable (song) שירה is employed demonstrating the monotonous prophetic theme in a vivid manner.[6] It appears, then, that standard biblical notions are not shared by the common Israelite audience, who reveal an apparently sceptical attitude towards major principles of the biblical religion. The opinionative and graphical style of Ps 1 indicates that the poem falls into the category of persuasive religious discourse.

Focusing on Ps 1, we notice that the poem starts with a word indicating a familiar formula of "well wishing". The Hebrew word אשרי, the plural construct form of the noun אשר, to quote M. Buber, connotes "a joyful exclamation and an enthusiastic observation".[7] A comparison with other citations of אשרי is illuminating:

אשרי הגוי אשר־ה' אלהיו העם בחר לנחלה לו

Blessed is the nation whose God is the Lord,
the nation that he has chosen as his heritage. (Ps 33:12)

אשרי הגבר יחסה־בו

Blessed is the man who takes refuge with him. (Ps 34:9)

---

[5] For convenient biblical poetics references consult W.G.E. Watson, *Classical Hebrew Poetry* (Sheffield: The University of Sheffield, 1984), L. Alonso Schökel, *A Manual of Hebrew Poetics* (Roma: Editrice Pontificio Istituto Biblico, 1988). Also see R. Alter, *The Art of Biblical Poetry* (New York: Basic Books, 1985).

[6] See Y. Gitay, "The Place and Function of the Song of the Vineyard in Isaiah's Prophecy," in *The Bible*, (ed. H. Bloom; New York: Chelsea House, 1987) 195-203. Also see Y. Gitay, *Isaiah and His Audience* (Assen: Van Gorcum, 1991) 87-116.

[7] M. Buber, *Recht und Unrecht*, cited in H.J. Kraus, *Psalms 1-59* (Minneapolis: Augsburg, 1988) 115. See in there for further bibliography. Also see H. Cazelles, אשרי in *Theological Dictionary of the Old Testament, Vol. 1* (eds G.J. Botterweck and H. Ringgren; Grand Rapids: Eerdmans, 1977) 445-448.

אשרי הגבר אשר־שם ה' מבטחו

Blessed is the one who sets his trust in God. (Ps 40:5)

אשרי יושבי ביתך

Blessed are those who live in your House. (Ps 84:5)

The formulaic statements of אשרי provide full affirmative declarations. Ps 1:1, however, is exceptional. The definition of the objective of the אשרי:

כי אם בתורת ה' חפצו ובתורתו יהגה יומם ולילה

but who has delight in Yahweh's instruction and, reading His Torah he meditates day and night, (v. 2)

is delayed, and instead a long sentence of negatives is inserted. The unexpected lines create a dramatic tension. K. Burke explains:

> Form is the creation of an appetite in the mind of the auditor, and the adequate satisfying of that appetite. This satisfaction - complicated in the human mechanism - at times involves a temporary set of frustrations, but in the end these frustrations prove to be simply a more involved kind of satisfaction, and furthermore serve to make the satisfaction or fulfilment more intense. A work of art ... also involves desires and their appeasement.[8]

The broken pattern makes noticeable the poem's deliberate attempt to capture the audience's full attention. A formulaic pattern might be dismissed by the listeners as a cliche, removing their attention. The need to arouse the audience's interest in a supposedly routine message calls for the dramatical and unexpected structure. The unexpected stimulates curiosity, and both content and form are now the object of the audience's concentration.[9]

The formulaic אשרי is then interrupted with the series of three negatives:

אשר לא הלך בעצת רשעים
ובדרך חטאים לא עמד
ובמושב לצים לא ישב

... who walks not in the counsel of the wicked
nor stands in the way of the sinners
nor sits in the circle of scoffers.

As pointed out above the series of negatives has a rhetorical significance:

> Negation expresses the opposite affirmative with peculiar emphasis.[10]

---

[8] K. Burke, *Counter Statement* (Chicago: The University of Chicago, 1957) 31.

[9] For the question of the cliché and the broken pattern in biblical poetry, consult Y. Gitay, "Deutero-Isaiah: Oral or written?," *JBL* 99 (1980) 185-197.

[10] J. Jebb, *Sacred Literature* (London, 1820) 36, cited in Gitay, *Isaiah*, 45.

The immediate negation rapidly creates a sense of sharp tension between two alternatives one of which is strongly contradicted. The poet furthermore stresses the opposition with the support of stylistic devices. In the first two verses the negative and the positive affirmation employ a deliberate use of tenses, connoting a sense of discontinuity (/לא/ הלך, עמד, ישב). By contrast, the positive, the desirable, is conveyed through a noun (חפצו) and the imperfect (יהגה); connoting therefore a sense of endlessness:

> The imperfect, as opposed to the perfect, represents actions, events, or states which are regarded by the speaker at any moment as still continuing ...[11]

Attention should be given to the vocabulary. As a rule, the Hebrew poets used a selection of stock of word-pairs, creating a common code of communication.[12] However, the choice of the words proclaiming the desirable behaviour: חפצו and יהגה as a pair is irregular.[13] The peculiarity, as R. Alter explains, produces a strong rhetorical impact. He writes thus:

> The process of literary creation ... is an unceasing dialectic between the necessity to use established forms in order to be able to communicate coherently and the necessity to break and remake those forms because they are arbitrary restrictions and because what is merely repeated automatically no longer conveys a message.[14]

The irregular compels the hearers to listen to the words and to concentrate on the description of the righteous.

The wicked are represented as the רשעים, חטאים and לצים ("scoffer", compare Isa 28:15; those who "open their mouth"). However, the objective of the righteous, the Torah, is twice repeated - the same word with no variation - in the two parallel lines of v. 1c. A specific code of biblical prosody, the word-pairs, has again been broken:

> There seems to be an emphasis here on the word Torah that is stronger than the rules of poetry. We must respect the fact that it was more important for the poet than his rule of style.[15]

The repetition is functional; it increases the feeling of existence.[16] The repetition, which attracts attention also through its unconventional prosodic form conveys the validity of the unaltered meaning of the Torah. This stands in contrast with the

---

[11] *Gesenius' Hebrew Grammar*, edited by E. Kautzsch and revise by A.E. Cowley (Oxford: Clarendon Press, 1910) §107a.

[12] See Watson, *Hebrew Poetry*, 128-144.

[13] The common counterpart of הגה is דבר, for instance, Isa 59:13, Job 27:4, Ps 37:30, 38:13, Prov 24:2.

[14] R. Alter, *The Art of Biblical Narrative* (New York: Basic Books, 1981) 62.

[15] H.W. Wolff, "Psalm 1," *EvTH* 9 (1949/50) 389. Compare Kraus, *Psalms 1-59*, 113.

[16] See Ch. Perelman and L. Olbrechts-Tyteca, *The New Rhetoric* (Notre Dame/London: University of Notre Dame, 1969) 174-175.

various sorts of wickedness (the three synonyms) whose instability is symbolized through the alternative terms.

We should pay attention to the ending of the lines comprising vv. 1-2. The first verse ends in closed syllables: ישב , עמד , חטאים , רשעים , הלך while v. 2 ends with open syllables: ולילה , חפצ. Sound and content harmonize: closed-end: the wicked; versus open-continuation: the righteous.

Thus far our discussion has focused on the stylistic and rhetorical devices employed in the psalm to convey a distinct religious concept that contradicts its opposition. This considerable rhetorical effort has not grown in a vacuum; the rhetorical means of dramatization and the stylistic devices of concentration reveal that the language of the psalm is not designed for an objective informative delivery. The poet's choice of language shows an argumentative tension. Perelman and Olbrechts-Tyteca shed light on the question of the deliberate use of language in argumentative discourse:

> The presentation of data is necessarily connected with problems of language. Choice of terms to express the speaker's thought is rarely without significance in the argumentation. But as regards their use by a speaker in a particular speech, the equivalence of synonyms can only be assured by taking account of the total situation into which the speech is fitted, and more particularly, of the social conventions to which the speech may be subject ... In general an indication of the argumentative intent is given by the use of the term representing a departure from ordinary language ... broadly speaking, a term that passes unnoticed may be considered ordinary.[17]

The psalm's stylistic choices and the careful selection of its terms present it as an argumentative discourse, aimed to be noticed through its unusual stylistic choice. The psalm's considerable rhetorical efforts indicate a complex persuasive task. What is the argumentative situation, the problem?

The psalm proclaims a belief:

כי־יודע ה' דרך צדיקים ודרך רשעים תאבד

For Yahweh knows about the way of the righteous, but the way of the wicked leads to destruction. (v. 6)

This is a religious premise shared by the convinced believer. However, this statement might be considered as an opinion by the unconvinced audience. The case of Ps 73 may illustrate the religious scepticism and consequently the argumentative problem. The poet, who sought to be a true believer, notices that the "real world" turns upside down his own religious world view; s/he "saw the prosperity of the wicked" (v. 3b). However, the poet of Ps 73 bolstered her unshaken belief in God's justice through a profound personal religious experience

---

17 Perelman and Olbrechts-Tyteca, *Rhetoric*, 149.

(v. 17).[18] In any event, Ps 73 presents an autobiographical experience while Ps 1 manifests a programmatic call to follow God's way: learning the Torah. The language and the literary structure of the psalm show that its reassuring religious thesis is stated as an argumentative response to the opponents who reject the Torah as the way of life.

The statement regarding the righteous' consistent study of the Torah is succeeded by the tree metaphor (v. 3). The metaphor is functional, aiming to give concrete form to the abstract concept of belief. It is the familiar depiction of the blossoming tree, a characteristic element in the geographical landscape of the Middle East.[19] The following Egyptian citation taken from the instruction of *Amenemope* exemplifies the function of the tree metaphor as an argumentative means for giving concrete form to a point of view. We read:

> As for the hot man in the temple,
> he is like a tree growing inside.
> Only for a moment does it bring forth young greenery.
> It finds its end in the channel,
> it goes far from its home,
> or the flames become its pyre.
> But the truly silent man holds himself apart.
> He is like a tree which grows in the sunlight.
> It grows green and doubles its fruits,
> it stands before its Lord,
> its fruits are sweet, its shade is pleasant,
> and it finds its end as a statue.[20]

The metaphor of the tree is also employed in Prov 3:17-18:

> דרכיה דרכי־נעם וכל־נתיבתיה שלום
> עץ־חיים היא למחזיקים בה ותמכיה מאשר
> Her ways [the Torah] are ways of pleasantness, and all her paths are peace.
> She is a tree of life to those who lay hold of her;
> Those who hold her fast are called happy.[21]

---

[18] Consult M. Buber, "The Heart Determines" in *On the Bible* (New York: Schocken, 1982) 199-210. Also see J.L. Crenshaw, *Old Testament Wisdom* (Atlanta: John Knox, 1981) 183.

[19] Consult G. Widengren, *The King and the Tree of Life in Ancient Near Eastern Religions* (Uppsala: Uppsala Universitets Arsskrift, 1951). For the cultural and mythical concept of the tree see also K. Nielsen, *There is Hope for a Tree* (Sheffield: Sheffield University, 1989) 74-85. For the place of trees in the context of the history of religion see P.R. Frese and S.J.M. Gray, "Trees," in *The Encyclopedia of Religion* (ed. M. Eliade; New York/London: Macmillan, 1987) vol. 15, pp. 26-33 (including bibliography).

[20] Cited in W. Beyerlin, ed., *Near Eastern Religious Texts* (Philadelphia: Westminster, 1978) p. 52 (with illuminations).

[21] Compare Isa 9:15.

These two verses effectively summarize Ps 1.

The citation from Prov employs a specific sort of metaphor in which the element of comparison, "the servant" (or "the vehicle") is inserted without the comparative introduction such as "as", כ "like" (or the verb "is" in English). This is the implicit metaphor regarded as one of the peaks of sublime poetry.[22] Ps 1, however, employs the explicit metaphor:

והיה כעץ שתול על־פלגי מים...

כי אם־כמץ אשר־תדפנו רוח

He is *like* a tree planted by streams of water ...

like chaff that the wind drives away. (vv. 3-5)[23]

The comparative vehicle, the particle כ "like" is explicit. Thus we observe two different categories of metaphors, dealing with the same theme.

Rhetorically the metaphor used in Ps 1 has an advantage over the perhaps more literarily sophisticated figure of Prov 3: it opens the door for analogical deduction. The persuasive goal is to establish a relationship between the rewarding future for the righteous and the destructive ending for the wicked. Seeking to persuade this sort of opposition must be factually presented. However, the matter under discussion (the future of the believer versus the fate of the nonbeliever) does not entail sterilized facts that are mathematically provable.[24] Consequently, an unscientific, non-mathematically provable discourse, that seeks to carry away its audience, to affect them, must use quasi-logical argumentation.

The issue at stake is the manner of arguing a case which is opinionative versus reasoning a scientific discourse. This matter already occupied the attention of early rhetoricians such as the sophist Gorgias, who made the distinction between *logos* and *doxa* (opinion) as D.L. Sullivan has pointed out:

> Persuasion from *doxa* depends on rational arguments in which one opinion seeks to contradict or abolish the other one.[25]

And Gorgias himself explained thus:

> To understand that persuasion ... is to impress the soul as it wishes. One must study the words of the astronomers who, substituting opinion for opinion ... make what is incredible and unclear seem true to the eye of opinion.[26]

---

22 See N. Frye, *The Great Code* (San Diego: Harcourt Brace Jovanovich, 1981) 54-74.

23 The NRSV (New York/Oxford: Oxford University, 1989) in its translation of Ps 1:3,5 replaces the original singular, third person masculine of האיש with plural in order to provide a political gender-correct version.

24 For the distinction between the factual discourse and the opinionative discourse, see R. Barilli, *Rhetoric* (Minneapolis: University of Minnesota, 1989) pp. ix-x.

25 D.L. Sullivan, "Kairos and Rhetoric of Belief," *Quarterly Journal of Speech* 78 (1992) 319.

26 Cited in R.K. Sprauge, *The Older Sophists* (Columbia, South Carolina: University of South Carolina, 1972) 53.

The ultimate success of the argument regarding matters of opinion (and beliefs) depends on the speaker's skill in presenting the contrasting view as meaningless.

The biblical poets, prophets and psalmists, employ various modes of appeal while practising the quasi-logical arguments in order to persuade their audience. For instance, Deutero-Isaiah uses the quasi-logical argument, depicting the foreign gods as worthless:

הפסל נסך חרש...
המסכן תרומה עץ לא־ירקב יבחר חרש חכם
יבקש־לו להכין פסל לא ימוט

An idol? - A workman casts it ... as a gift one chooses mulberry wood - wood that will not rot - then seeks out a skilled artisan to set up an image that will not topple. (Isa 40:19-20)[27]

The prophet avoids a philosophical-theological argument regarding the merit of the gods; there is no end to such a debate. Instead, the argument is based on probabilities, which can distort and magnify: how can a piece of wood be the real god!?[28]

Ps 1, however, employs through metaphor the strategy of the quasi-logical argument in order to persuade its readers or listeners to adopt the psalmist's religious view of the bright future of the righteous. The analogy (metaphor) is a useful method for drawing logical conclusions regarding unscientific matters. In the first place the metaphor portrays the argumentative matter in terms that are conceived by our senses. Cicero explained it thus:

> When something that can scarcely be conveyed by the proper term is expressed metaphorically, this meaning we desire to convey is made clear by the resemblance of the thing that we have expressed by the word that does not belong ... every metaphor ... has a direct appeal to the senses, especially the sense of sight, which is the keenest ... (*De Oratore*, 3.155-161)

However, the metaphor is not merely one object which resembles another one, "an extra trick with words". The metaphor is not disconnected from the message itself. Thus Riffaterre explains the issue:

> When the reader assumes that figurative description is there to duplicate and confirm literal description, he is rationalizing ... he reads wrongly ... in fact the image should be seen not as referring to an object but as a different discourse. The image will be interpreting it ... Its primary purpose is not to offer a representation, but to dictate an interpretation.[29]

---

[27] For the verses and the versions see C.R. North, *The Second Isaiah* (Oxford: Clarendon Press, 1964) 82-83.

[28] For the argument of probability rather than scientific facts, see Plato, *Phaedrus* 267a6. Consult G.A. Kennedy, *The Art of Persuasion in Greece* (Princeton: Princeton University, 1963) 62-63.

[29] M. Riffaterre, "Descriptive Imagery," *Yale French Studies* 61 (1981) 108,125.

The context of the poem (psalm) dominates the reading of the metaphor not as a depiction of an external reality but as the poem's theme. Thus the relationship between the two components of the analogy, the *phoros* ("the bearer" or "the servant") and the theme is a "resemblance of relationship".[30] In other words, the image of the blossoming tree, the *phoros*, of Ps 1 is not merely an illustration but is the argument itself. The metaphor of the tree is the poem's religious reality. The image of the blossoming tree is the undeniable existence of the cosmological reality rather than a matter of opinion or belief.

A close reading of the description of the metaphor of Ps 1 reveals that the tree is not spontaneously growing by itself in the wilderness. This is in sharp contrast to the image of the worship of Baal, which takes place "under every green tree" (Jer 3:13, Deut 12:2, 1 Kgs 14:23, and more). The tree of Ps 1 has been deliberately "planted" (v. 3); an effort has been made to secure its growth. The tree is furthermore watered by the (י)פלג, "streams of water" (ibid.). The use of the noun פלג suggests that these streams of water have been created artificially (cf. Ps 46:5). Planned preparation and careful labour have guaranteed the successful growth of the tree. Thus the reward of the righteous is secured, who make a constant effort to follow God's way through the learning of the Torah.

In conclusion, Psalm 1 portrays a world of reality through a metaphor. We do not perceive the abstract concept of faith as the surrounding reality. The psalm, referring to the spiritual sphere of religious belief, seeks to transfer the world of belief to the seen world of nature. The religious world is not merely the world of the believers but reality as it is. The tree in the context of Ps 1 is not a simple botanical phenomenon; rather, it is the righteous as they are. The metaphor is therefore the vehicle employed by the religious poet of Ps 1 who transfers the unseen and unprovable onto the undeniable reality. The metaphor used in the psalm happens to be the reality itself rather than a stylistic decoration. Ps 1 demonstrates how a religious subject seeking to persuade uses secular descriptive language in metaphor as a rhetorical tool to force the reality of existence to concur with the religious ideal.

The structure of the psalm shows a planned rhetorical design. The metaphor is used only after the psalmist has called attention to his dispute with his opponents, and only after the psalmist has formulated his choice of the righteous way of life. The psalm's strong opinionative orientation is then followed by the metaphor, and the reader's interpretation has been determined. Now we can answer our earlier question as to why this psalm starts the canonical lyrical religious poetry of ancient Israel. We may point to its superb rhetorical design and its remarkable stylistic mixture of the sphere of religious belief and the realm of natural reality for introducing the happy future of the truly righteous.

---

[30] Compare Perelman and Olbrechts-Tyteca, *New Rhetoric*, 372-373.

III. EPILOGUE

HEBREW RHETORIC AND THE TRANSLATOR

JAN DE WAARD

Introductory Remarks

The last article of this volume is supposed to deal with the implications of the preceding contributions for translation. However, since this should remain an article and not become a preliminary study of a still missing "Handbook on Hebrew Rhetoric", it can impossibly deal with all the implications of all the contributions for translation. Selection is therefore an imperative and the principle of selection will be the relatively unexplored character of certain rhetorical features in translation studies. Mainly for reasons of practical organization, the features on the level of macrostructures of texts will be dealt with first and those on the level of microstructures last. However, this is also in agreement with what should be the first move of the translator: descending from the higher levels of the hierarchy of the discourse to the lower ones.

A second caveat concerns the typology of translation. It will hopefully be clear that most of the findings of this volume can only be applied in a functional equivalence type of translation, be it on a literary or a common language level. The reasons for this are apparent: most rhetorical features are language specific, making any kind of formal correspondence between languages impossible. Therefore, not the rhetorical features as such have to be rendered, but their function. That sometimes also translations belonging to another type (interlinear, literal, philological, linguistic) are quoted, relates to the fact that especially Bible translations present a strange and unsatisfactory mixture of different translational types. Lack of detailed, explicit formulation of underlying principles and procedures, ideological considerations, and the wish to satisfy target audience expectations (real or imaginary) are no doubt all factors causing such a state of affairs.

Rhetorical Features of Macrostructures

Although the question can be rightfully asked whether textual structures only exist in the brain of the researcher, a number of contributions to this volume (Bailey, Boadt, Fokkelman) make it far more likely that they do not. The first and the last one effectively deal with what could be called mirror arrangements of the discourse, and they add to the significant material already existing. This topic has been in vogue for more than twenty years and its bibliography alone easily exceeds the pages of this volume. It is not only confined to smaller discourse units at and beyond the paragraph level, but it also extends in a daring way to the entire discourse of whole biblical books such as Ruth, Ecclesiastes, Song of Songs, Ezekiel, Amos and Joel, the last one showing both patterns of parallelism and inverted parallelism.[1] In fact, so many concentric patterns have been discovered that the question can be raised whether quantity is not inversely proportional to significance.

Anyway, significance of structures, in particular for the translator, is the issue here, and one can only be grateful for the attention paid by most contributors to such a perspective.[2] So with regard to macrostructures, Bailey especially aims at the device of formatting of the receptor text. This is an important insight since the analysis of "poetry" always presupposes some kind of spatial arrangement of the sequence of words, phrases and sentences in temporal discourse.[3] Therefore, a format consisting of a system of indented lines, perhaps reinforced by identical capitalized letters in the margin indicating parallel sequences, may be the only means to make arrangements visible. However, unless the aim of the translation is to instruct the audience about the formal characteristics of Hebrew rhetoric, one cannot imagine translators to follow such procedure with any regularity. It will be reserved for very exceptional cases such as the rendering of the literary unit Amos 5:1-17. The structural analysis of this passage proposed elsewhere[4] has generally been accepted by modern scholarship and it has, for example, in a slightly more pedagogical and less sophisticated way been taken over in GN. This simply was a must for the German translators, for when competent Hebrew scholars have been unable to discern the arrangement of sequences, how will the lay reader of a translation be capable to distinguish it?

However, even such a procedure is not necessarily the last to be applied. Decisions can hardly be taken on the level of one rhetorical unit in a whole book. If our analysis of the global concentric structure of Amos is correct, even the discourse unit

---

[1] For Ruth see Murray D. Gow, *The Book of Ruth, Its Structure, Theme and Purpose.* Leicester: Apollos. 1992; for Ecclesiastes compare my article on "The Structure of Qoheleth", *Proceedings of the Eighth World Congress of Jewish Studies.* Jerusalem. 1992. 57-64 and for Amos: J. de Waard and W.A. Smalley, *A Translator's Handbook on the Book of Amos.* New York: United Bible Societies. 1979. For Ezekiel see the two volumes commentary of Brian Tidiman, *Le livre d'Ezéchiel.* Vaux-sur Seine: Edifac. 1985-1987 and for Joel: Irene Grunewald, *Joel, een structuuranalyse.* Doctoraalscriptie Semitische Talen. Amsterdam. 1993.

[2] Occasionally important translational observations are made on details of structures, such as Fokkelman's complaint about the failure to appreciate the syntactical status of the adjective רעה in twenty modern versions of Gen 37:2 in five languages. Taking note of the renderings in REB: "and he told tales about them to their father", and GNB: "He brought bad reports to his father about what his brothers were doing", may nevertheless be an encouragement to the author.

[3] See Daniel Lafarriere, Automorphic Structures in the Poem's Grammatical Space. *Semiotica* 10. 1974. 333-350.

[4] The Chiastic Structure of Amos V 1-17. *Vetus Testamentum* xxvii, 1977. 170-177. For the last discussion of the subject see P.R. Noble, The Literary Structure of Amos: A Thematic Analysis. *Journal of Biblical Literature* 114. 1995. 209-226 and the literature mentioned in footnotes 2 and 3.

5:1-17 may have to be subdivided as has partly been done in TILC.[5] However, it may well last till the end of next century before we will be able to satisfactorily describe the primary, secondary and tertiary structures of the discourse of an entire book. And it is not something which can simply be left to translators as part of their preparatory work!

This raises the question whether so much time and energy should be invested in such a research for translational purposes. A question which can only be answered one way or another when one would have a clear picture of what the function of such structures is. In spite of everything which has been said, such a clear picture is still lacking. If, for example, the function would be purely mnemotechnic, the structures described above would be hardly relevant to the translator rendering the source text for a modern religious community in which memorization of sacred texts does not play an important part at all. If in addition the function would be liturgical - in addition, for "mnemotechnical" and "liturgical" are not mutually exclusive -, the translator producing target texts not intended for liturgical recitation, would hardly feel concerned. Only if these structures would turn out to be bearers of rhetorical meaning, translators will have to find out what these particular meanings precisely are and how they can functionally be matched in the target language.

Although we still are at the very beginning of research, it seems already clear that rhetorical meaning of these structures cannot be excluded. Moreover, there appears to be consensus with regard to a few rhetorical functions: the overall function would be to enhance vividness by breaking the monotony of direct parallelism, whereas some of the specific functions would be to mark the boundaries of discourse and to highlight the information which is contained in the centre or the hinge of the construction which serves semantically as the climax of the communication everywhere where it is present. Lack of the turning point should be indicated by "zero" and be defined as a meaningful absence of something.[6]

These insights are, of course, of utmost translational importance. How can translators effectively match these rhetorical functions? One of the answers, not easily to be dismissed, would be: by restructuring. In fact, restructuring on sentence, and even on paragraph level has become a current practice in Bible translation, and there is no reason of principle why restructuring should end with the paragraph boundaries. However, a few caveats are not superfluous. Although inverted parallelism has been described at some length for North Eastern and North Western Semitic as well as for Greek and Latin (compare the Homeric *hysteron proteron*

---

[5]   In fact, the analysis contained in the Appendix to the Handbook (189-214) is only an excerpt from a very detailed discourse analysis of 130 pages by Dr. Smalley which remained unpublished. See, however, W.A. Smalley, Recursion Patterns and the Sectioning of Amos. *The Bible Translator* 30. 1979. 118-127.

[6]   Some progress has been made since Nils W. Lund's notorious study *Chiasmus in the New Testament*. Chapel Hill: University of North Caroline Press. 1942. Especially to be singled out for the translator in the interlingual communication situation is John W. Welch (Ed.), *Chiasmus in Antiquity. Structures, Analyses, Exegesis*. Hildesheim: Gerstenberg Verlag. 1981.

technique),[7] the present writer is not aware of the existence of any elaborate research of inverted parallelism in any other language of the world. It may be true that pure envelope structures especially those with identical topics, are more widely attested. Such a frequency, however, has not been established for structures in which an expectancy of a climax in the centre is gradually built up.[8] Therefore, the universality of such a structure not having been proven, a plea could be made for restructuring. However, such a restructuring also presents problems. For example, how does it affect other structural relationships in the same text? Where should it start and where should it end? In Amos 5:1-17 e.g. NEB and NAB combine C and C' (verses 7 and 10) and they put the centre of the structure E (verse 8d) after D'. But why not combine the informations contained in B and B'? On the other hand, for the translators of REB the restructuring of NEB apparently went too far, because they restore the centre in its place and only maintain the C-C' combination.[9]

One can therefore conclude that in the present state of our knowledge restructuring remains a risky endeavour. In fact, the only time the present writer advised translation teams in some languages to do important restructuring, a New Testament text was concerned which should really be looked at at the interface of structural analysis and hermeneutics, namely Luke 9:57-62.[10] This text presents a triptych of three episodes, and the emphasis is put upon the central part and particularly upon the last colon of it, the only element which is not matched anywhere in the structure: "but as for you, go and proclaim the kingdom of God". By these words and by a highly complex system of elaborated paradoxes the concept of "following" has been redefined. The tripartite arrangement is not logical, but stylistic only. In a logical arrangement the central part would come at the end. Readers in many languages in

---

[7]   See e.g. John Welch's contribution about "Chiasmus in Ancient Greek and Latin Literatures" in the work quoted at the end of the preceding note (250-268) and the literature cited there.

[8]   It is evident that one has to face a conscious rhetorical technique of which the target audience was aware. For that reason, glossators who wanted to give a *relecture* of an existing text with "zero" centre, could use the "zero" slot in order to communicate a new actualizing information to new readers. See my treatment of Isaiah 7:1-17 in "Quel texte traduire? Le traducteur face au conflit des interprétations". *Meta* 32.1987. 16-20.

[9]   Most probably, however, such changes were not based upon structural insights of the translators at all nor on the legitimate concern with the intelligibility of the receptor text on the side of the prospective readers. More likely, these translators judged the source text to be in disorder and they reconstructed it according to what they considered to be its more original precanonical form. This raises the interesting question whether translators are only allowed to render the base text in its final redactional form, or whether they can also render a reconstructed form belonging to the supposed prehistory of the text. The limitations of this article forbid to enter into a detailed answer to such an important question.

[10] R. Morgenthaler (*Die lukanische Geschichtsschreibung als Zeugnis.* 1948) has clearly demonstrated the Lukan preference of a threefold structural pattern. It is difficult to decide whether one has to see here Semitic or Greek literary influences. In view of the fact that a colon structure analysis according to the canons of Greek rhetoric (Aristotle, *Rhetoric* III.9.5; Demetrius, περὶ ἑρμηνείας I; Hermogenes, περὶ εὑρέσεως IV) can naturally be applied to this text (see Johannes P. Louw, Discourse Analysis and the Greek New Testament. *The Bible Translator* 24. 1973. 101-118), Greek literary influences may be more probable. See especially R. Meynet, *Quelle est donc cette parole? Lecture rhétorique de l'évangile de Luc. Vol. 1 and 2.* Paris: Les éditions du Cerf. 1979.

which climaxes naturally come at the end of the total discourse, will also expect it there. They will be unable to follow the shift of expectancy towards the end of the central part. The more so since they will be distracted by the extremely mysterious proverbial language. A restructuring of the text according to which the second episode is presented last, therefore seems a necessity.[11]

In addition to the structural debate, the contribution by Boadt is of great indirect importance to translators for two other reasons. In the first place it dwells considerably upon the rhetorical function of "coherence", that is, the way in which the text of Ezekiel fits or coheres to the world view of the participants in the communication,[12] and, secondly, it highlights particularly the rhetorical functions of "progression" and "cohesion" in the same discourse. "Progression" is here defined as the manner in which the movement of the discourse from one episode or argument to the next has been marked, and "cohesion" involves the different ways in which the various units of the Ezekiel discourse have been connected one with the other. It cannot sufficiently be underlined that without a proper insight into these rhetorical functions, a text cannot be understood, and, therefore, not be translated.

Rhetorical Features of Microstructures

It is not suggested here that borderlines between macro- and microstructures can be neatly indicated nor that such a distinction is essential. It is only introduced as a commodity for pragmatic purposes. In the descending order the first rhetorical feature to be met is that of literary insertion as described by Tsumura since it can manifest itself on the sentence and beyond the sentence level.

With regard to the AXB surface structure, it may semantically not be so easy to distinguish between insertion and inversion patterns as has been suggested, especially when the question of rhetorical function is raised. However, for analytical purposes, the insertion of information after the breaking up of composite units, is a useful description of a consciously applied rhetorical technique.

The greatest problem for translators is the recognition of the existence of such a technique. Here the case of 1 Sam 8:16 is rather revealing. It shows the additional complication of a textual problem, but the thesis can be defended that the

---

[11] In translations allowing for footnotes, on the other hand, the possibility exists to explain either the stylistic arrangement as such or the climax itself in a non-technical language thereby respecting the Lukan stylistic pattern. For such a solution see the note in SEB.

[12] The definition of "coherence" could also be worded as "the requirement that texts hang together conceptually" (B. Hatim and I. Mason, *Discourse and the Translator*. London and New York: Longman. 1990. 239). There are, of course, different types of coherence. Intratextual coherence precedes the intertextual coherence subject to the following rule: "*Miteinander kohärent sein müssen (1) die vom Produzenten im Ausgangstext enkodierte Nachricht in der Rezeptionsweise durch den Translator, (2) die vom Translator als Rezipient dieser Nachricht interpetierte Nachricht, (3) die vom rezipierenden Translator als (Re-)Produzent enkodierte Nachricht für den Zielrezipienten*" (K. Reiß and H.J. Vermeer, *Grundlegung einer allgemeinen Translationstheorie*. Tübingen: Max Niemeyer Verlag. 1984.114).

non-recognition of subtle rhetorical features frequently creates pseudo-textual problems. In this case, G, by reading "your cattle" (בקריכם) for "your young men" (בחוריכם) changes the alternation pattern animal-man into a coordinate word pair, providing therefore a secondary contextual harmonization. That the textual issue is not unrelated to the discussion of the inserted element הטובים can be seen in the reading of καὶ τὰ ἀγαθὰ of codex B. First of all translators should take the B evaluation given by the Hebrew Old Testament Project Committee to the reading of M seriously,[13] and not follow the vast majority of modern versions (RSV, NRSV, NEB, REB, JB, GNB, NIV) in their adaptation of G. What should they do, however, with regard to the inserted element? If the analysis offered by Tsumura is correct, they should not take it as modifying only the preceding noun (RSV, JPS, NEB, REB) or as modifying all the preceding nouns (NAV) or all the preceding nouns plus the following one (JB), but they should consider it to modify the composite unit "your young men and asses". Hence a new rendering, unattested up till now, will have to be proposed: "and the best of your young men and donkeys".[14]

A second problem translators are faced with is the correct interpretation of the rhetorical function of the technique described above. In fact, rhetorical processes are more and more accurately outlined, but their possible rhetorical functions are not frequently elaborated. This is e.g. the case in the treatment of 2 Sam 1:21, "*l'un des lieux les plus inutilement torturés de la Bible*".[15] If Tsumura's interpretation which implies a return to a position held already by Cappel in the seventeenth century, is accepted, the topic "mountains of Gilboa" and "fields of the heights" is interrupted by a comment "no dew nor rain upon you" which seems to bear rhetorical focus. Such a rhetorical focus seems in many languages to come more naturally at the end, hence the (also interpretationally) acceptable solution of NAV: *"Gilboaberge! Offerland! Nòg dou, nòg reën vir jullie!"*. Of course, if interpretationally a part to a whole relationship is taken to exist between the envelopes, rhetorical focus could come equally naturally at the very beginning, as in GNB: "May no rain or dew fall on Gilboa's hills; may its fields be always barren!".

Without the complication of textual problems patterns become frequently straightforward, and in a case like 1 Sam 28:19 there can be no doubt about the function of rhetorical focus upon the inserted element "and tomorrow you and your sons shall be with me". NEB and REB try to render the rhetorical focus by introducing the inserted element with the clause: "What is more,". Taking emphasis also to be the rhetorical function of repetition, NEB introduces the repeated element in addition with: "Yes, indeed", whereas REB more formally starts it with: "I tell you again:". Such renderings may seem to be useful attempts at an adequate

---

[13] See Dominique Barthélemy, *Critique textuelle de l'Ancien Testament I*. OBO 50/1. Fribourg and Göttingen: Editions universitaires and Vandenhoeck & Ruprecht. 1982. 158-159.

[14] GNB: "Your best cattle and donkeys" is a combination of wrong textual decision and correct rhetorical translation. For a more complex and expanded AXYB pattern in Psalm 24:6, its non-recognition in G and its recognition in two antipodal modern versions (Buber and GN) see my "Die hermeneutischen Prinzipien der 'Bibel in heutigem Deutsch'" in: J. Gnilka and H.P. Rüger (Eds), *Die Übersetzung der Bibel - Aufgabe der Theologie*. Bielefeld: Luther Verlag. 1985. 169-186.

[15] So Barthélemy, 227.

translation of rhetorical meaning, but in reality they miss the whole point. In fact, the repetition does not have the purpose to emphasize the information it contains, but to shift the emphasis to the insertion.[16] A real functional equivalence translation would therefore have to abandon the formal stylistic arrangement, to telescope in some way the informations of the AB pattern, and to put the climactic information of the insertion, though formulated in an understandable way, at the very end. GN is a good example of such an approach: "*....wird er dich und das Heer Israels in die Gewalt der Philister geben. Morgen wirst du mit deinen Söhnen bei mir in der Totenwelt sein*".

It is far more difficult to know what the rhetorical function of the insertion of one word into a broken construct chain is. Freedman has given quite some examples of this stylistic phenomenon in Hosea, among others 6:9: דרך ירצחו שכמה.[17] By extrapolation, one may want to hypothesize a same function as in the preceding cases. If so, in spite of some details depending upon the solution of some textual and interpretational problems,[18] the total verse may have to be translationally restructured, and the rendering of the inserted element may have to figure as a climax at the end. Such was at least the intention of GN: "*An der Straße nach Sichem liegen Priester auf der Lauer wie eine Räuberbande. Sie treten das Gesetz mit Füßen, sie morden*".

There also are highly debatable issues as to which the present writer is at a loss. For example, in 2 Sam 12:9 the AXB pattern can be syntactically analyzed as a means-purpose-means pattern, and such a pattern can be explicitly handled in different ways as, e.g. in TILC: "*Tu hai fatto morire in battaglia Uriah l'Ittita. Per prenderti in moglie la sua sposa, hai agito in modo che Uria fosse ucciso dagli Ammoniti*". It is, however, also suggested that there would be a rhetorical pattern in which the inserted element has the rhetorical function of impact, i.e. psychologically on the mind of David in the interaction prophet-king. The element involved in the impact would then be relevance. One should, however, note that there normally is no coincidence between syntactical/logical patterns and rhetorical ones, since the very essence of rhetoric consists of the breaking of syntactical rules. It seems therefore preferable to analyze the text either syntactically or rhetorically. In the last case, one could then end up with a rendering such as given by REB: "You have struck down Uriah the Hittite with the sword; the man himself you murdered by the sword of the Ammonites, and you have stolen his wife".

That, remaining on the sentence level, impact based on novelty and emphasis are the two functions of rhetorical questions, is sufficiently known. The different ways in which these functions can be matched in translation, have been described in detail by de Regt. To be singled out is the particular case in which a rhetorical question is

---

[16] For that reason, P. Kyle McCarter, failing to appreciate the rhetorical structure, can speak of a conflation of two versions of one clause (*I Samuel.* New York: Doubleday. 1980. 419).

[17] D.N. Freedman, The Broken Construct Chain. *Biblica* 53. 1972. 534-536.

[18] Compare the discussion in Dominique Barthélemy, *Critique textuelle de l'Ancien Testament 3.* OBO 50/3. Fribourg and Göttingen: Editions universitaires and Vandenhoeck & Ruprecht. 1992. 531-533.

an implicit quotation of an existing wisdom thesis with negative bias. Far more research is needed with regard to such phenomena and three major reasons can be quoted as to the urgency of their research: (1) they are very hard to spot; (2) they are difficult to translate; (3) they may be more frequent than generally believed.

Building on the cited case of Job 12:12, if one refuses to do minor surgery on the text by shifting the final לו of verse 11 as a mistake for the negation לוא to the beginning of verse 12: "wisdom is not with the aged",[19] 12:12 should be preferably taken as a rhetorical question denying implicitly a conventional belief.[20] However, if such is the case, a functional equivalence translation according to the definition of the present author, cannot consider it to be sufficient to formulate the question in such a way that the negative answer shines through. For the receptor audience of the translation cannot be persuaded of the incorrectness of a belief in the first receptor culture which it does not necessarily share. Hence the necessity of a rendering like in GN: "*Man sagt, die alten Leute hätten Weisheit, ihr hohes Alter gäbe ihnen Einsicht. Bei Gott ist wirklich Weisheit, Rat und Einsicht und auch die Macht, Geplantes auszuführen*". In fact, this is not a recent translational insight. Already RV had in margin: "With the old men, ye say, is wisdom" and Moffatt in the text of his translation: "Wisdom, you argue, lies with aged men, a long life means intelligence? Nay, wisdom and authority belong to God; strength and knowledge are his own" (compare also Job 31:3 and its translation in W and FC).

At the clause level, the discourse implications of resumption in Hebrew אשר clauses in Genesis have been described by Van Dyke Parunak. In most cases, the translational conclusions can be easily drawn. If the unusual pattern עם אשר תמצא את אלהיך in stead of אשר*[21] תמצא את אלהיך עמו in Gen 31:32 really expresses heightened vividness of an episode climax, that feature is perfectly matched in a rendering such as given in GN: "*Aber deine Götter? Bei wem du sie findest, der soll sterben!*".

Other issues, however, are translationally far more problematic. If the אשר clause with participial predicate: אשר אסורים בבית הסהר in Gen 40:5 really serves the rhetorical function of focus, such a prominence is certainly not rendered by putting the information between hyphens in the translation (RSV, NRSV, NIV). It is even less rendered by its total omission! (GN) Nevertheless, one should see that the information concerned is completely redundant in the immediate context and that, unlike in Hebrew, repetition of information in other languages not always serves the rhetorical function of emphasis. Therefore, in cases of redundancy like here the question has at least to be raised whether implicitness of information does not have to be preferred. Translation is in the first place the art of leaving superfluous information implicit, and only secondly of making necessary information explicit.

---

[19] So in the traces of Beer, Stevenson and Fohrer lately H.H. Rowley, *The Book of Job* . Grand Rapids and London: Wm. B. Eerdmans & Marshall, Morgan & Scott. 1980.94.

[20] As defended already by Strahan, Hölscher and Tur-Sinai.

[21] The reconstruction as offered by P. Joüon and T. Muraoka (*A Grammar of Biblical Hebrew III: Syntax*. Roma: Editrice pontificio istituto biblico. 1993. § 158m) is preferred.

Combining the information of the end of verse 4 with that of verse 5 may come in as a handy narrative solution as e.g. in JPS: "When they had been in custody for some time..." (so also in a different way REB), but such a procedure shifts the attention to the rather doubtful time element, especially when it outgrows Hebrew grammar as in GrN: "*toen ze al geruime tijd gevangen zaten*".[22] The only solution to all these problems may be shifting the final information of the verse to a near sentence initial position, reinforcing it, as in GNB: "One night there in prison", or to introduce a kind of "suspense" note as in TILC: "*sempre in prigione*".

Descending to the word level one arrives finally at the arrangements of participants in compound clausal elements (de Regt). Difficult to handle translationally remains the rhetorical significance of a chiastic pattern of participants, if there is any. The present writer wonders whether the exceptional arrangement prophets - worshippers - priests in 2 Kings 10:19 could not be analyzed as such a pattern in which the lay people are sandwiched between the two groups of professionals. Although there is the complication of a textual problem, there can be very little doubt about the originality of M, at least at the level of the final redaction.[23] The shift of the worshippers to the end in the Antiochian recension of G and in S should only be considered as a "*manifestation anachronique du sens hiérarchique*".[24] However, when a modern translation such as GN does the same, and certainly not for textual reasons, should such a rendering be evaluated as the correct rendering of a Hebrew rhetorical meaning? Or, if the last one cannot be defined, what is wrong with the adaptation to an ordering pattern of a receptor culture?

Some chiastic pairings of participants pass totally unnoticed in translation, e.g. Mahlon-Kilyon (Ruth 1:2 and 5) over against Kilyon-Mahlon in 4:9. Interestingly, in the traces of Rahlfs's L and C group, S and the Kennicott manuscripts 167,218,600 and de Rossi's manuscript 586, JB transposes the second pair, assimilating it to the first. However, in order to get the marriage relations correct, the opposite should be done![25] At least in some cultures, such a correct knowledge at the outset may have priority over any stylistic arrangement in spite of its presupposed rhetorical meaning.

---

[22] For ימים see E. Kautzsch and A.E. Cowley, *Gesenius' Hebrew Grammar*. Oxford: Clarendon Press. 1990. § 139h.

[23] The expression כלעבדיו has been left untranslated in BJ and C. The note in BJ seems to suggest that it is considered to be a later intrusion from verses 21-23 as suggested by J.A. Montgomery and H. Snyder Gehman, *A Critical and Exegetical Commentary on the Books of Kings*. Edinburgh: T. & T. Clark. 1967. 411. The critical notes in BHK and BHS as well as the recommendation to delete the expression in some of the commentaries since Klostermann may also have influenced this decision. Montgomery's and Gehman's observation that mss 170 and 174 omit the expression, taken over in BHS, is erroneous. See J.B. de Rossi, *Variae lectiones veteris testamenti I*. Amsterdam: Philo Press. 1969. 240. Omission in translation may also have been inspired by the vocalization עֲבָדָיו of some Hebrew manuscripts which would make the servants belong to a specific class, providing in this way a redundant information. So: A.B. Ehrlich, *Randglossen zur hebräischen Bibel 7*. Hildesheim: Georg Olms. 1968. 303.

[24] So Barthélemy, 1982. 396.

[25] See the discussion in E. Campbell, *Ruth*. New York: Doubleday. 1975. 151.

Concluding Observations

The discussion contained in this article is full of lacunae. It does not elaborate all the rich rhetorical insights of this volume putting them into a translational perspective. Without forcing this contribution into an "envelope structure", it can only be hoped that the interrogation of the selected materials has at least intensified the felt need of a handbook on Hebrew rhetoric for translators. Could this volume even be a first step, to be followed by others, on the long road to such an end?

ABBREVIATIONS

AB	Anchor Bible
ABD	*Anchor Bible Dictionary*
AdvPh	Adverbial Phrase
AnBib	Analecta biblica
ANEP	J.B. Pritchard (ed.), *Ancient Near East in Pictures*
ANET	J.B. Pritchard (ed.), *Ancient Near Eastern Texts*
ATD	Das Alte Testament Deutsch
AV	Authorized Version
BASOR	*Bulletin of the American Schools of Oriental Research*
BBB	Bonner biblische Beiträge
BDB	F. Brown, S.R. Driver, and C.A. Briggs, *Hebrew and English Lexicon of the Old Testament*
BEvT	Beiträge zur evangelischen Theologie
BETL	Bibliotheca ephemeridum theologicarum lovaniensium
BFC	Bible en français courant
BHS	*Biblia hebraica stuttgartensia*
Bib	*Biblica*
Bi(b)Or	Biblica et Orientalia
BJ/BdJ	Bible de Jérusalem
BKAT	Biblischer Kommentar: Altes Testament
BWA(N)T	Beiträge zur Wissenschaft vom Alten und Neuen Testament
BZAW	Beihefte zur *ZAW*
C	Petrus Canisius Translation
CBQ	*Catholic Biblical Quarterly*
CCL	Corpus christianorum, series latina
CD	Cairo Geniza Text of the *Damascus Document*
CRINT	Compendia rerum iudaicarum ad novum testamentum
CSEL	Corpus scriptorum ecclesiasticorum latinorum
CTA	A. Herdner, *Corpus des tablettes en cunéiformes alphabétiques*
Ebib	Etudes bibliques
EKKNT	Evangelisch-katholischer Kommentar zum Neuen Testament
EvT	*Evangelische Theologie*
FC	La Bible en Français Courant
FRLANT	Forschungen zur Religion und Literatur des Alten und Neuen Testaments
G	Old Greek
GN	Der Bibel in heutigem Deutsch
GNB	Good News Bible: Today's English Version

Gr N	Groot Nieuws Bijbel
HAL	L. Koehler and W. Baumgartner, *Hebräisches und aramäisches Lexikon zum Alten Testament*
HAT	Handbuch zum Alten Testament
HKAT	Handkommentar zum Alten Testament
HNT	Handbuch zum Neuen Testament
HTKNT	Herders theologischer Kommentar zum Neuen Testament
HUCA	*Hebrew Union College Annual*
ICC	International Critical Commentary
JAC	Jahrbuch für Antike und Christentum
JB	Jerusalem Bible
JBL	*Journal of Biblical Literature*
JPS	Jewish Publication Society of America; the second edition of its Tanakh translation, 1985.
JQR	*Jewish Quarterly Review*
JSJ	*Journal for the Study of Judaism in the Persian, Hellenistic and Roman Period*
JSOT	*Journal for the Study of the Old Testament*
JSOTS	Journal for the Study of the Old Testament - Supplement Series.
KAT	Kommentar zum Alten Testament
KBS	Katholieke Bijbelstichting (Dutch foundation responsible for the Willibrord Translation)
KJV	King James Version
LXX	Septuagint
MDAIK	*Mitteilungen des Deutschen Archeologischen Instituts. Abteilung Kairo*
MT/TM	Masoretic Text
NAB	New American Bible
NAG	J.P. Fokkelman, Narrative Art in Genesis, Assen 1975, (reprinted, 2nd edition, Sheffield 1991)
NAPS	J.P. Fokkelman, *Narrative Art and Poetry in the Books of Samuel, a full interpretation based on stylistic and structural analyses*, Assen 1981-1993, four volumes.
NAV	New Afrikaans Version
NEB	New English Bible
NFB	Nije Fryske Bibeloersetting
NICOT	New International Commentary on the Old Testament
NIV	New International Version
NP	Nominal Phrase
NRSV	New Revised Standard Version
OBO	Orbis biblicus et orientalis
OTL	Old Testament Library
OTS	Oudtestamentische Studiën
1QH	*Hôdāyōt (Thanksgiving Hymns) from Qumran Cave 1*
1QM	*Milḥāmāh (War Scroll)*
4QTestim	*Testimonia* text form Qumran Cave 4

REB   Revised English Bible
RLÜ   Revidierte Lutherübersetzung
RSV   Revised Standard Version
RV   Revised Version
S(yr)   Old Syriac
SANT   Studien zum Alten und Neuen Testament
SBLSCS   SBL Septuagint and Cognate Studies
SEB   Stuttgarter Erklärungsbibel
SPB   Studia postbiblica
SSN   Studia semitica neerlandica
SubBib   Subsidia biblica
SVT   Supplements to *VT*
THAT   E. Jenni and C. Westermann (eds.), *Theologisches Handwörterbuch
            zum Alten Testament*
TILC   Traduzione interconfessionale in lingua corrente
TOB   Traduction oecuménique de la Bible
TWAT   G.J. Botterweck and H. Ringgren (eds.), *Theologisches Wörterbuch
            zum Alten Testament*
UF   *Ugarit Forschungen*
VP   Verb phrase
VT   *Vetus Testamentum*
W   Willibrord Translation
WMANT   Wissenschaftliche Monographien zum Alten und Neuen Testament
ZAW   *Zeitschrift für die alttestamentliche Wissenschaft*
ZNW   *Zeitschrift für die neutestamentliche Wissenschaft*

INDEX OF BIBLICAL REFERENCES

LIST OF CONTRIBUTORS

Kenneth E. Bailey
Research Scholar in Middle Eastern New Testament Studies
New Wilmington, PA, USA

Pancratius C. Beentjes
Catholic Theological University
Utrecht, The Netherlands

Lawrence E. Boadt, C.S.P.
Saint Paul's College
Washington DC, USA

Lyle M. Eslinger
The University of Calgary
Calgary, Alberta, Canada

Jan P. Fokkelman
Leiden University
Leiden, The Netherlands

Yehoshua Gitay
University of Cape Town
Rondebosch, Republic of South Africa

Rabbi Jonathan Magonet
Leo Baeck College
London, England

Jean-Claude Margot
United Bible Societies
Etoy, Switzerland

Takamitsu Muraoka
Leiden University
Leiden, The Netherlands

Henry Van Dyke Parunak
Industrial Technology Institute
Ann Arbor, MI, USA

Lénart J. de Regt
Free University
Amsterdam, The Netherlands

David Toshio Tsumura
Japan Bible Seminary
Hamura, Tokyo, Japan

Jan de Waard
Free University
Amsterdam, The Netherlands

Ellen J. van Wolde
Tilburg University
Tilburg, The Netherlands

DATE DUE

APR 1 8 2000			
NOV 0 6 2002			
			Printed in USA

HIGHSMITH #45230